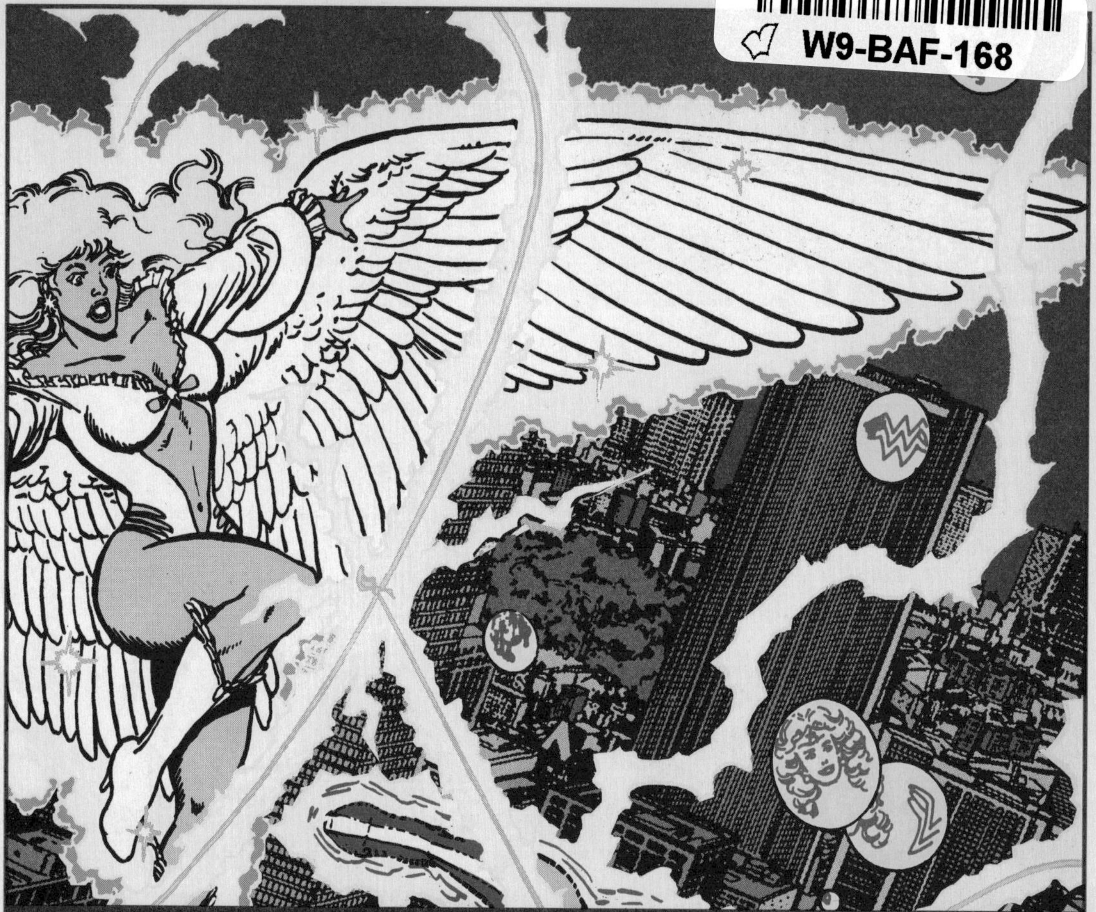

WONDER WOMAN

BEAUTY and the BEASTS

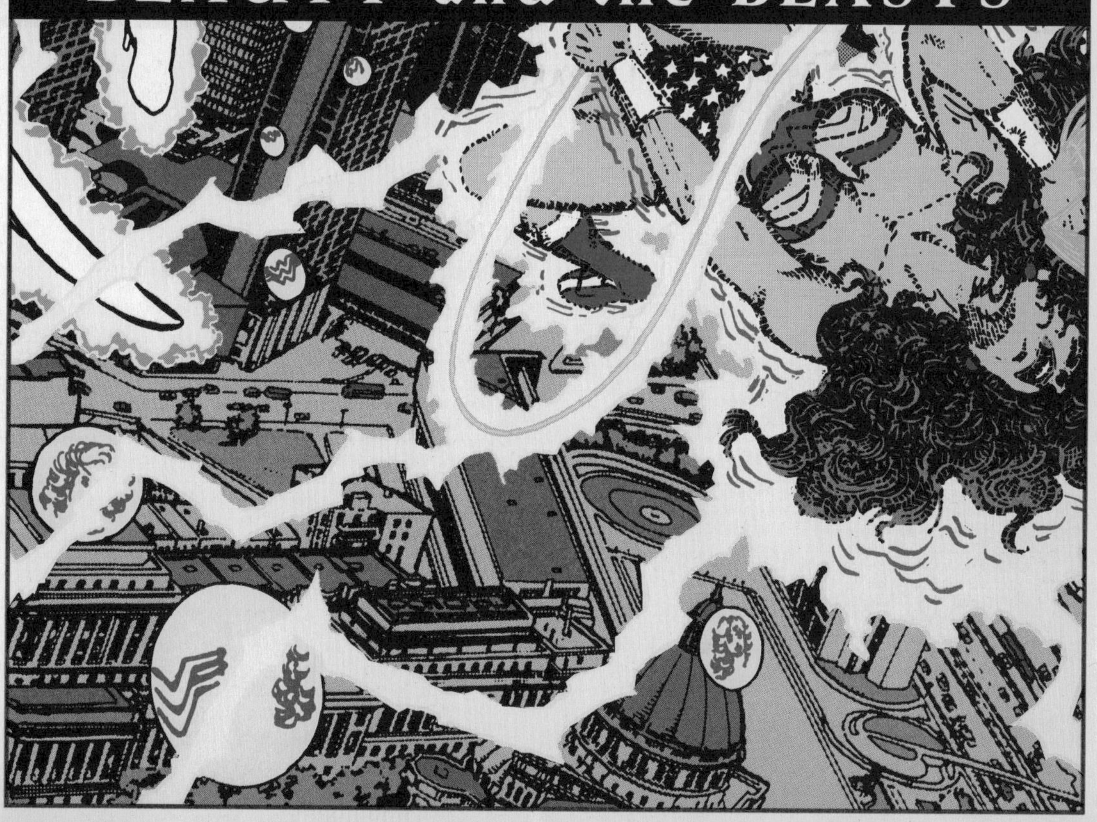

HARRISON BRANCH

WONDER WOMAN: BEAUTY AND THE BEASTS

Published by DC Comics. Cover and compilation copyright © 2005 DC Comics.
All Rights Reserved.

Originally published in single magazine form in WONDER WOMAN #15-19 and
ACTION COMICS #600. Copyright © 1988 DC Comics. All Rights Reserved.
All characters, their distinctive likenesses and related elements featured in
this publication are trademarks of DC Comics. The stories, characters and
incidents featured in this publication are entirely fictional. DC Comics does
not read or accept unsolicited submissions of ideas, stories or artwork.

DC Comics, 1700 Broadway, New York, NY 10019
A Warner Bros. Entertainment Company
Printed in Canada
First Printing
ISBN: 1-4012-0484-8

Cover art by George Pérez
Cover color by Tom Smith

WONDER WOMAN
BEAUTY and the BEASTS

GEORGE PÉREZ   JOHN BYRNE   LEN WEIN   Writers

GEORGE PÉREZ   JOHN BYRNE   Pencillers

DICK GIORDANO   GEORGE PÉREZ   BRUCE PATTERSON
BOB SMITH   FRANK McLAUGHLIN   Inkers

CARL GAFFORD   TOM ZIUKO   Original Colorists

JOHN COSTANZA   Letterer

GEORGE PÉREZ   Original Series Covers

Heroic Age   Color reconstruction and enhancement

Wonder Woman created by William Moulton Marston

OUR STORY SO FAR...

Over three thousand years ago, the goddess Artemis proposed to the Olympian gods that a new race of mortal human beings be created, which she would call Amazons — a female race that would set an example to the rest of humanity and promote equality between the sexes. Artemis, along with Athena, Aphrodite, Demeter, and Hestia, created the Amazons from the souls of women who were killed before their time due to violence by men. The first to be reborn, Hippolyte, was designated as the queen.

The Amazons founded a city-state called Themyscira, where compassion and justice would reign. But the war god Ares found the Amazons an obstacle to his quest for absolute power, and so had a pawn taunt the demigod Heracles with false reports that Hippolyte was besmirching his reputation. Heracles tricked the Amazons into a celebratory gathering with his warriors — but the Amazons were caught off-guard, and Heracles and his men treacherously attacked, defeated, and enslaved them.

Hippolyte prayed to the goddesses for forgiveness. Athena appeared to her and said she would be free if she rededicated herself to her ideals. Hippolyte escaped her cell, freed the other Amazons, and led them in defeating their captors.

The goddesses decreed that Hippolyte and her Amazons do penance for failing to lead humanity to establish new ways of justice and equality. Therefore, the goddesses sent Hippolyte's Amazons to a distant island, beneath which lay a source of great evil. As long as Amazons served to keep that evil from menacing humanity, the Amazons would be immortal.

Hippolyte's Amazons established a new city-state on Paradise Island, and the Amazons renewed their sense of purpose and self-discipline as the centuries passed. Various Amazons were killed over the years in carrying out the difficult task of keeping the great evil confined underground. During all this time, the Amazons of Paradise Island had no contact with the outside world.

Hippolyte was the only one of the Amazons who was pregnant when she was killed in her previous incarnation. The soul of Hippolyte's unborn daughter was still waiting to be reborn. On Artemis' instructions, Hippolyte formed the image of a baby from the clay of Paradise Island. The five goddesses who were the Amazons' patrons, along with Hermes, endowed the unborn soul with various gifts, including super-human strength and speed and the power of flight. Then the unborn soul entered the clay form which came to life as a real baby. The child was named Diana, after a revered warrior who had died to save the Amazon race.

After Hippolyte's daughter had grown to adulthood, the gods revealed to the Amazons that Ares had gone insane and might destroy all of Earth with a terrible source of power. The gods decreed that the Amazons choose through a tournament a champion who could confront Ares in the world outside Paradise Island.

Diana asked to participate in the tournament but was forbidden to do so by Hippolyte. Nonetheless, urged on by Athena, a disguised Diana entered the tournament and won. Unable to defy the gods' will, Hippolyte agreed to let Diana be the champion to be sent against Ares. Diana was given a costume bearing the standard of her deceased namesake.

Hermes transported Diana to Boston, Massachusetts, where she met a professor of classical Greek history named Julia Kapatelis, who taught her how to speak English and serves as her guide to contemporary civilization. Diana presented herself as an ambassador from Paradise Island to the rest of society, here to teach the ways of her just and peaceful civilization to a violent world.

Diana ultimately accomplished the mission for which she was sent to Man's World, defeating Ares before the god could bring about a third World War. The media dubbed her "Wonder Woman," and she became an overnight sensation — while also gaining a publicist in Myndi Mayer.

Julia and her daughter Vanessa took Diana into their home, but soon after the Princess was summoned to face a challenge from Zeus to prove the Amazons' worth. Diana encountered obstacle after obstacle while uncovering the truth about the mysterious heroine for whom she was named — which turned out to be the mother of pilot Steve Trevor. Plus, Diana learned of the terrible evil that lies beneath Paradise Island, which her fellow Amazons were charged with keeping contained for all time.

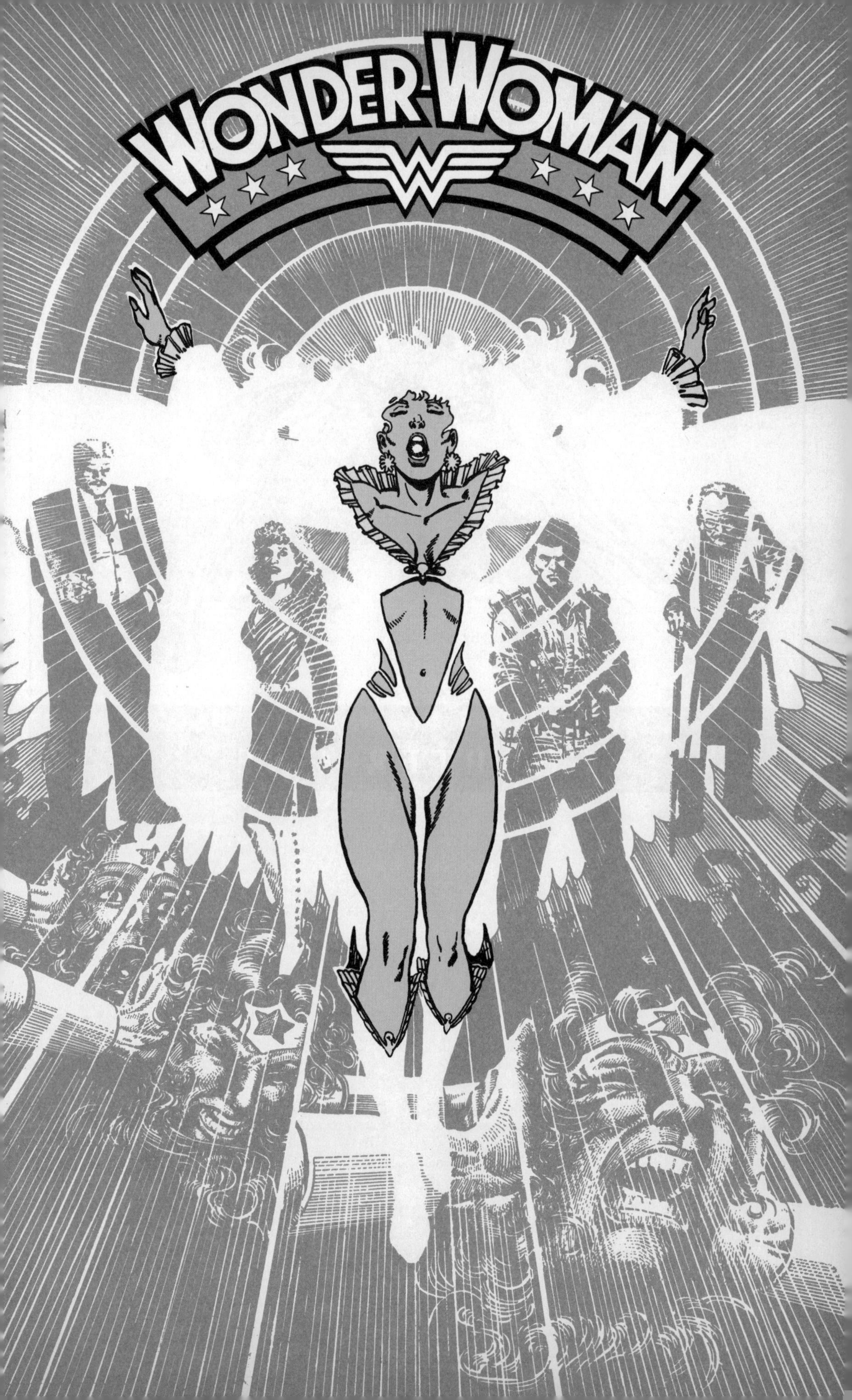
WONDER WOMAN

WONDER WOMAN

CHAPTER ONE

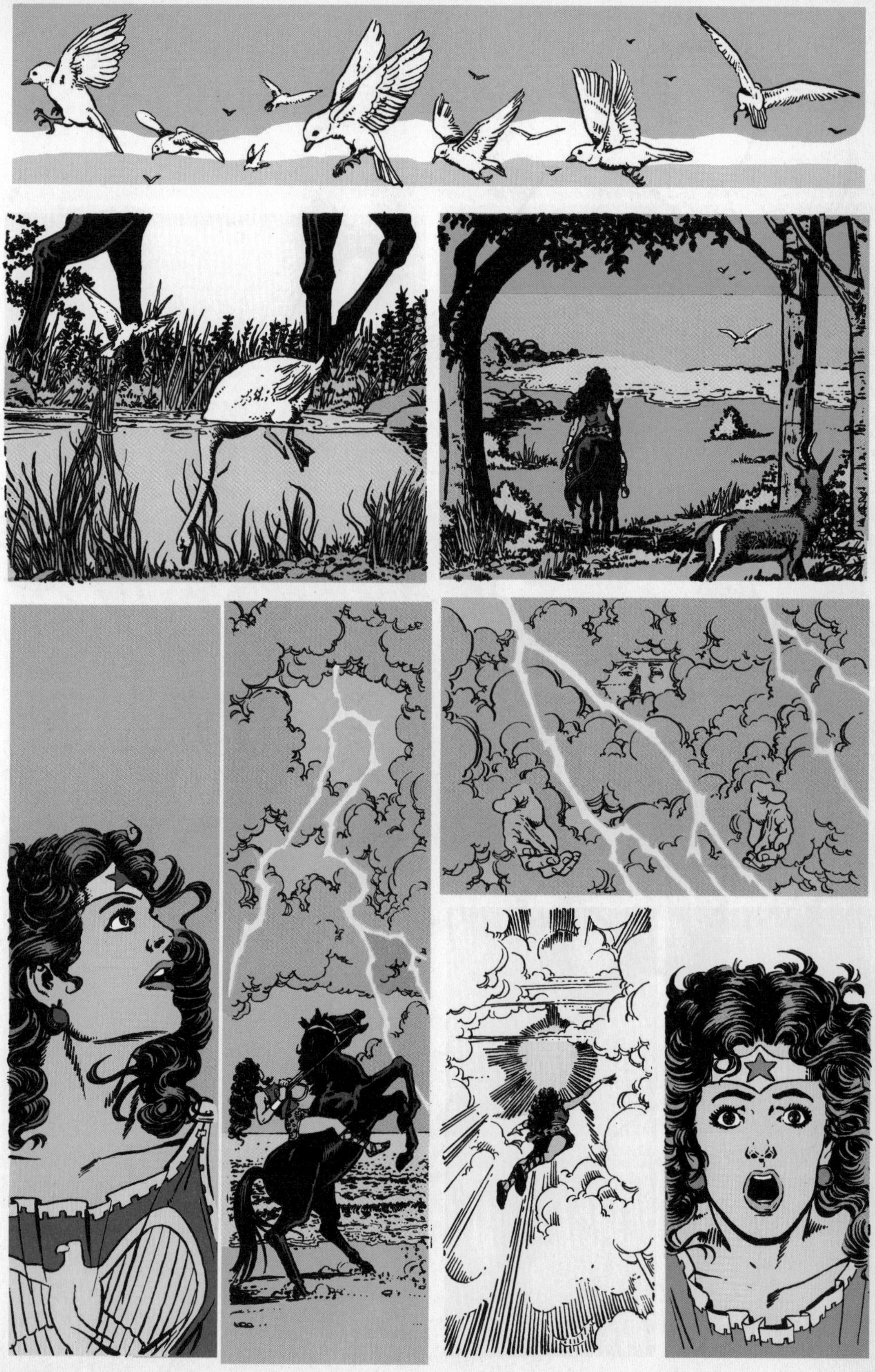

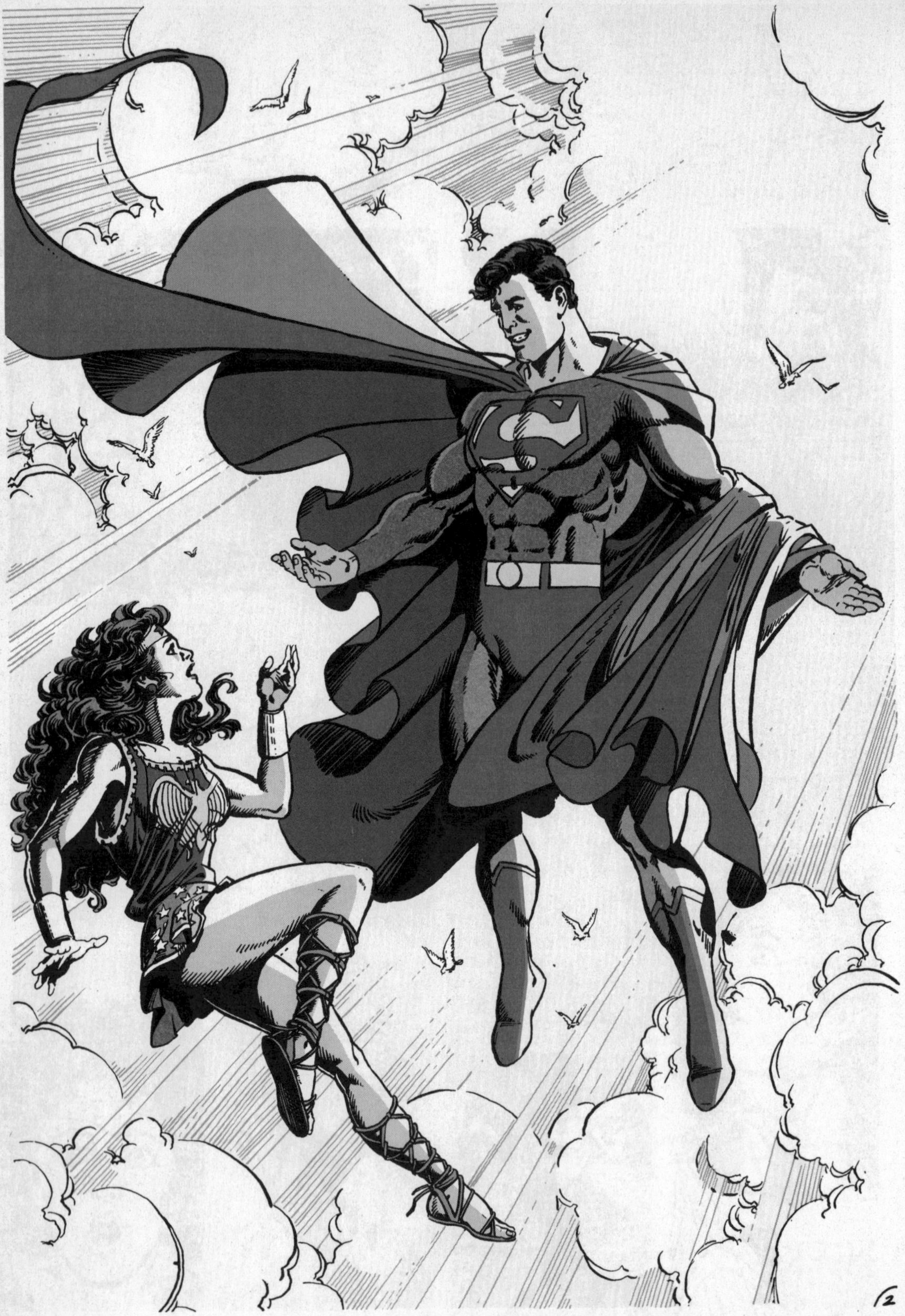

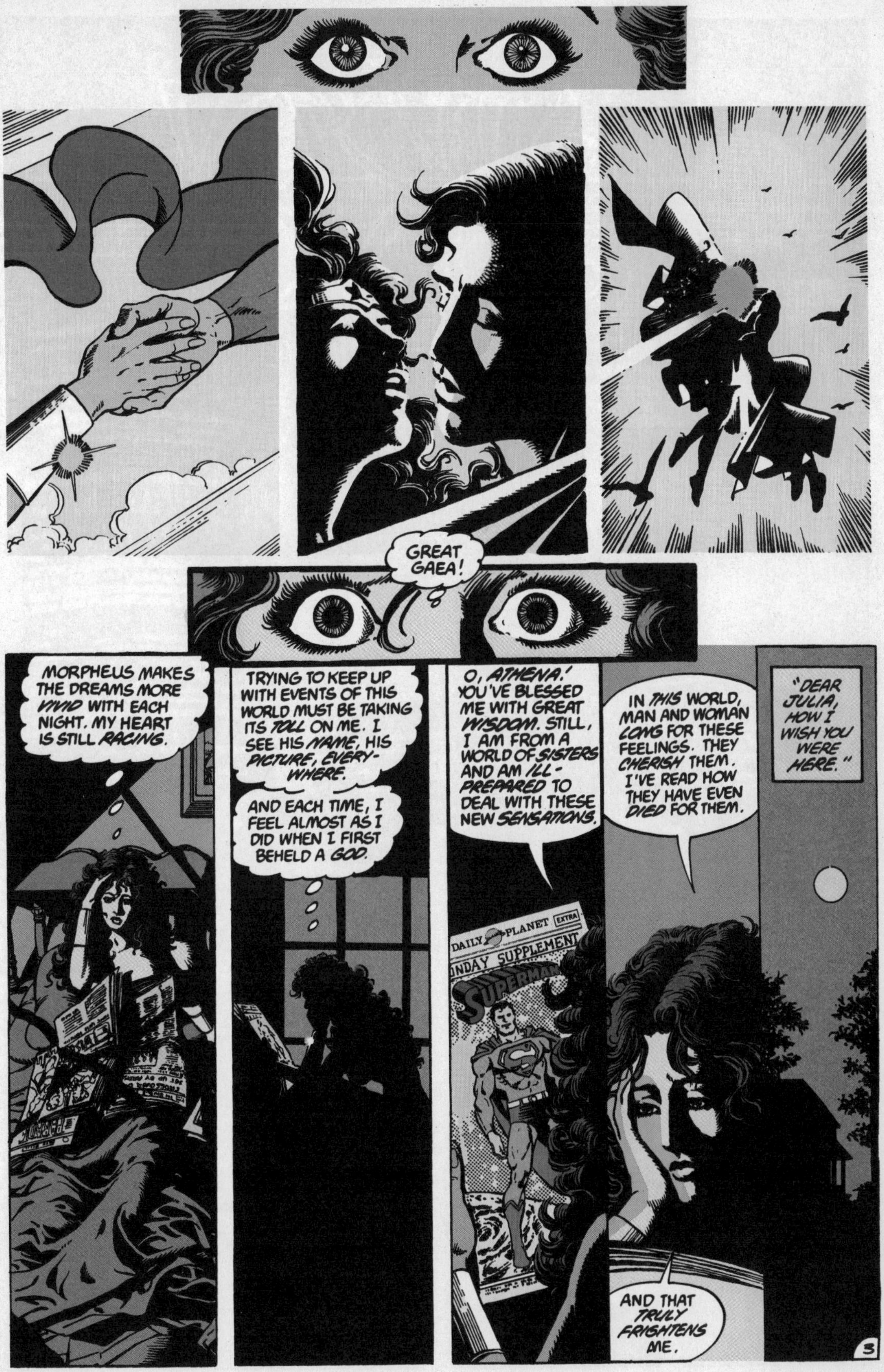
GREAT GAEA!
MORPHEUS MAKES THE DREAMS MORE VIVID WITH EACH NIGHT. MY HEART IS STILL RACING.
TRYING TO KEEP UP WITH EVENTS OF THIS WORLD MUST BE TAKING ITS TOLL ON ME. I SEE HIS NAME, HIS PICTURE, EVERY-WHERE.
AND EACH TIME, I FEEL ALMOST AS I DID WHEN I FIRST BEHELD A GOD.
O, ATHENA! YOU'VE BLESSED ME WITH GREAT WISDOM. STILL, I AM FROM A WORLD OF SISTERS AND AM ILL-PREPARED TO DEAL WITH THESE NEW SENSATIONS.
DAILY PLANET
EXTRA
IN THIS WORLD, MAN AND WOMAN LONG FOR THESE FEELINGS. THEY CHERISH THEM. I'VE READ HOW THEY HAVE EVEN DIED FOR THEM.
"DEAR JULIA, HOW I WISH YOU WERE HERE."
AND THAT TRULY FRIGHTENS ME.
3

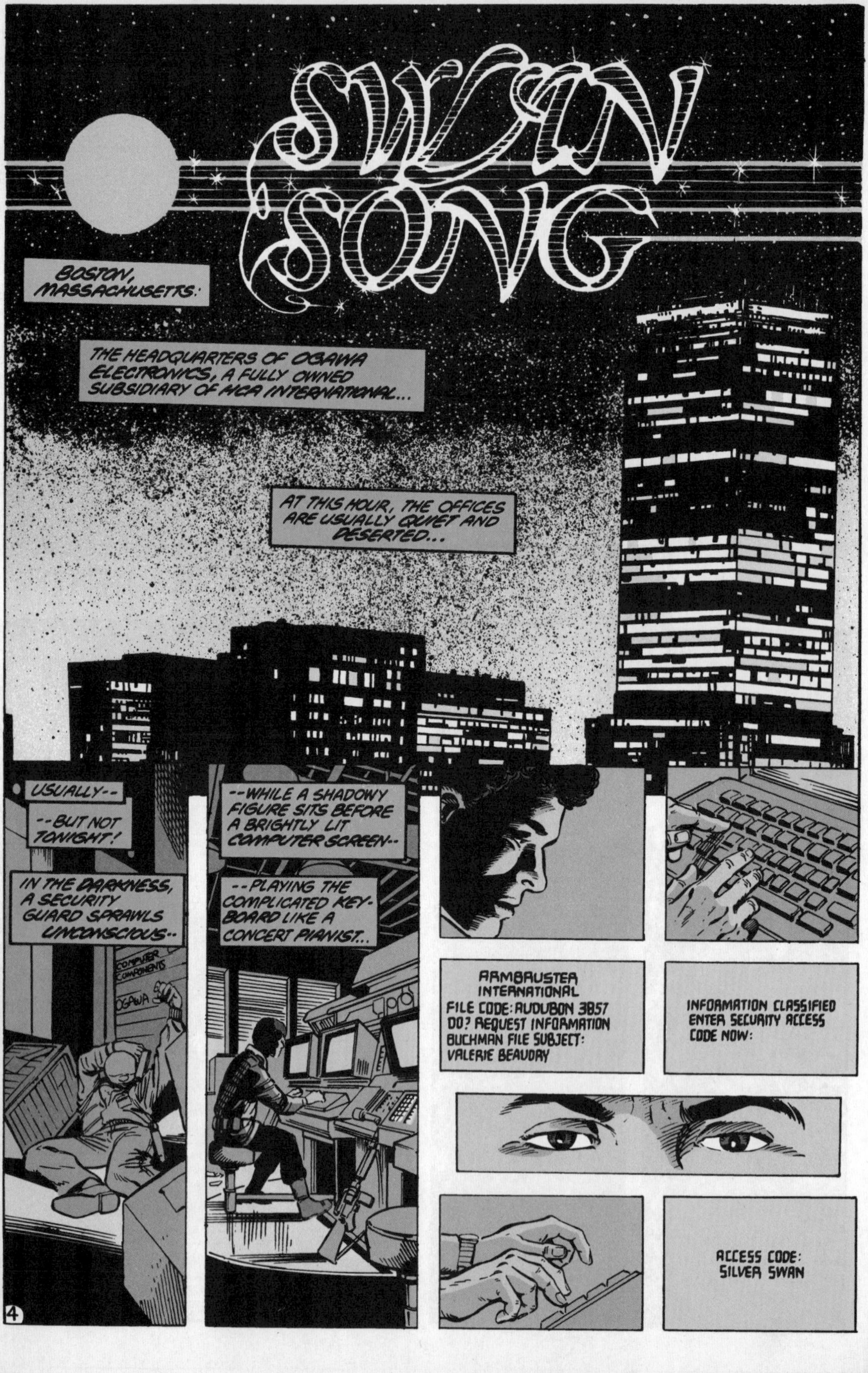
SWAN SONG
BOSTON, MASSACHUSETTS:
THE HEADQUARTERS OF OGAWA ELECTRONICS, A FULLY OWNED SUBSIDIARY OF KGA INTERNATIONAL...
AT THIS HOUR, THE OFFICES ARE USUALLY QUIET AND DESERTED...
USUALLY--
--BUT NOT TONIGHT!
IN THE DARKNESS, A SECURITY GUARD SPRAWLS UNCONSCIOUS--
COMPUTER COMPONENTS
OGAWA
--WHILE A SHADOWY FIGURE SITS BEFORE A BRIGHTLY LIT COMPUTER SCREEN--
--PLAYING THE COMPLICATED KEY-BOARD LIKE A CONCERT PIANIST...
ARMBRUSTER INTERNATIONAL
FILE CODE: AUDUBON 3B57
DO? REQUEST INFORMATION
BUCHMAN FILE SUBJECT:
VALERIE BEAUDRY
INFORMATION CLASSIFIED
ENTER SECURITY ACCESS
CODE NOW:
ACCESS CODE:
SILVER SWAN
4

HEY, MURRAY!!

MURRAY? C'MON, MAN--YOU WERE SUPPOSED TO BE BACK BY NOW!

MURRAY, I'M SERIOUS, MAN-- THIS IS STARTIN' TA SPOOK ME!

MURRAY, EITHER YOU ANSWER ME, MAN--

--OR I'M GONNA ASSUME THE WORST!!

SECURITY, DANGER CODE: SILVER SWAN TARGET: STERNBACH, MAXINE

I'M WARNIN' YA, MAN--!

IF I GOTTA COME IN THERE AFTER YOU--

TEK TOK TAK

--I'M COMIN' IN ARMED AND DANGER--

--UUNNHH!!

HHUNNFF!!

NEXT TIME, FRIEND--

--DON'T ANNOUNCE YOURSELF!

YOU'LL LIVE A LOT LONGER THAT WAY!

5

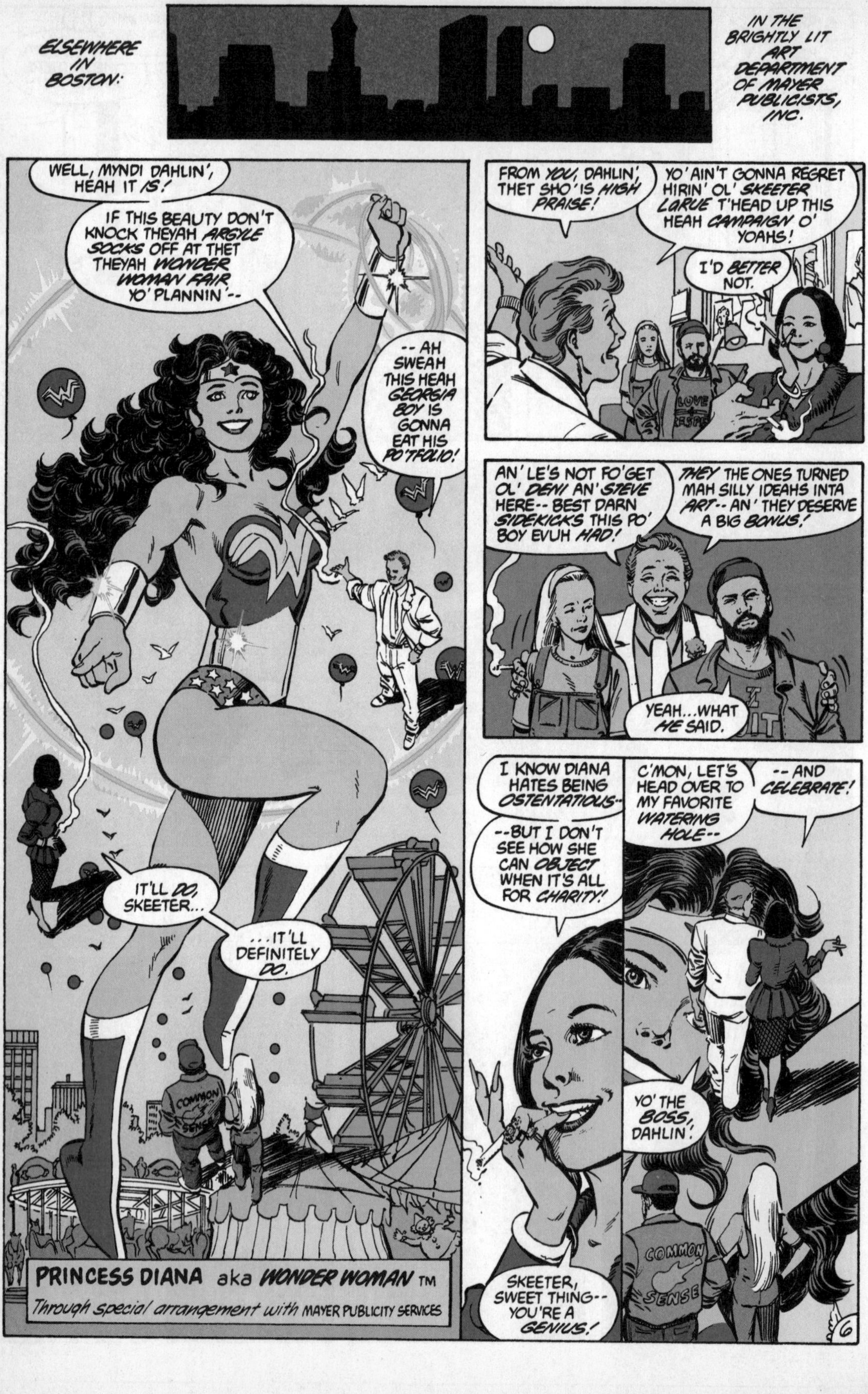
ELSEWHERE IN BOSTON:
IN THE BRIGHTLY LIT ART DEPARTMENT OF MAYER PUBLICISTS, INC.
WELL, MYNDI DAHLIN', HEAH IT IS!
IF THIS BEAUTY DON'T KNOCK THEYAH ARGYLE SOCKS OFF AT THET THEYAH WONDER WOMAN FAIR YO' PLANNIN'--
--AH SWEAH THIS HEAH GEORGIA BOY IS GONNA EAT HIS PO'TFOLIO!
IT'LL DO, SKEETER...
...IT'LL DEFINITELY DO.
COMMON SENSE
PRINCESS DIANA aka WONDER WOMAN ™
Through special arrangement with MAYER PUBLICITY SERVICES
FROM YOU, DAHLIN', THET SHO' IS HIGH PRAISE!
YO' AIN'T GONNA REGRET HIRIN' OL' SKEETER LARUE T'HEAD UP THIS HEAH CAMPAIGN O' YOAHS!
I'D BETTER NOT.
AN' LE'S NOT FO'GET OL' DENI AN' STEVE HERE-- BEST DARN SIDEKICKS THIS PO' BOY EVUH HAD!
THEY THE ONES TURNED MAH SILLY IDEAHS INTA ART-- AN' THEY DESERVE A BIG BONUS!
YEAH...WHAT HE SAID.
I KNOW DIANA HATES BEING OSTENTATIOUS--
--BUT I DON'T SEE HOW SHE CAN OBJECT WHEN IT'S ALL FOR CHARITY!
C'MON, LET'S HEAD OVER TO MY FAVORITE WATERING HOLE--
--AND CELEBRATE!
YO' THE BOSS, DAHLIN'.
COMMON SENSE
SKEETER, SWEET THING-- YOU'RE A GENIUS!
6

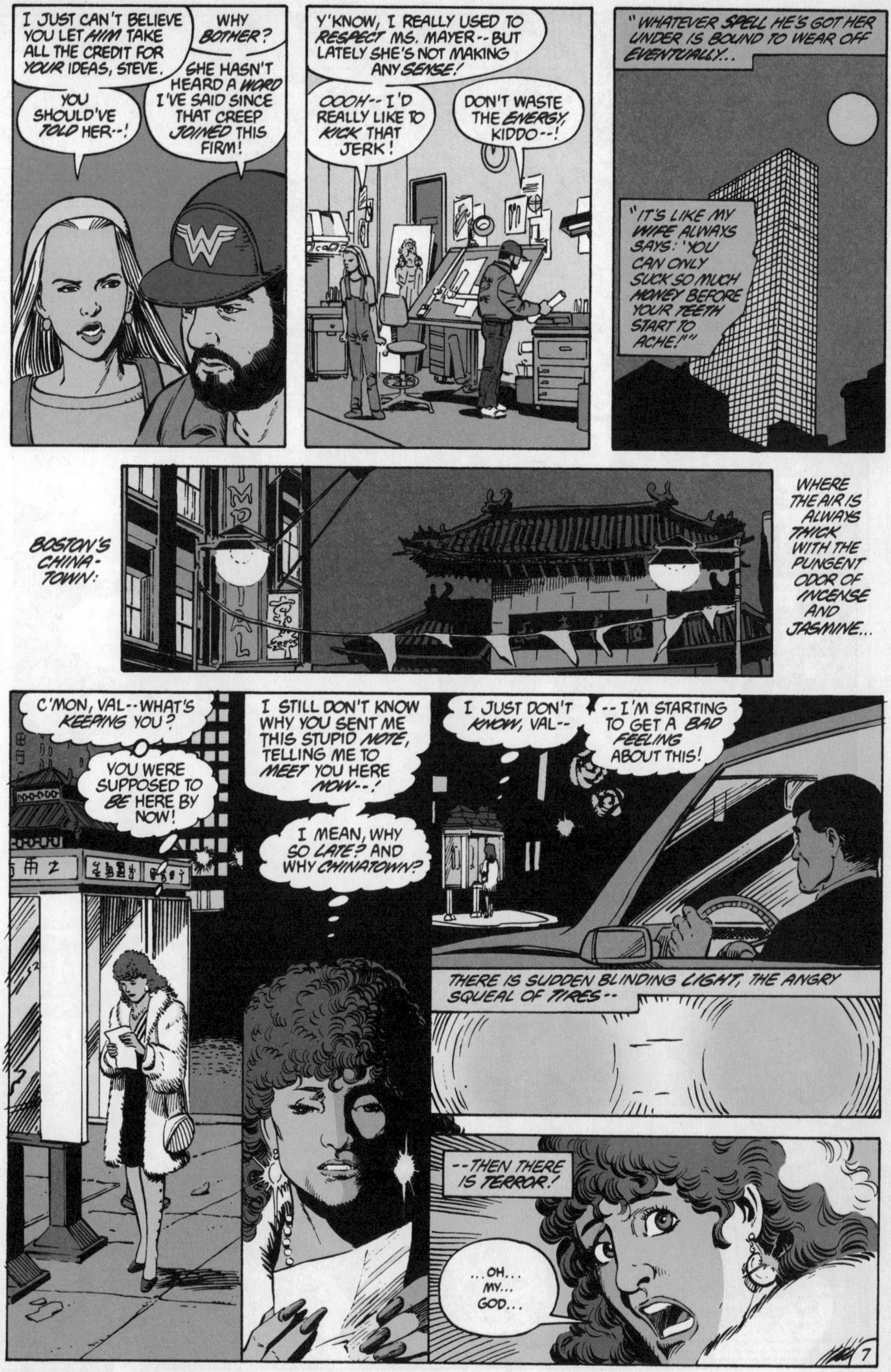
I JUST CAN'T BELIEVE YOU LET HIM TAKE ALL THE CREDIT FOR YOUR IDEAS, STEVE.
WHY BOTHER?
YOU SHOULD'VE TOLD HER--!
SHE HASN'T HEARD A WORD I'VE SAID SINCE THAT CREEP JOINED THIS FIRM!
Y'KNOW, I REALLY USED TO RESPECT MS. MAYER--BUT LATELY SHE'S NOT MAKING ANY SENSE!
OOOH--I'D REALLY LIKE TO KICK THAT JERK!
DON'T WASTE THE ENERGY, KIDDO--!
"WHATEVER SPELL HE'S GOT HER UNDER IS BOUND TO WEAR OFF EVENTUALLY...
"IT'S LIKE MY WIFE ALWAYS SAYS: 'YOU CAN ONLY SUCK SO MUCH MONEY BEFORE YOUR TEETH START TO ACHE!'"
BOSTON'S CHINA-TOWN:
WHERE THE AIR IS ALWAYS THICK WITH THE PUNGENT ODOR OF INCENSE AND JASMINE...
C'MON, VAL--WHAT'S KEEPING YOU?
YOU WERE SUPPOSED TO BE HERE BY NOW!
I STILL DON'T KNOW WHY YOU SENT ME THIS STUPID NOTE, TELLING ME TO MEET YOU HERE NOW--!
I MEAN, WHY SO LATE? AND WHY CHINATOWN?
I JUST DON'T KNOW, VAL--
--I'M STARTING TO GET A BAD FEELING ABOUT THIS!
THERE IS SUDDEN BLINDING LIGHT, THE ANGRY SQUEAL OF TIRES--
--THEN THERE IS TERROR!
...OH... MY... GOD...
7

AND REFLEX FASTER THAN *THOUGHT!*

AAAAAAHH!!

THAT WAS NO *ACCIDENT!*

THAT CAR DELIBERATELY TRIED TO *KILL* ME!

"BUT WHY--?!?"

THOUGHT I COULD *LOSE* HIM IN THIS *ALLEY--* BUT HE'S *GAINING--!*

PLEASE, SOMEBODY-- HELP ME!

I DON'T WANT TO *DIE!*

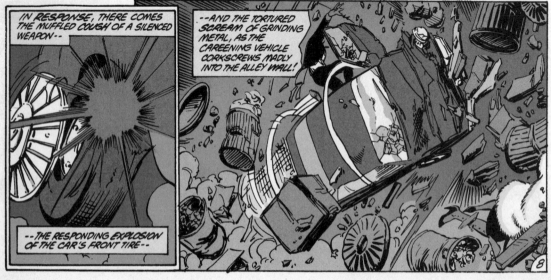

IN RESPONSE, THERE COMES THE MUFFLED COUGH OF A SILENCED WEAPON--

--THE RESPONDING EXPLOSION OF THE CAR'S FRONT TIRE--

--AND THE TORTURED SCREAM OF GRINDING METAL, AS THE CAREENING VEHICLE CORKSCREWS MADLY INTO THE ALLEY WALL!

8

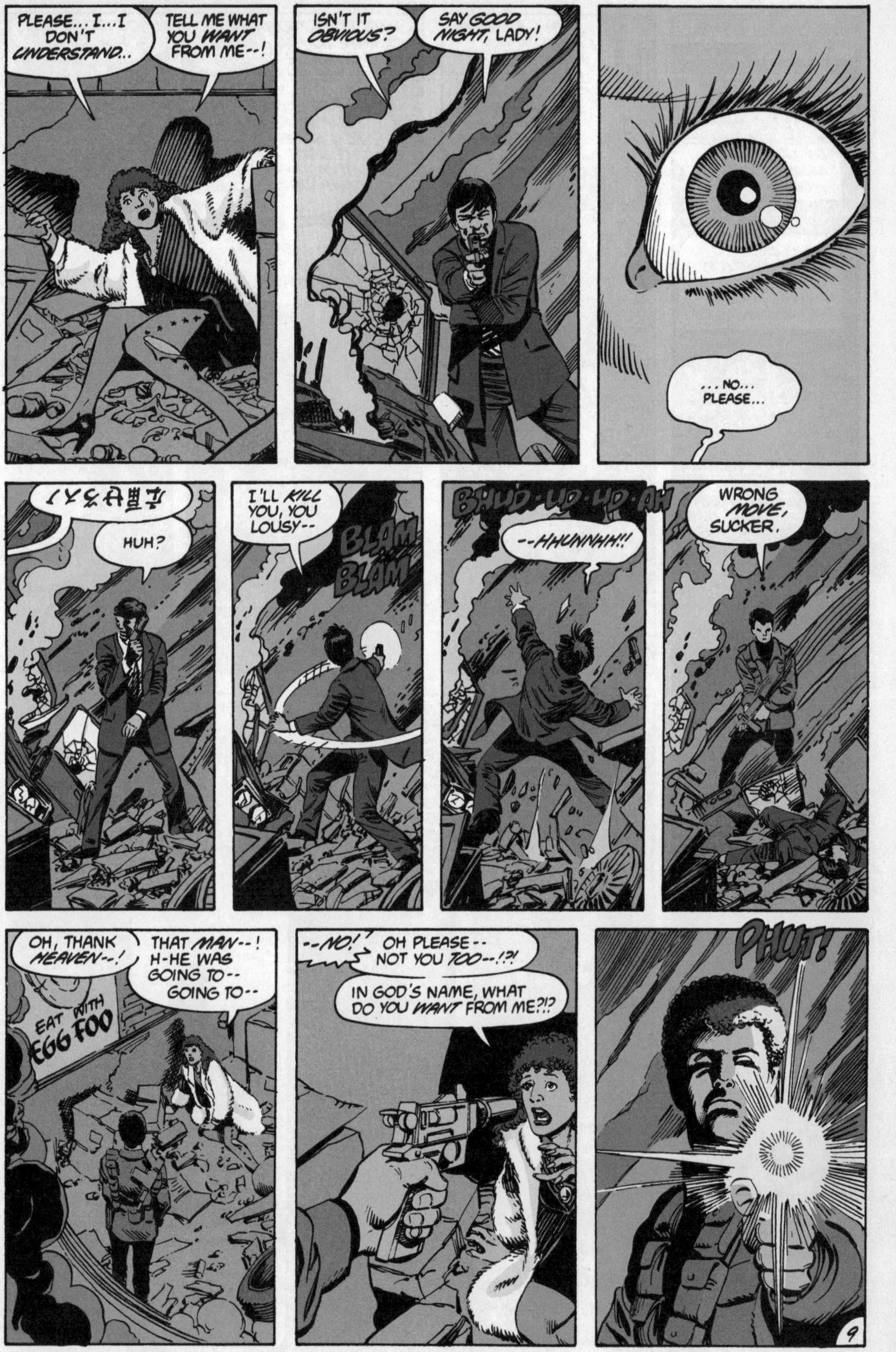
PLEASE... I...I DON'T UNDERSTAND...
TELL ME WHAT YOU WANT FROM ME--!
ISN'T IT OBVIOUS?
SAY GOOD NIGHT, LADY!
... NO... PLEASE...
HUH?
I'LL KILL YOU, YOU LOUSY--
BLAM BLAM
BHUD-UD-UD-AH
--HHUNNHH!!
WRONG MOVE, SUCKER.
OH, THANK HEAVEN--!
THAT MAN--! H-HE WAS GOING TO-- GOING TO--
EAT WITH EGG FOO
--NO!
OH PLEASE-- NOT YOU TOO--!?!
IN GOD'S NAME, WHAT DO YOU WANT FROM ME?!?
PHUT!
9

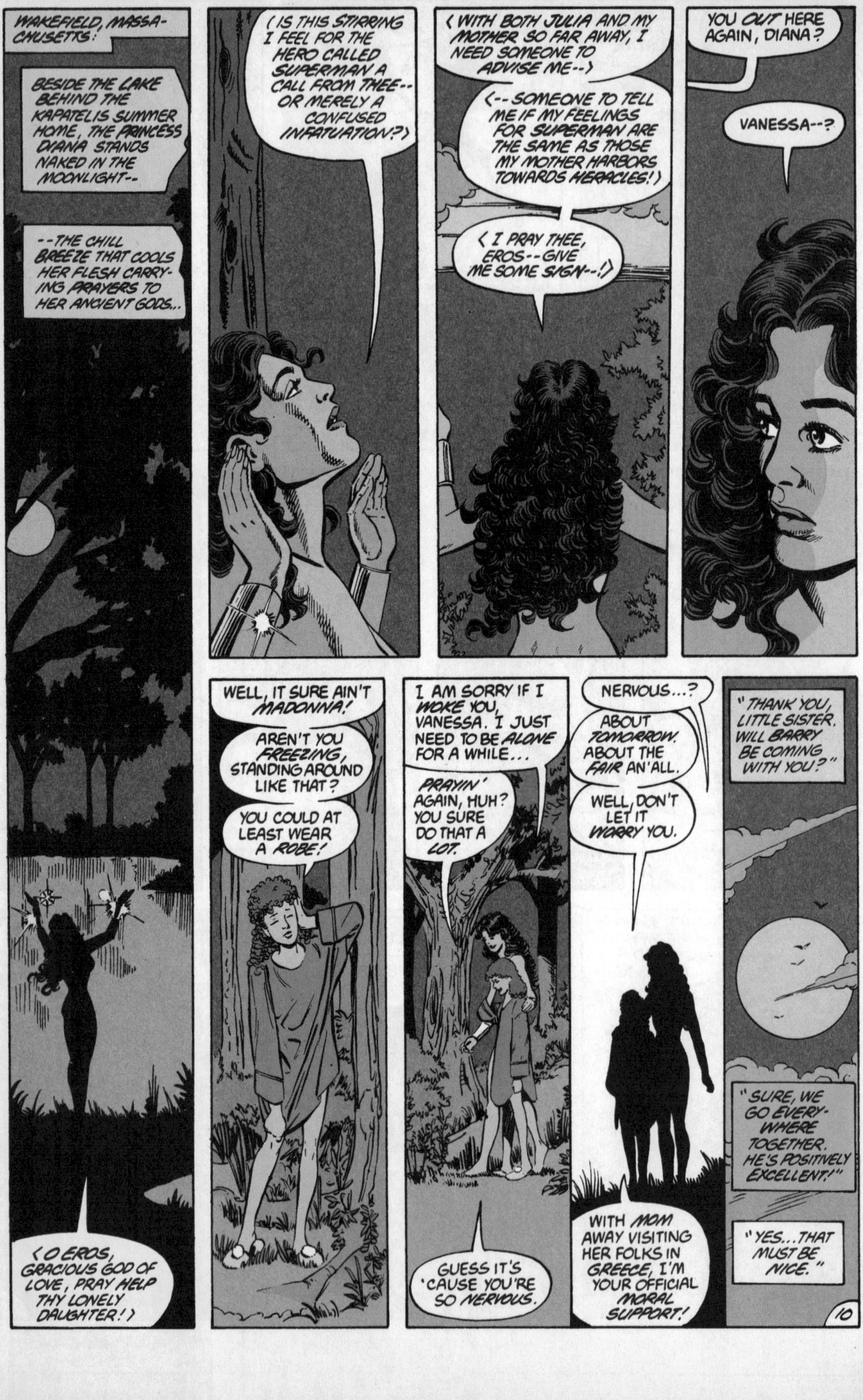

WAKEFIELD, MASSA-CHUSETTS:
BESIDE THE LAKE BEHIND THE KAPATELIS SUMMER HOME, THE PRINCESS DIANA STANDS NAKED IN THE MOONLIGHT--
--THE CHILL BREEZE THAT COOLS HER FLESH CARRY-ING PRAYERS TO HER ANCIENT GODS...
⟨ O EROS, GRACIOUS GOD OF LOVE, PRAY HELP THY LONELY DAUGHTER! ⟩
⟨ IS THIS STIRRING I FEEL FOR THE HERO CALLED SUPERMAN A CALL FROM THEE--OR MERELY A CONFUSED INFATUATION? ⟩
⟨ WITH BOTH JULIA AND MY MOTHER SO FAR AWAY, I NEED SOMEONE TO ADVISE ME-- ⟩
⟨ --SOMEONE TO TELL ME IF MY FEELINGS FOR SUPERMAN ARE THE SAME AS THOSE MY MOTHER HARBORS TOWARDS HERACLES! ⟩
⟨ I PRAY THEE, EROS--GIVE ME SOME SIGN--! ⟩
YOU OUT HERE AGAIN, DIANA?
VANESSA--?
WELL, IT SURE AIN'T MADONNA!
AREN'T YOU FREEZING, STANDING AROUND LIKE THAT?
YOU COULD AT LEAST WEAR A ROBE!
I AM SORRY IF I WOKE YOU, VANESSA. I JUST NEED TO BE ALONE FOR A WHILE...
PRAYIN' AGAIN, HUH? YOU SURE DO THAT A LOT.
GUESS IT'S 'CAUSE YOU'RE SO NERVOUS.
NERVOUS...?
ABOUT TOMORROW. ABOUT THE FAIR AN'ALL.
WELL, DON'T LET IT WORRY YOU.
WITH MOM AWAY VISITING HER FOLKS IN GREECE, I'M YOUR OFFICIAL MORAL SUPPORT!
"THANK YOU, LITTLE SISTER. WILL BARRY BE COMING WITH YOU?"
"SURE, WE GO EVERY-WHERE TOGETHER. HE'S POSITIVELY EXCELLENT!"
"YES...THAT MUST BE NICE."
10

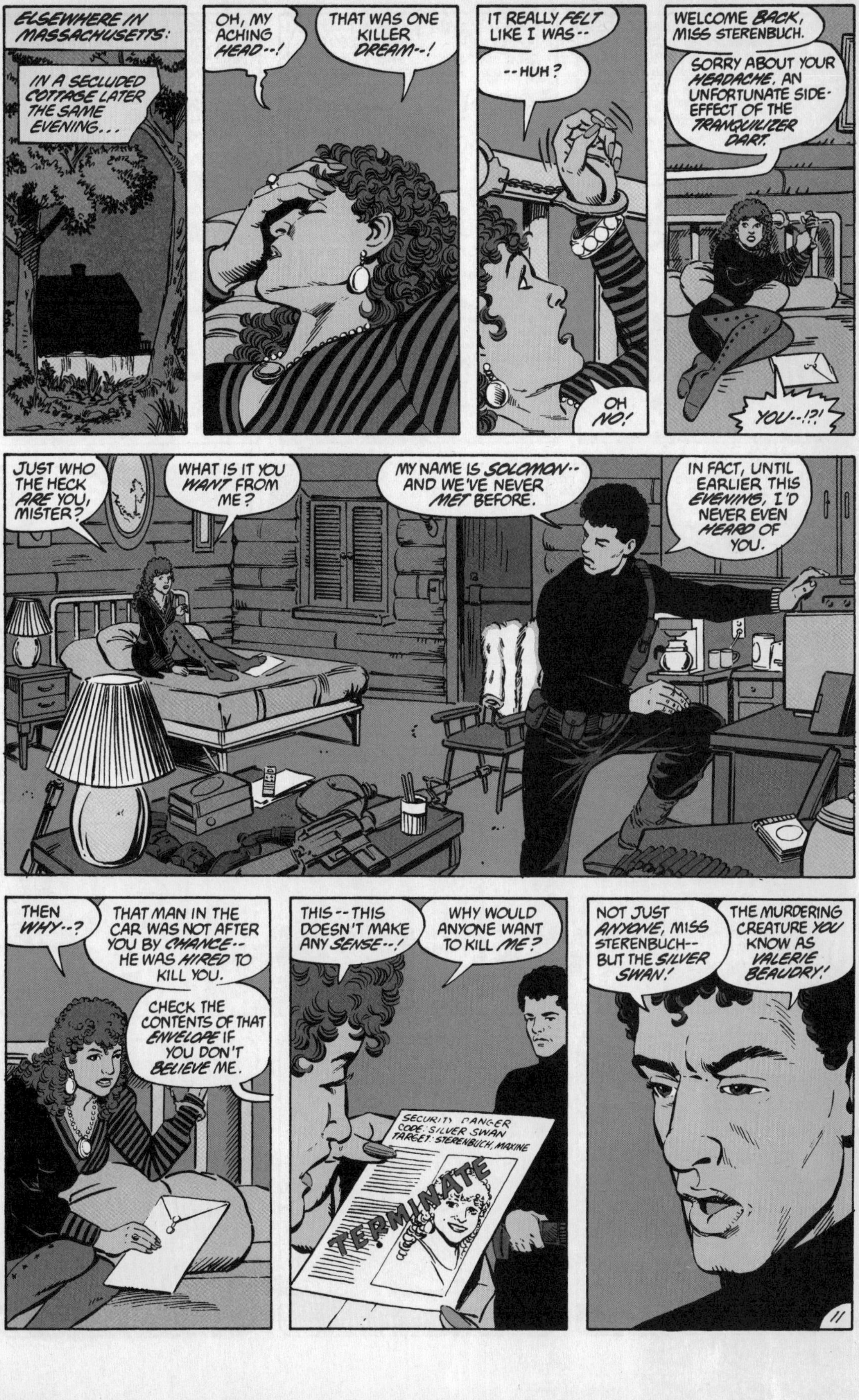
ELSEWHERE IN MASSACHUSETTS:
IN A SECLUDED COTTAGE LATER THE SAME EVENING...
OH, MY ACHING HEAD--!
THAT WAS ONE KILLER DREAM--!
IT REALLY FELT LIKE I WAS--
--HUH?
OH NO!
WELCOME BACK, MISS STERENBUCH.
SORRY ABOUT YOUR HEADACHE. AN UNFORTUNATE SIDE-EFFECT OF THE TRANQUILIZER DART.
YOU--!?!
JUST WHO THE HECK ARE YOU, MISTER?
WHAT IS IT YOU WANT FROM ME?
MY NAME IS SOLOMON--AND WE'VE NEVER MET BEFORE.
IN FACT, UNTIL EARLIER THIS EVENING, I'D NEVER EVEN HEARD OF YOU.
THEN WHY--?
THAT MAN IN THE CAR WAS NOT AFTER YOU BY CHANCE--HE WAS HIRED TO KILL YOU.
CHECK THE CONTENTS OF THAT ENVELOPE IF YOU DON'T BELIEVE ME.
THIS--THIS DOESN'T MAKE ANY SENSE--!
WHY WOULD ANYONE WANT TO KILL ME?
SECURITY DANGER
CODE: SILVER SWAN
TARGET: STERENBUCH, MAXINE
TERMINATE
NOT JUST ANYONE, MISS STERENBUCH--BUT THE SILVER SWAN!
THE MURDERING CREATURE YOU KNOW AS VALERIE BEAUDRY!
11

YOU'RE *CRAZY!* VAL WOULD *NEVER* DO ANY SUCH *THING!*

NO, *ARMBRUSTER* PUT YOU UP TO THIS, DIDN'T HE? HE *ARRANGED* ALL THIS JUST TO KEEP ME *AWAY* FROM VAL--!

SURE, *THAT'S* IT--YOU'RE ONLY TRYING TO *SCARE* ME--!

IF WHAT YOU'RE SAYING WERE *TRUE,* MISS STERENBUCH--

--IT WOULD HAVE BEEN A GREAT DEAL EASIER MERELY TO *KILL* YOU.

BESIDES, I AM WELL AWARE THAT YOU AND THE SILVER SWAN HAD NOT EVEN *MET* UNTIL A FEW SHORT *MONTHS* AGO.

STOP *CALLING* HER THAT! HER NAME IS *VALERIE!*

AND WE *ARE* FRIENDS-- *TRUE* FRIENDS!

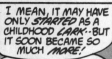

I MEAN, IT MAY HAVE ONLY *STARTED* AS A CHILDHOOD *LARK*--BUT IT SOON BECAME SO MUCH *MORE!*

Y'SEE, WHEN I WAS *FIFTEEN,* I THOUGHT IT WOULD BE FUN TO HAVE A *PEN-PAL...*

"THEN, AN AD IN ONE OF THOSE *TEEN MAGAZINES* CAUGHT MY EYE..."

PEN-PAL WANTED: Do you want a *real* friend--a REAL friend? Warm, sensitive 15-year-old girl seeks new girlfriend to share thoughts. LOVE: poetry, bike-riding, old movies, singing, and Janis Ian. HATE: Superficial people. A true friend is the most treasured thing in the world. Please, if you want a heart to share, write to Valerie Beaudry, P.O. Box 23, Woodworth, ND. No photo

"VAL WROTE BACK IMMEDIATELY--THE MOST BEAUTIFUL LETTER I'D EVER READ..."

"FROM THEN ON, WE WERE *CONFIDANTS,* SHARING EVERY EVENT, EVERY *FEELING.* SHE WAS *WARM...* AND *GIVING...* AND NEVER ASKED ANYTHING MORE THAN TO BE MY FRIEND..."

"WHEN I TURNED *SIXTEEN,* I SENT HER MY *PICTURE,* SO SHE WOULD KNOW THE FACE BEHIND MY *HEART*--"

"--BUT SHE NEVER SENT A PICTURE *BACK!*"

"STILL, SHE WAS ALWAYS *WITH* ME--"

"--AT MY *SENIOR* PROM--"

"--THROUGH EVERY *BREAK-UP* WITH EVERY NEW BOYFRIEND--"

"--VAL GREW UP WITH ME, AND THE *POEMS* SHE WROTE ME WERE MORE *COMFORTING* THAN A MOTHER'S *KISS...*"

12

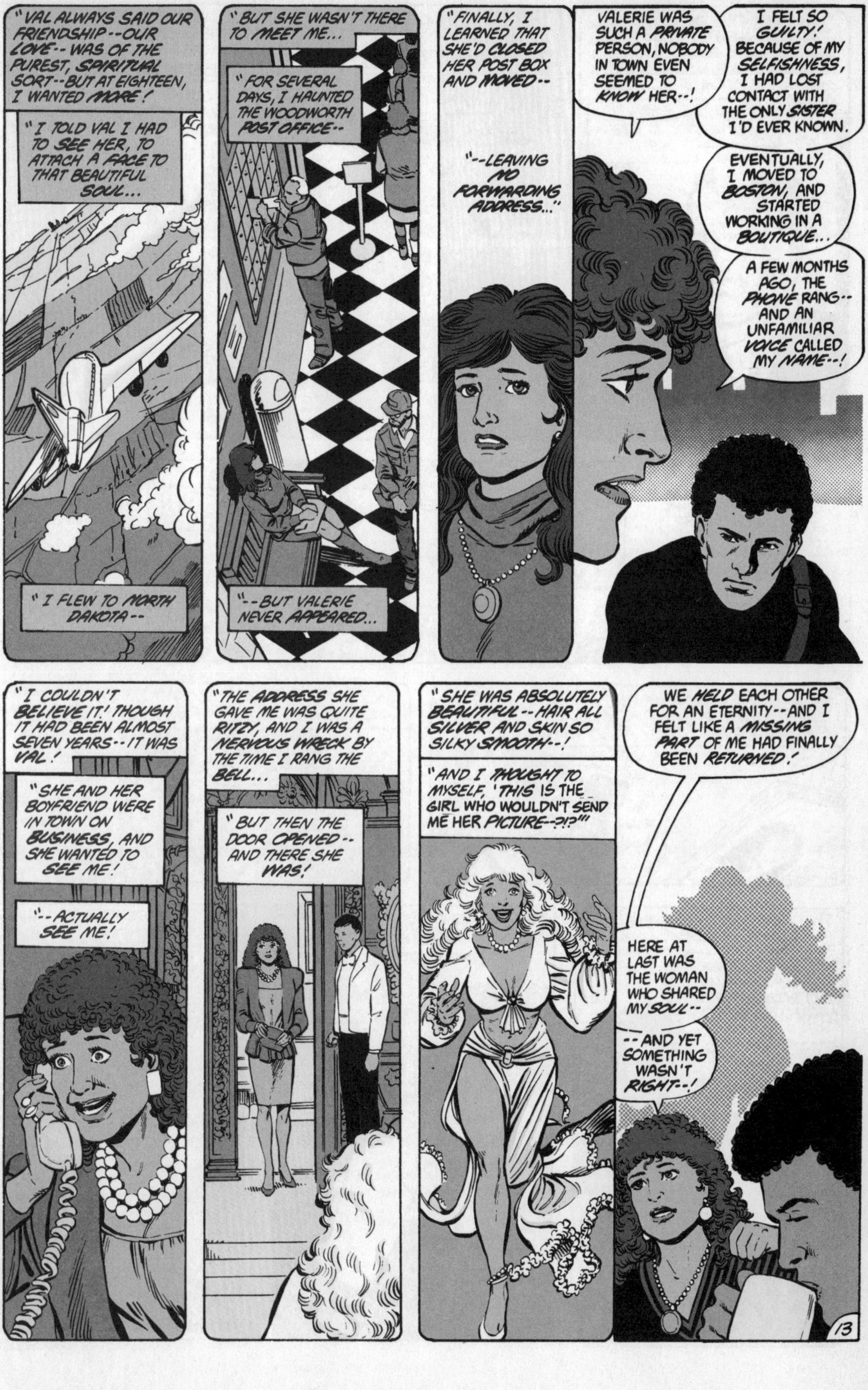
"VAL ALWAYS SAID OUR FRIENDSHIP--OUR LOVE--WAS OF THE PUREST, SPIRITUAL SORT--BUT AT EIGHTEEN, I WANTED MORE!
"I TOLD VAL I HAD TO SEE HER, TO ATTACH A FACE TO THAT BEAUTIFUL SOUL...
"I FLEW TO NORTH DAKOTA--
"BUT SHE WASN'T THERE TO MEET ME...
"FOR SEVERAL DAYS, I HAUNTED THE WOODWORTH POST OFFICE--
"--BUT VALERIE NEVER APPEARED...
"FINALLY, I LEARNED THAT SHE'D CLOSED HER POST BOX AND MOVED--
"--LEAVING NO FORWARDING ADDRESS..."
VALERIE WAS SUCH A PRIVATE PERSON, NOBODY IN TOWN EVEN SEEMED TO KNOW HER--!
I FELT SO GUILTY! BECAUSE OF MY SELFISHNESS, I HAD LOST CONTACT WITH THE ONLY SISTER I'D EVER KNOWN.
EVENTUALLY, I MOVED TO BOSTON, AND STARTED WORKING IN A BOUTIQUE...
A FEW MONTHS AGO, THE PHONE RANG--AND AN UNFAMILIAR VOICE CALLED MY NAME--!
"I COULDN'T BELIEVE IT! THOUGH IT HAD BEEN ALMOST SEVEN YEARS--IT WAS VAL!
"SHE AND HER BOYFRIEND WERE IN TOWN ON BUSINESS, AND SHE WANTED TO SEE ME!
"--ACTUALLY SEE ME!
"THE ADDRESS SHE GAVE ME WAS QUITE RITZY, AND I WAS A NERVOUS WRECK BY THE TIME I RANG THE BELL...
"BUT THEN THE DOOR OPENED--AND THERE SHE WAS!
"SHE WAS ABSOLUTELY BEAUTIFUL--HAIR ALL SILVER AND SKIN SO SILKY SMOOTH--!
"AND I THOUGHT TO MYSELF, 'THIS IS THE GIRL WHO WOULDN'T SEND ME HER PICTURE--?!?'"
WE HELD EACH OTHER FOR AN ETERNITY--AND I FELT LIKE A MISSING PART OF ME HAD FINALLY BEEN RETURNED!
HERE AT LAST WAS THE WOMAN WHO SHARED MY SOUL--
--AND YET SOMETHING WASN'T RIGHT--!
13

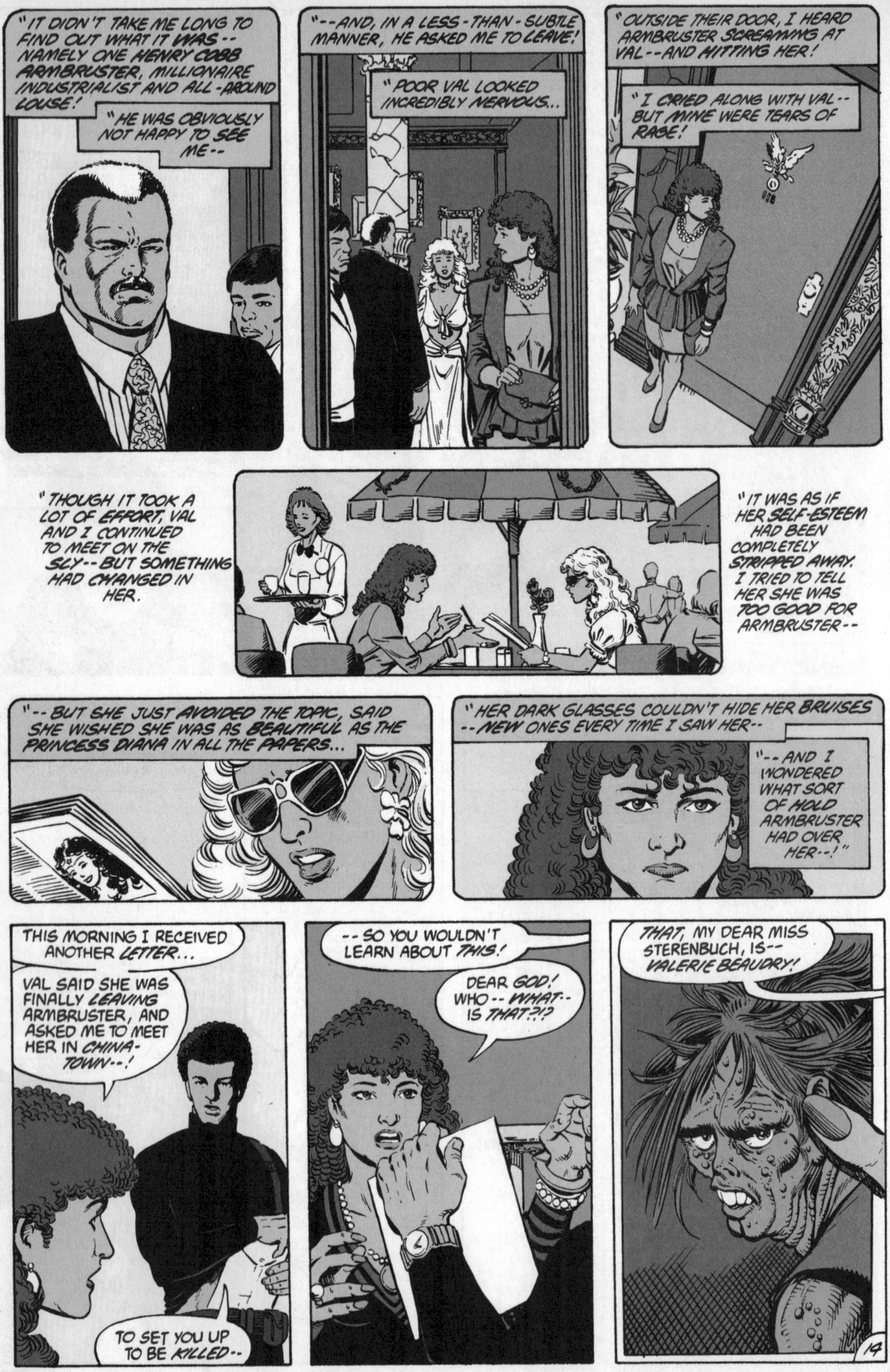
"IT DIDN'T TAKE ME LONG TO FIND OUT WHAT IT WAS -- NAMELY ONE HENRY COBB ARMBRUSTER, MILLIONAIRE INDUSTRIALIST AND ALL-AROUND LOUSE!
"HE WAS OBVIOUSLY NOT HAPPY TO SEE ME --
"-- AND, IN A LESS-THAN-SUBTLE MANNER, HE ASKED ME TO LEAVE!
"POOR VAL LOOKED INCREDIBLY NERVOUS...
"OUTSIDE THEIR DOOR, I HEARD ARMBRUSTER SCREAMING AT VAL -- AND HITTING HER!
"I CRIED ALONG WITH VAL -- BUT MINE WERE TEARS OF RAGE!
"THOUGH IT TOOK A LOT OF EFFORT, VAL AND I CONTINUED TO MEET ON THE SLY -- BUT SOMETHING HAD CHANGED IN HER.
"IT WAS AS IF HER SELF-ESTEEM HAD BEEN COMPLETELY STRIPPED AWAY. I TRIED TO TELL HER SHE WAS TOO GOOD FOR ARMBRUSTER --
"-- BUT SHE JUST AVOIDED THE TOPIC, SAID SHE WISHED SHE WAS AS BEAUTIFUL AS THE PRINCESS DIANA IN ALL THE PAPERS...
"HER DARK GLASSES COULDN'T HIDE HER BRUISES -- NEW ONES EVERY TIME I SAW HER --
"-- AND I WONDERED WHAT SORT OF HOLD ARMBRUSTER HAD OVER HER --!"
THIS MORNING I RECEIVED ANOTHER LETTER...
VAL SAID SHE WAS FINALLY LEAVING ARMBRUSTER, AND ASKED ME TO MEET HER IN CHINA-TOWN --!
TO SET YOU UP TO BE KILLED --
-- SO YOU WOULDN'T LEARN ABOUT THIS!
DEAR GOD! WHO -- WHAT -- IS THAT?!?
THAT, MY DEAR MISS STERENBUCH, IS -- VALERIE BEAUDRY!
14

BUT *WHY*-- *HOW*--?!? HER *PARENTS* WERE BOTH EXPOSED TO EARLY *NUCLEAR TESTS*. THEY'RE *DEAD* NOW.

THAT PHOTO WAS TAKEN *FIVE YEARS AGO*--WHEN SHE WAS THE SUBJECT OF AN *EXPERIMENT* CODE-NAMED *SILVER SWAN!*

ACCORDING TO THESE *RECORDS* I STOLE, BEAUDRY DEVELOPED *MUTANT SONIC-DISRUPTION ABILITIES*..

--WHICH *ARMBRUSTER INTERNATIONAL* INTENDED TO DEVELOP FOR ITS OWN *USE.*

LOOK, I SPLICED THIS *TAPE* TOGETHER FROM SCRAPS THAT SURVIVED THE EXPLOSION OF *HCA LABS' ALASKAN BRANCH.*

YOU'LL NOTICE THAT ITS *SOUNDTRACK* HAS BEEN *INEXPLICABLY ERASED.*

PAY PARTICULAR ATTENTION TO THE *OLD MAN* ON THE SCREEN...

"THAT IS MY FATHER--PROFESSOR BENJAMIN BUCHMAN--IN MORTAL FEAR FOR HIS LIFE! I'VE MEMORIZED EVERY INCH OF THIS TAPE...THE TERROR IN MY FATHER'S EYES...THE EXPLOSIONS...HIS FUTILE EFFORTS TO ESCAPE...

"...AND HIS PURSUER...THE THING HE HAD CREATED...STALKING HIM THROUGH THE RUINS...ITS FEET NEVER TOUCHING THE FLOOR...FINALLY CORNERING HIM...SILVER-BLUE EYES FILLED WITH A COLD, CALCULATING MADNESS THAT IGNITED THE AIR AROUND HER...

...THEN THAT SCREAM I CANNOT HEAR... AND ALL THAT REMAINED OF MY FATHER WAS A PUDDLE!

"YOUR PRECIOUS FRIEND IS ARMBRUSTER'S FRANKEN-STEIN, MISS STERENBUCH... THE SILVER SWAN..."

...THE *MONSTER* I HAVE SWORN TO *DESTROY!*

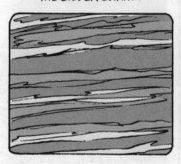

KLIK

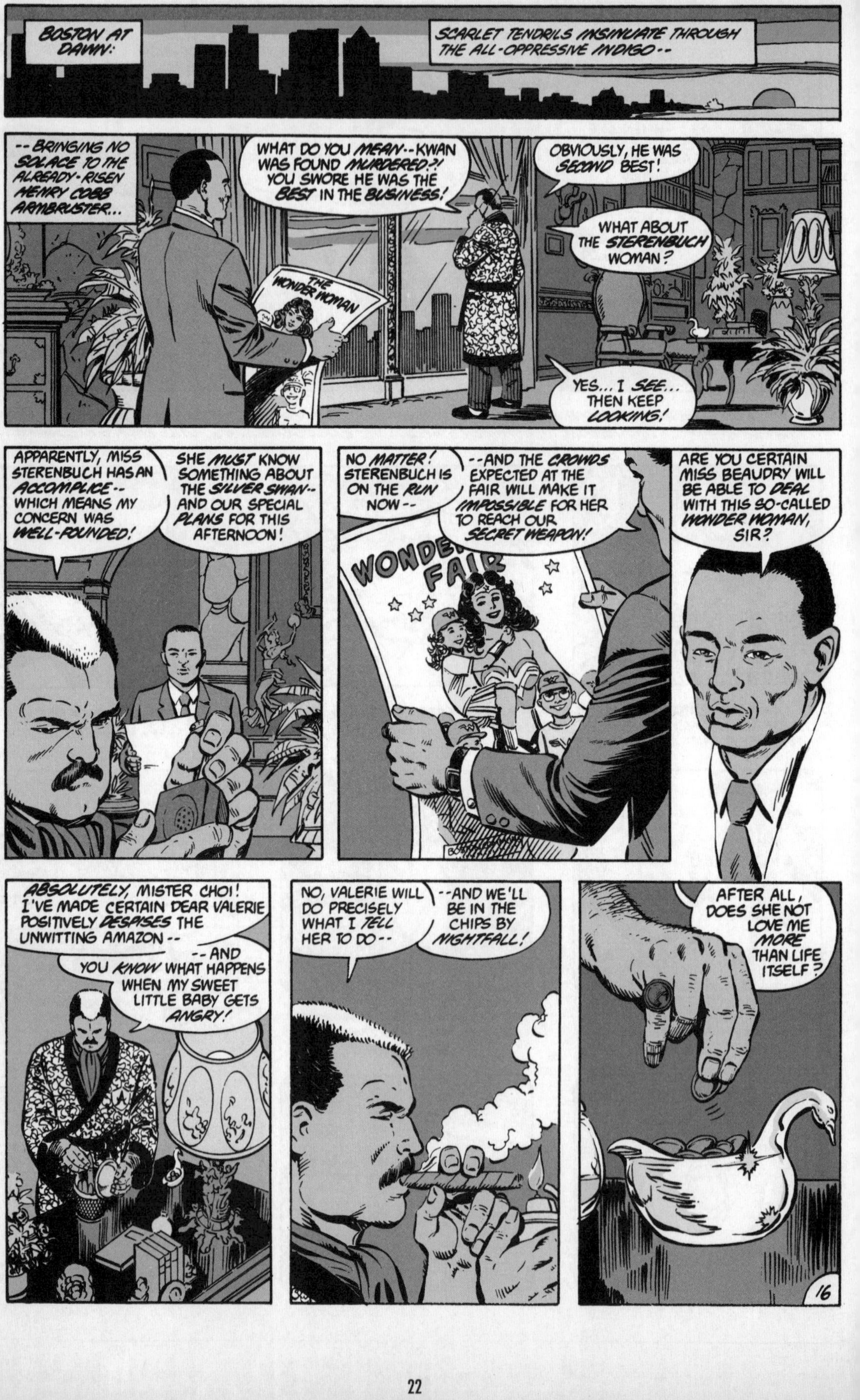

BOSTON AT DAWN:
SCARLET TENDRILS INSINUATE THROUGH THE ALL-OPPRESSIVE INDIGO--
--BRINGING NO SOLACE TO THE ALREADY-RISEN HENRY COBB ARMBRUSTER...
WHAT DO YOU MEAN--KWAN WAS FOUND MURDERED?! YOU SWORE HE WAS THE BEST IN THE BUSINESS!
OBVIOUSLY, HE WAS SECOND BEST!
WHAT ABOUT THE STERENBUCH WOMAN?
YES... I SEE... THEN KEEP LOOKING!
THE WONDER WOMAN
APPARENTLY, MISS STERENBUCH HAS AN ACCOMPLICE-- WHICH MEANS MY CONCERN WAS WELL-FOUNDED!
SHE MUST KNOW SOMETHING ABOUT THE SILVER SWAN-- AND OUR SPECIAL PLANS FOR THIS AFTERNOON!
NO MATTER! STERENBUCH IS ON THE RUN NOW--
--AND THE CROWDS EXPECTED AT THE FAIR WILL MAKE IT IMPOSSIBLE FOR HER TO REACH OUR SECRET WEAPON!
ARE YOU CERTAIN MISS BEAUDRY WILL BE ABLE TO DEAL WITH THIS SO-CALLED WONDER WOMAN, SIR?
ABSOLUTELY, MISTER CHOI! I'VE MADE CERTAIN DEAR VALERIE POSITIVELY DESPISES THE UNWITTING AMAZON--
--AND YOU KNOW WHAT HAPPENS WHEN MY SWEET LITTLE BABY GETS ANGRY!
NO, VALERIE WILL DO PRECISELY WHAT I TELL HER TO DO--
--AND WE'LL BE IN THE CHIPS BY NIGHTFALL!
AFTER ALL, DOES SHE NOT LOVE ME MORE THAN LIFE ITSELF?
16

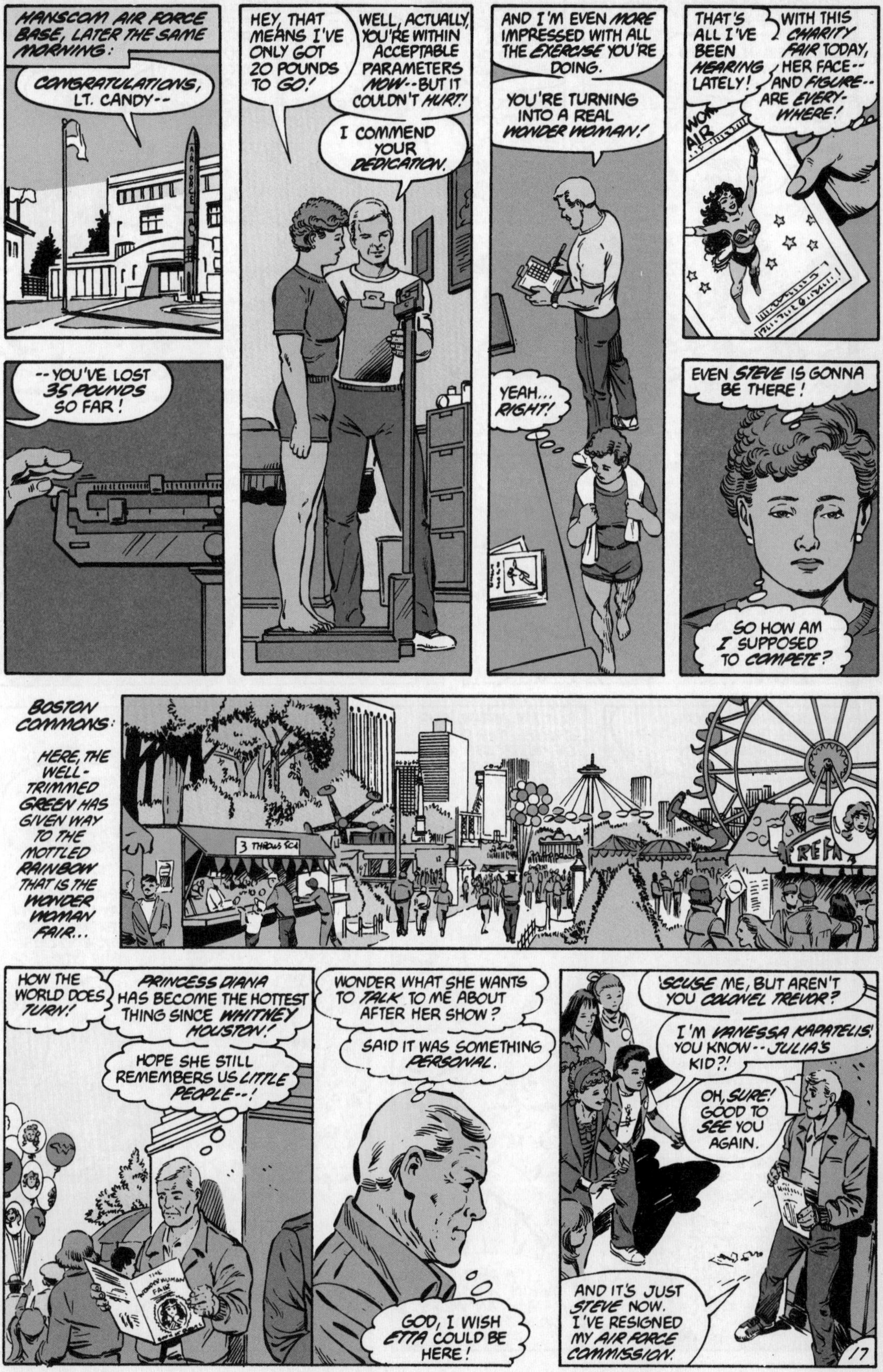
HANSCOM AIR FORCE BASE, LATER THE SAME MORNING:
CONGRATULATIONS, LT. CANDY--
--YOU'VE LOST 35 POUNDS SO FAR!
HEY, THAT MEANS I'VE ONLY GOT 20 POUNDS TO GO!
WELL, ACTUALLY, YOU'RE WITHIN ACCEPTABLE PARAMETERS NOW--BUT IT COULDN'T HURT!
I COMMEND YOUR DEDICATION.
AND I'M EVEN MORE IMPRESSED WITH ALL THE EXERCISE YOU'RE DOING.
YOU'RE TURNING INTO A REAL WONDER WOMAN!
YEAH... RIGHT!
THAT'S ALL I'VE BEEN HEARING LATELY!
WITH THIS CHARITY FAIR TODAY, HER FACE--AND FIGURE--ARE EVERYWHERE!
EVEN STEVE IS GONNA BE THERE!
SO HOW AM I SUPPOSED TO COMPETE?
BOSTON COMMONS:
HERE, THE WELL-TRIMMED GREEN HAS GIVEN WAY TO THE MOTTLED RAINBOW THAT IS THE WONDER WOMAN FAIR...
3 THROWS
HOW THE WORLD DOES TURN!
PRINCESS DIANA HAS BECOME THE HOTTEST THING SINCE WHITNEY HOUSTON!
HOPE SHE STILL REMEMBERS US LITTLE PEOPLE--!
WONDER WHAT SHE WANTS TO TALK TO ME ABOUT AFTER HER SHOW?
SAID IT WAS SOMETHING PERSONAL.
GOD, I WISH ETTA COULD BE HERE!
'SCUSE ME, BUT AREN'T YOU COLONEL TREVOR?
I'M VANESSA KAPATELIS! YOU KNOW--JULIA'S KID?!
OH, SURE! GOOD TO SEE YOU AGAIN.
AND IT'S JUST STEVE NOW. I'VE RESIGNED MY AIR FORCE COMMISSION.
17

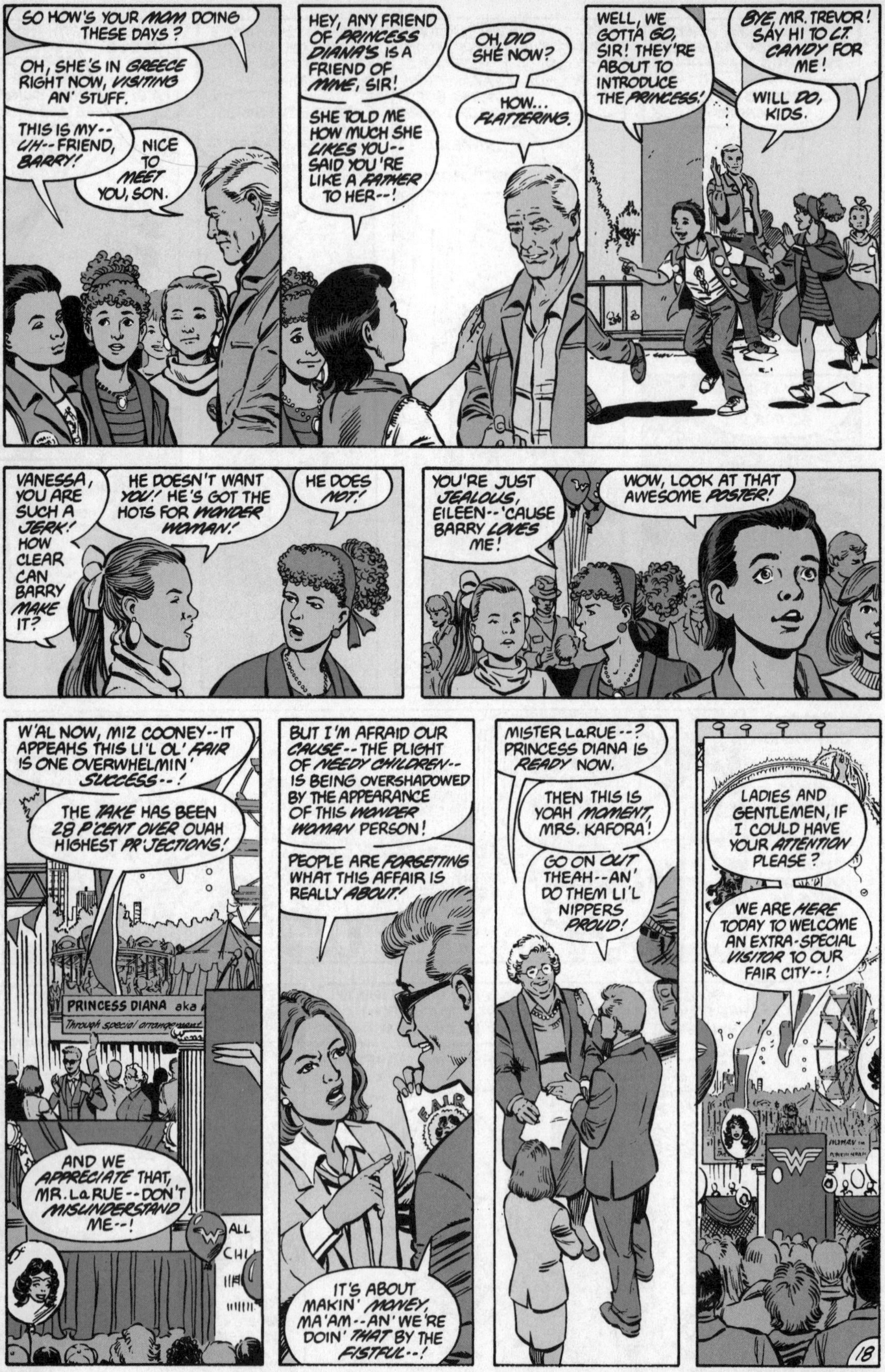

SO HOW'S YOUR MOM DOING THESE DAYS?
OH, SHE'S IN GREECE RIGHT NOW, VISITING AN' STUFF.
THIS IS MY-- UH-- FRIEND, BARRY!
NICE TO MEET YOU, SON.
HEY, ANY FRIEND OF PRINCESS DIANA'S IS A FRIEND OF MINE, SIR!
SHE TOLD ME HOW MUCH SHE LIKES YOU-- SAID YOU'RE LIKE A FATHER TO HER--!
OH, DID SHE NOW?
HOW... FLATTERING.
WELL, WE GOTTA GO, SIR! THEY'RE ABOUT TO INTRODUCE THE PRINCESS!
BYE, MR. TREVOR! SAY HI TO LT. CANDY FOR ME!
WILL DO, KIDS.
VANESSA, YOU ARE SUCH A JERK! HOW CLEAR CAN BARRY MAKE IT?
HE DOESN'T WANT YOU! HE'S GOT THE HOTS FOR WONDER WOMAN!
HE DOES NOT!
YOU'RE JUST JEALOUS, EILEEN--'CAUSE BARRY LOVES ME!
WOW, LOOK AT THAT AWESOME POSTER!
W'AL NOW, MIZ COONEY--IT APPEAHS THIS LI'L OL' FAIR IS ONE OVERWHELMIN' SUCCESS--!
THE TAKE HAS BEEN 28 P'CENT OVER OUAH HIGHEST PR'JECTIONS!
PRINCESS DIANA aka
Through special arrangement
AND WE APPRECIATE THAT, MR. LaRUE--DON'T MISUNDERSTAND ME--!
BUT I'M AFRAID OUR CAUSE--THE PLIGHT OF NEEDY CHILDREN--IS BEING OVERSHADOWED BY THE APPEARANCE OF THIS WONDER WOMAN PERSON!
PEOPLE ARE FORGETTING WHAT THIS AFFAIR IS REALLY ABOUT!
IT'S ABOUT MAKIN' MONEY, MA'AM--AN' WE'RE DOIN' THAT BY THE FISTFUL--!
MISTER LaRUE--? PRINCESS DIANA IS READY NOW.
THEN THIS IS YOAH MOMENT, MRS. KAFORA!
GO ON OUT THEAH--AN' DO THEM LI'L NIPPERS PROUD!
LADIES AND GENTLEMEN, IF I COULD HAVE YOUR ATTENTION PLEASE?
WE ARE HERE TODAY TO WELCOME AN EXTRA-SPECIAL VISITOR TO OUR FAIR CITY--!
18

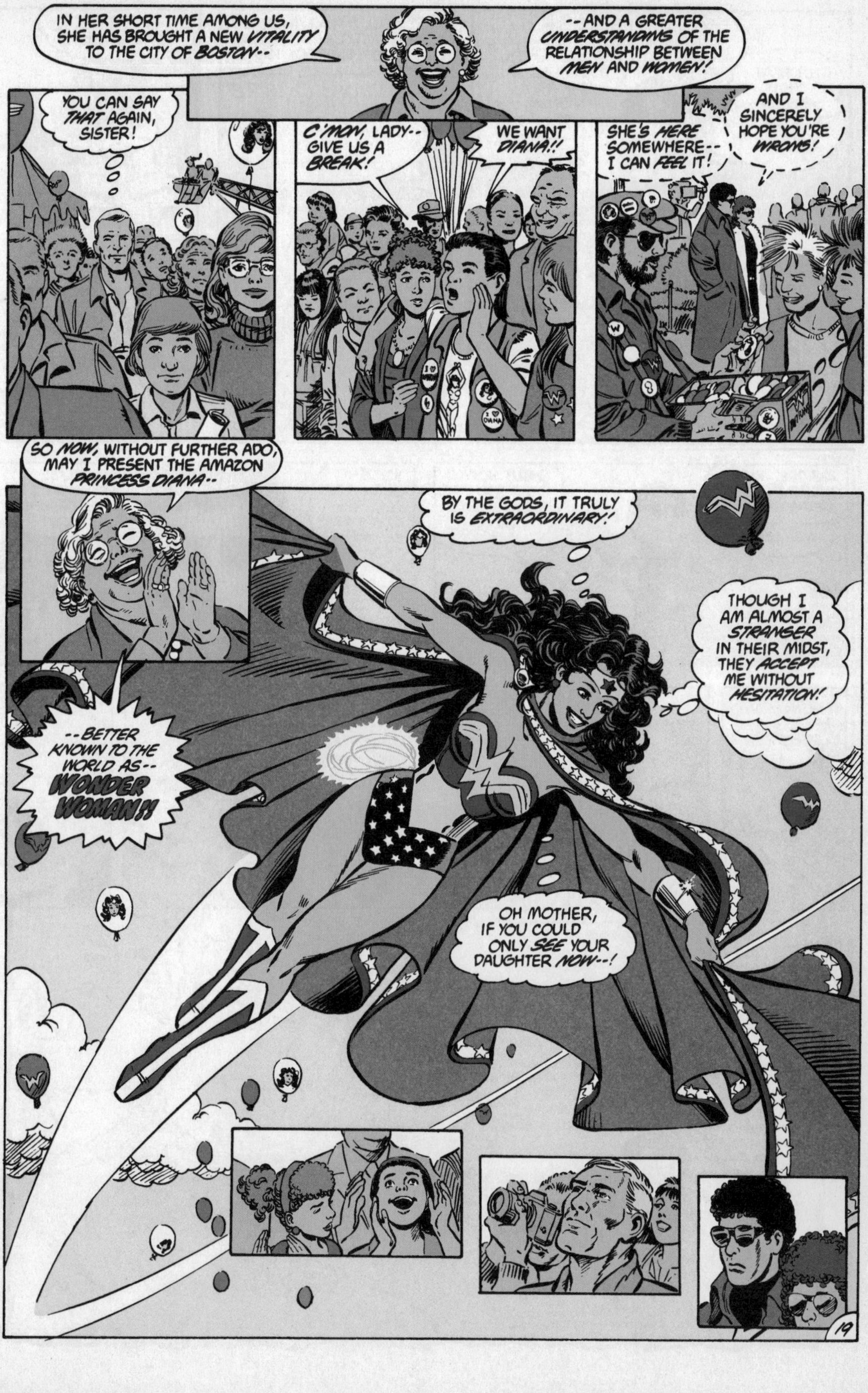
IN HER SHORT TIME AMONG US, SHE HAS BROUGHT A NEW VITALITY TO THE CITY OF BOSTON--
--AND A GREATER UNDERSTANDING OF THE RELATIONSHIP BETWEEN MEN AND WOMEN!
YOU CAN SAY THAT AGAIN, SISTER!
C'MON, LADY-- GIVE US A BREAK!
WE WANT DIANA!!
SHE'S HERE SOMEWHERE-- I CAN FEEL IT!
AND I SINCERELY HOPE YOU'RE WRONG!
SO NOW, WITHOUT FURTHER ADO, MAY I PRESENT THE AMAZON PRINCESS DIANA--
BY THE GODS, IT TRULY IS EXTRAORDINARY!
THOUGH I AM ALMOST A STRANGER IN THEIR MIDST, THEY ACCEPT ME WITHOUT HESITATION!
--BETTER KNOWN TO THE WORLD AS-- WONDER WOMAN!!
OH MOTHER, IF YOU COULD ONLY SEE YOUR DAUGHTER NOW--!
19

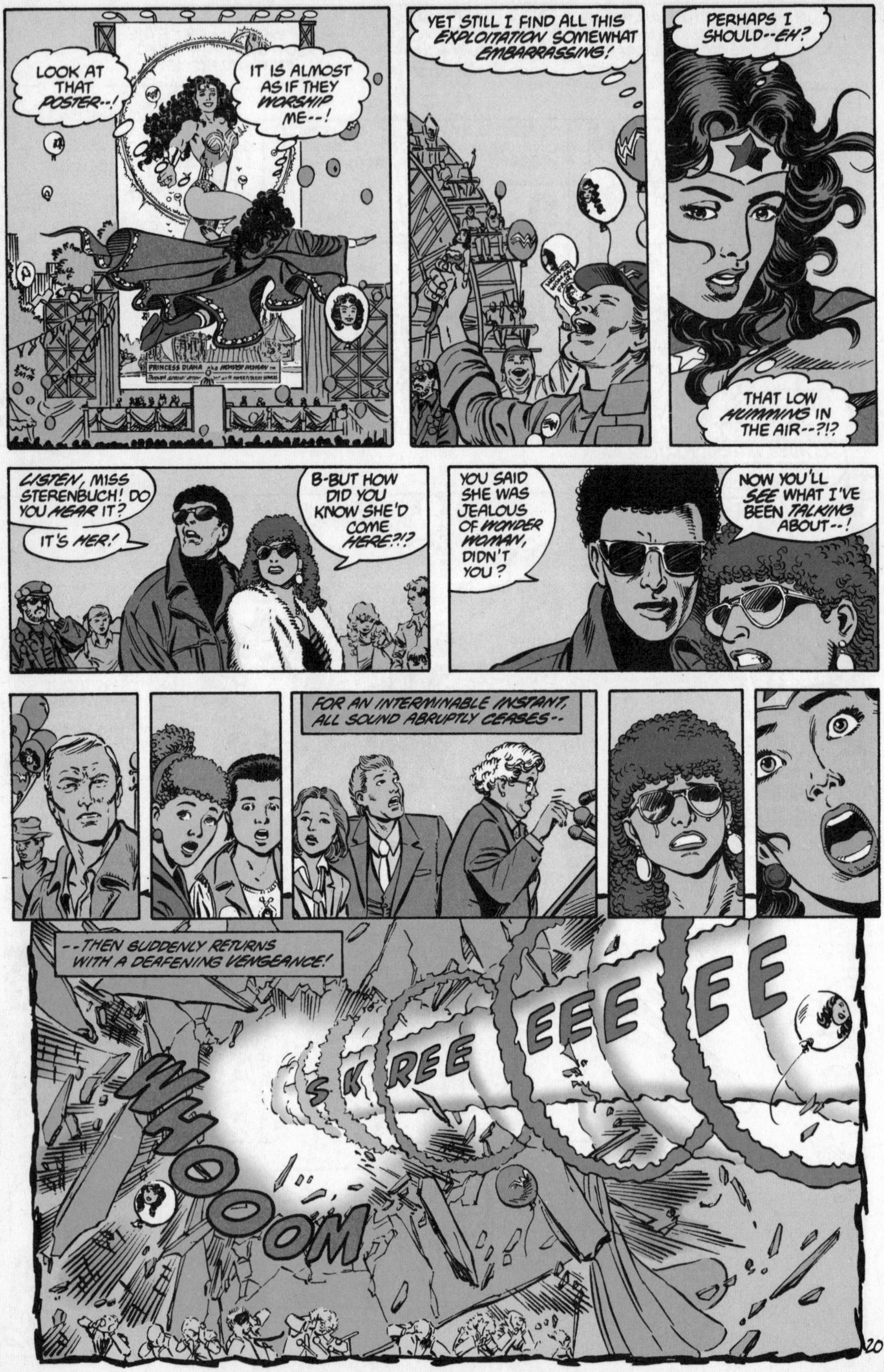
LOOK AT THAT POSTER--!
IT IS ALMOST AS IF THEY WORSHIP ME--!
PRINCESS DIANA aka WONDER WOMAN
YET STILL I FIND ALL THIS EXPLOITATION SOMEWHAT EMBARRASSING!
PERHAPS I SHOULD--EH?
THAT LOW HUMMING IN THE AIR--?!?
LISTEN, MISS STERENBUCH! DO YOU HEAR IT?
IT'S HER!
B-BUT HOW DID YOU KNOW SHE'D COME HERE?!?
YOU SAID SHE WAS JEALOUS OF WONDER WOMAN, DIDN'T YOU?
NOW YOU'LL SEE WHAT I'VE BEEN TALKING ABOUT--!
FOR AN INTERMINABLE INSTANT, ALL SOUND ABRUPTLY CEASES--
--THEN SUDDENLY RETURNS WITH A DEAFENING VENGEANCE!
WHOOOOM
SKREEEEEEE
20

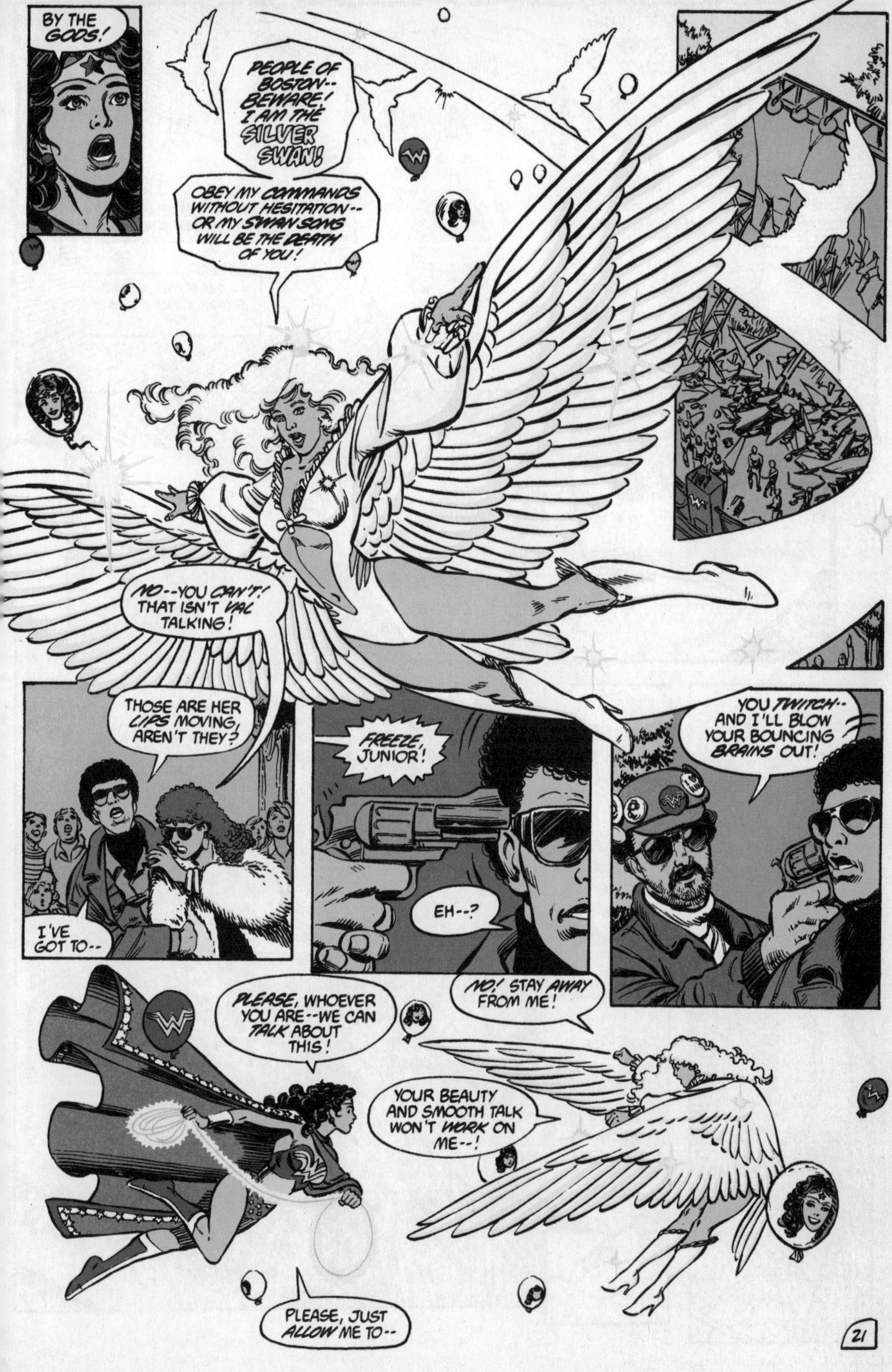

BY THE GODS!
PEOPLE OF BOSTON-- BEWARE! I AM THE SILVER SWAN!
OBEY MY COMMANDS WITHOUT HESITATION-- OR MY SWAN SONGS WILL BE THE DEATH OF YOU!
NO--YOU CAN'T! THAT ISN'T VAL TALKING!
THOSE ARE HER LIPS MOVING, AREN'T THEY?
I'VE GOT TO--
FREEZE, JUNIOR!
EH--?
YOU TWITCH-- AND I'LL BLOW YOUR BOUNCING BRAINS OUT!
PLEASE, WHOEVER YOU ARE--WE CAN TALK ABOUT THIS!
NO! STAY AWAY FROM ME!
YOUR BEAUTY AND SMOOTH TALK WON'T WORK ON ME--!
PLEASE, JUST ALLOW ME TO--
21

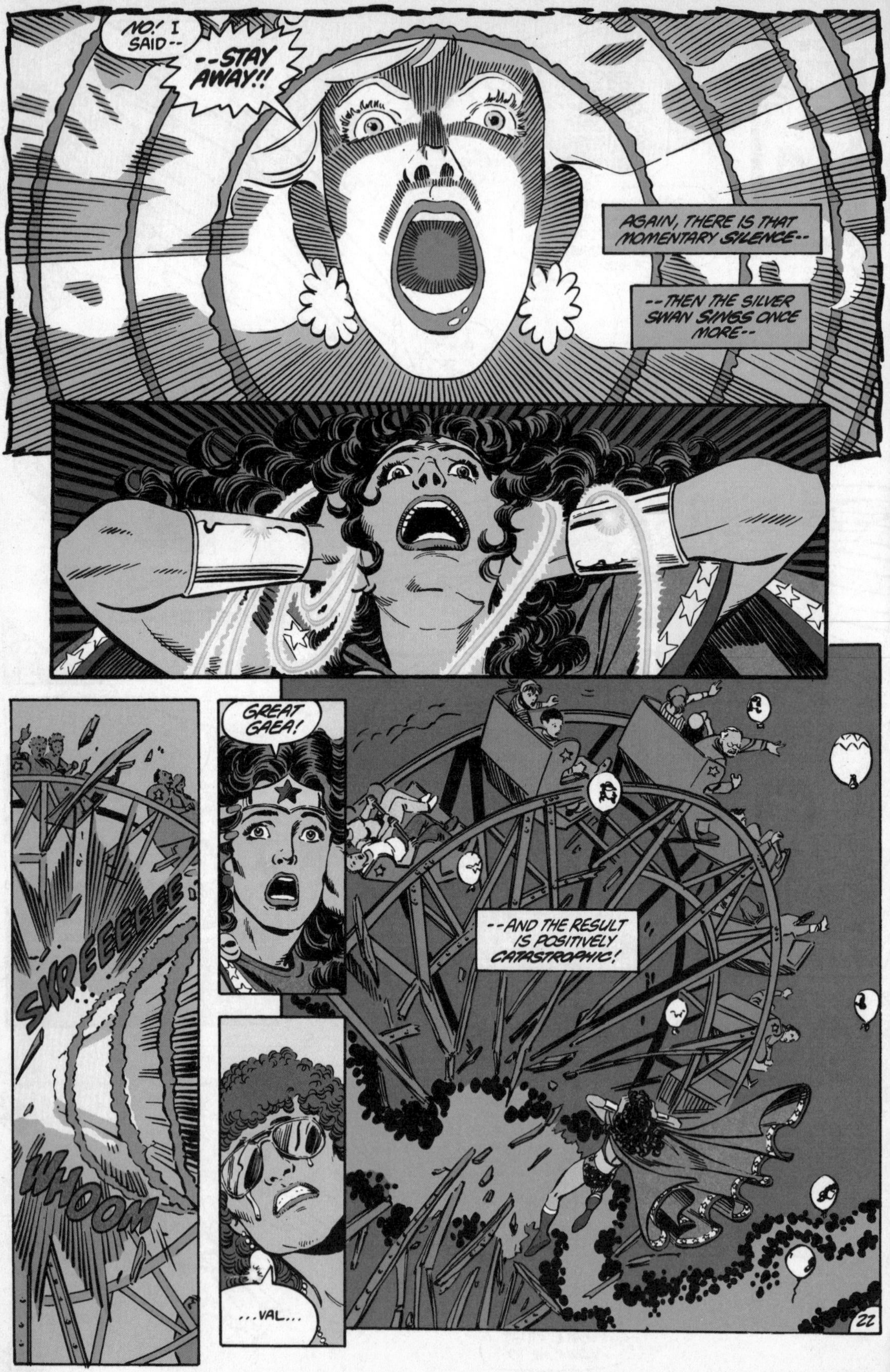
NO! I SAID--
--STAY AWAY!!
AGAIN, THERE IS THAT MOMENTARY SILENCE--
--THEN THE SILVER SWAN SINGS ONCE MORE--
SKREEEEEEEE
WHOOM
GREAT GAEA!
...VAL...
--AND THE RESULT IS POSITIVELY CATASTROPHIC!
22

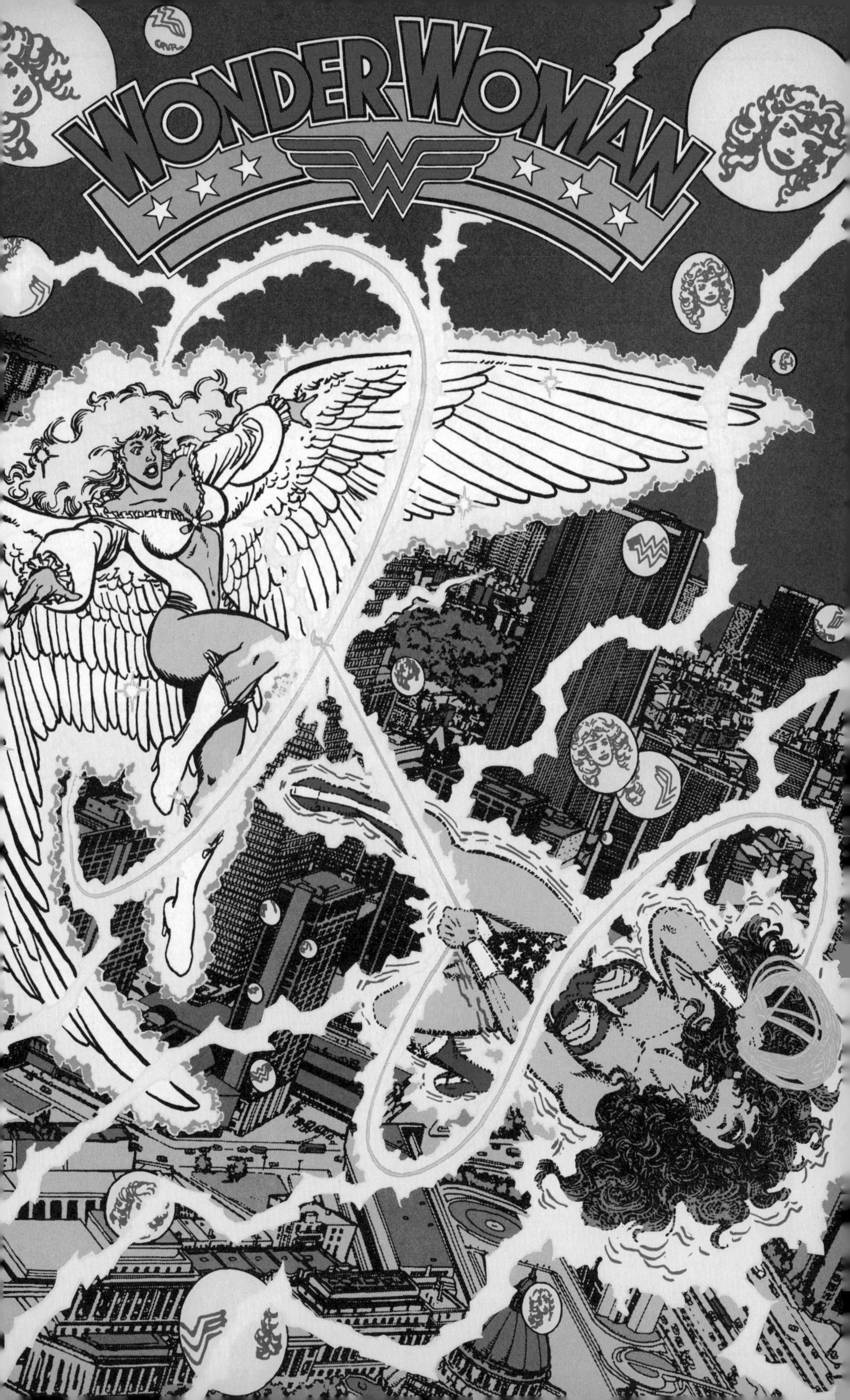
WONDER WOMAN

WONDER WOMAN

CHAPTER TWO

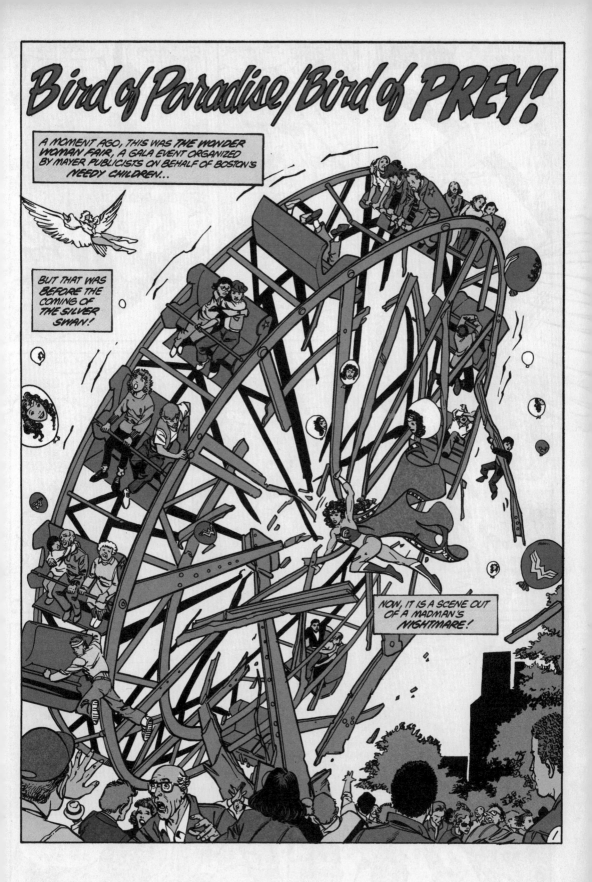

Bird of Paradise/Bird of PREY!

A MOMENT AGO, THIS WAS THE WONDER WOMAN FAIR, A GALA EVENT ORGANIZED BY MAYER PUBLICISTS ON BEHALF OF BOSTON'S NEEDY CHILDREN...

BUT THAT WAS BEFORE THE COMING OF THE SILVER SWAN!

NOW, IT IS A SCENE OUT OF A MADMAN'S NIGHTMARE!

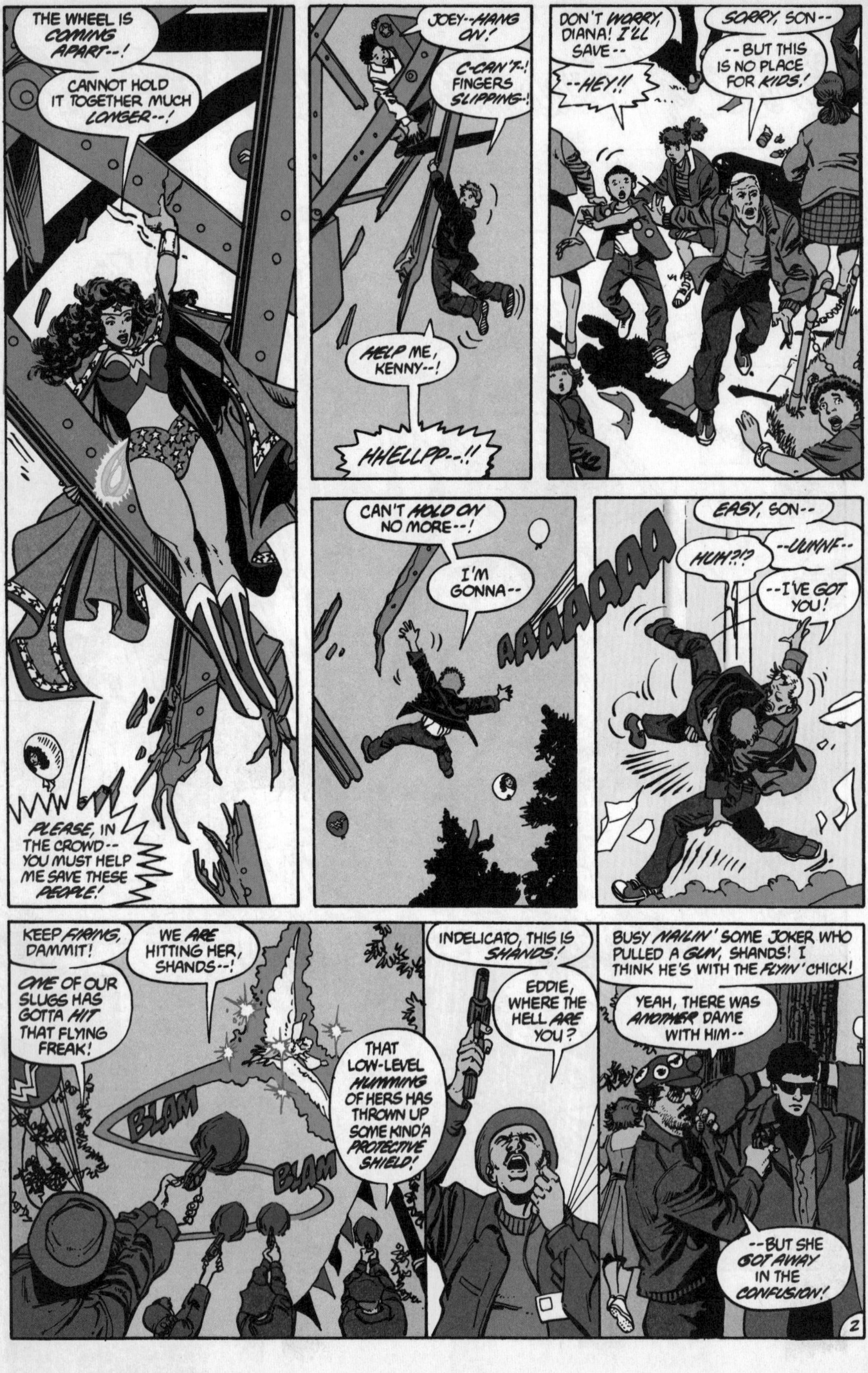
THE WHEEL IS COMING APART--!
CANNOT HOLD IT TOGETHER MUCH LONGER--!
PLEASE, IN THE CROWD-- YOU MUST HELP ME SAVE THESE PEOPLE!
JOEY--HANG ON!
C-CAN'T-! FINGERS SLIPPING-!
HELP ME, KENNY--!
HHELLPP--!!
DON'T WORRY, DIANA! I'LL SAVE--
--HEY!!
SORRY, SON--
--BUT THIS IS NO PLACE FOR KIDS!
CAN'T HOLD ON NO MORE--!
I'M GONNA--
AAAAAAAA
EASY, SON--
HUH?!?
--UUNNF--
--I'VE GOT YOU!
KEEP FIRING, DAMMIT!
WE ARE HITTING HER, SHANDS--!
ONE OF OUR SLUGS HAS GOTTA HIT THAT FLYING FREAK!
THAT LOW-LEVEL HUMMING OF HERS HAS THROWN UP SOME KIND'A PROTECTIVE SHIELD!
BLAM
BLAM
INDELICATO, THIS IS SHANDS!
EDDIE, WHERE THE HELL ARE YOU?
BUSY NAILIN' SOME JOKER WHO PULLED A GUN, SHANDS! I THINK HE'S WITH THE FLYIN' CHICK!
YEAH, THERE WAS ANOTHER DAME WITH HIM--
--BUT SHE GOT AWAY IN THE CONFUSION!
2

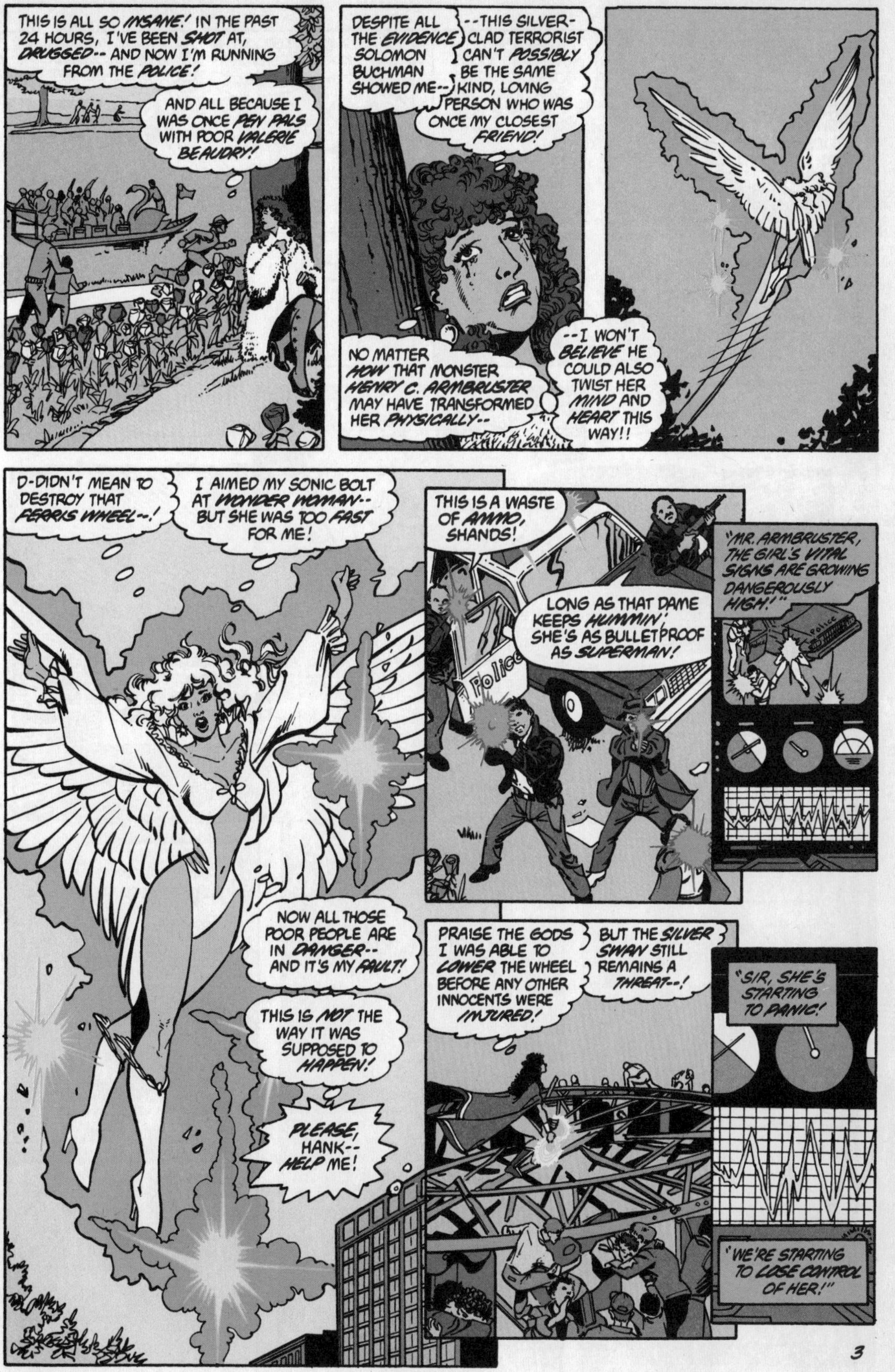
THIS IS ALL SO INSANE! IN THE PAST 24 HOURS, I'VE BEEN SHOT AT, DRUGGED-- AND NOW I'M RUNNING FROM THE POLICE!
AND ALL BECAUSE I WAS ONCE PEN PALS WITH POOR VALERIE BEAUDRY!
DESPITE ALL THE EVIDENCE SOLOMON BUCHMAN SHOWED ME--
--THIS SILVER-CLAD TERRORIST CAN'T POSSIBLY BE THE SAME KIND, LOVING PERSON WHO WAS ONCE MY CLOSEST FRIEND!
NO MATTER HOW THAT MONSTER HENRY C. ARMBRUSTER MAY HAVE TRANSFORMED HER PHYSICALLY--
--I WON'T BELIEVE HE COULD ALSO TWIST HER MIND AND HEART THIS WAY!!
D-DIDN'T MEAN TO DESTROY THAT FERRIS WHEEL--!
I AIMED MY SONIC BOLT AT WONDER WOMAN-- BUT SHE WAS TOO FAST FOR ME!
NOW ALL THOSE POOR PEOPLE ARE IN DANGER-- AND IT'S MY FAULT!
THIS IS NOT THE WAY IT WAS SUPPOSED TO HAPPEN!
PLEASE, HANK-- HELP ME!
THIS IS A WASTE OF AMMO, SHANDS!
LONG AS THAT DAME KEEPS HUMMIN', SHE'S AS BULLETPROOF AS SUPERMAN!
Police
"MR. ARMBRUSTER, THE GIRL'S VITAL SIGNS ARE GROWING DANGEROUSLY HIGH!"
PRAISE THE GODS I WAS ABLE TO LOWER THE WHEEL BEFORE ANY OTHER INNOCENTS WERE INJURED!
BUT THE SILVER SWAN STILL REMAINS A THREAT--!
"SIR, SHE'S STARTING TO PANIC!"
"WE'RE STARTING TO LOSE CONTROL OF HER!"
3

GIVE ME THAT *MICROPHONE,* IDIOT!

VALERIE?! NOW YOU *LISTEN* TO ME, HONEY-- AND YOU LISTEN *GOOD!*

YOU *PANIC* NOW -- AND YOU'RE GOING TO *RUIN* EVERYTHING WE'VE *WORKED* FOR!

YOU'VE GOT TO KEEP *COOL,* SUGAR-- AND REMEMBER EVERYTHING I'VE *TAUGHT* YOU!

SO YOU JUST *CALM* YOURSELF, HONEY--

-- AND PREPARE FOR A *LEVEL THREE FORCE BLAST!*

LEVEL THREE?!?

BUT WE MIGHT ACCIDENTALLY *HURT* SOMEBODY WITH--

DAMMIT, VAL-- DON'T *ARGUE* WITH ME!

INITIATE *FORCE LEVEL THREE* -- --*NOW!!*

HESITANTLY AT FIRST, THE *SILVER-HAIRED* YOUNG WOMAN PURSES HER *TREMBLING LIPS* --

-- AND A *TERRIFYING SILENCE* SUDDENLY DOMINATES THE *ENTIRE AREA* --

-- FOLLOWED AN INSTANT LATER BY A *SCREAM* THAT IS EVERY BIT AS *LOUD* --

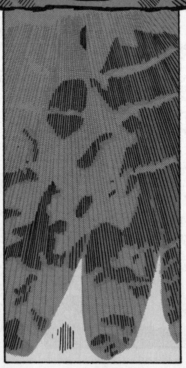

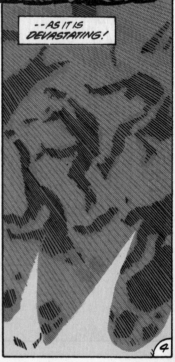

-- AS IT IS *DEVASTATING!*

4

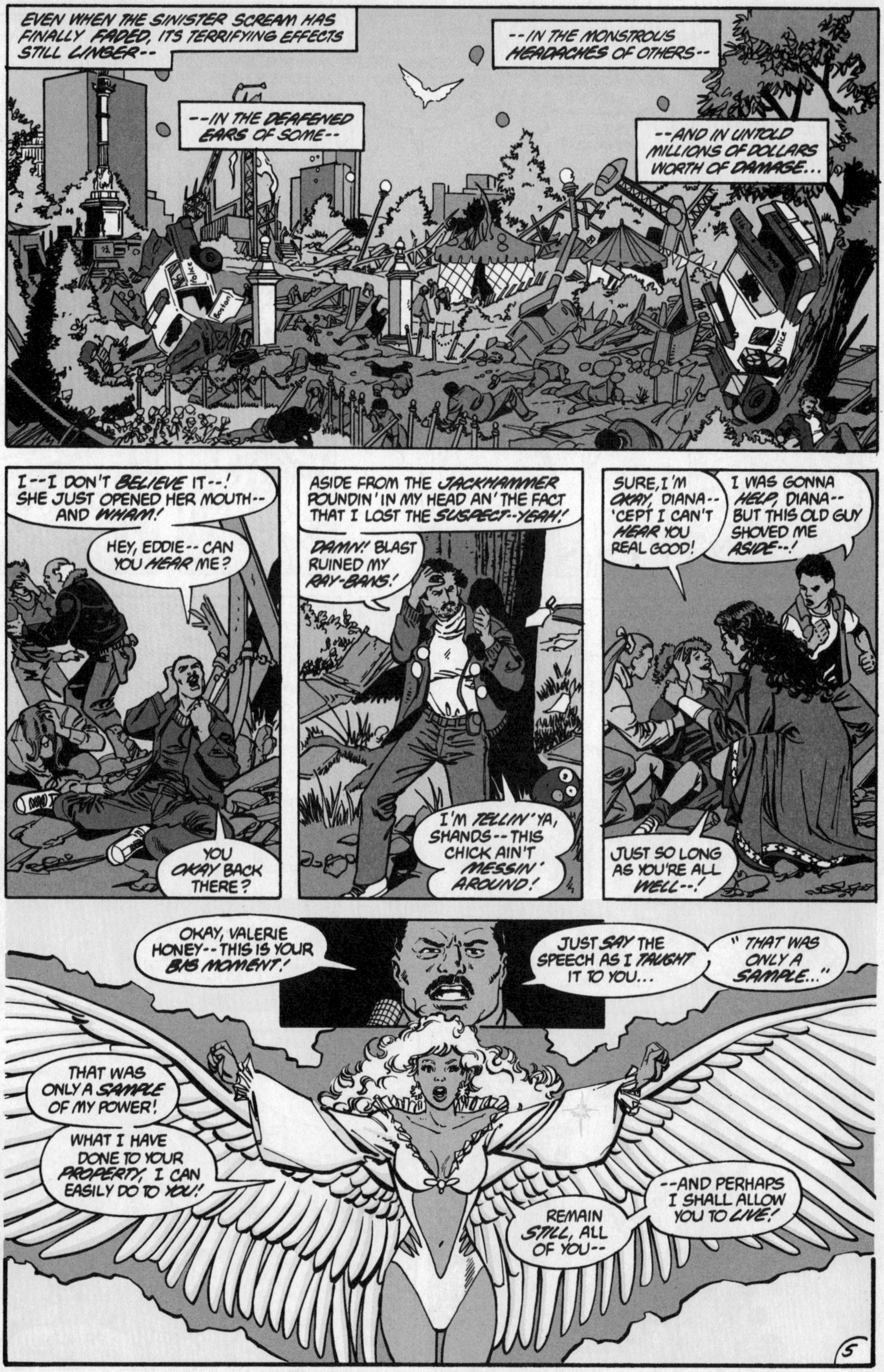
EVEN WHEN THE SINISTER SCREAM HAS FINALLY FADED, ITS TERRIFYING EFFECTS STILL LINGER--
--IN THE DEAFENED EARS OF SOME--
--IN THE MONSTROUS HEADACHES OF OTHERS--
--AND IN UNTOLD MILLIONS OF DOLLARS WORTH OF DAMAGE...
POLICE
BOSTON
POLICE
I--I DON'T BELIEVE IT--! SHE JUST OPENED HER MOUTH--AND WHAM!
HEY, EDDIE--CAN YOU HEAR ME?
YOU OKAY BACK THERE?
ASIDE FROM THE JACKHAMMER POUNDIN' IN MY HEAD AN' THE FACT THAT I LOST THE SUSPECT--YEAH!
DAMN! BLAST RUINED MY RAY-BANS!
I'M TELLIN' YA, SHANDS--THIS CHICK AIN'T MESSIN' AROUND!
SURE, I'M OKAY, DIANA--'CEPT I CAN'T HEAR YOU REAL GOOD!
I WAS GONNA HELP, DIANA--BUT THIS OLD GUY SHOVED ME ASIDE--!
JUST SO LONG AS YOU'RE ALL WELL--!
OKAY, VALERIE HONEY--THIS IS YOUR BIG MOMENT!
JUST SAY THE SPEECH AS I TAUGHT IT TO YOU...
" THAT WAS ONLY A SAMPLE..."
THAT WAS ONLY A SAMPLE OF MY POWER!
WHAT I HAVE DONE TO YOUR PROPERTY, I CAN EASILY DO TO YOU!
REMAIN STILL, ALL OF YOU--
--AND PERHAPS I SHALL ALLOW YOU TO LIVE!
5

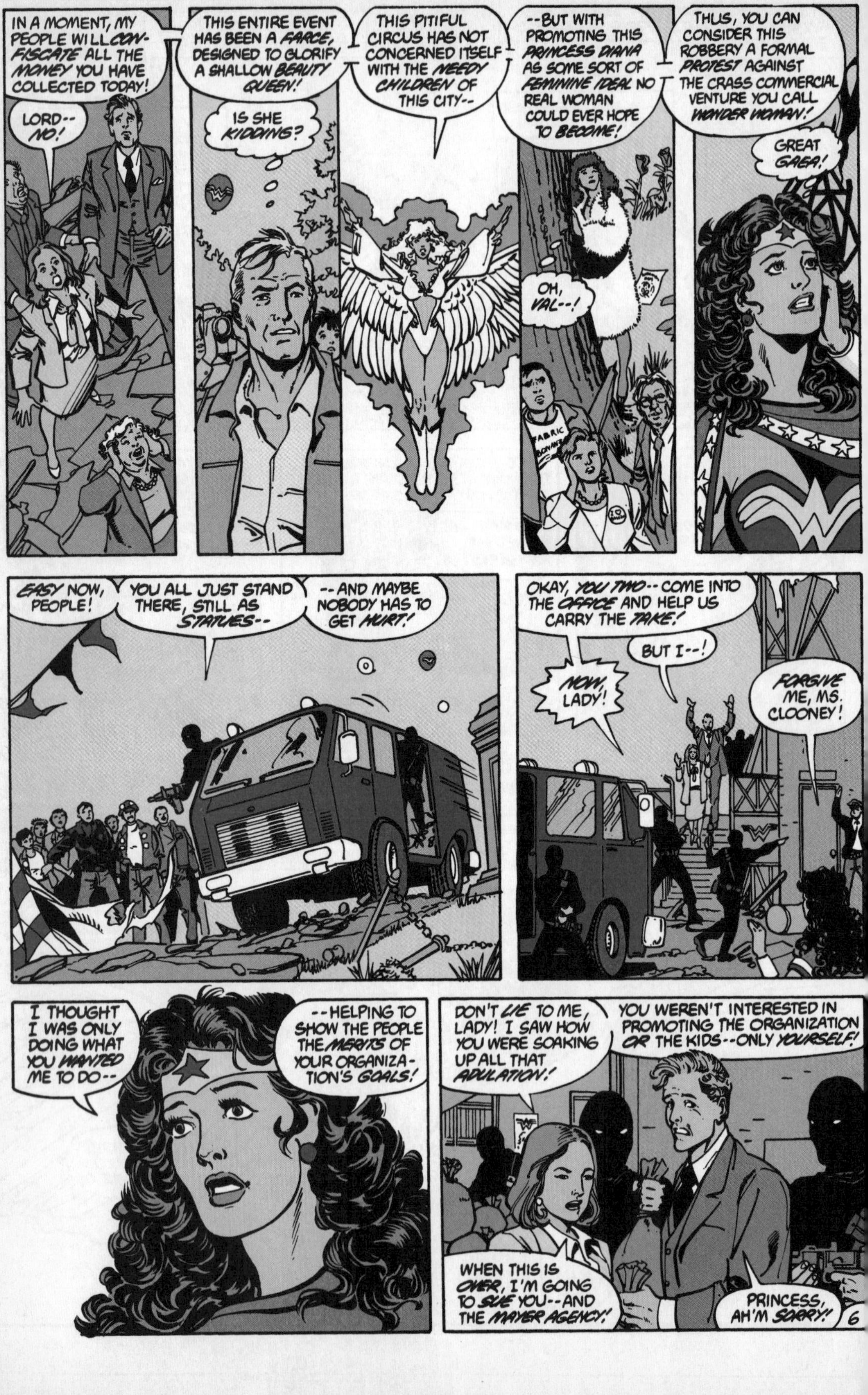

IN A MOMENT, MY PEOPLE WILL CONFISCATE ALL THE MONEY YOU HAVE COLLECTED TODAY!
LORD-- NO!
THIS ENTIRE EVENT HAS BEEN A FARCE, DESIGNED TO GLORIFY A SHALLOW BEAUTY QUEEN!
IS SHE KIDDING?
THIS PITIFUL CIRCUS HAS NOT CONCERNED ITSELF WITH THE NEEDY CHILDREN OF THIS CITY--
--BUT WITH PROMOTING THIS PRINCESS DIANA AS SOME SORT OF FEMININE IDEAL NO REAL WOMAN COULD EVER HOPE TO BECOME!
OH, VAL--!
THUS, YOU CAN CONSIDER THIS ROBBERY A FORMAL PROTEST AGAINST THE CRASS COMMERCIAL VENTURE YOU CALL WONDER WOMAN!
GREAT GAEA!
EASY NOW, PEOPLE!
YOU ALL JUST STAND THERE, STILL AS STATUES--
--AND MAYBE NOBODY HAS TO GET HURT!
OKAY, YOU TWO--COME INTO THE OFFICE AND HELP US CARRY THE TAKE!
BUT I--!
NOW, LADY!
FORGIVE ME, MS. CLOONEY!
I THOUGHT I WAS ONLY DOING WHAT YOU WANTED ME TO DO--
--HELPING TO SHOW THE PEOPLE THE MERITS OF YOUR ORGANIZATION'S GOALS!
DON'T LIE TO ME, LADY! I SAW HOW YOU WERE SOAKING UP ALL THAT ADULATION!
YOU WEREN'T INTERESTED IN PROMOTING THE ORGANIZATION OR THE KIDS--ONLY YOURSELF!
WHEN THIS IS OVER, I'M GOING TO SUE YOU--AND THE MAYER AGENCY!
PRINCESS, AH'M SORRY!
6

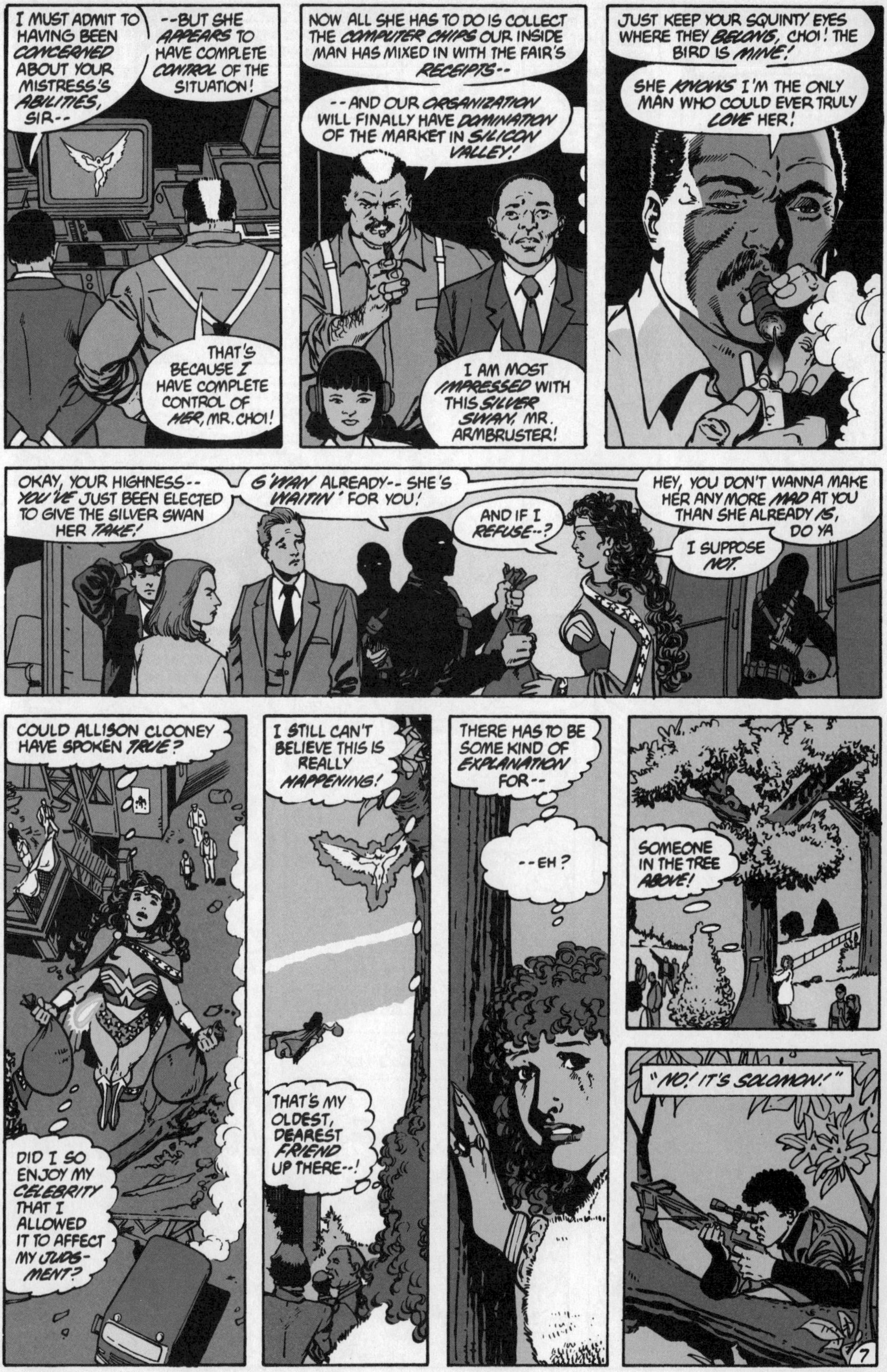
I MUST ADMIT TO HAVING BEEN CONCERNED ABOUT YOUR MISTRESS'S ABILITIES, SIR--
--BUT SHE APPEARS TO HAVE COMPLETE CONTROL OF THE SITUATION!
THAT'S BECAUSE I HAVE COMPLETE CONTROL OF HER, MR. CHOI!
NOW ALL SHE HAS TO DO IS COLLECT THE COMPUTER CHIPS OUR INSIDE MAN HAS MIXED IN WITH THE FAIR'S RECEIPTS--
--AND OUR ORGANIZATION WILL FINALLY HAVE DOMINATION OF THE MARKET IN SILICON VALLEY!
I AM MOST IMPRESSED WITH THIS SILVER SWAN, MR. ARMBRUSTER!
JUST KEEP YOUR SQUINTY EYES WHERE THEY BELONG, CHOI! THE BIRD IS MINE!
SHE KNOWS I'M THE ONLY MAN WHO COULD EVER TRULY LOVE HER!
OKAY, YOUR HIGHNESS-- YOU'VE JUST BEEN ELECTED TO GIVE THE SILVER SWAN HER TAKE!
G'WAN ALREADY-- SHE'S WAITIN' FOR YOU!
AND IF I REFUSE--?
HEY, YOU DON'T WANNA MAKE HER ANY MORE MAD AT YOU THAN SHE ALREADY IS, DO YA
I SUPPOSE NOT.
COULD ALLISON CLOONEY HAVE SPOKEN TRUE?
DID I SO ENJOY MY CELEBRITY THAT I ALLOWED IT TO AFFECT MY JUDGMENT?
I STILL CAN'T BELIEVE THIS IS REALLY HAPPENING!
THAT'S MY OLDEST, DEAREST FRIEND UP THERE--!
THERE HAS TO BE SOME KIND OF EXPLANATION FOR--
--EH?
SOMEONE IN THE TREE ABOVE!
"NO! IT'S SOLOMON!"
7

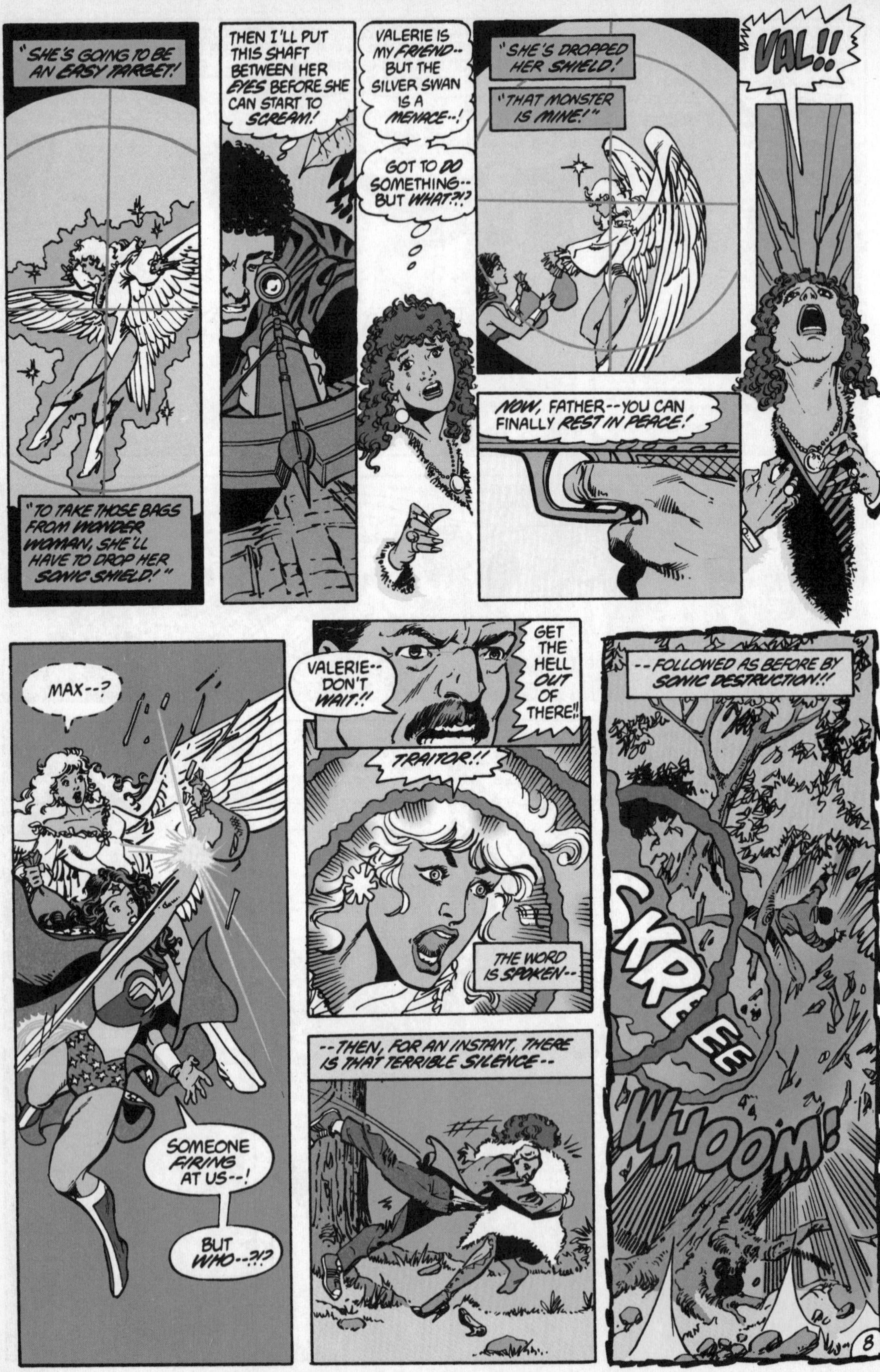
"SHE'S GOING TO BE AN EASY TARGET!
"TO TAKE THOSE BAGS FROM WONDER WOMAN, SHE'LL HAVE TO DROP HER SONIC SHIELD!"
THEN I'LL PUT THIS SHAFT BETWEEN HER EYES BEFORE SHE CAN START TO SCREAM!
VALERIE IS MY FRIEND-- BUT THE SILVER SWAN IS A MENACE--!
GOT TO DO SOMETHING-- BUT WHAT?!?
"SHE'S DROPPED HER SHIELD!
"THAT MONSTER IS MINE!"
NOW, FATHER--YOU CAN FINALLY REST IN PEACE!
VAL!!
MAX--?
SOMEONE FIRING AT US--!
BUT WHO--?!?
VALERIE-- DON'T WAIT!!
GET THE HELL OUT OF THERE!!
TRAITOR!!
THE WORD IS SPOKEN--
--THEN, FOR AN INSTANT, THERE IS THAT TERRIBLE SILENCE--
--FOLLOWED AS BEFORE BY SONIC DESTRUCTION!!
SKREEE
WHOOM!
8

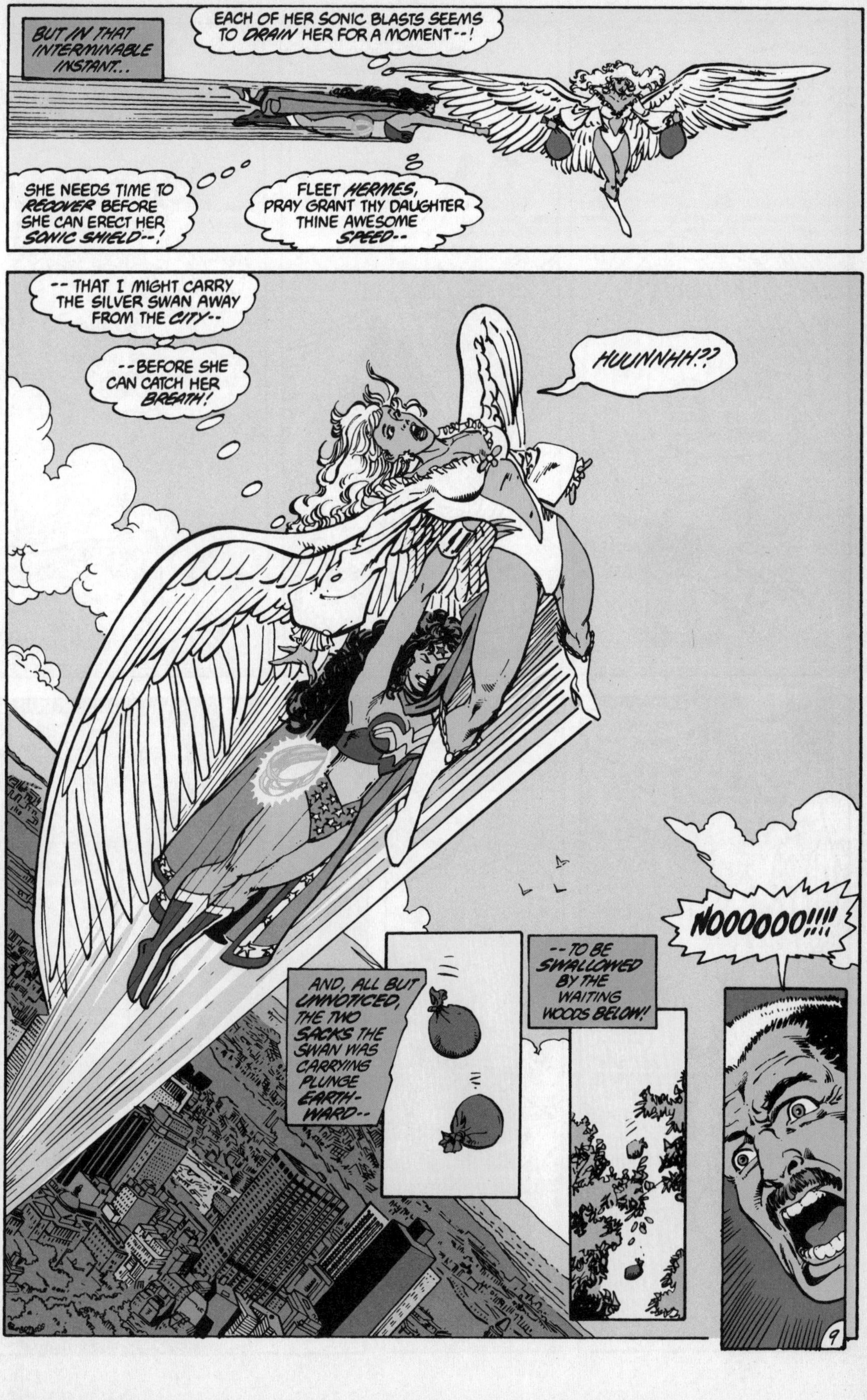
BUT IN THAT INTERMINABLE INSTANT...
EACH OF HER SONIC BLASTS SEEMS TO DRAIN HER FOR A MOMENT--!
SHE NEEDS TIME TO RECOVER BEFORE SHE CAN ERECT HER SONIC SHIELD--!
FLEET HERMES, PRAY GRANT THY DAUGHTER THINE AWESOME SPEED--
--THAT I MIGHT CARRY THE SILVER SWAN AWAY FROM THE CITY--
--BEFORE SHE CAN CATCH HER BREATH!
HUUNNHH??
AND, ALL BUT UNNOTICED, THE TWO SACKS THE SWAN WAS CARRYING PLUNGE EARTH-WARD--
--TO BE SWALLOWED BY THE WAITING WOODS BELOW!
NOOOOOO!!!!
9

NO! KEEP AWAY FROM ME!

YOU'LL SPOIL EVERYTHING--!

SHE MANEUVERS WITH THE GRACE OF HER AVIAN NAMESAKE--

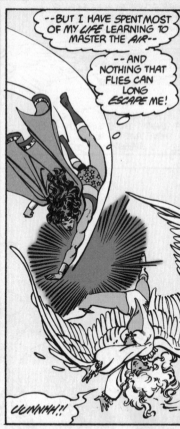

--BUT I HAVE SPENT MOST OF MY *LIFE* LEARNING TO MASTER THE *AIR*--

--AND NOTHING THAT FLIES CAN LONG *ESCAPE* ME!

UUNNHH!!

MY OPEN-HANDED SLAP *STUNNED* HER AS I'D HOPED--

--SO THAT I MAY *BIND* HER WITH MY *LASSO OF TRUTH*--

--AND FINALLY GET TO THE *HEART* OF THIS INSANITY--!

VALERIE-- *WAKE UP!!*

YOU CAN'T LET HER CAPTURE YOU!

INITIATE DEFENSE MANEUVER SIX!

BUT I--

SIX, HONEY-- NOW!!

AT HER MASTER'S *COMMAND,* THE SILVER SWAN BEGINS TO EMIT A LOW, THROATY *HUM*--

--WHICH REACTIVATES HER *SONIC SHIELD*--

--AND THUS SENDS AN *ENERGY BACKLASH* SIZZLING ALONG THE LENGTH OF THE *GOLDEN LASSO*--

-- AND *THROUGH* THE WRITHING BODY OF THE *AMAZON PRINCESS!*

10

40

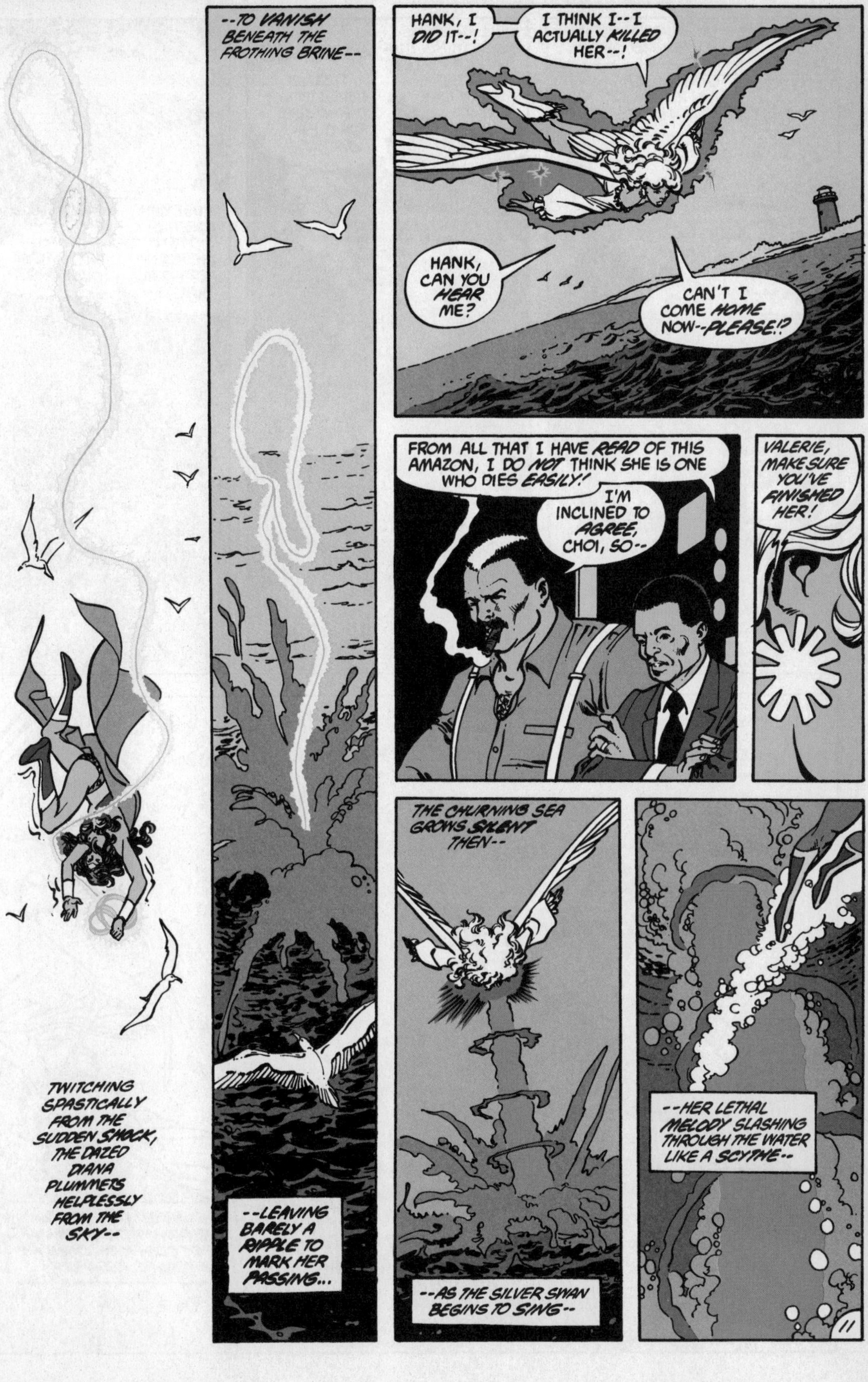
TWITCHING SPASTICALLY FROM THE SUDDEN SHOCK, THE DAZED DIANA PLUMMETS HELPLESSLY FROM THE SKY--
--TO VANISH BENEATH THE FROTHING BRINE--
--LEAVING BARELY A RIPPLE TO MARK HER PASSING...
HANK, I DID IT--!
I THINK I--I ACTUALLY KILLED HER--!
HANK, CAN YOU HEAR ME?
CAN'T I COME HOME NOW--PLEASE!?
FROM ALL THAT I HAVE READ OF THIS AMAZON, I DO NOT THINK SHE IS ONE WHO DIES EASILY!
I'M INCLINED TO AGREE, CHOI, SO--
VALERIE, MAKE SURE YOU'VE FINISHED HER!
THE CHURNING SEA GROWS SILENT THEN--
--AS THE SILVER SWAN BEGINS TO SING--
--HER LETHAL MELODY SLASHING THROUGH THE WATER LIKE A SCYTHE--
11

--PASSING BARELY A HAIR'S-BREADTH FROM ITS INTENDED TARGET!

CANNOT STAY UNDER MUCH LONGER--!

DID NOT HAVE TIME TO TAKE A BREATH--!

MUST FIND SOME WAY TO MUFFLE THE SWAN'S CRIES-- BUT HOW?

WELL, THERE IS SOMETHING THAT VANESSA TAUGHT ME AT THE BEACH ONE DAY--

--THOUGH I NEVER THOUGHT I'D FIND USE FOR IT IN BATTLE!

MUST WAIT FOR THE MOMENT BETWEEN HER SONIC BURSTS--

--WHEN SHE IS MOST VULNERABLE--

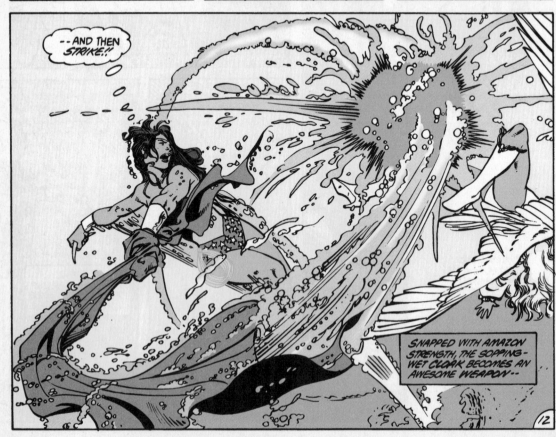

--AND THEN STRIKE!!

SNAPPED WITH AMAZON STRENGTH, THE SOPPING-WET CLOAK BECOMES AN AWESOME WEAPON--

12

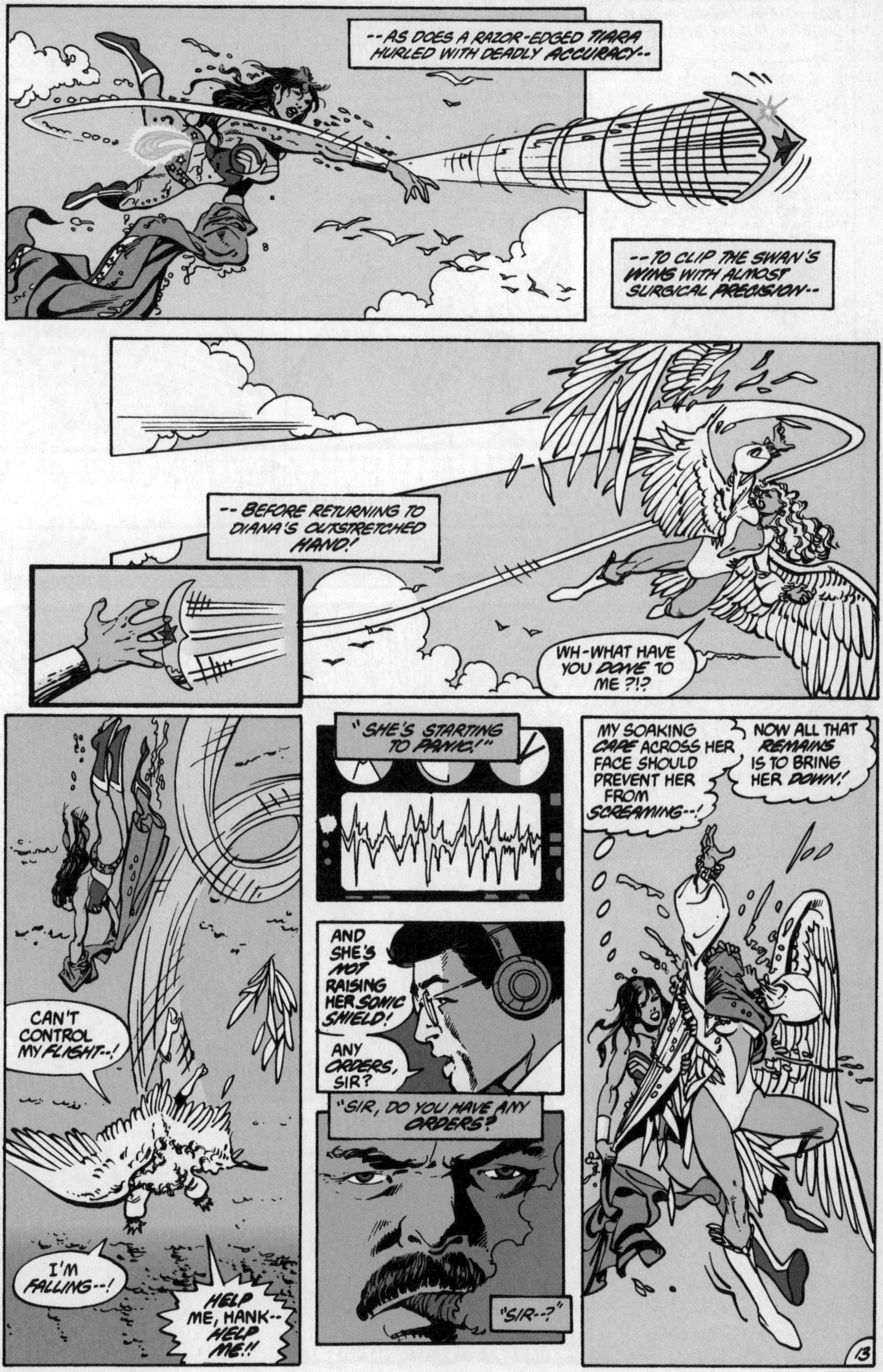
--AS DOES A RAZOR-EDGED TIARA HURLED WITH DEADLY ACCURACY--
--TO CLIP THE SWAN'S WINGS WITH ALMOST SURGICAL PRECISION--
-- BEFORE RETURNING TO DIANA'S OUTSTRETCHED HAND!
WH-WHAT HAVE YOU DONE TO ME ?!?
CAN'T CONTROL MY FLIGHT--!
I'M FALLING--!
HELP ME, HANK-- HELP ME!!
"SHE'S STARTING TO PANIC!"
AND SHE'S NOT RAISING HER SONIC SHIELD!
ANY ORDERS, SIR?
"SIR, DO YOU HAVE ANY ORDERS?"
"SIR--?"
MY SOAKING CAPE ACROSS HER FACE SHOULD PREVENT HER FROM SCREAMING--!
NOW ALL THAT REMAINS IS TO BRING HER DOWN!
13

YOU FOUGHT *PASSIONATELY*, SISTER-- BUT THE BATTLE IS *ENDED!*

I URGE YOU TO *SURRENDER!*

SISTER, *PLEASE*--STOP *STRUGGLING!* I HAVE NO WISH TO *HARM* YOU!

JUST TELL ME WHY YOU *HATE* ME SO, AND PERHAPS I CAN HELP.

THEN THERE IS *SILENCE*--

--SILENCE THAT SWALLOWS ALL *SANITY*--

"SIR, HER *PULSE* IS ALMOST OFF THE SCALE--!"

"SIR, SHE'S *LOSING* IT COMPLETELY--!"

"SHE'S REACHING *CRITICAL LEVEL*--!"

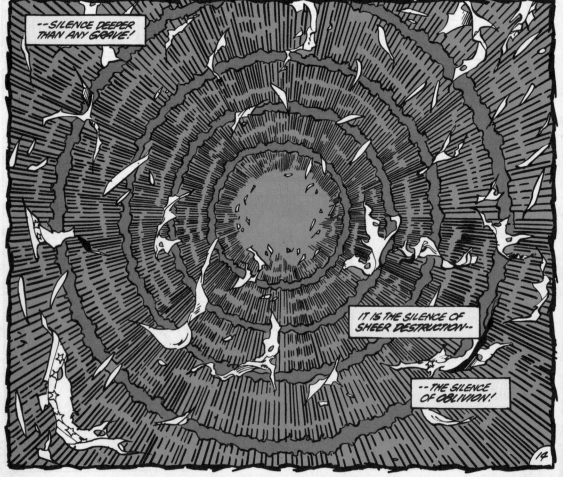

--SILENCE DEEPER THAN ANY *GRAVE!*

IT IS THE SILENCE OF *SHEER DESTRUCTION*--

--THE SILENCE OF *OBLIVION!*

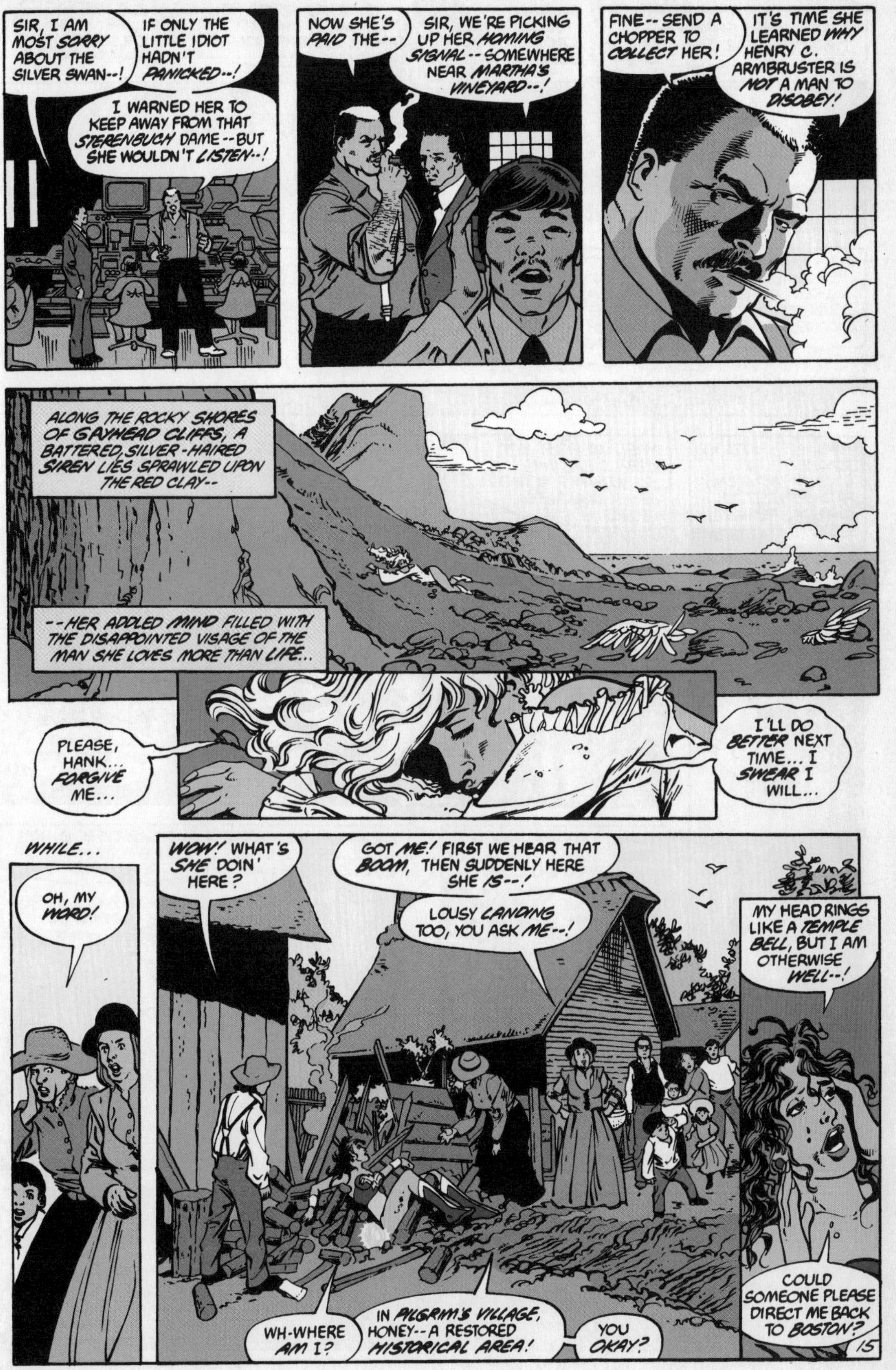
SIR, I AM MOST SORRY ABOUT THE SILVER SWAN--!
IF ONLY THE LITTLE IDIOT HADN'T PANICKED--!
I WARNED HER TO KEEP AWAY FROM THAT STERENBUCH DAME--BUT SHE WOULDN'T LISTEN--!
NOW SHE'S PAID THE--
SIR, WE'RE PICKING UP HER HOMING SIGNAL--SOMEWHERE NEAR MARTHA'S VINEYARD--!
FINE--SEND A CHOPPER TO COLLECT HER!
IT'S TIME SHE LEARNED WHY HENRY C. ARMBRUSTER IS NOT A MAN TO DISOBEY!
ALONG THE ROCKY SHORES OF GAYHEAD CLIFFS, A BATTERED, SILVER-HAIRED SIREN LIES SPRAWLED UPON THE RED CLAY--
--HER ADDLED MIND FILLED WITH THE DISAPPOINTED VISAGE OF THE MAN SHE LOVES MORE THAN LIFE...
PLEASE, HANK... FORGIVE ME...
I'LL DO BETTER NEXT TIME... I SWEAR I WILL...
WHILE...
OH, MY WORD!
WOW! WHAT'S SHE DOIN' HERE?
GOT ME! FIRST WE HEAR THAT BOOM, THEN SUDDENLY HERE SHE IS--!
LOUSY LANDING TOO, YOU ASK ME--!
WH-WHERE AM I?
IN PILGRIM'S VILLAGE, HONEY--A RESTORED HISTORICAL AREA!
YOU OKAY?
MY HEAD RINGS LIKE A TEMPLE BELL, BUT I AM OTHERWISE WELL--!
COULD SOMEONE PLEASE DIRECT ME BACK TO BOSTON?
15

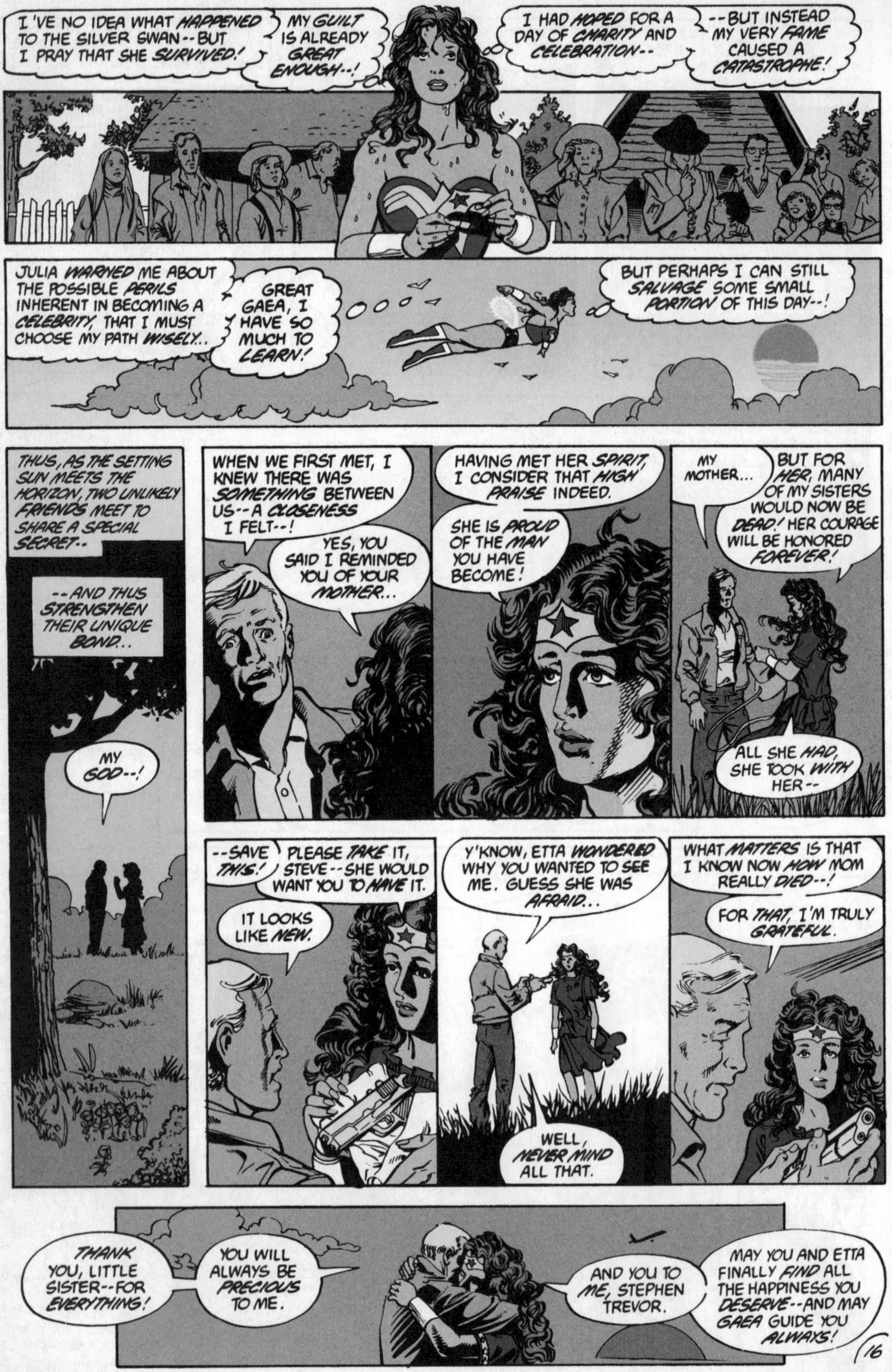

I'VE NO IDEA WHAT HAPPENED TO THE SILVER SWAN--BUT I PRAY THAT SHE SURVIVED!
MY GUILT IS ALREADY GREAT ENOUGH--!
I HAD HOPED FOR A DAY OF CHARITY AND CELEBRATION--
--BUT INSTEAD MY VERY FAME CAUSED A CATASTROPHE!
JULIA WARNED ME ABOUT THE POSSIBLE PERILS INHERENT IN BECOMING A CELEBRITY, THAT I MUST CHOOSE MY PATH WISELY...
GREAT GAEA, I HAVE SO MUCH TO LEARN!
BUT PERHAPS I CAN STILL SALVAGE SOME SMALL PORTION OF THIS DAY--!
THUS, AS THE SETTING SUN MEETS THE HORIZON, TWO UNLIKELY FRIENDS MEET TO SHARE A SPECIAL SECRET--
--AND THUS STRENGTHEN THEIR UNIQUE BOND...
MY GOD--!
WHEN WE FIRST MET, I KNEW THERE WAS SOMETHING BETWEEN US--A CLOSENESS I FELT--!
YES, YOU SAID I REMINDED YOU OF YOUR MOTHER...
HAVING MET HER SPIRIT, I CONSIDER THAT HIGH PRAISE INDEED.
SHE IS PROUD OF THE MAN YOU HAVE BECOME!
MY MOTHER...
BUT FOR HER, MANY OF MY SISTERS WOULD NOW BE DEAD! HER COURAGE WILL BE HONORED FOREVER!
ALL SHE HAD, SHE TOOK WITH HER--
--SAVE THIS!
PLEASE TAKE IT, STEVE--SHE WOULD WANT YOU TO HAVE IT.
IT LOOKS LIKE NEW.
Y'KNOW, ETTA WONDERED WHY YOU WANTED TO SEE ME. GUESS SHE WAS AFRAID...
WELL, NEVER MIND ALL THAT.
WHAT MATTERS IS THAT I KNOW NOW HOW MOM REALLY DIED--!
FOR THAT, I'M TRULY GRATEFUL.
THANK YOU, LITTLE SISTER--FOR EVERYTHING!
YOU WILL ALWAYS BE PRECIOUS TO ME.
AND YOU TO ME, STEPHEN TREVOR.
MAY YOU AND ETTA FINALLY FIND ALL THE HAPPINESS YOU DESERVE--AND MAY GAEA GUIDE YOU ALWAYS!
16

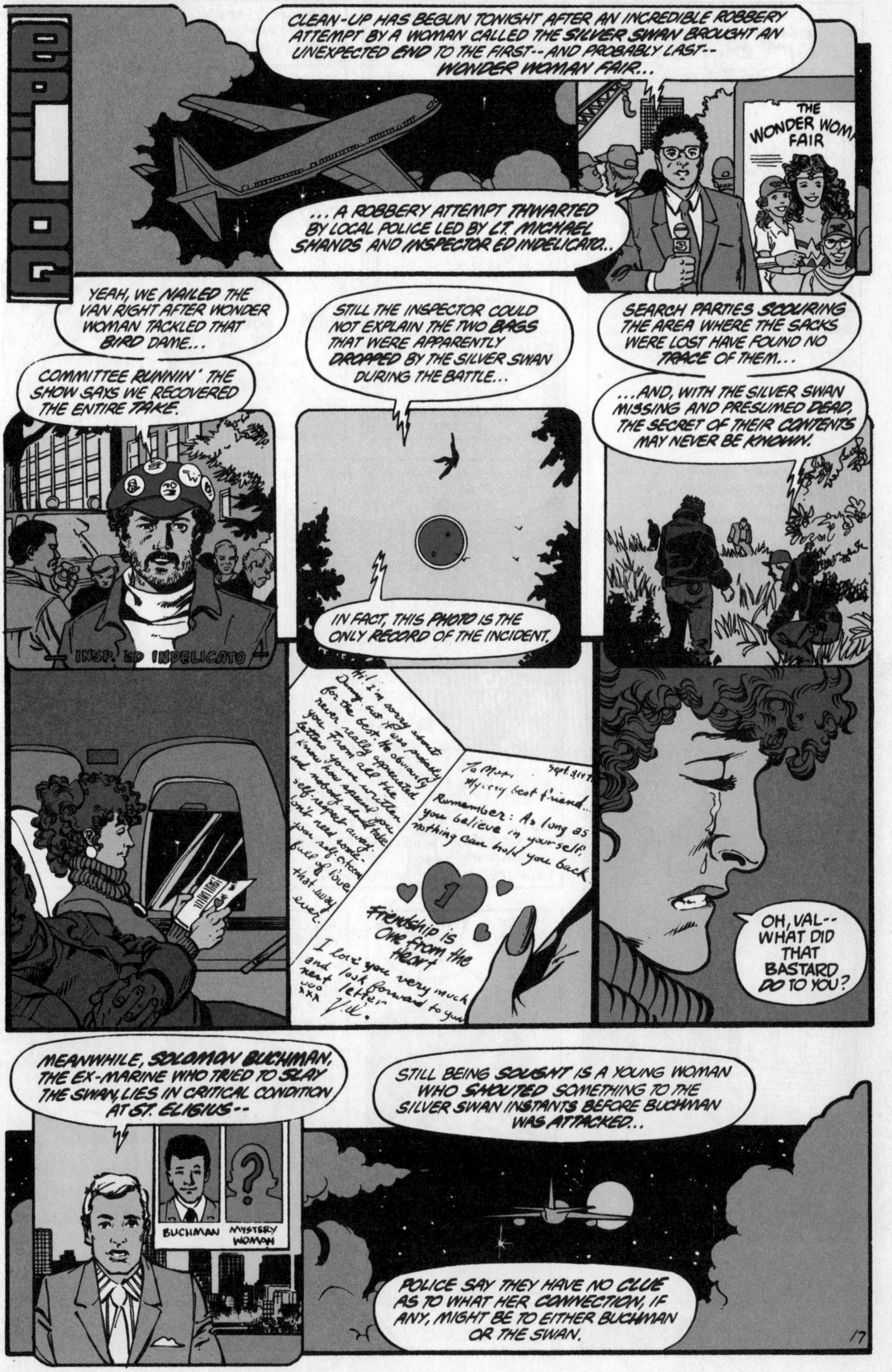
EPILOG
CLEAN-UP HAS BEGUN TONIGHT AFTER AN INCREDIBLE ROBBERY ATTEMPT BY A WOMAN CALLED THE SILVER SWAN BROUGHT AN UNEXPECTED END TO THE FIRST-- AND PROBABLY LAST-- WONDER WOMAN FAIR...
THE WONDER WOM FAIR
... A ROBBERY ATTEMPT THWARTED BY LOCAL POLICE LED BY LT. MICHAEL SHANDS AND INSPECTOR ED INDELICATO...
YEAH, WE NAILED THE VAN RIGHT AFTER WONDER WOMAN TACKLED THAT BIRD DAME...
COMMITTEE RUNNIN' THE SHOW SAYS WE RECOVERED THE ENTIRE TAKE.
INSP. ED INDELICATO
STILL THE INSPECTOR COULD NOT EXPLAIN THE TWO BAGS THAT WERE APPARENTLY DROPPED BY THE SILVER SWAN DURING THE BATTLE...
IN FACT, THIS PHOTO IS THE ONLY RECORD OF THE INCIDENT.
SEARCH PARTIES SCOURING THE AREA WHERE THE SACKS WERE LOST HAVE FOUND NO TRACE OF THEM...
...AND, WITH THE SILVER SWAN MISSING AND PRESUMED DEAD, THE SECRET OF THEIR CONTENTS MAY NEVER BE KNOWN.
Friendship is One from the Heart
OH, VAL-- WHAT DID THAT BASTARD DO TO YOU?
MEANWHILE, SOLOMON BUCHMAN, THE EX-MARINE WHO TRIED TO SLAY THE SWAN, LIES IN CRITICAL CONDITION AT ST. ELIGIUS--
BUCHMAN
MYSTERY WOMAN
STILL BEING SOUGHT IS A YOUNG WOMAN WHO SHOUTED SOMETHING TO THE SILVER SWAN INSTANTS BEFORE BUCHMAN WAS ATTACKED...
POLICE SAY THEY HAVE NO CLUE AS TO WHAT HER CONNECTION, IF ANY, MIGHT BE TO EITHER BUCHMAN OR THE SWAN.
17

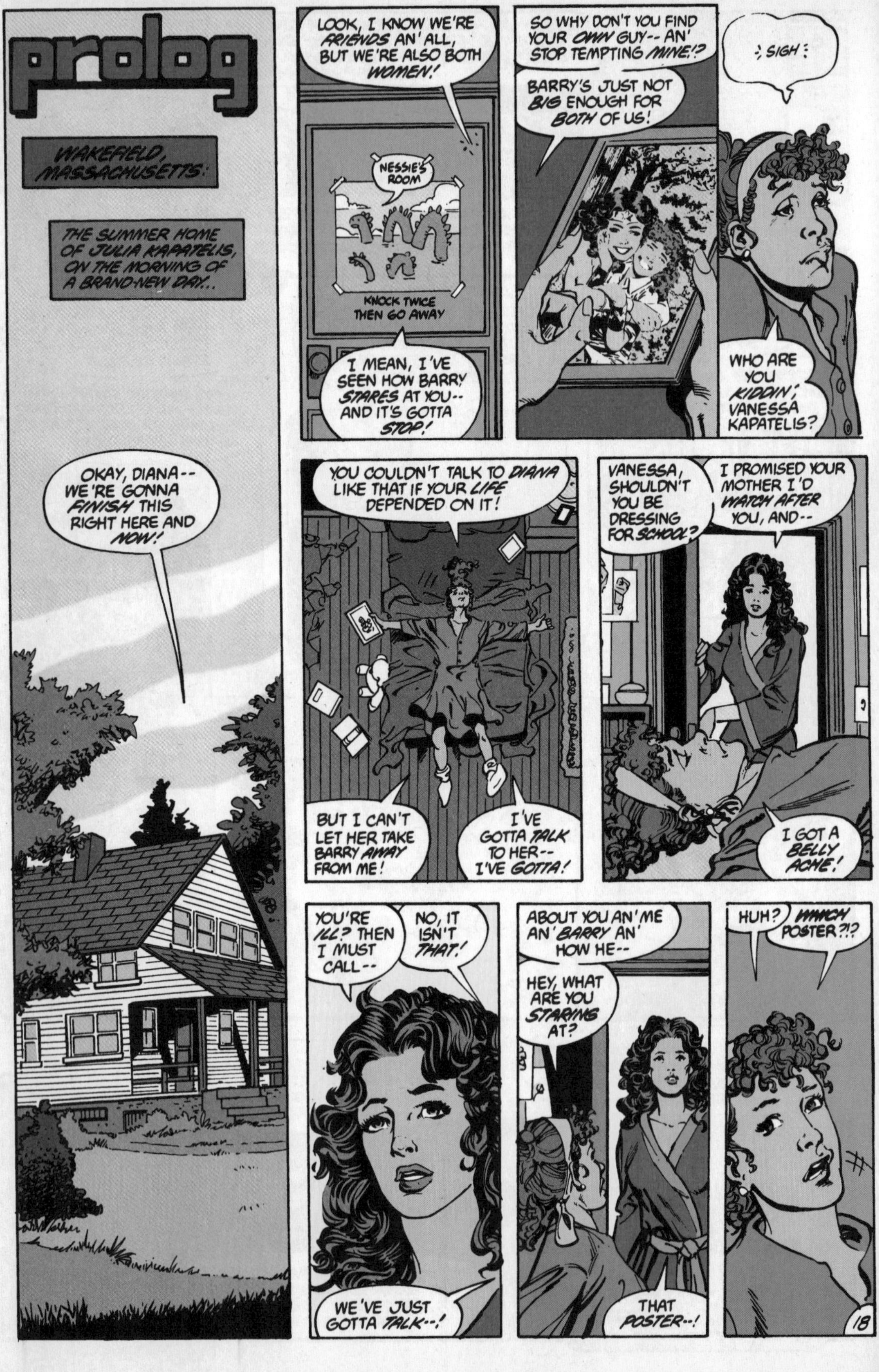
prolog
WAKEFIELD, MASSACHUSETTS:
THE SUMMER HOME OF JULIA KAPATELIS, ON THE MORNING OF A BRAND-NEW DAY...
OKAY, DIANA-- WE'RE GONNA FINISH THIS RIGHT HERE AND NOW!
LOOK, I KNOW WE'RE FRIENDS AN' ALL, BUT WE'RE ALSO BOTH WOMEN!
NESSIE'S ROOM
KNOCK TWICE THEN GO AWAY
I MEAN, I'VE SEEN HOW BARRY STARES AT YOU-- AND IT'S GOTTA STOP!
SO WHY DON'T YOU FIND YOUR OWN GUY-- AN' STOP TEMPTING MINE!?
BARRY'S JUST NOT BIG ENOUGH FOR BOTH OF US!
SIGH
WHO ARE YOU KIDDIN', VANESSA KAPATELIS?
YOU COULDN'T TALK TO DIANA LIKE THAT IF YOUR LIFE DEPENDED ON IT!
BUT I CAN'T LET HER TAKE BARRY AWAY FROM ME!
I'VE GOTTA TALK TO HER-- I'VE GOTTA!
VANESSA, SHOULDN'T YOU BE DRESSING FOR SCHOOL?
I PROMISED YOUR MOTHER I'D WATCH AFTER YOU, AND--
I GOT A BELLY ACHE!
YOU'RE ILL? THEN I MUST CALL--
NO, IT ISN'T THAT!
WE'VE JUST GOTTA TALK--!
ABOUT YOU AN' ME AN' BARRY AN' HOW HE--
HEY, WHAT ARE YOU STARING AT?
THAT POSTER--!
HUH? WHICH POSTER?!?
18

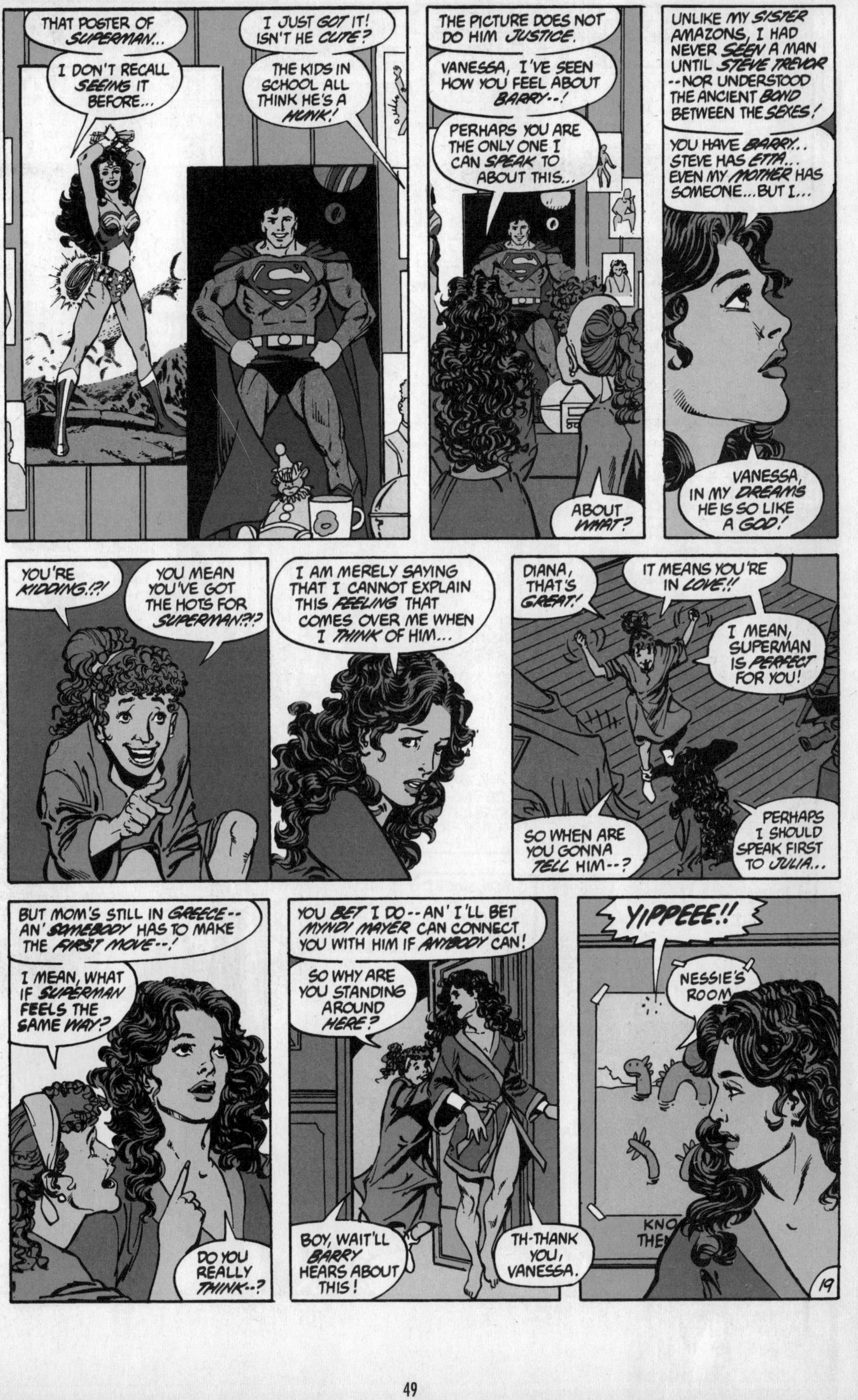
THAT POSTER OF SUPERMAN...
I DON'T RECALL SEEING IT BEFORE...
I JUST GOT IT! ISN'T HE CUTE?
THE KIDS IN SCHOOL ALL THINK HE'S A HUNK!
THE PICTURE DOES NOT DO HIM JUSTICE.
VANESSA, I'VE SEEN HOW YOU FEEL ABOUT BARRY--!
PERHAPS YOU ARE THE ONLY ONE I CAN SPEAK TO ABOUT THIS...
ABOUT WHAT?
UNLIKE MY SISTER AMAZONS, I HAD NEVER SEEN A MAN UNTIL STEVE TREVOR --NOR UNDERSTOOD THE ANCIENT BOND BETWEEN THE SEXES!
YOU HAVE BARRY... STEVE HAS ETTA... EVEN MY MOTHER HAS SOMEONE... BUT I...
VANESSA, IN MY DREAMS HE IS SO LIKE A GOD!
YOU'RE KIDDING!?!
YOU MEAN YOU'VE GOT THE HOTS FOR SUPERMAN?!?
I AM MERELY SAYING THAT I CANNOT EXPLAIN THIS FEELING THAT COMES OVER ME WHEN I THINK OF HIM...
DIANA, THAT'S GREAT!
IT MEANS YOU'RE IN LOVE!!
I MEAN, SUPERMAN IS PERFECT FOR YOU!
SO WHEN ARE YOU GONNA TELL HIM--?
PERHAPS I SHOULD SPEAK FIRST TO JULIA...
BUT MOM'S STILL IN GREECE-- AN' SOMEBODY HAS TO MAKE THE FIRST MOVE--!
I MEAN, WHAT IF SUPERMAN FEELS THE SAME WAY?
DO YOU REALLY THINK--?
YOU BET I DO--AN' I'LL BET MYNDI MAYER CAN CONNECT YOU WITH HIM IF ANYBODY CAN!
SO WHY ARE YOU STANDING AROUND HERE?
BOY, WAIT'LL BARRY HEARS ABOUT THIS!
TH-THANK YOU, VANESSA.
YIPPEEE!!
NESSIE'S ROOM
19

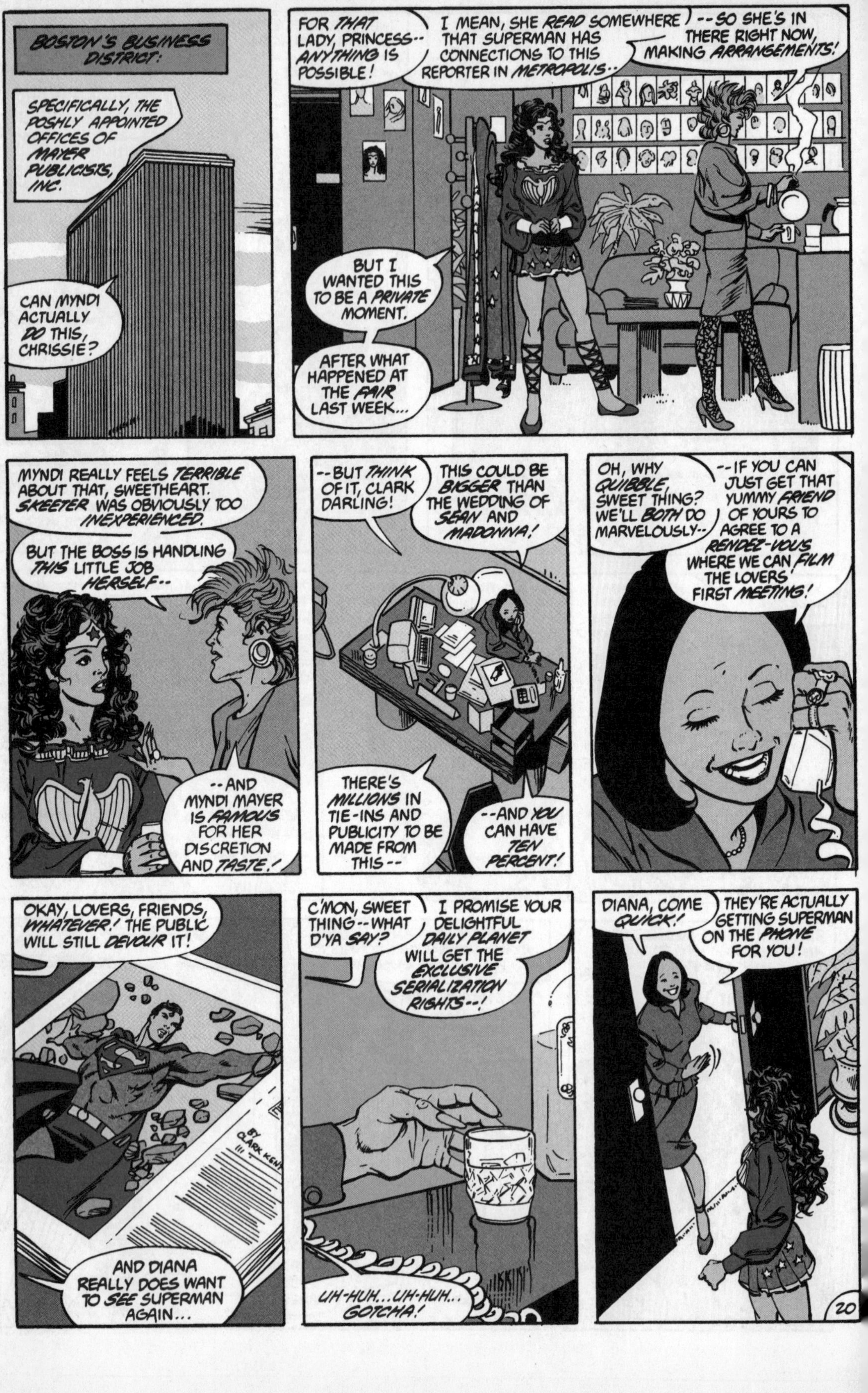

BOSTON'S BUSINESS DISTRICT:
SPECIFICALLY, THE POSHLY APPOINTED OFFICES OF MAYER PUBLICISTS, INC.
CAN MYNDI ACTUALLY DO THIS, CHRISSIE?
FOR THAT LADY, PRINCESS-- ANYTHING IS POSSIBLE!
I MEAN, SHE READ SOMEWHERE THAT SUPERMAN HAS CONNECTIONS TO THIS REPORTER IN METROPOLIS..
--SO SHE'S IN THERE RIGHT NOW, MAKING ARRANGEMENTS!
BUT I WANTED THIS TO BE A PRIVATE MOMENT.
AFTER WHAT HAPPENED AT THE FAIR LAST WEEK...
MYNDI REALLY FEELS TERRIBLE ABOUT THAT, SWEETHEART. SKEETER WAS OBVIOUSLY TOO INEXPERIENCED.
BUT THE BOSS IS HANDLING THIS LITTLE JOB HERSELF--
--AND MYNDI MAYER IS FAMOUS FOR HER DISCRETION AND TASTE!
--BUT THINK OF IT, CLARK DARLING!
THIS COULD BE BIGGER THAN THE WEDDING OF SEAN AND MADONNA!
THERE'S MILLIONS IN TIE-INS AND PUBLICITY TO BE MADE FROM THIS--
--AND YOU CAN HAVE TEN PERCENT!
OH, WHY QUIBBLE, SWEET THING? WE'LL BOTH DO MARVELOUSLY--
--IF YOU CAN JUST GET THAT YUMMY FRIEND OF YOURS TO AGREE TO A RENDEZ-VOUS WHERE WE CAN FILM THE LOVERS' FIRST MEETING!
OKAY, LOVERS, FRIENDS, WHATEVER! THE PUBLIC WILL STILL DEVOUR IT!
BY CLARK KENT
AND DIANA REALLY DOES WANT TO SEE SUPERMAN AGAIN...
C'MON, SWEET THING--WHAT D'YA SAY?
I PROMISE YOUR DELIGHTFUL DAILY PLANET WILL GET THE EXCLUSIVE SERIALIZATION RIGHTS--!
UH-HUH...UH-HUH... GOTCHA!
DIANA, COME QUICK!
THEY'RE ACTUALLY GETTING SUPERMAN ON THE PHONE FOR YOU!
20

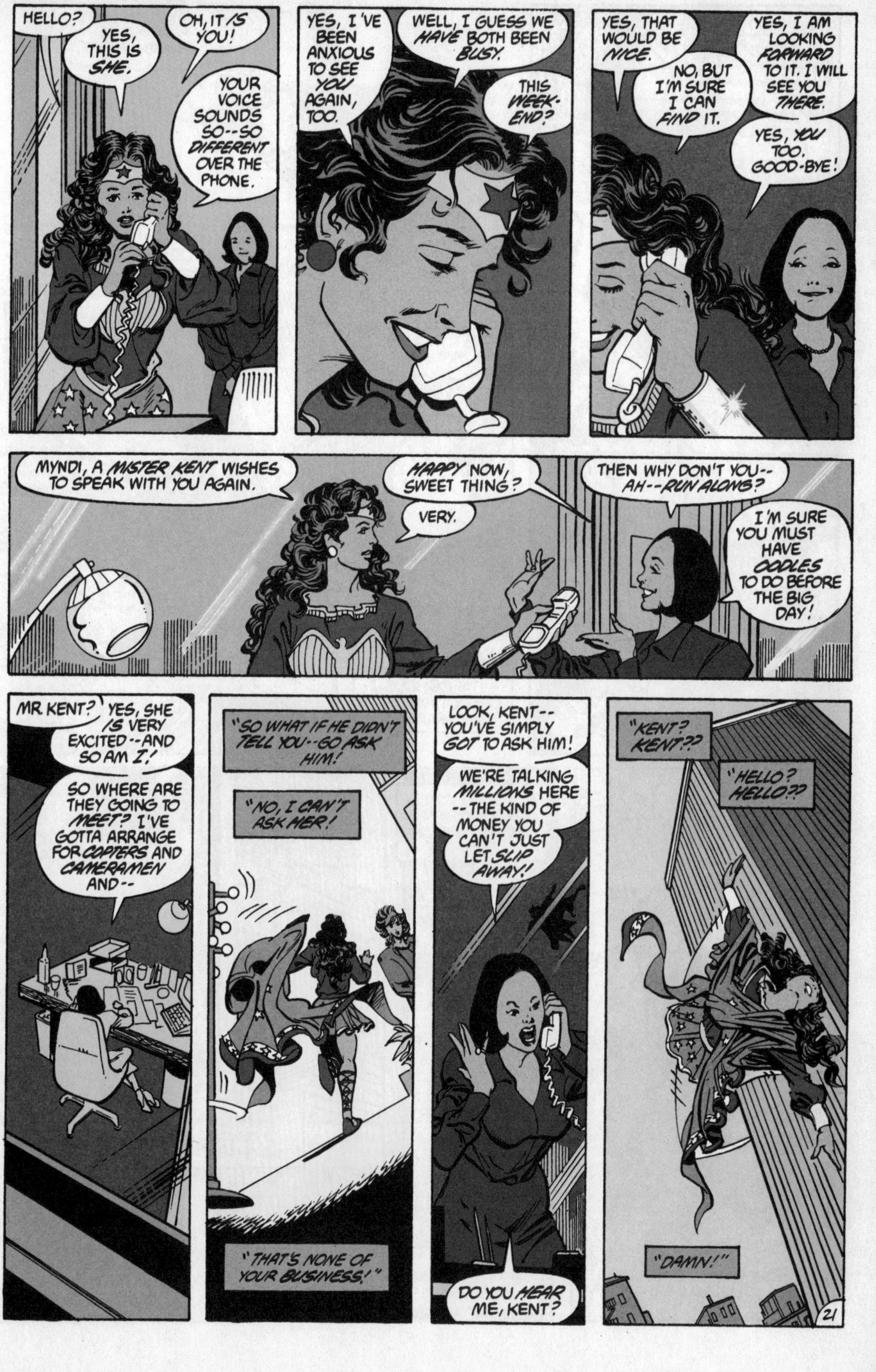
HELLO?
YES, THIS IS SHE.
OH, IT IS YOU!
YOUR VOICE SOUNDS SO--SO DIFFERENT OVER THE PHONE.
YES, I'VE BEEN ANXIOUS TO SEE YOU AGAIN, TOO.
WELL, I GUESS WE HAVE BOTH BEEN BUSY.
THIS WEEK-END?
YES, THAT WOULD BE NICE.
NO, BUT I'M SURE I CAN FIND IT.
YES, I AM LOOKING FORWARD TO IT. I WILL SEE YOU THERE.
YES, YOU TOO. GOOD-BYE!
MYNDI, A MISTER KENT WISHES TO SPEAK WITH YOU AGAIN.
HAPPY NOW, SWEET THING?
VERY.
THEN WHY DON'T YOU-- AH--RUN ALONG?
I'M SURE YOU MUST HAVE OODLES TO DO BEFORE THE BIG DAY!
MR. KENT? YES, SHE IS VERY EXCITED--AND SO AM I!
SO WHERE ARE THEY GOING TO MEET? I'VE GOTTA ARRANGE FOR COPTERS AND CAMERAMEN AND--
"SO WHAT IF HE DIDN'T TELL YOU--GO ASK HIM!
"NO, I CAN'T ASK HER!
"THAT'S NONE OF YOUR BUSINESS!"
LOOK, KENT-- YOU'VE SIMPLY GOT TO ASK HIM!
WE'RE TALKING MILLIONS HERE --THE KIND OF MONEY YOU CAN'T JUST LET SLIP AWAY!
DO YOU HEAR ME, KENT?
"KENT? KENT??
"HELLO? HELLO??
"DAMN!"
21

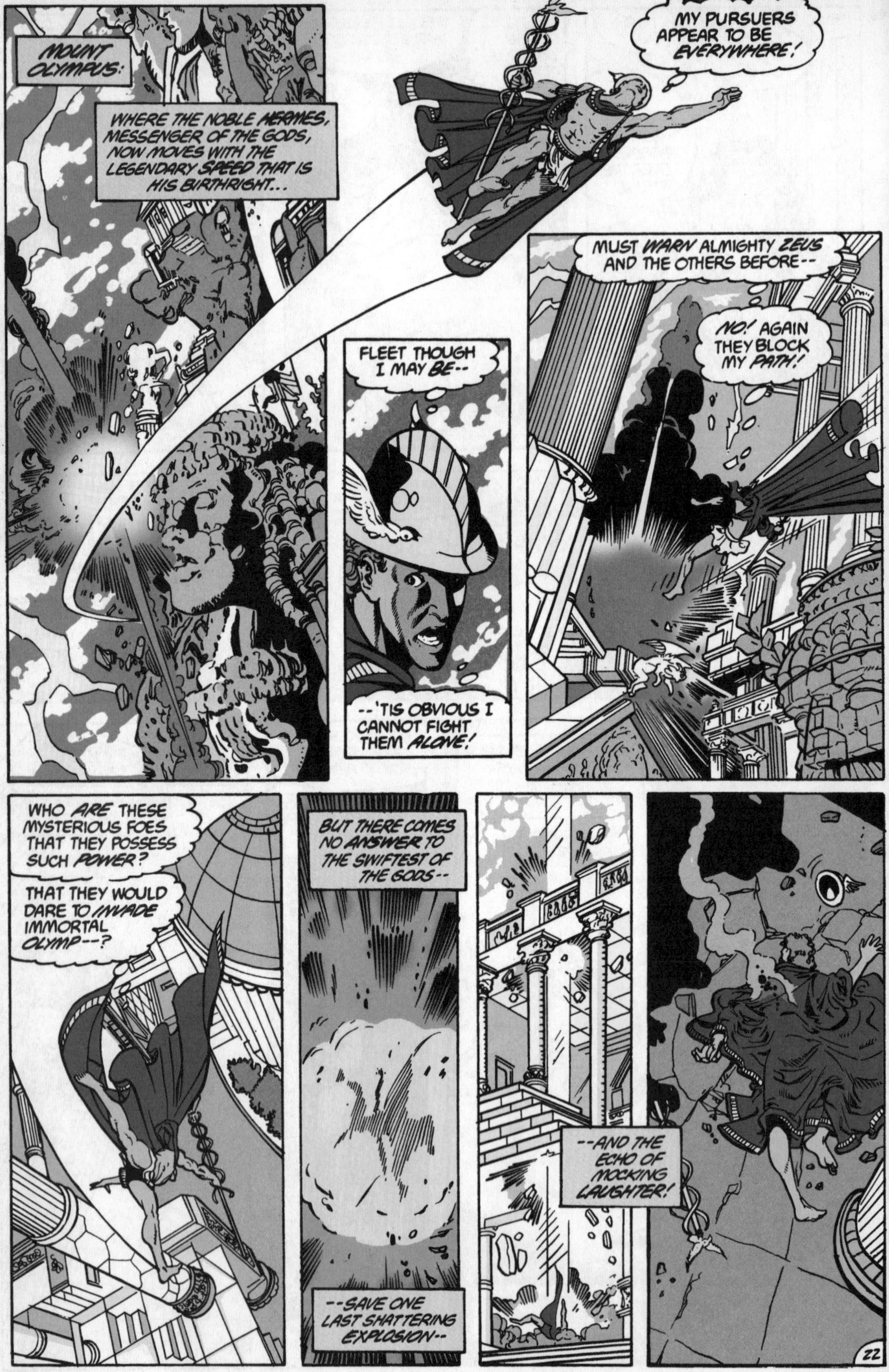

MOUNT OLYMPUS:
WHERE THE NOBLE HERMES, MESSENGER OF THE GODS, NOW MOVES WITH THE LEGENDARY SPEED THAT IS HIS BIRTHRIGHT...
MY PURSUERS APPEAR TO BE EVERYWHERE!
FLEET THOUGH I MAY BE--
--'TIS OBVIOUS I CANNOT FIGHT THEM ALONE!
MUST WARN ALMIGHTY ZEUS AND THE OTHERS BEFORE--
NO! AGAIN THEY BLOCK MY PATH!
WHO ARE THESE MYSTERIOUS FOES THAT THEY POSSESS SUCH POWER?
THAT THEY WOULD DARE TO INVADE IMMORTAL OLYMP--?
BUT THERE COMES NO ANSWER TO THE SWIFTEST OF THE GODS--
--SAVE ONE LAST SHATTERING EXPLOSION--
--AND THE ECHO OF MOCKING LAUGHTER!
22

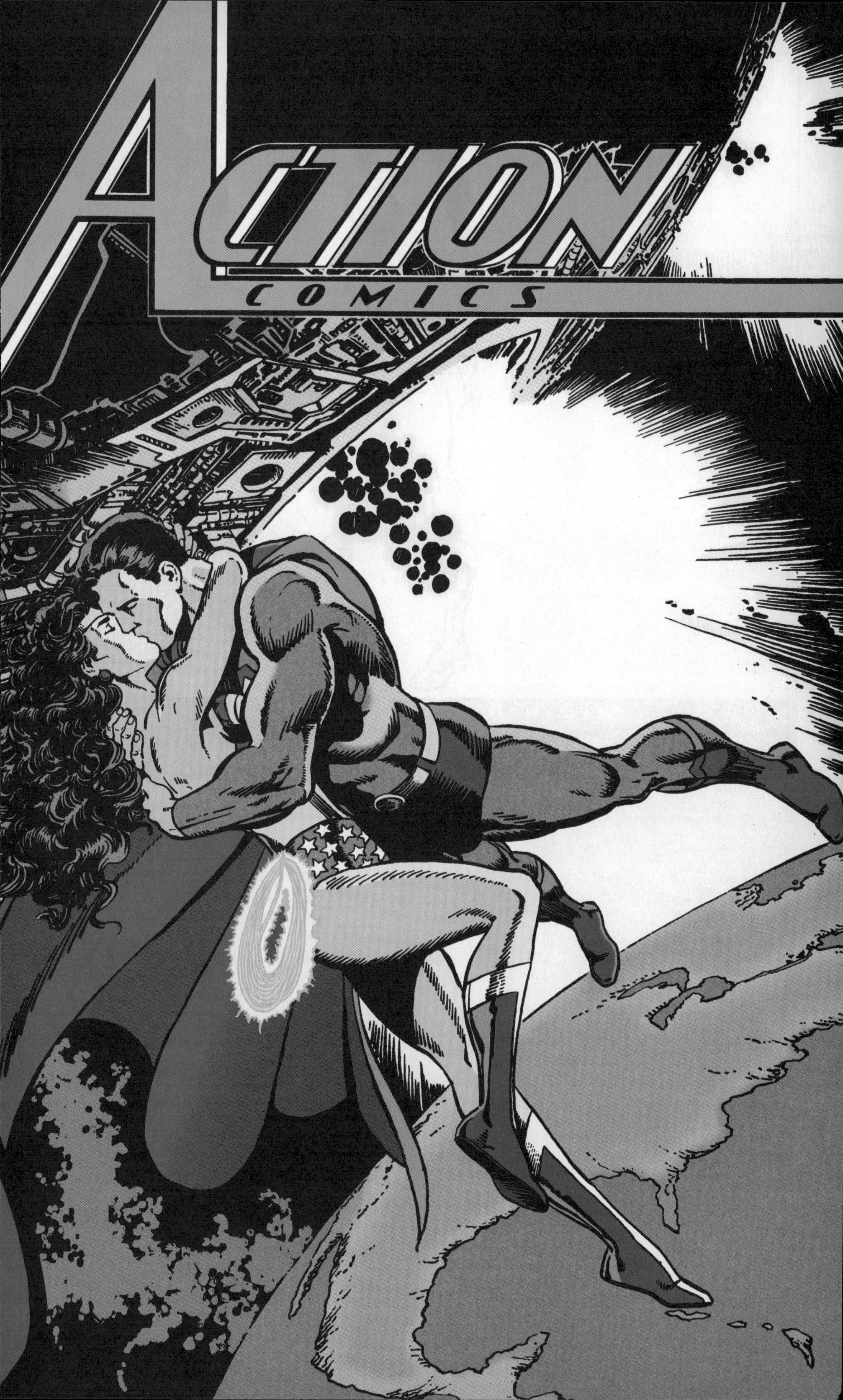
ACTION
COMICS

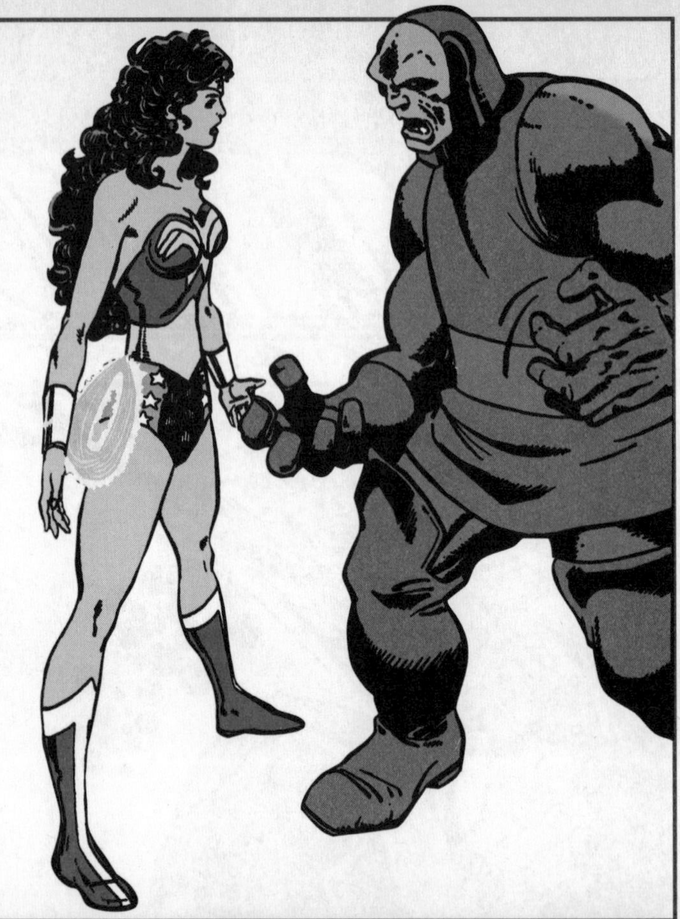

WONDER WOMAN

CHAPTER THREE

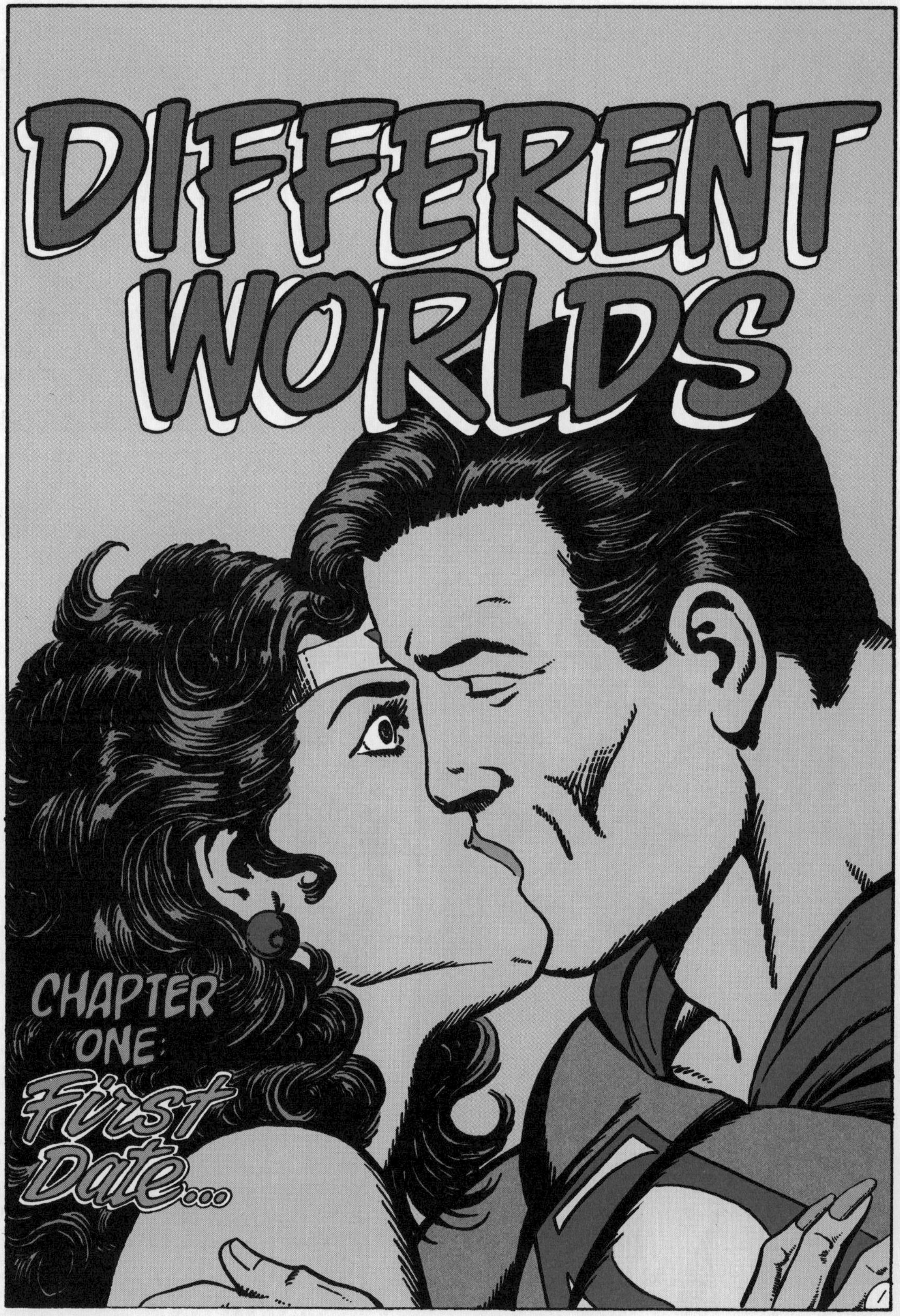
DIFFERENT WORLDS
CHAPTER ONE:
First Date...

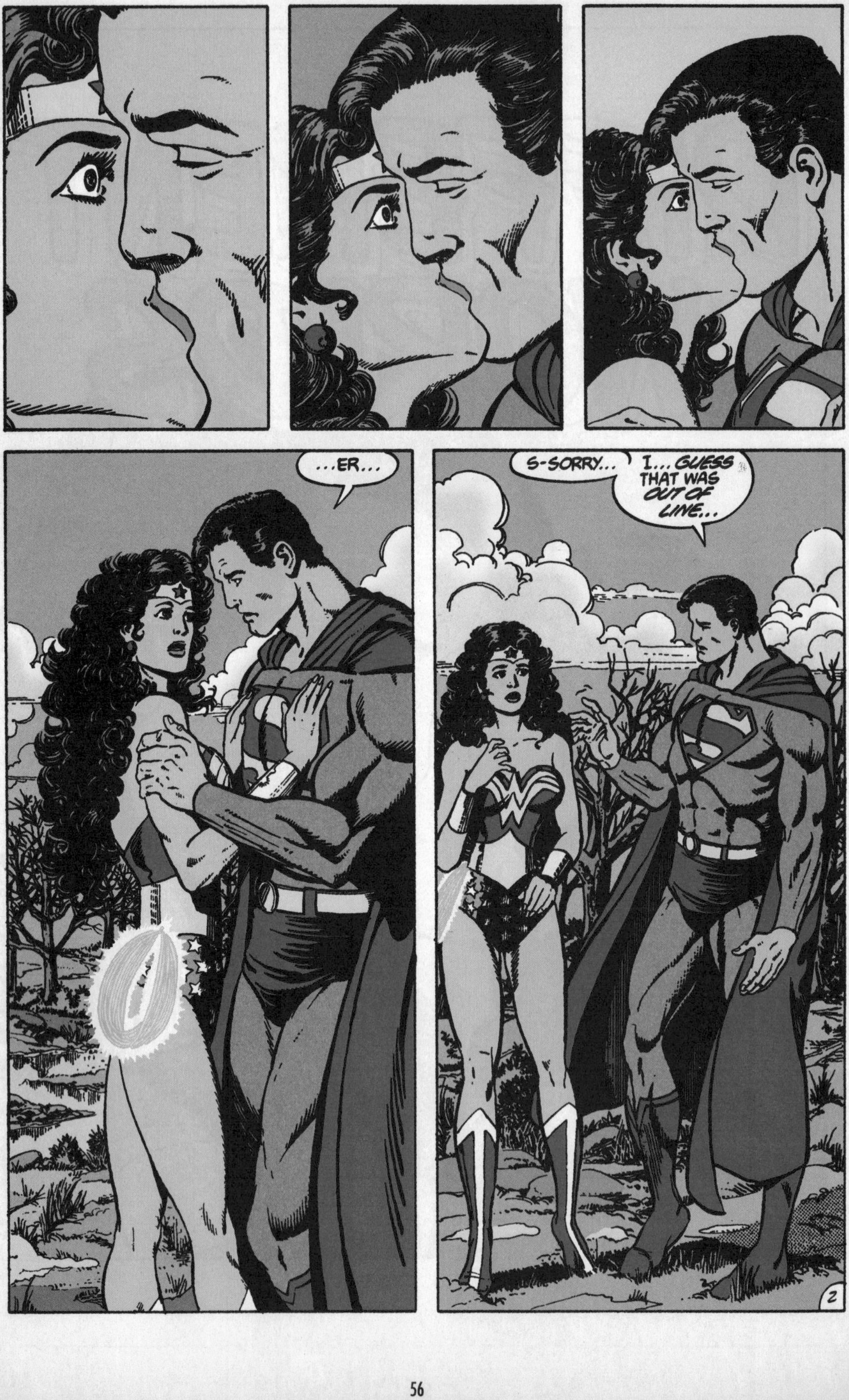
...ER...
S-SORRY...
I... GUESS THAT WAS OUT OF LINE...
2

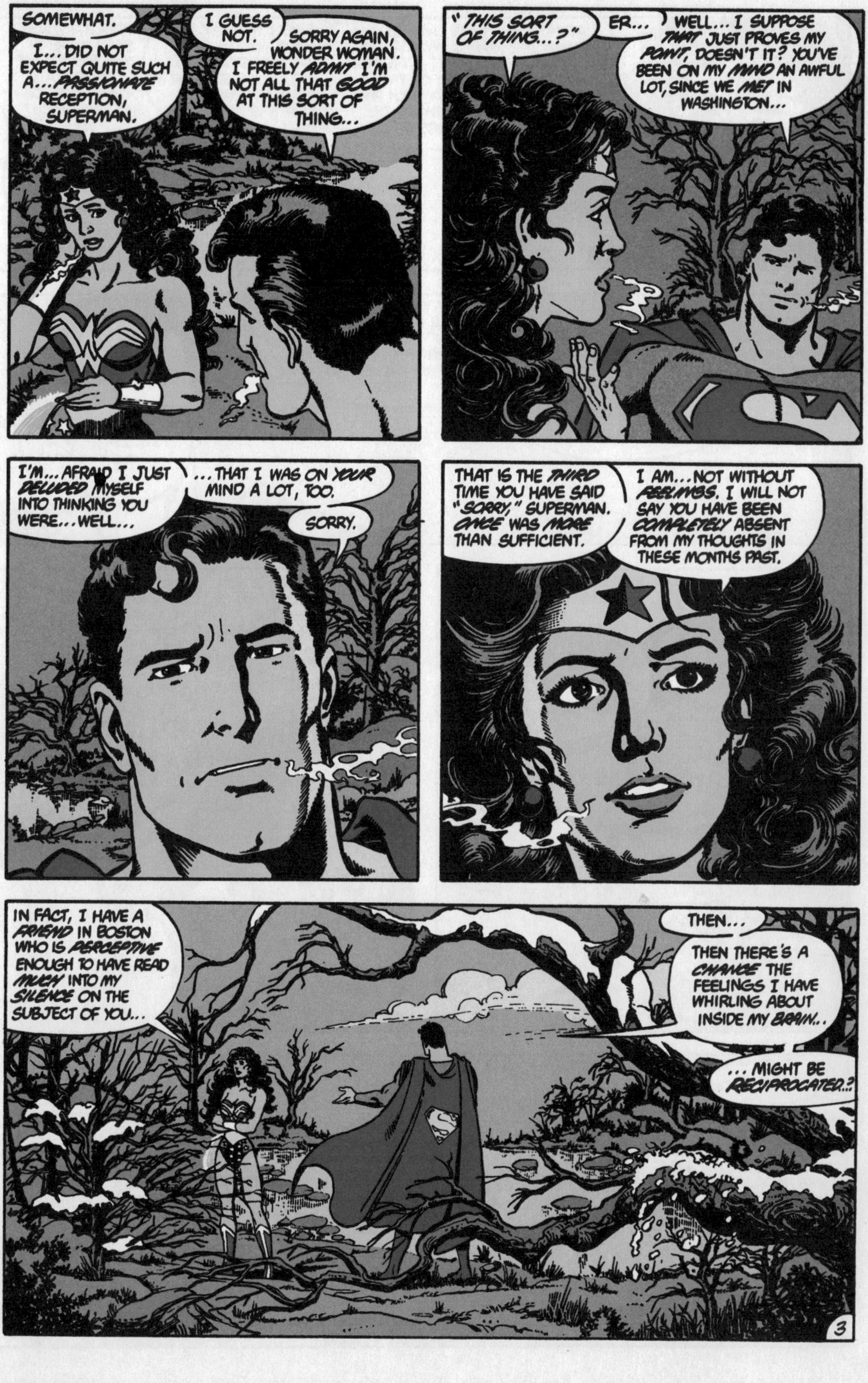
SOMEWHAT.
I... DID NOT EXPECT QUITE SUCH A... PASSIONATE RECEPTION, SUPERMAN.
I GUESS NOT.
SORRY AGAIN, WONDER WOMAN. I FREELY ADMIT I'M NOT ALL THAT GOOD AT THIS SORT OF THING...
"THIS SORT OF THING...?"
ER...
WELL... I SUPPOSE THAT JUST PROVES MY POINT, DOESN'T IT? YOU'VE BEEN ON MY MIND AN AWFUL LOT, SINCE WE MET IN WASHINGTON...
I'M... AFRAID I JUST DELUDED MYSELF INTO THINKING YOU WERE... WELL...
...THAT I WAS ON YOUR MIND A LOT, TOO.
SORRY.
THAT IS THE THIRD TIME YOU HAVE SAID "SORRY," SUPERMAN. ONCE WAS MORE THAN SUFFICIENT.
I AM... NOT WITHOUT FEELINGS. I WILL NOT SAY YOU HAVE BEEN COMPLETELY ABSENT FROM MY THOUGHTS IN THESE MONTHS PAST.
IN FACT, I HAVE A FRIEND IN BOSTON WHO IS PERCEPTIVE ENOUGH TO HAVE READ MUCH INTO MY SILENCE ON THE SUBJECT OF YOU...
THEN...
THEN THERE'S A CHANCE THE FEELINGS I HAVE WHIRLING ABOUT INSIDE MY BRAIN...
...MIGHT BE RECIPROCATED..?
3

I... DO NOT *KNOW*, SUPERMAN.

I HAVE LIVED IN *MAN'S WORLD* ONLY A SHORT TIME, AND SO MANY OF THE EMOTIONS WHICH PASS FREELY BETWEEN THE SEXES ARE STILL...

I WILL NOT SAY I HAVE *NOT* THOUGHT OF YOU SINCE THE AFFAIR OF G. *GORDON GODFREY* ENDED IN YOUR WASHINGTON...

IN FACT, IT HAS BEEN MORE IN THE FASHION OF A DELIBERATE *AVOIDANCE* OF THOUGHTS ABOUT YOU...

IN MANY WAYS A *GREATER* STRAIN THAN FACING ANY FEELINGS *OUTRIGHT*.

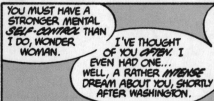

YOU MUST HAVE A STRONGER MENTAL *SELF-CONTROL* THAN I DO, WONDER WOMAN.

I'VE THOUGHT OF YOU *OFTEN*. I EVEN HAD ONE... WELL, A RATHER *INTENSE* DREAM ABOUT YOU, SHORTLY AFTER WASHINGTON.

THAT WAS WHEN I STARTED TO WONDER IF IT MIGHT NOT BE MY *HEART* TRYING TO COME TO *TERMS* WITH SOMETHING MY *BRAIN* HAD YET TO SEE...

YOU SPEAK IN MOST *COMPELLING* TERMS, SUPERMAN.

I HAVE A *WARRIOR'S HEART*, BUT I AM NOT *UNMOVED* BY YOUR WORDS.

BUT YOU MAINTAIN YOUR *DISTANCE*, WONDER WOMAN.

YOU STILL EXPRESS YOUR FEELINGS IN TERMS OF WHAT THEY'RE *NOT*-- *NOT* THINKING OF ME, *NOT* UNMOVED BY MY WORDS...

YES...

BUT THIS IS MY *PREROGATIVE*, IS IT NOT? TO USE THE LANGUAGE OF THIS LAND, THIS IS OUR... *FIRST DATE*.

WE SEEK HERE *UNDERSTANDING*, NOT *CONSUMMATION*.

AM I *RIGHT*?

YES. ABSOLUTELY.

ALL RIGHT, WONDER WOMAN, WILL YOU COME WITH ME NOW, SO I CAN *INTRODUCE* MYSELF MORE *PROPERLY*?

SUPERMAN... I WOULD BE *HONORED*...

BUT, PLEASE, MY NAME IS DIANA!

4

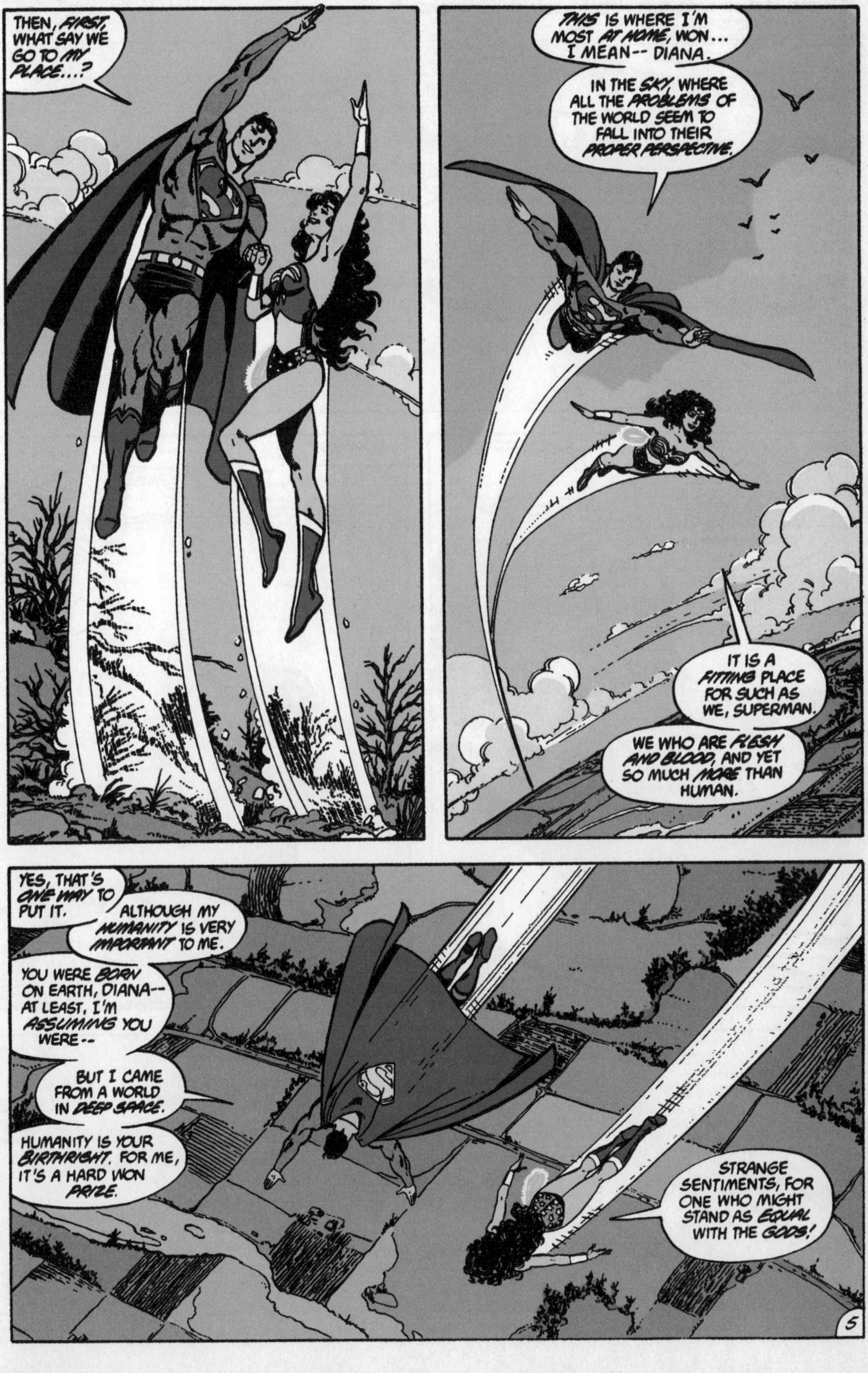
THEN, FIRST, WHAT SAY WE GO TO MY PLACE...?
THIS IS WHERE I'M MOST AT HOME, WON... I MEAN-- DIANA.
IN THE SKY, WHERE ALL THE PROBLEMS OF THE WORLD SEEM TO FALL INTO THEIR PROPER PERSPECTIVE.
IT IS A FITTING PLACE FOR SUCH AS WE, SUPERMAN.
WE WHO ARE FLESH AND BLOOD, AND YET SO MUCH MORE THAN HUMAN.
YES, THAT'S ONE WAY TO PUT IT.
ALTHOUGH MY HUMANITY IS VERY IMPORTANT TO ME.
YOU WERE BORN ON EARTH, DIANA-- AT LEAST, I'M ASSUMING YOU WERE--
BUT I CAME FROM A WORLD IN DEEP SPACE.
HUMANITY IS YOUR BIRTHRIGHT. FOR ME, IT'S A HARD WON PRIZE.
STRANGE SENTIMENTS, FOR ONE WHO MIGHT STAND AS EQUAL WITH THE GODS!
5

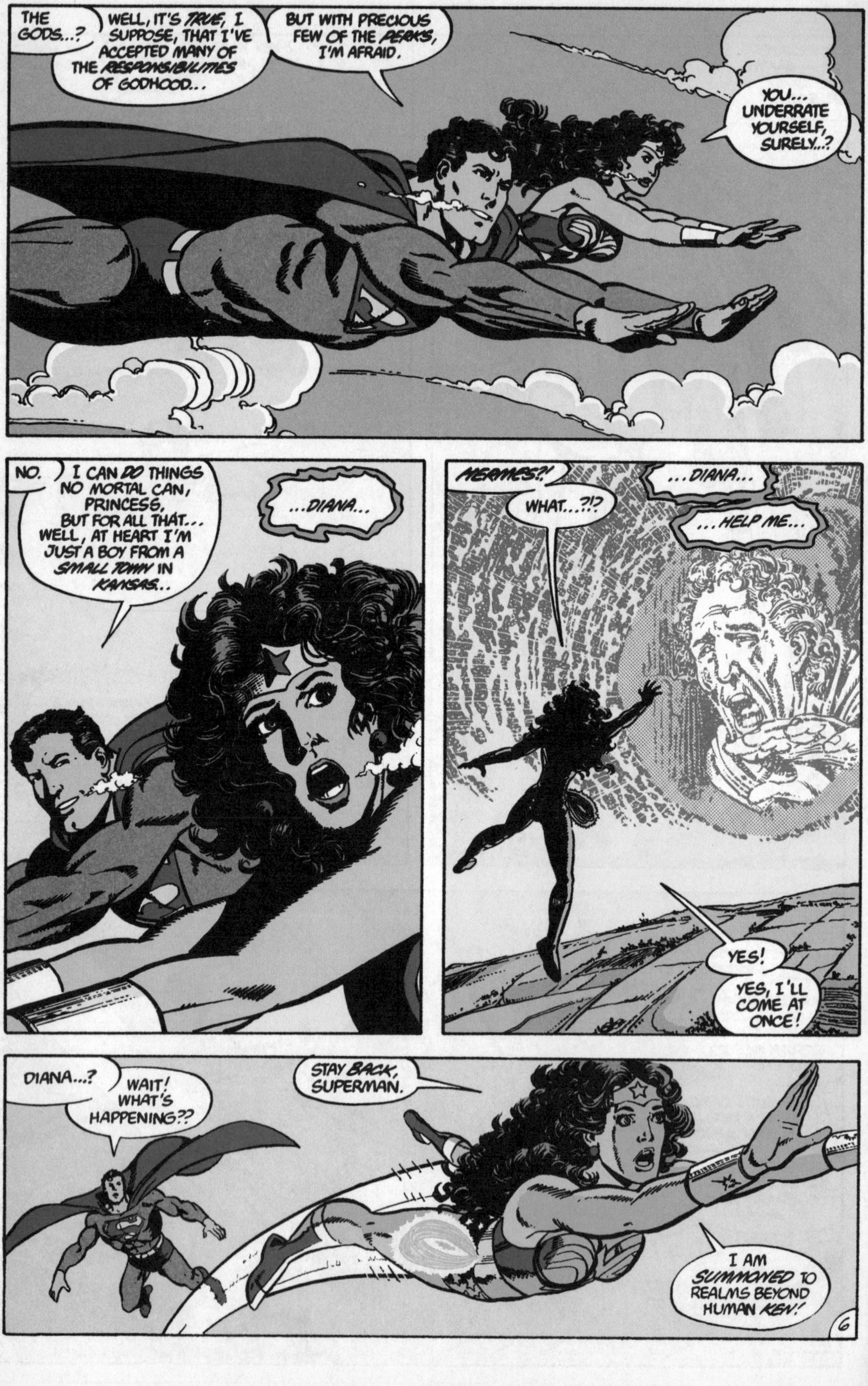
THE GODS...?
WELL, IT'S TRUE, I SUPPOSE, THAT I'VE ACCEPTED MANY OF THE RESPONSIBILITIES OF GODHOOD...
BUT WITH PRECIOUS FEW OF THE PERKS, I'M AFRAID.
YOU... UNDERRATE YOURSELF, SURELY...?
NO.
I CAN DO THINGS NO MORTAL CAN, PRINCESS, BUT FOR ALL THAT... WELL, AT HEART I'M JUST A BOY FROM A SMALL TOWN IN KANSAS...
...DIANA...
HERMES?!
WHAT...?!?
...DIANA...
...HELP ME...
YES!
YES, I'LL COME AT ONCE!
DIANA...?
WAIT! WHAT'S HAPPENING??
STAY BACK, SUPERMAN.
I AM SUMMONED TO REALMS BEYOND HUMAN KEN!
6

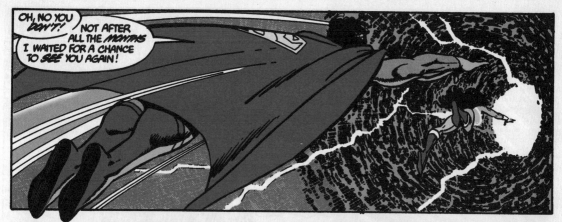

OH, NO YOU *DON'T!* NOT AFTER ALL THE *MONTHS* I WAITED FOR A CHANCE TO *SEE* YOU AGAIN!

I'M COMING *WITH...*

...YOU...

OH-HHH-H

:UNGH!:

WHAT IN...??

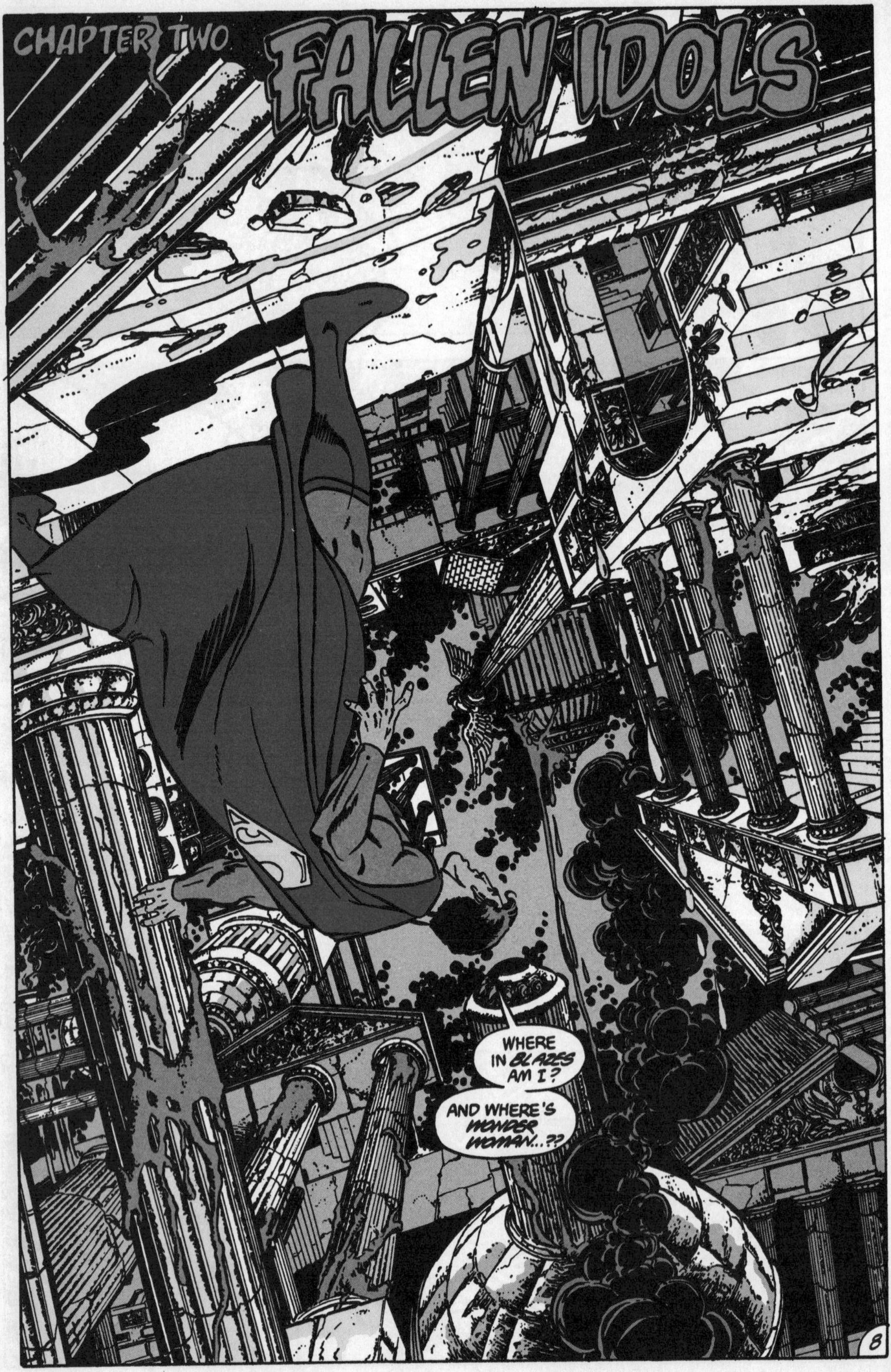
CHAPTER TWO
FALLEN IDOLS
WHERE IN BLAZES AM I?
AND WHERE'S WONDER WOMAN...??
8

SHE'S NOWHERE IN MY *DIRECT* LINE OF SIGHT.

MAYBE MY *TELESCOPIC VISION* WILL...

OH...NOW *THAT* IS *TOO WEIRD!*

THAT'S *ME!* SEEN AS IF I'M SOMEHOW *BEHIND* MYSELF!

WHICH TENDS TO RENDER MY *VISION* POWERS EVER SO SLIGHTLY *USELESS!*

ALL RIGHT, WE'LL DO THIS THE *HARD* WAY.

I'LL FIND HER IF I HAVE TO SEARCH EVERY *INCH* OF THIS...

HUM...?

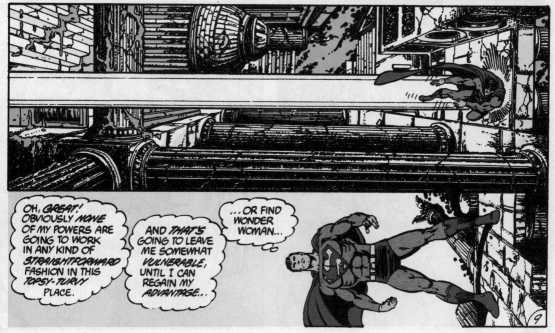

OH, *GREAT!* OBVIOUSLY *NONE* OF MY POWERS ARE GOING TO WORK IN ANY KIND OF *STRAIGHTFORWARD* FASHION IN THIS *TOPSY-TURVY* PLACE.

AND *THAT'S* GOING TO LEAVE ME SOMEWHAT *VULNERABLE,* UNTIL I CAN REGAIN MY *ADVANTAGE...*

...OR FIND WONDER WOMAN...

9

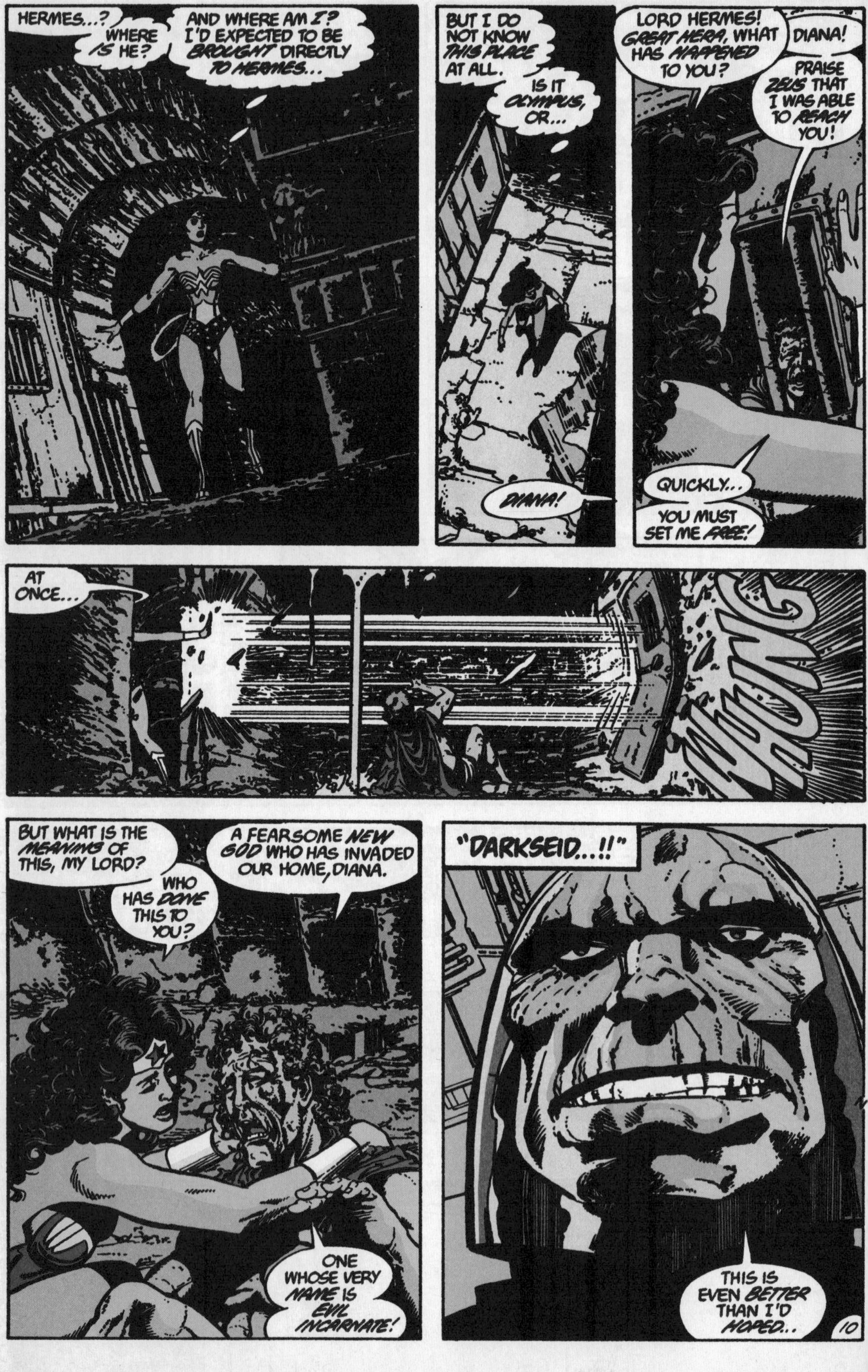
HERMES...? WHERE IS HE?
AND WHERE AM I? I'D EXPECTED TO BE BROUGHT DIRECTLY TO HERMES...
BUT I DO NOT KNOW THIS PLACE AT ALL.
IS IT OLYMPUS, OR...
DIANA!
LORD HERMES! GREAT HERA, WHAT HAS HAPPENED TO YOU?
DIANA!
PRAISE ZEUS THAT I WAS ABLE TO REACH YOU!
QUICKLY...
YOU MUST SET ME FREE!
AT ONCE...
BUT WHAT IS THE MEANING OF THIS, MY LORD?
WHO HAS DONE THIS TO YOU?
A FEARSOME NEW GOD WHO HAS INVADED OUR HOME, DIANA.
ONE WHOSE VERY NAME IS EVIL INCARNATE!
"DARKSEID...!!"
THIS IS EVEN BETTER THAN I'D HOPED...
10

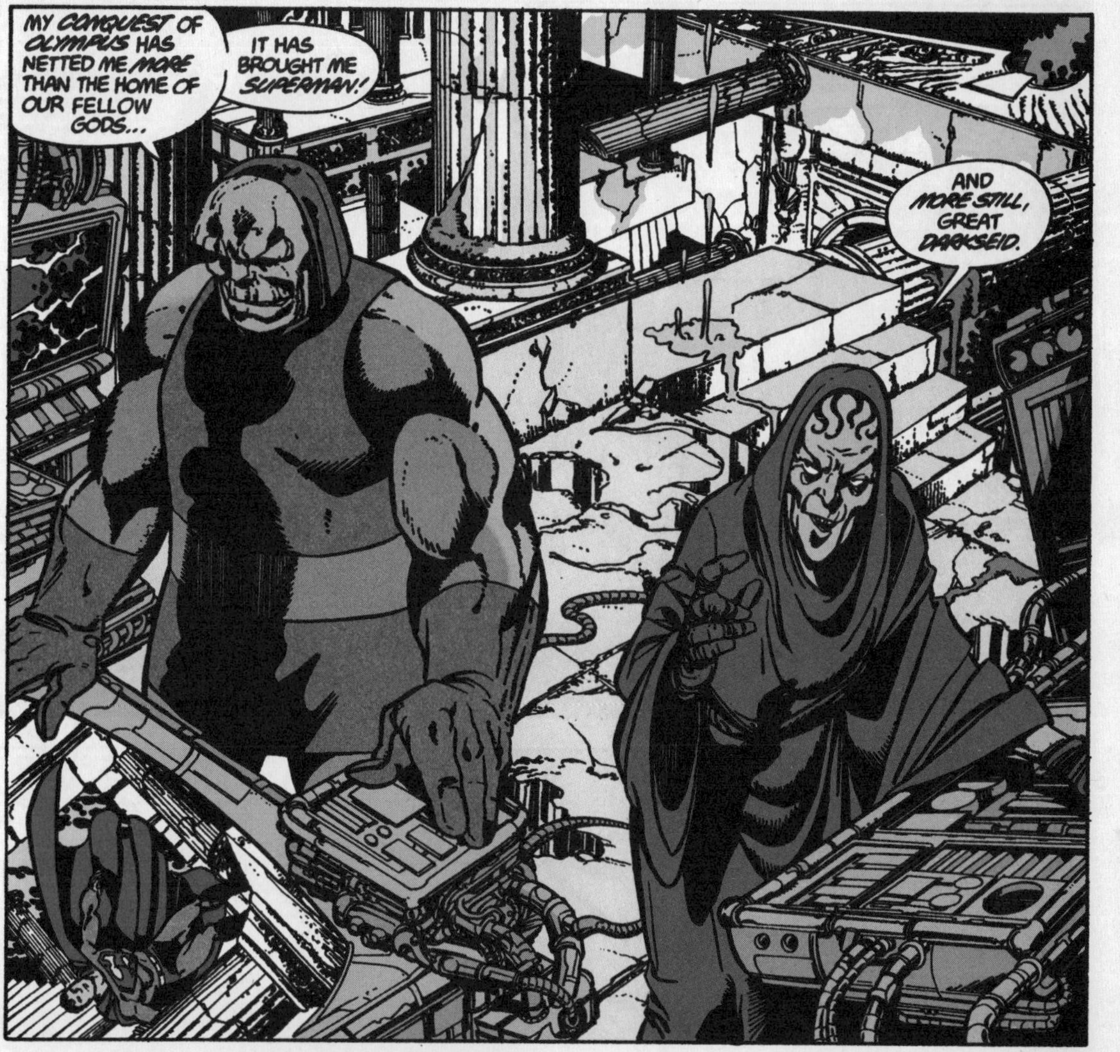
MY CONQUEST OF OLYMPUS HAS NETTED ME MORE THAN THE HOME OF OUR FELLOW GODS...
IT HAS BROUGHT ME SUPERMAN!
AND MORE STILL, GREAT DARKSEID.

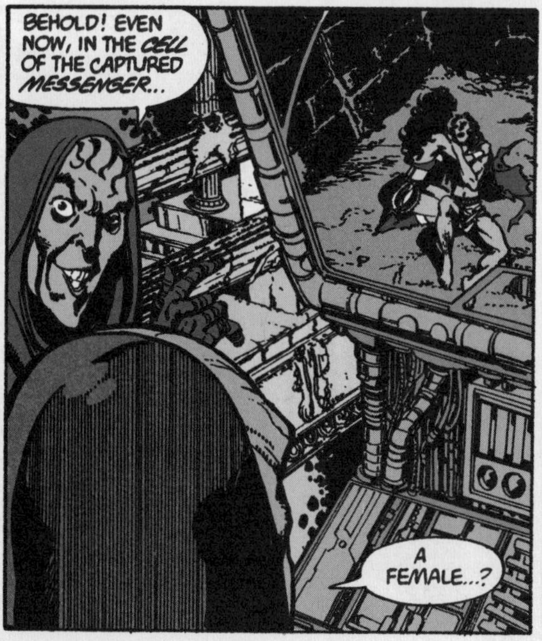
BEHOLD! EVEN NOW, IN THE CELL OF THE CAPTURED MESSENGER...
A FEMALE...?

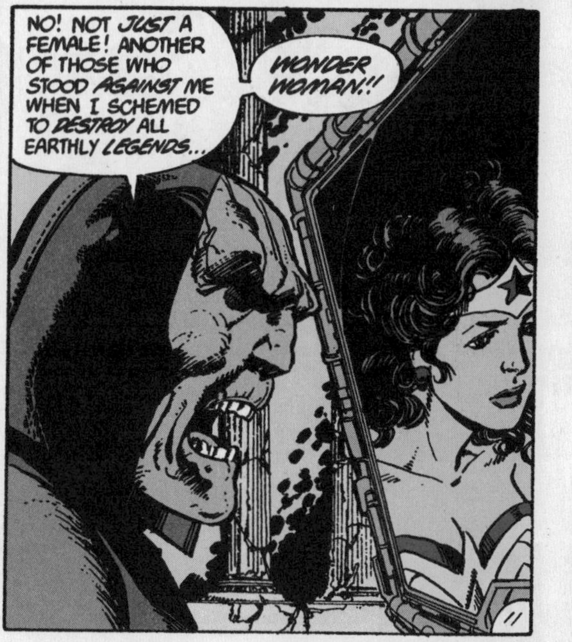
NO! NOT JUST A FEMALE! ANOTHER OF THOSE WHO STOOD AGAINST ME WHEN I SCHEMED TO DESTROY ALL EARTHLY LEGENDS...
WONDER WOMAN!!

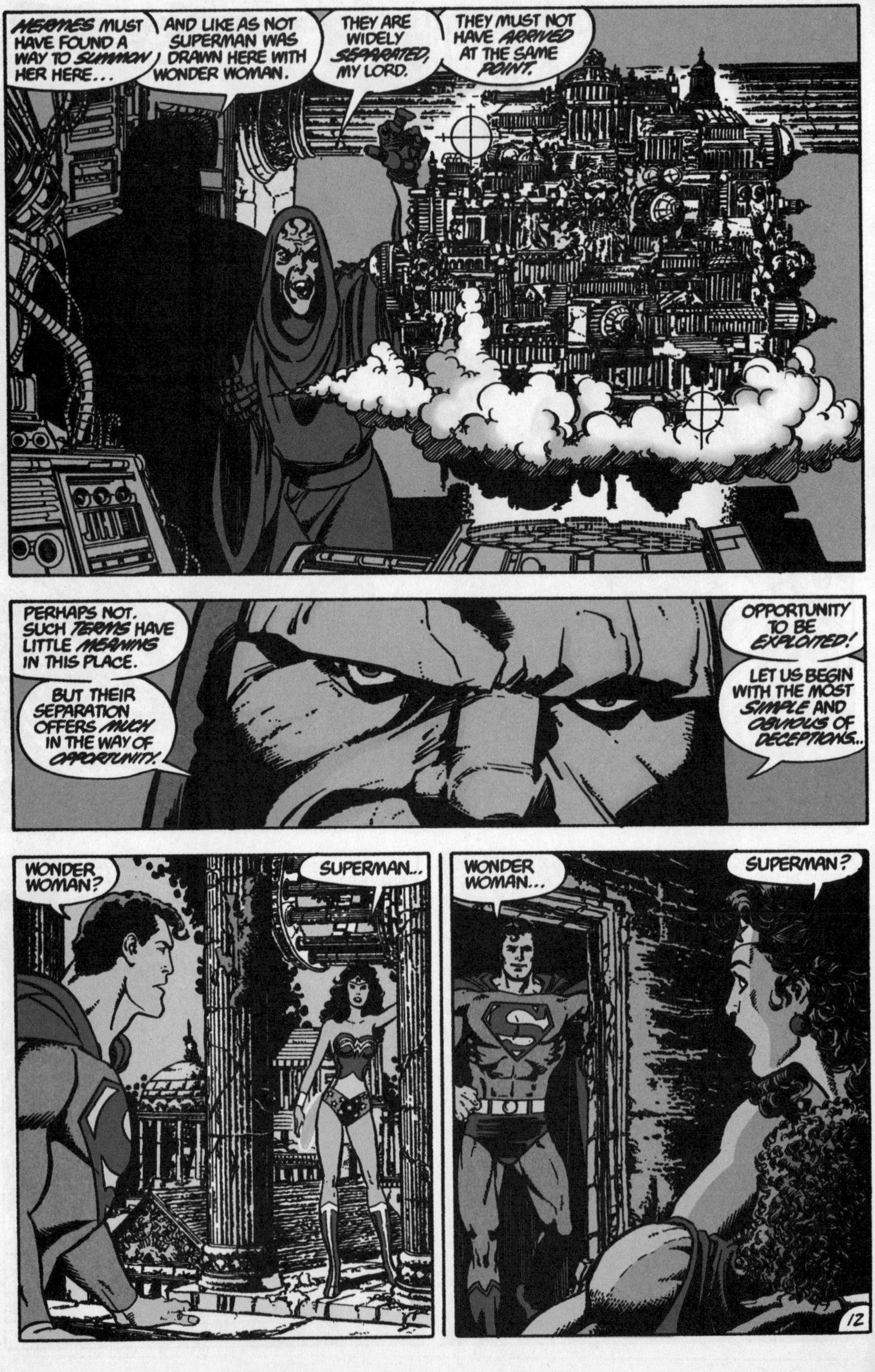
HERMES MUST HAVE FOUND A WAY TO SUMMON HER HERE...
AND LIKE AS NOT SUPERMAN WAS DRAWN HERE WITH WONDER WOMAN.
THEY ARE WIDELY SEPARATED, MY LORD.
THEY MUST NOT HAVE ARRIVED AT THE SAME POINT.
PERHAPS NOT. SUCH TERMS HAVE LITTLE MEANING IN THIS PLACE.
BUT THEIR SEPARATION OFFERS MUCH IN THE WAY OF OPPORTUNITY.
OPPORTUNITY TO BE EXPLOITED!
LET US BEGIN WITH THE MOST SIMPLE AND OBVIOUS OF DECEPTIONS...
WONDER WOMAN?
SUPERMAN...
WONDER WOMAN...
SUPERMAN?
12

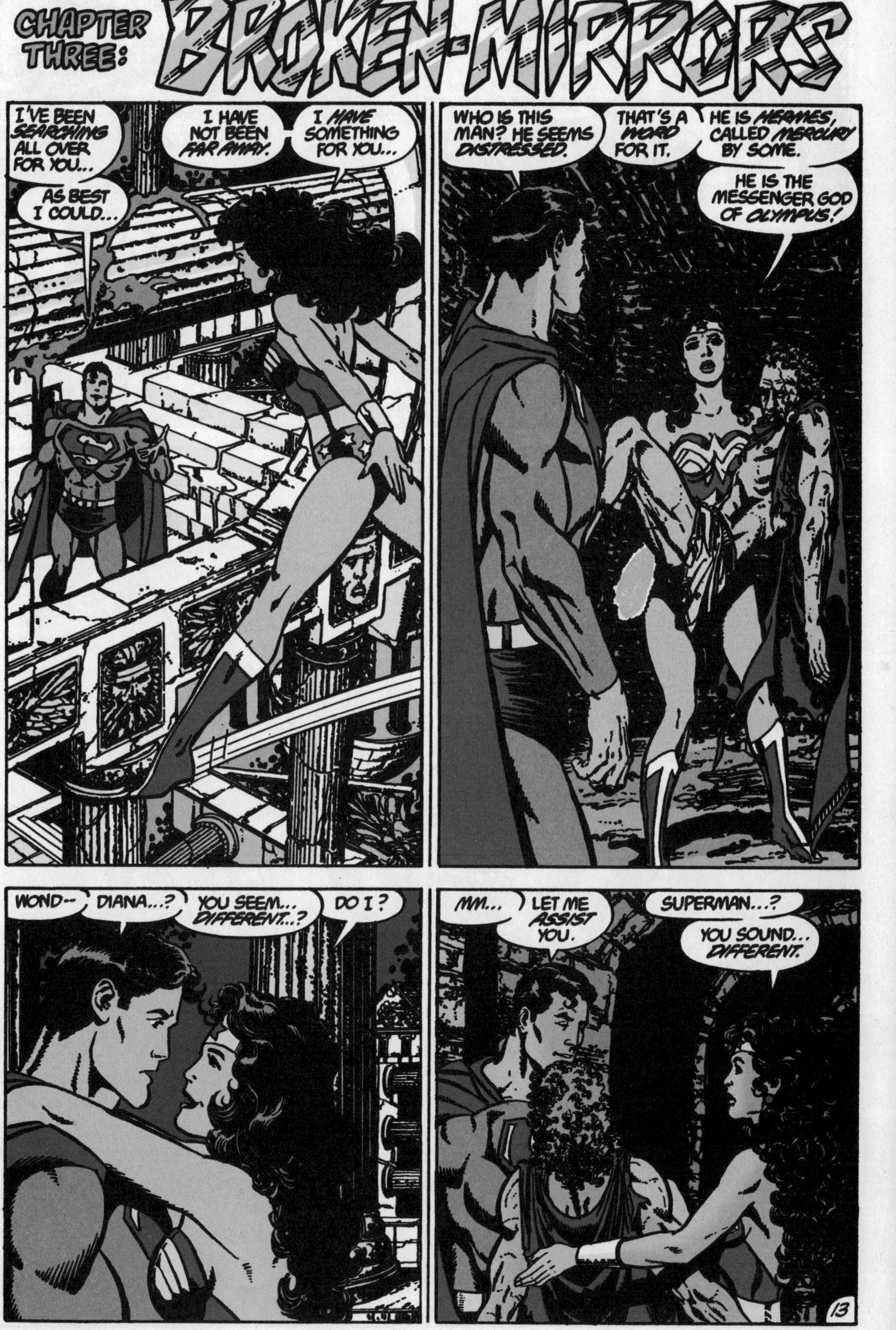
CHAPTER THREE: BROKEN-MIRRORS
I'VE BEEN SEARCHING ALL OVER FOR YOU...
AS BEST I COULD...
I HAVE NOT BEEN FAR AWAY.
I HAVE SOMETHING FOR YOU...
WHO IS THIS MAN? HE SEEMS DISTRESSED.
THAT'S A WORD FOR IT.
HE IS HERMES, CALLED MERCURY BY SOME.
HE IS THE MESSENGER GOD OF OLYMPUS!
WOND-- DIANA...?
YOU SEEM... DIFFERENT...?
DO I?
MM...
LET ME ASSIST YOU.
SUPERMAN...?
YOU SOUND... DIFFERENT.
13

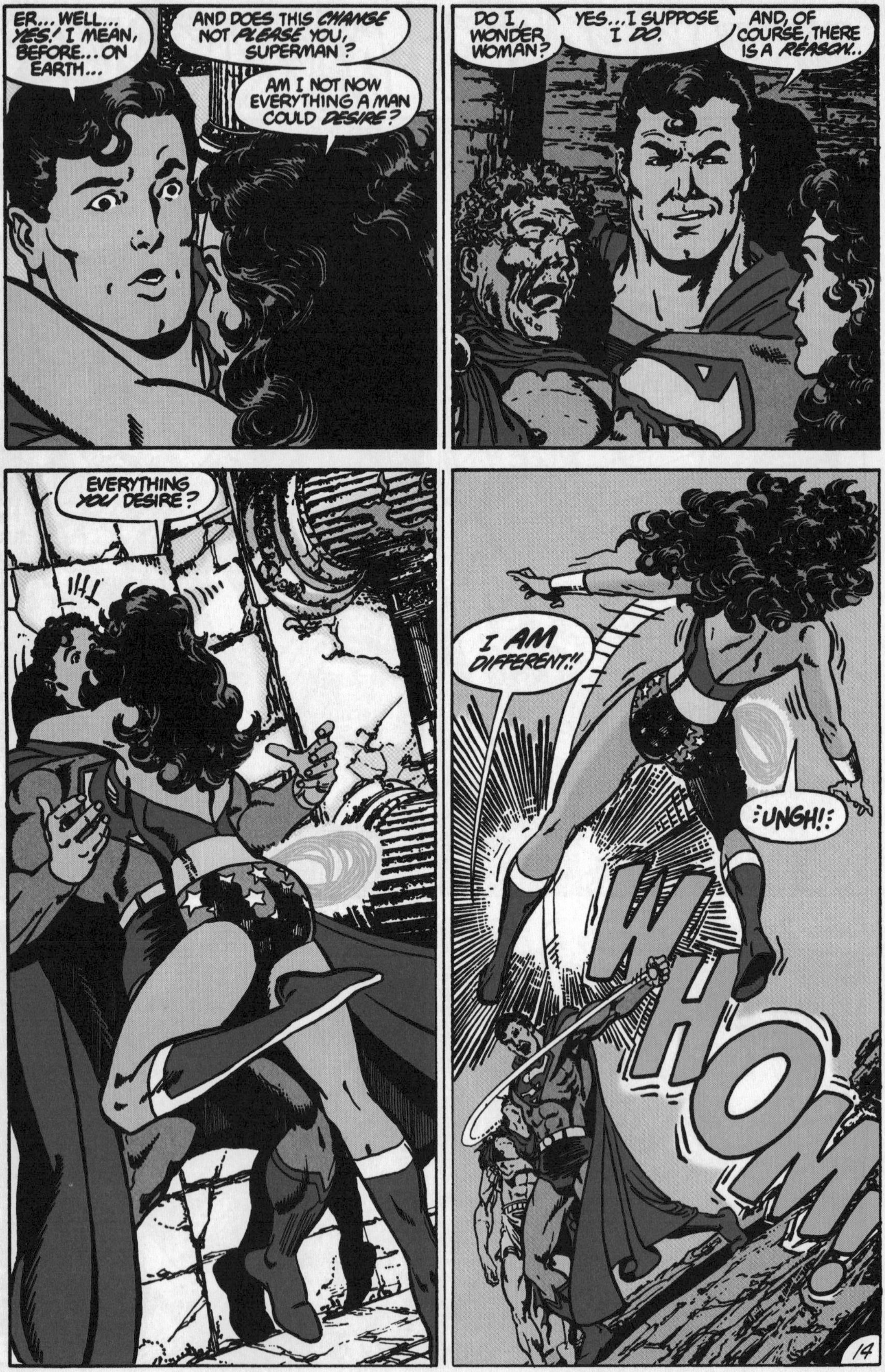

ER... WELL... YES! I MEAN, BEFORE... ON EARTH...
AND DOES THIS CHANGE NOT PLEASE YOU, SUPERMAN?
AM I NOT NOW EVERYTHING A MAN COULD DESIRE?
DO I, WONDER WOMAN?
YES... I SUPPOSE I DO.
AND, OF COURSE, THERE IS A REASON..
EVERYTHING YOU DESIRE?
THT!
I AM DIFFERENT!!
UNGH!!
WHOM!
14

HA HAHA HA HAH HA HAH HA HAHAH HAHA HA HAHA HA HA HA HA HA HA HA

DO YOU *APPRECIATE* THE DELICIOUS *IRONY* OF THE SITUATION, DESAAD?

DO YOU SEE HOW MY *CONSTRUCTS* PLAY OFF THE INNER *WEAKNESSES* OF EACH OF OUR UN-SUSPECTING *GUESTS*?

YES, GREAT DARKSEID...

BUT... IS THIS NOT *DANGEROUS*, MY LORD?

THUS FAR OUR... *YOUR* CONQUEST OF OLYMPUS HAS BEEN *WITH-OUT FLAW!*

SHOULD THESE *INTRUDERS* NOT BE SUMMARILY *DESTROYED,* RATHER THAN *TOYED* WITH?

STRANGE SENTIMENTS, FROM *YOU,* DESAAD.

YOU, WHOSE WHOLE *EXISTENCE* IS DEDICATED TO *CRUELTY* AND *SUFFERING.*

BUT *FRET NOT,* DESAAD. I HAVE WAITED *TOO LONG* TO LET THIS SMALL *DIVERSION* DISRUPT MY *MASTER PLAN.*

WAITED ALL THESE *CENTURIES* SINCE FIRST I LEARNED THE *TRUTH* ABOUT OLYMPUS.

"REMEMBER, DESAAD?

"REMEMBER THE GREAT *LEGENDS* OF HOW THE WORLD OF THE FIRST GODS, THE *OLD GODS,* DIED?

"SPLIT ASUNDER BY THE FURY OF THEIR FINAL *RAGNAROK...*

15

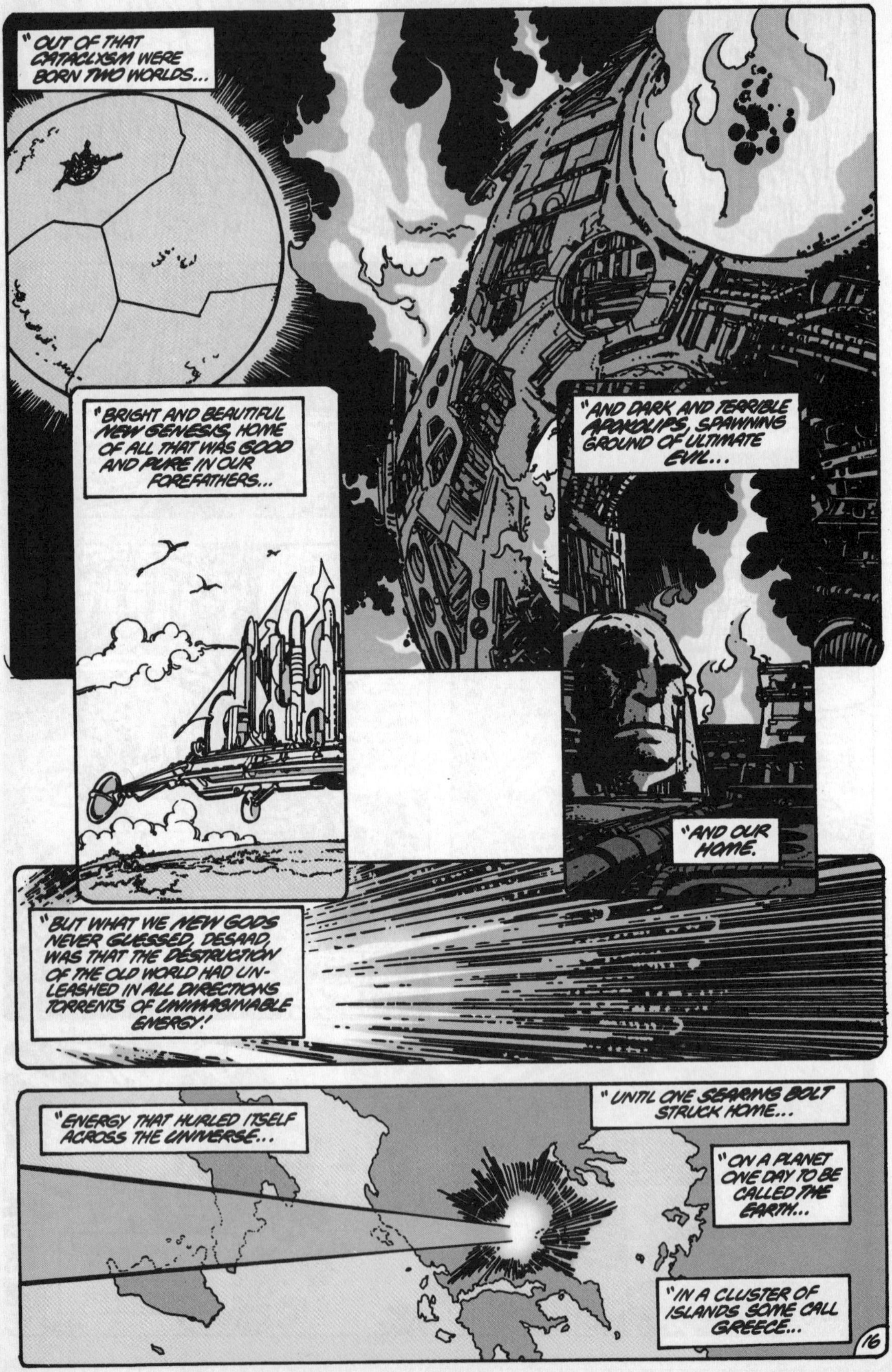
"OUT OF THAT CATACLYSM WERE BORN TWO WORLDS...
"BRIGHT AND BEAUTIFUL NEW GENESIS, HOME OF ALL THAT WAS GOOD AND PURE IN OUR FOREFATHERS...
"AND DARK AND TERRIBLE APOKOLIPS, SPAWNING GROUND OF ULTIMATE EVIL...
"AND OUR HOME.
"BUT WHAT WE NEW GODS NEVER GUESSED, DESAAD, WAS THAT THE DESTRUCTION OF THE OLD WORLD HAD UN-LEASHED IN ALL DIRECTIONS TORRENTS OF UNIMAGINABLE ENERGY!
"ENERGY THAT HURLED ITSELF ACROSS THE UNIVERSE...
"UNTIL ONE SEARING BOLT STRUCK HOME...
"ON A PLANET ONE DAY TO BE CALLED THE EARTH...
"IN A CLUSTER OF ISLANDS SOME CALL GREECE...
16

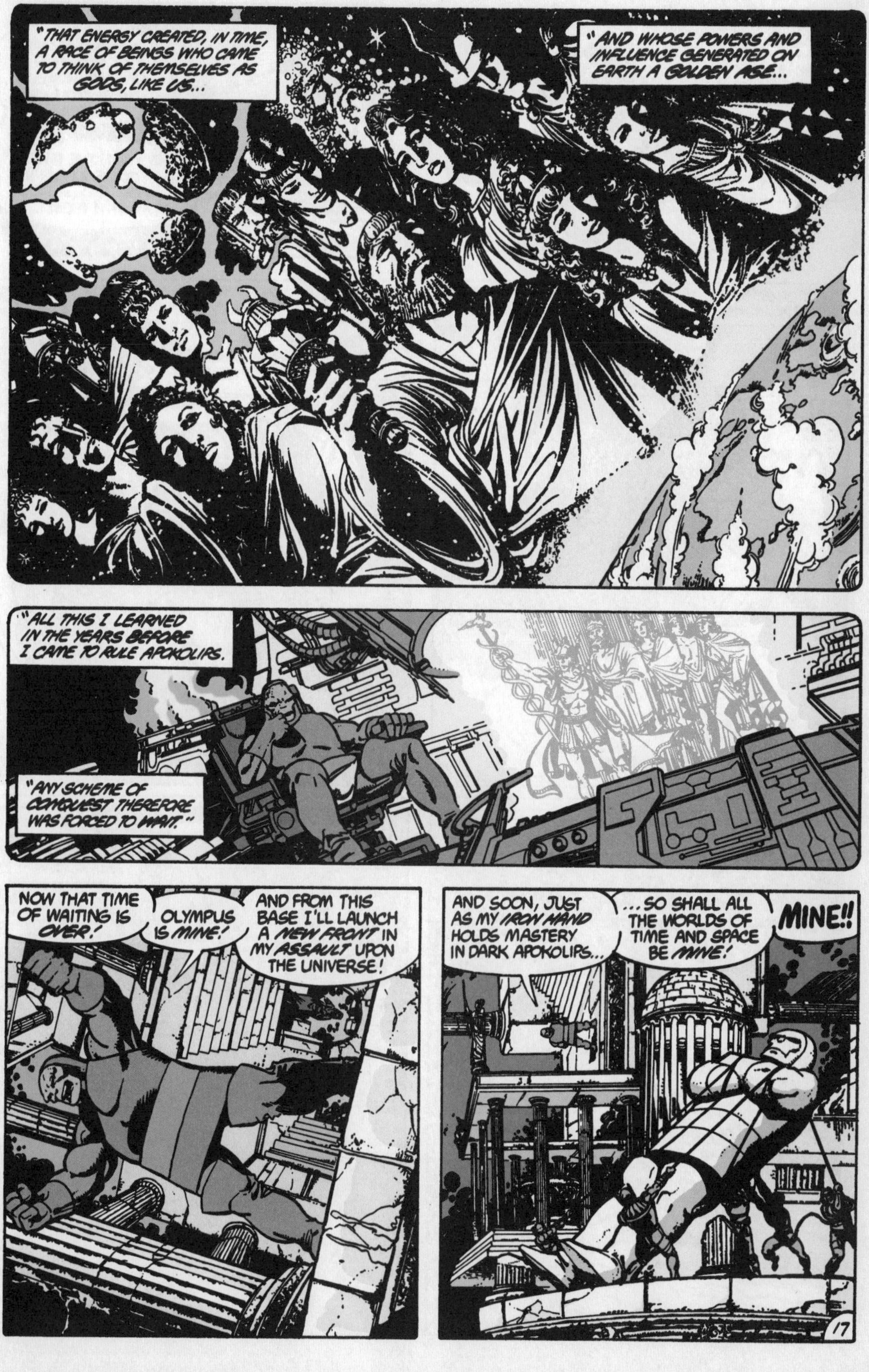
"THAT ENERGY CREATED, IN TIME, A RACE OF BEINGS WHO CAME TO THINK OF THEMSELVES AS GODS, LIKE US...
"AND WHOSE POWERS AND INFLUENCE GENERATED ON EARTH A GOLDEN AGE...
"ALL THIS I LEARNED IN THE YEARS BEFORE I CAME TO RULE APOKOLIPS.
"ANY SCHEME OF CONQUEST THEREFORE WAS FORCED TO WAIT."
NOW THAT TIME OF WAITING IS OVER!
OLYMPUS IS MINE!
AND FROM THIS BASE I'LL LAUNCH A NEW FRONT IN MY ASSAULT UPON THE UNIVERSE!
AND SOON, JUST AS MY IRON HAND HOLDS MASTERY IN DARK APOKOLIPS...
...SO SHALL ALL THE WORLDS OF TIME AND SPACE BE MINE!
MINE!!
17

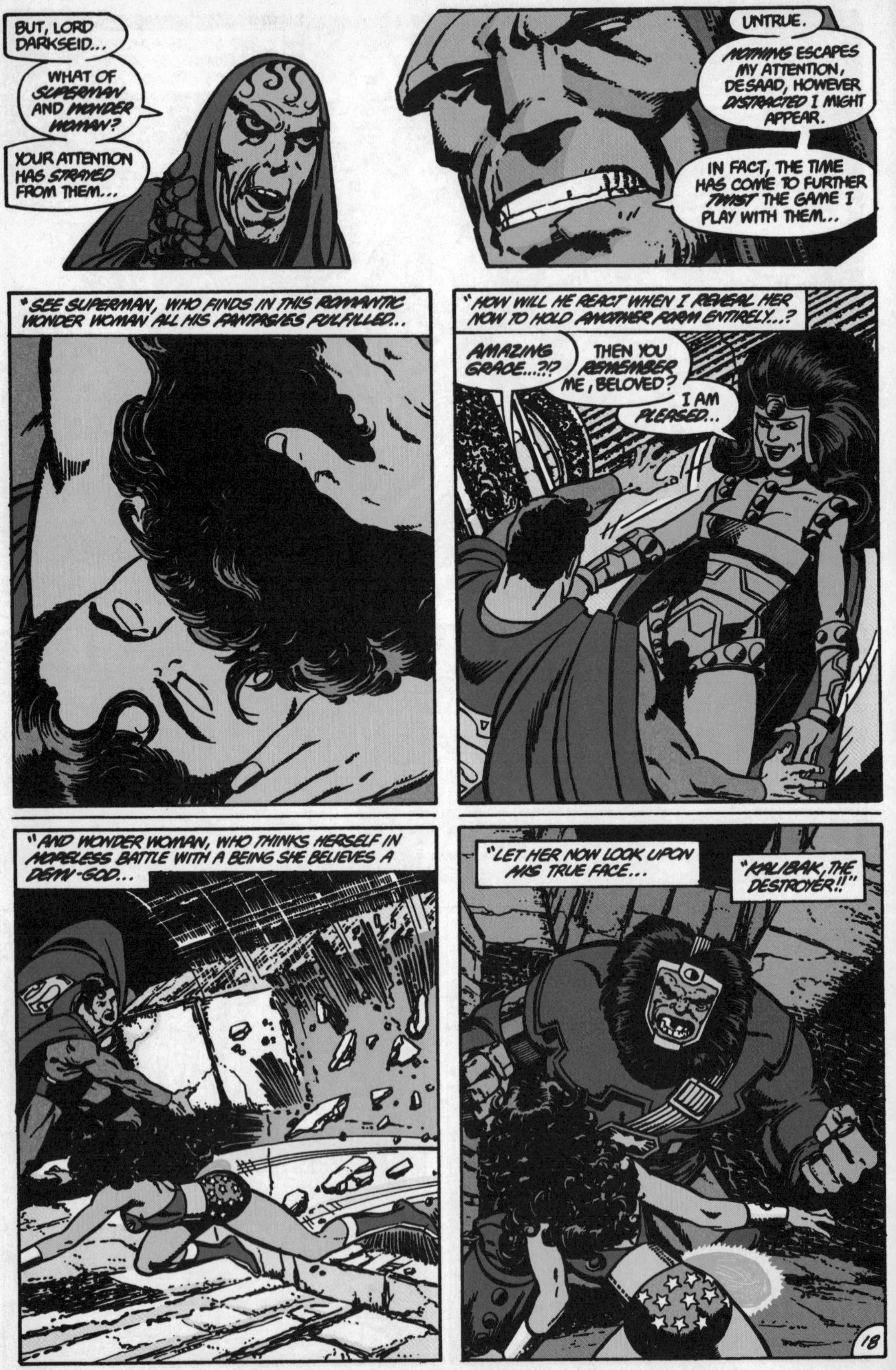
BUT, LORD DARKSEID...
WHAT OF SUPERMAN AND WONDER WOMAN?
YOUR ATTENTION HAS STRAYED FROM THEM...
UNTRUE.
NOTHING ESCAPES MY ATTENTION, DESAAD, HOWEVER DISTRACTED I MIGHT APPEAR.
IN FACT, THE TIME HAS COME TO FURTHER TWIST THE GAME I PLAY WITH THEM...
"SEE SUPERMAN, WHO FINDS IN THIS ROMANTIC WONDER WOMAN ALL HIS FANTASIES FULFILLED...
"HOW WILL HE REACT WHEN I REVEAL HER NOW TO HOLD ANOTHER FORM ENTIRELY...?
AMAZING GRACE...?!?
THEN YOU REMEMBER ME, BELOVED?
I AM PLEASED...
"AND WONDER WOMAN, WHO THINKS HERSELF IN HOPELESS BATTLE WITH A BEING SHE BELIEVES A DEMI-GOD...
"LET HER NOW LOOK UPON HIS TRUE FACE...
"KALIBAK, THE DESTROYER!!"
18

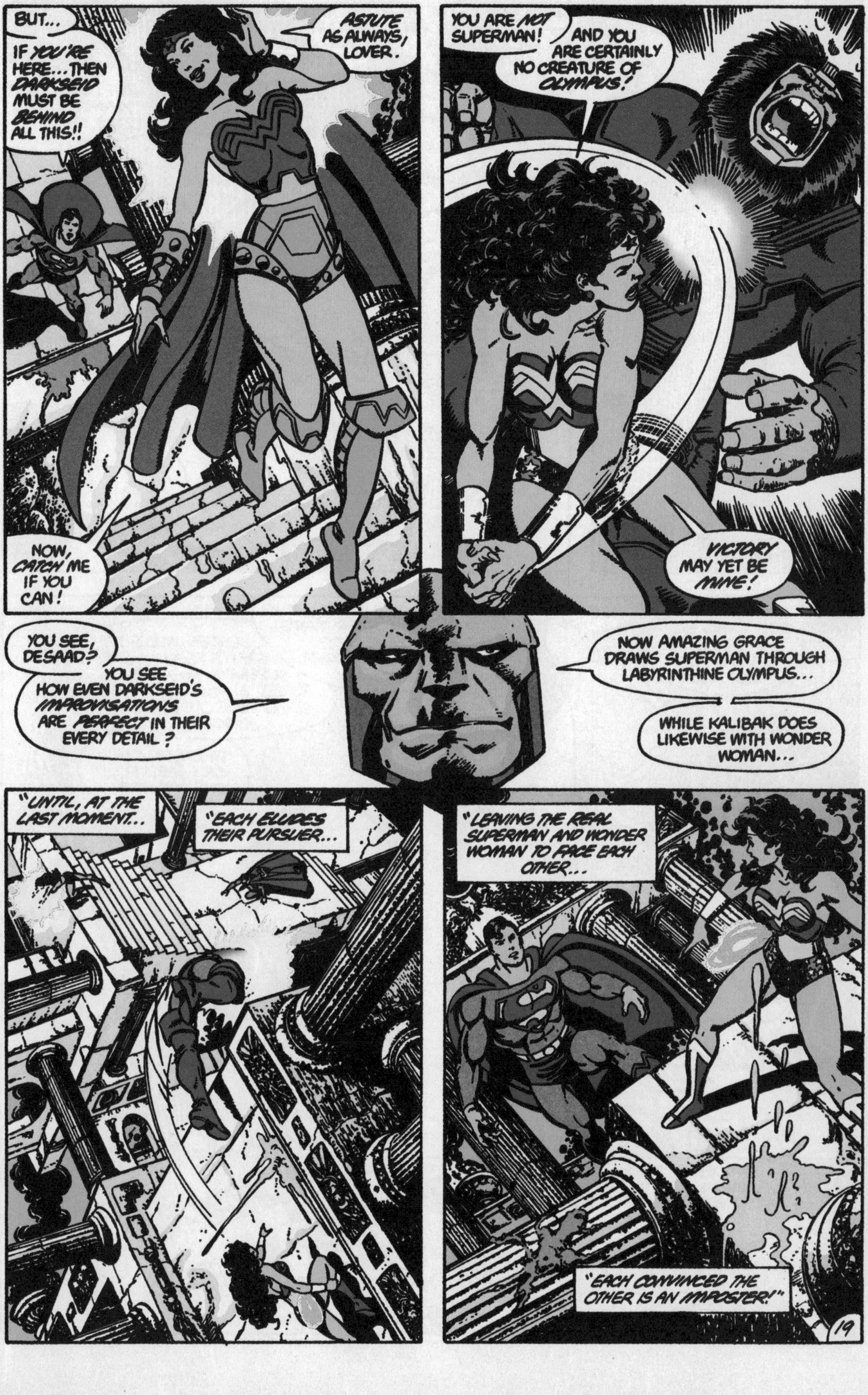
BUT...
IF YOU'RE HERE... THEN DARKSEID MUST BE BEHIND ALL THIS!!
ASTUTE AS ALWAYS, LOVER.
NOW, CATCH ME IF YOU CAN!
YOU ARE NOT SUPERMAN!
AND YOU ARE CERTAINLY NO CREATURE OF OLYMPUS!
VICTORY MAY YET BE MINE!
YOU SEE, DESAAD?
YOU SEE HOW EVEN DARKSEID'S IMPROVISATIONS ARE PERFECT IN THEIR EVERY DETAIL?
NOW AMAZING GRACE DRAWS SUPERMAN THROUGH LABYRINTHINE OLYMPUS...
WHILE KALIBAK DOES LIKEWISE WITH WONDER WOMAN...
"UNTIL, AT THE LAST MOMENT...
"EACH ELUDES THEIR PURSUER...
"LEAVING THE REAL SUPERMAN AND WONDER WOMAN TO FACE EACH OTHER...
"EACH CONVINCED THE OTHER IS AN IMPOSTER!"
19

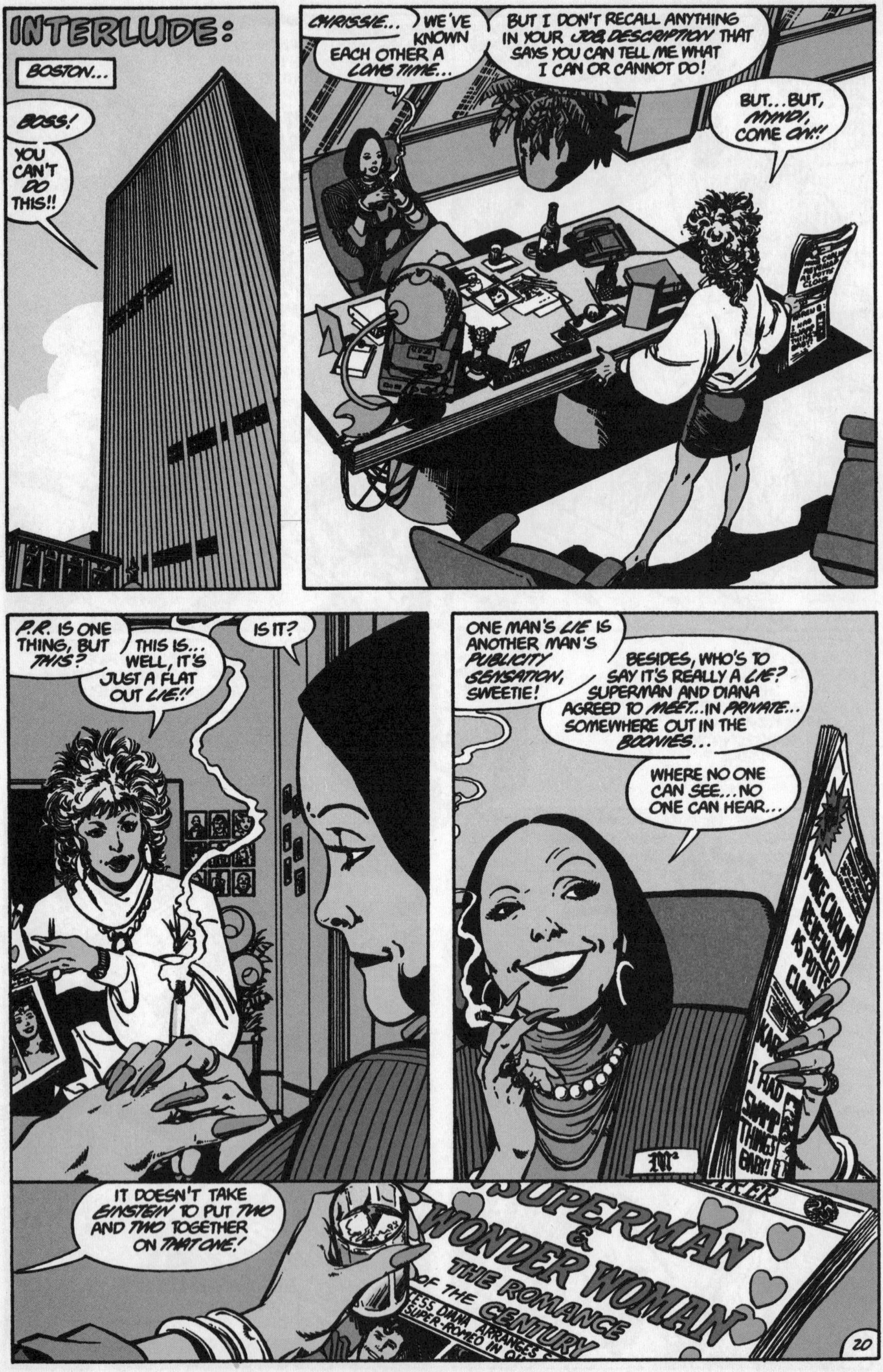
INTERLUDE:
BOSTON...
BOSS! YOU CAN'T DO THIS!!
CHRISSIE... WE'VE KNOWN EACH OTHER A LONG TIME...
BUT I DON'T RECALL ANYTHING IN YOUR JOB DESCRIPTION THAT SAYS YOU CAN TELL ME WHAT I CAN OR CANNOT DO!
BUT...BUT, MYNDI, COME ON!!
P.R. IS ONE THING, BUT THIS?
THIS IS... WELL, IT'S JUST A FLAT OUT LIE!!
IS IT?
ONE MAN'S LIE IS ANOTHER MAN'S PUBLICITY SENSATION, SWEETIE!
BESIDES, WHO'S TO SAY IT'S REALLY A LIE? SUPERMAN AND DIANA AGREED TO MEET...IN PRIVATE... SOMEWHERE OUT IN THE BOONIES...
WHERE NO ONE CAN SEE...NO ONE CAN HEAR...
IT DOESN'T TAKE EINSTEIN TO PUT TWO AND TWO TOGETHER ON THAT ONE!
SUPERMAN & WONDER WOMAN
THE ROMANCE OF THE CENTURY
20

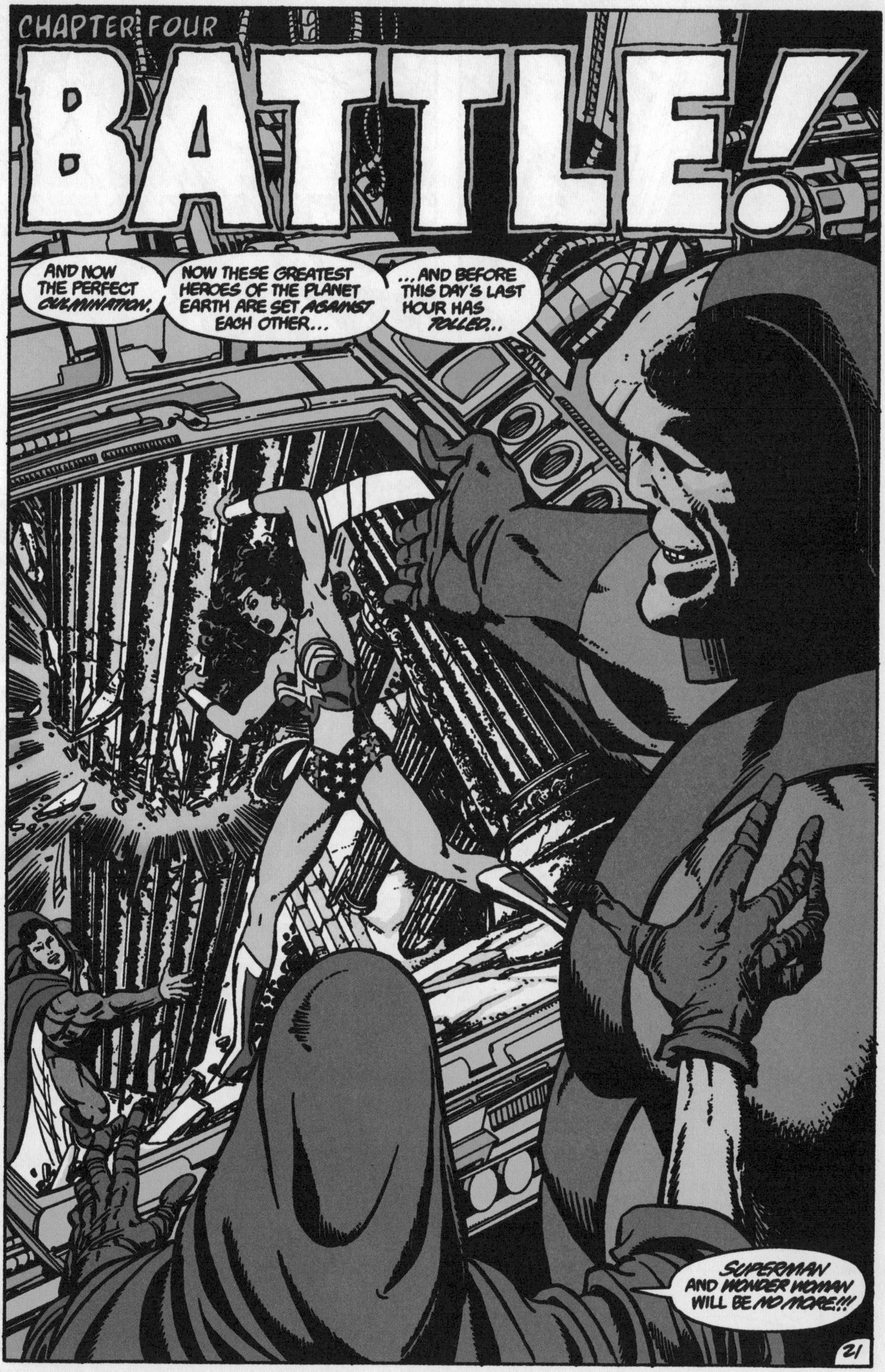
CHAPTER FOUR
BATTLE!
AND NOW THE PERFECT CULMINATION,
NOW THESE GREATEST HEROES OF THE PLANET EARTH ARE SET AGAINST EACH OTHER...
...AND BEFORE THIS DAY'S LAST HOUR HAS TOLLED...
SUPERMAN AND WONDER WOMAN WILL BE NO MORE!!!
21

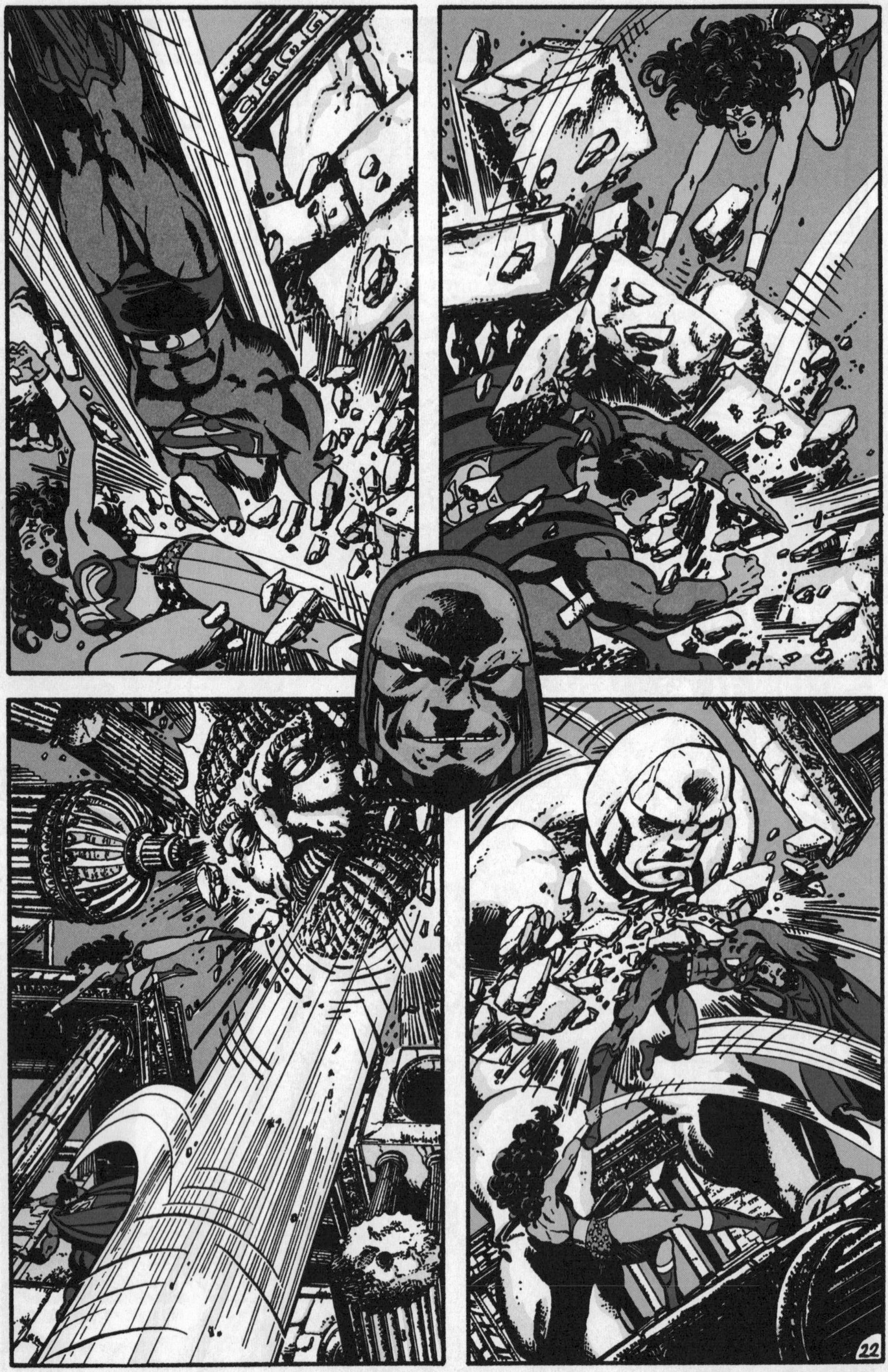
22

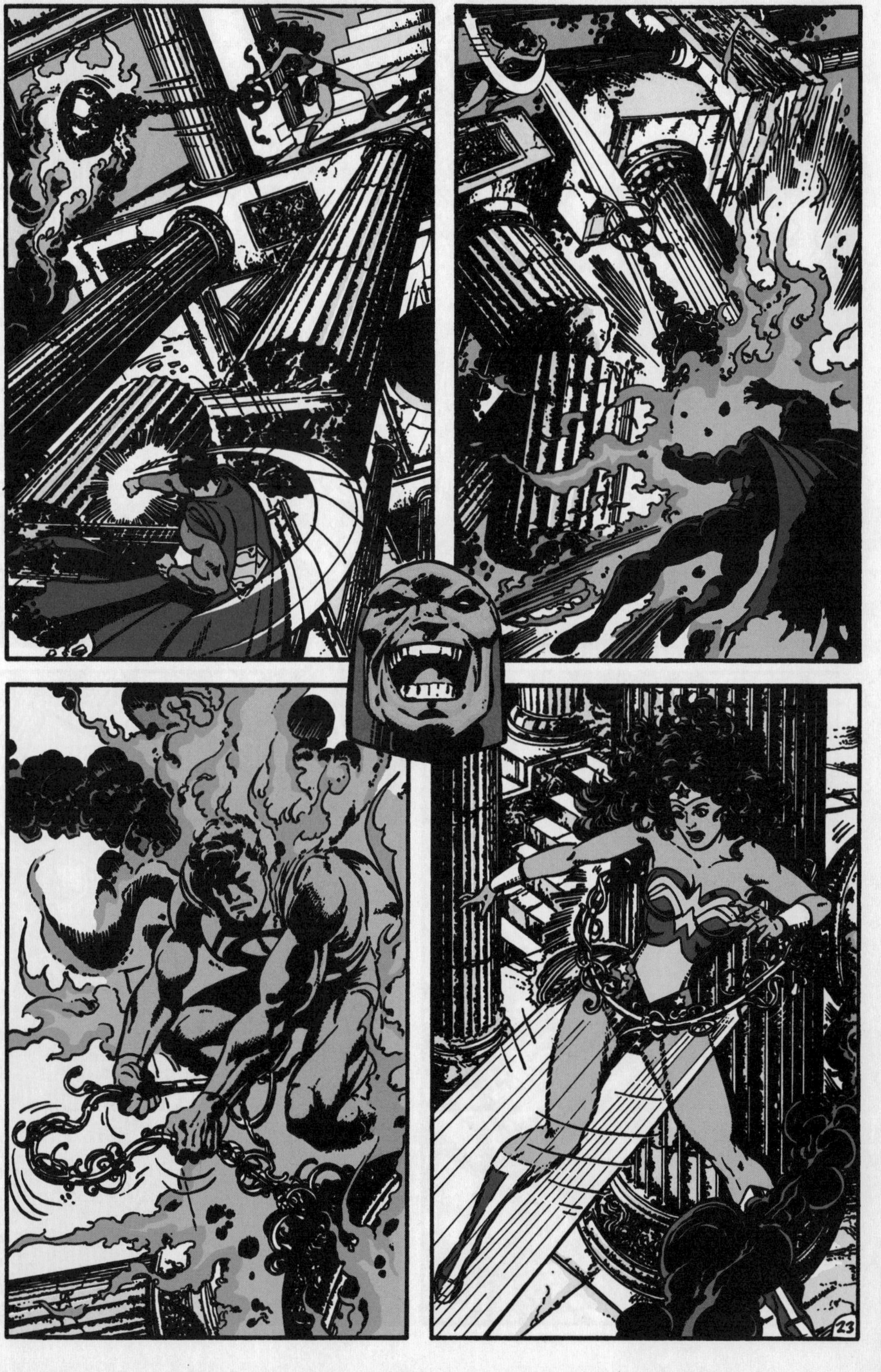
23

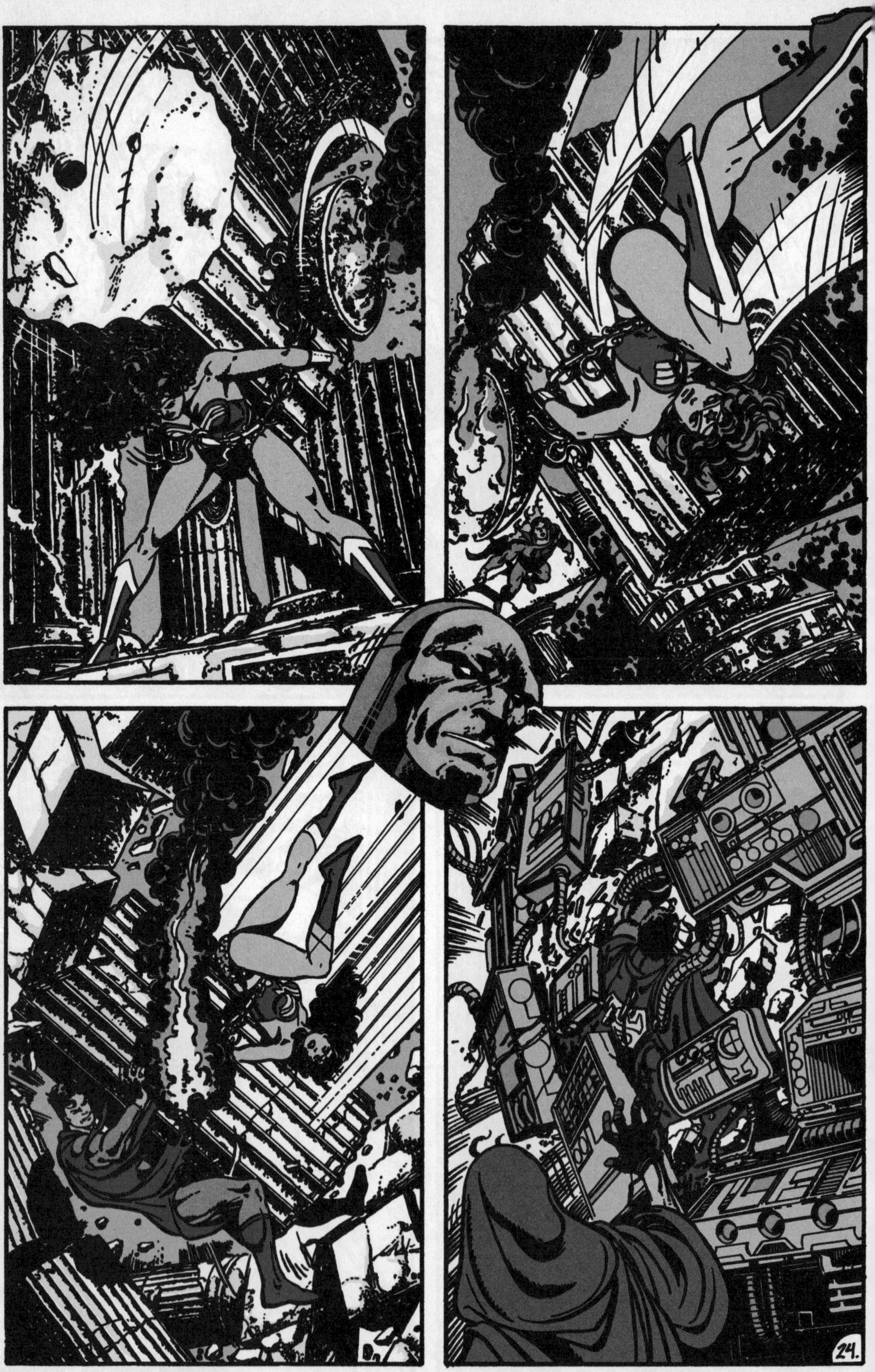
24.

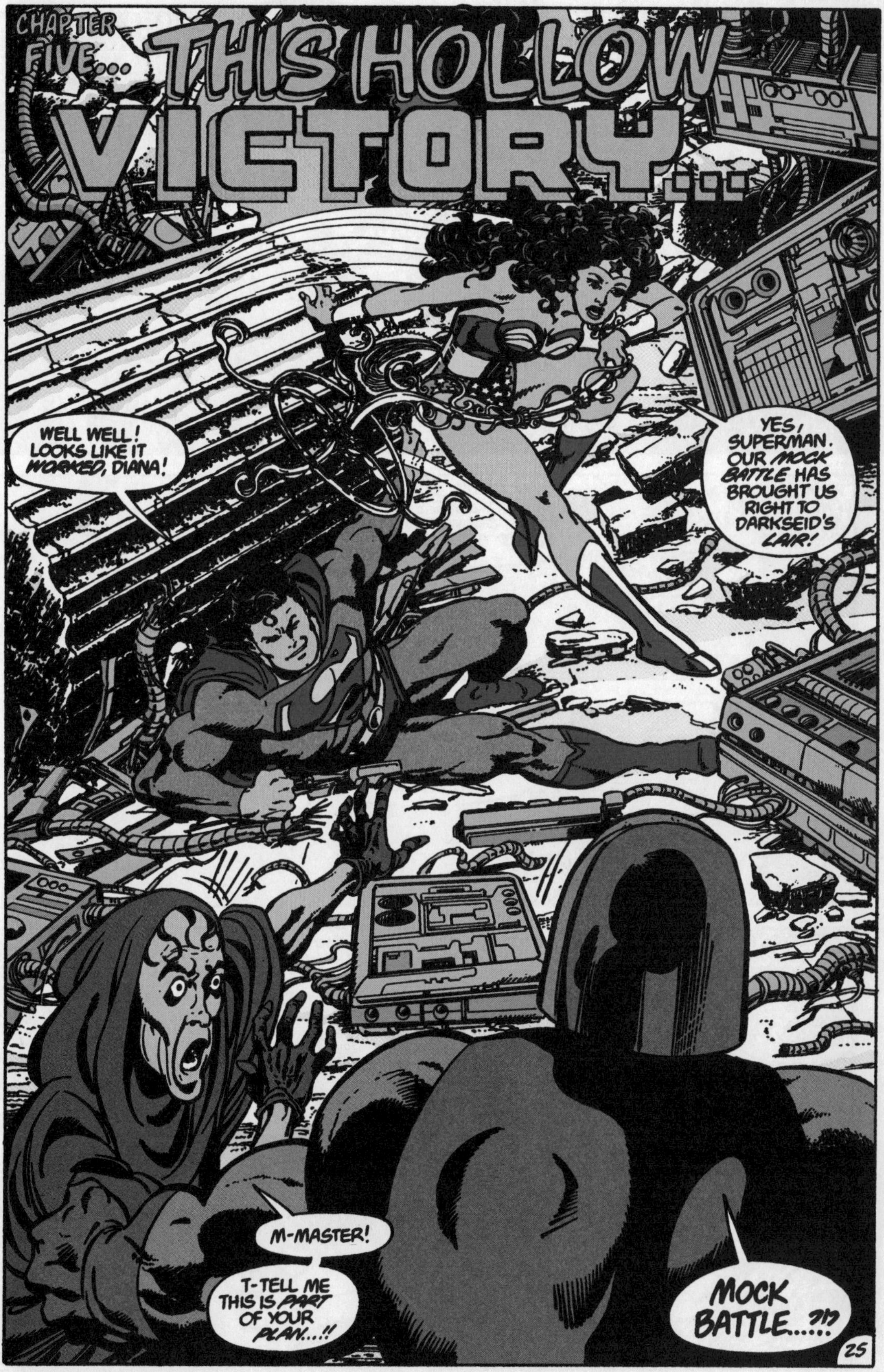
CHAPTER FIVE...
THIS HOLLOW VICTORY...
WELL WELL! LOOKS LIKE IT WORKED, DIANA!
YES, SUPERMAN. OUR MOCK BATTLE HAS BROUGHT US RIGHT TO DARKSEID'S LAIR!
M-MASTER!
T-TELL ME THIS IS PART OF YOUR PLAN...!!
MOCK BATTLE.....?!?
25

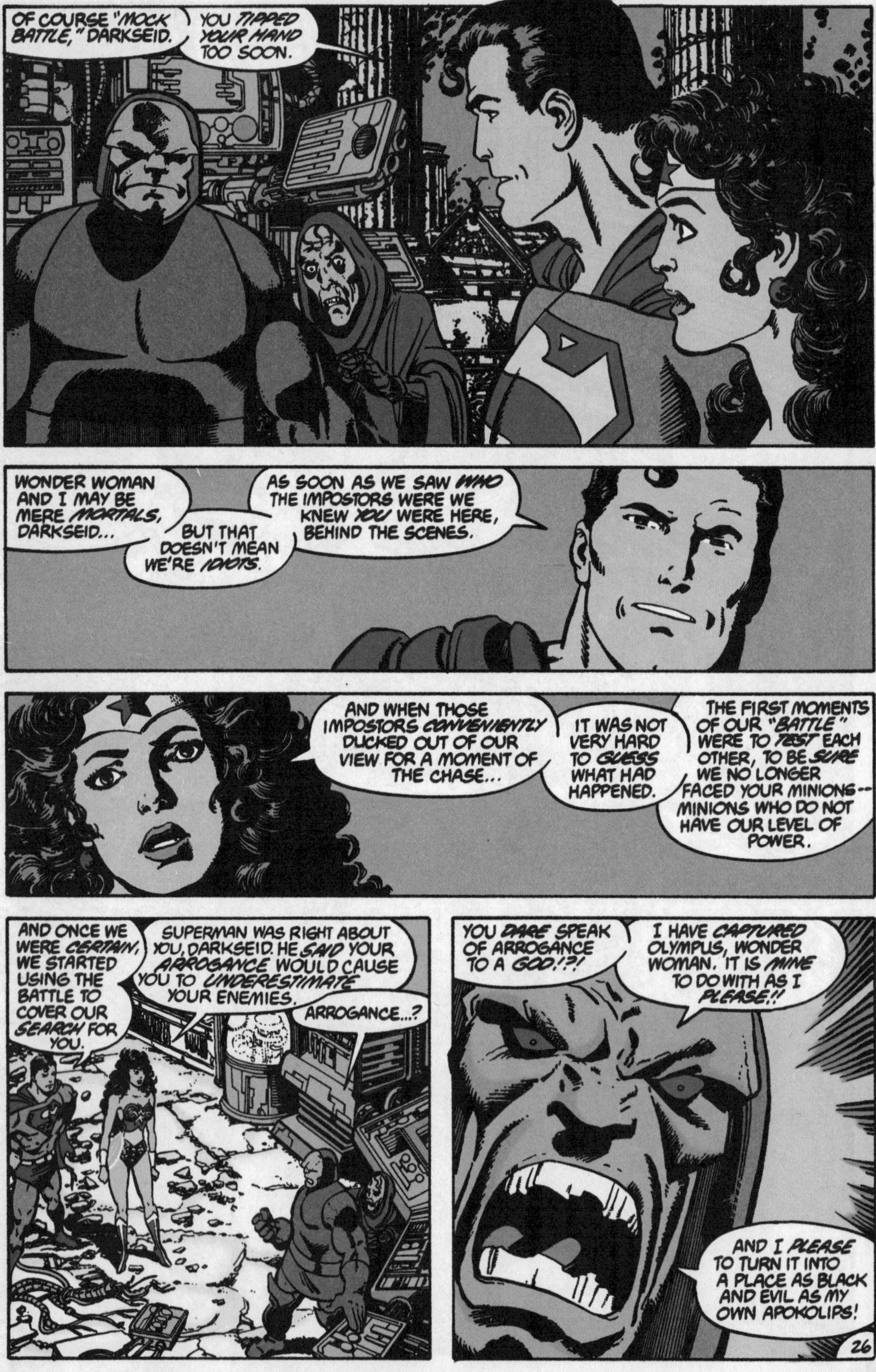
OF COURSE "MOCK BATTLE," DARKSEID.
YOU TIPPED YOUR HAND TOO SOON.
WONDER WOMAN AND I MAY BE MERE MORTALS, DARKSEID...
BUT THAT DOESN'T MEAN WE'RE IDIOTS.
AS SOON AS WE SAW WHO THE IMPOSTORS WERE WE KNEW YOU WERE HERE, BEHIND THE SCENES.
AND WHEN THOSE IMPOSTORS CONVENIENTLY DUCKED OUT OF OUR VIEW FOR A MOMENT OF THE CHASE...
IT WAS NOT VERY HARD TO GUESS WHAT HAD HAPPENED.
THE FIRST MOMENTS OF OUR "BATTLE" WERE TO TEST EACH OTHER, TO BE SURE WE NO LONGER FACED YOUR MINIONS-- MINIONS WHO DO NOT HAVE OUR LEVEL OF POWER.
AND ONCE WE WERE CERTAIN, WE STARTED USING THE BATTLE TO COVER OUR SEARCH FOR YOU.
SUPERMAN WAS RIGHT ABOUT YOU, DARKSEID. HE SAID YOUR ARROGANCE WOULD CAUSE YOU TO UNDERESTIMATE YOUR ENEMIES.
ARROGANCE...?
YOU DARE SPEAK OF ARROGANCE TO A GOD!?!
I HAVE CAPTURED OLYMPUS, WONDER WOMAN. IT IS MINE TO DO WITH AS I PLEASE!!
AND I PLEASE TO TURN IT INTO A PLACE AS BLACK AND EVIL AS MY OWN APOKOLIPS!
26

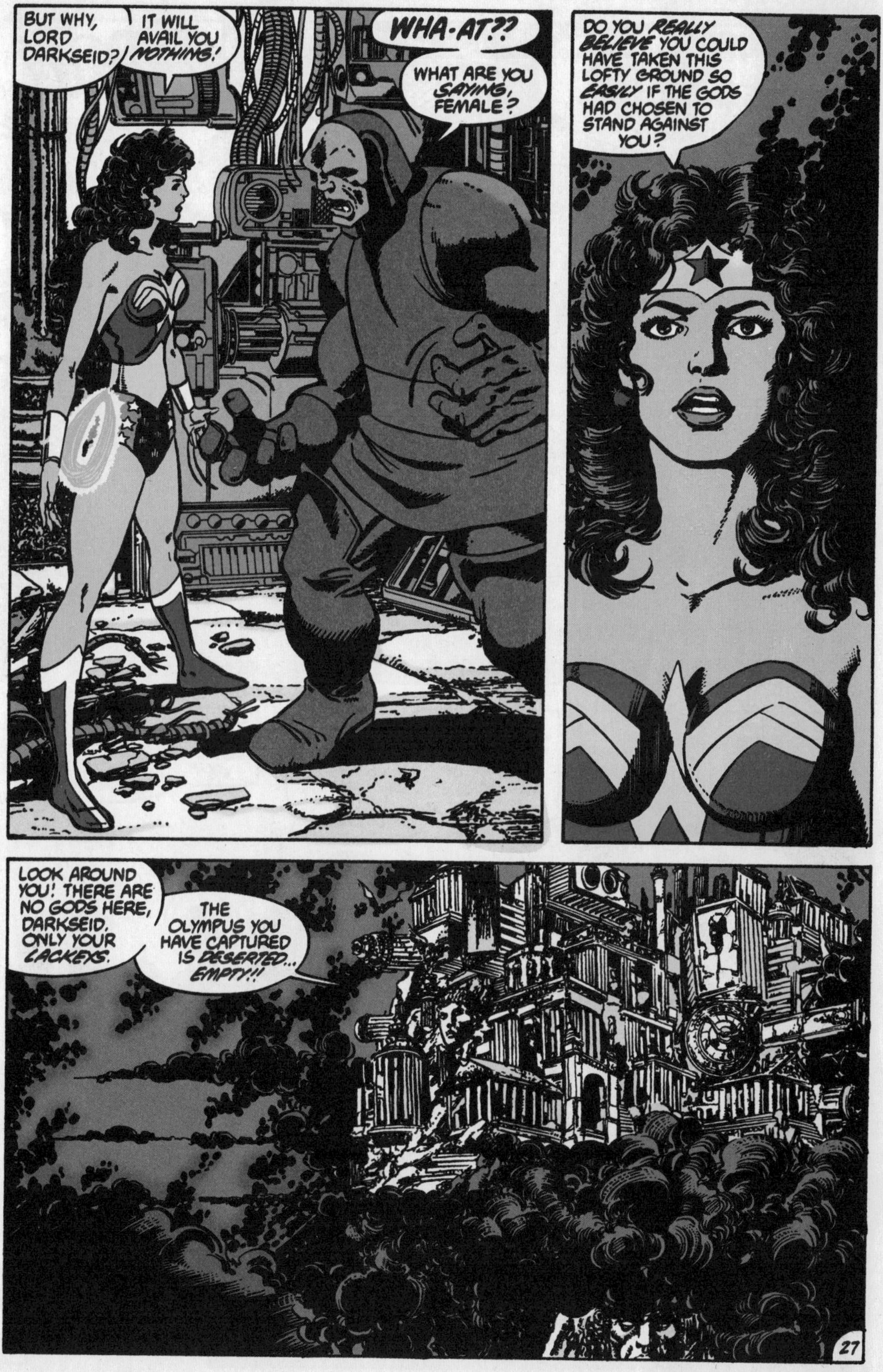

BUT WHY, LORD DARKSEID?
IT WILL AVAIL YOU NOTHING!
WHA-AT??
WHAT ARE YOU SAYING, FEMALE?
DO YOU REALLY BELIEVE YOU COULD HAVE TAKEN THIS LOFTY GROUND SO EASILY IF THE GODS HAD CHOSEN TO STAND AGAINST YOU?
LOOK AROUND YOU! THERE ARE NO GODS HERE, DARKSEID. ONLY YOUR LACKEYS.
THE OLYMPUS YOU HAVE CAPTURED IS DESERTED... EMPTY!!
27

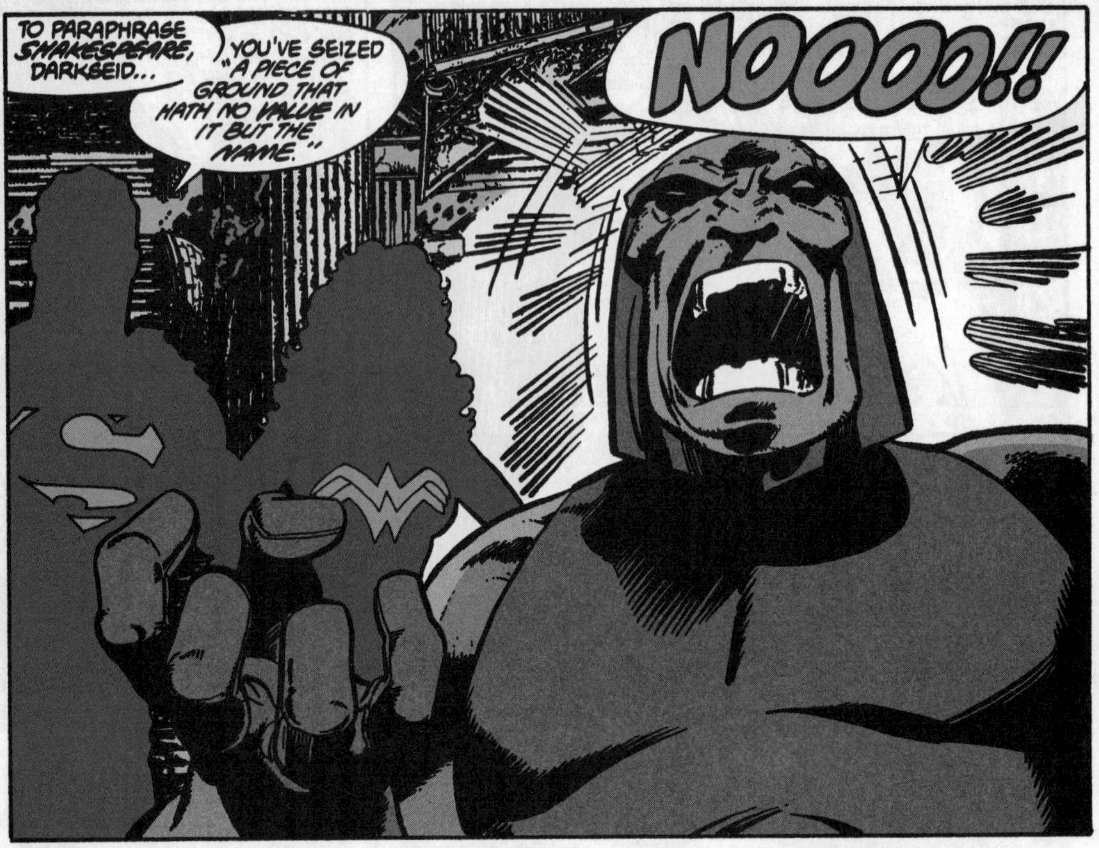
TO PARAPHRASE SHAKESPEARE, DARKSEID...
YOU'VE SEIZED "A PIECE OF GROUND THAT HATH NO VALUE IN IT BUT THE NAME."
NOOOO!!

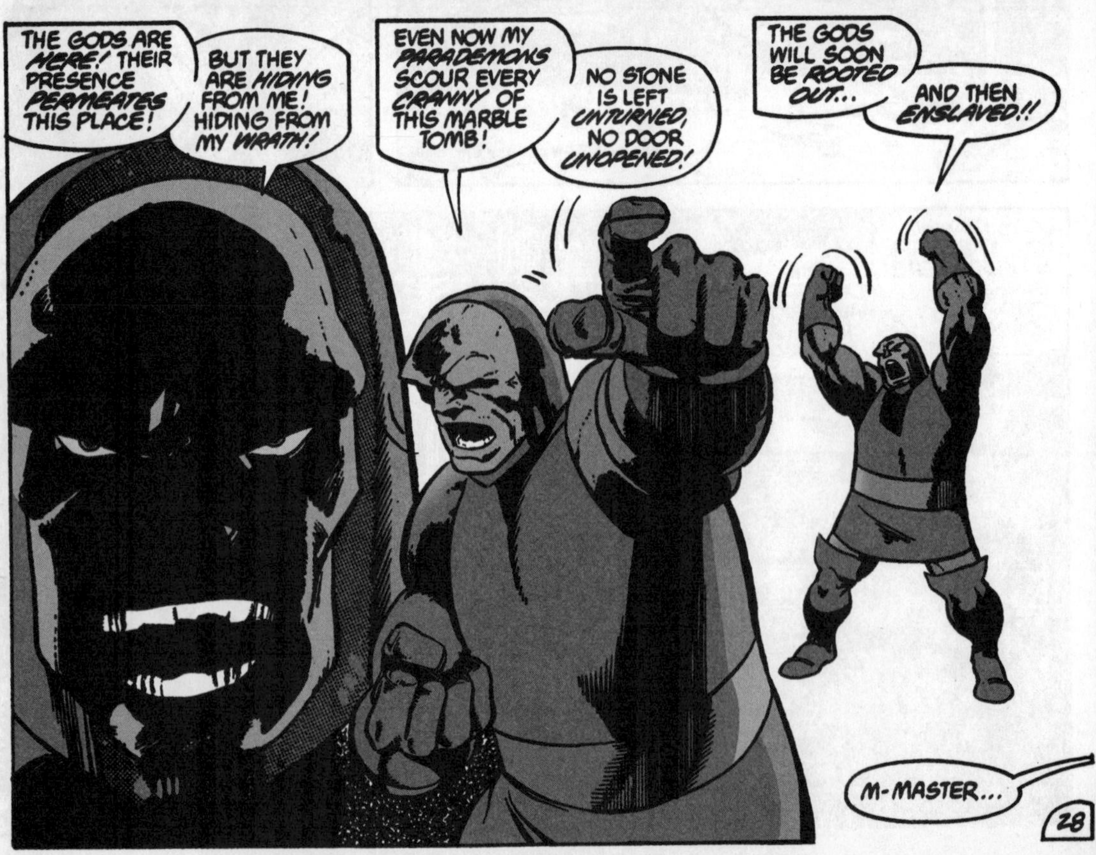
THE GODS ARE HERE! THEIR PRESENCE PERMEATES THIS PLACE!
BUT THEY ARE HIDING FROM ME! HIDING FROM MY WRATH!
EVEN NOW MY PARADEMONS SCOUR EVERY CRANNY OF THIS MARBLE TOMB!
NO STONE IS LEFT UNTURNED, NO DOOR UNOPENED!
THE GODS WILL SOON BE ROOTED OUT...
AND THEN ENSLAVED!!
M-MASTER...
28

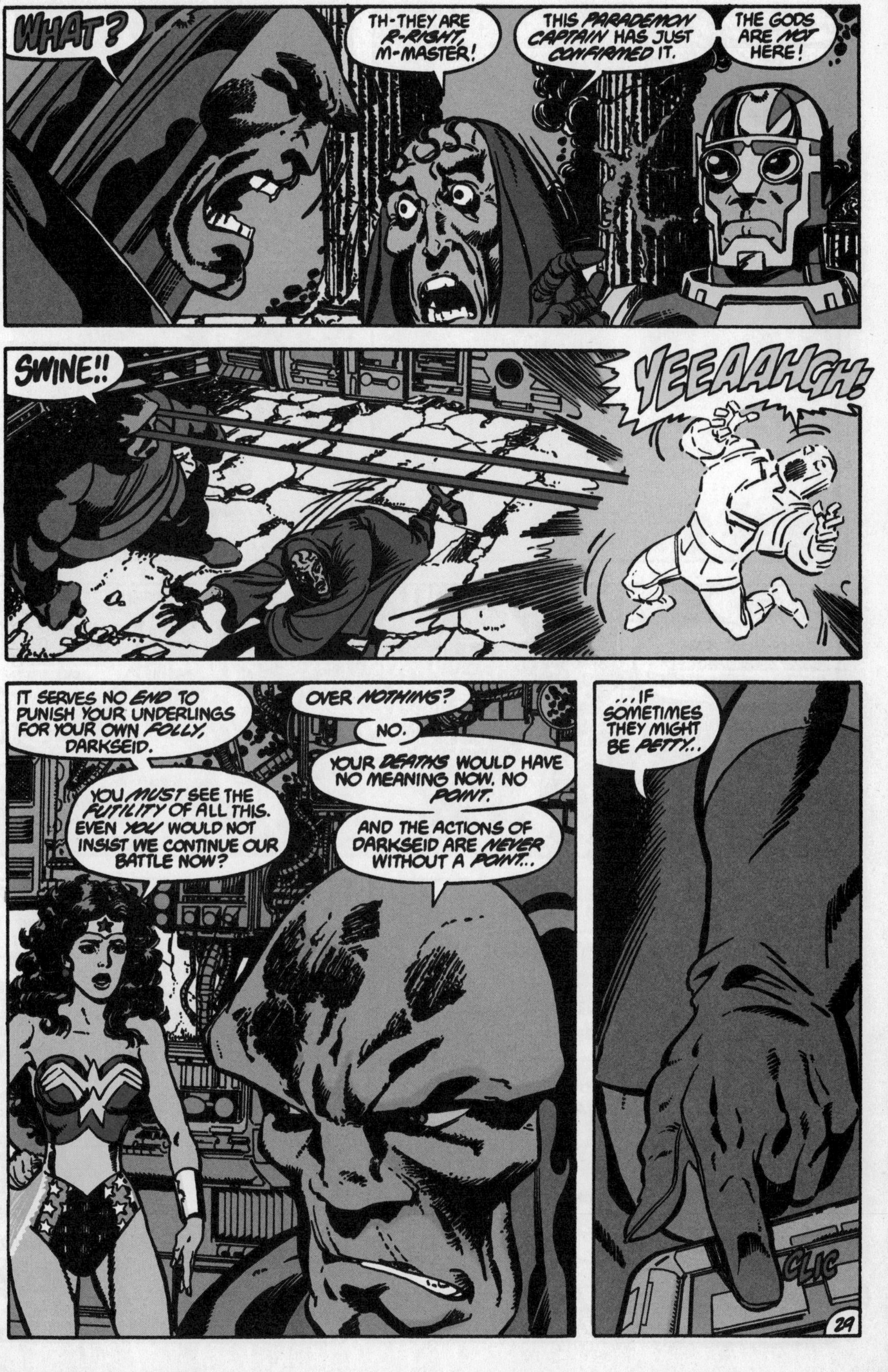
WHAT?
TH-THEY ARE R-RIGHT, M-MASTER!
THIS PARADEMON CAPTAIN HAS JUST CONFIRMED IT.
THE GODS ARE NOT HERE!
SWINE!!
YEEAAHGH!
IT SERVES NO END TO PUNISH YOUR UNDERLINGS FOR YOUR OWN FOLLY, DARKSEID.
YOU MUST SEE THE FUTILITY OF ALL THIS. EVEN YOU WOULD NOT INSIST WE CONTINUE OUR BATTLE NOW?
OVER NOTHING?
NO.
YOUR DEATHS WOULD HAVE NO MEANING NOW. NO POINT.
AND THE ACTIONS OF DARKSEID ARE NEVER WITHOUT A POINT...
...IF SOMETIMES THEY MIGHT BE PETTY...
CLIC
29

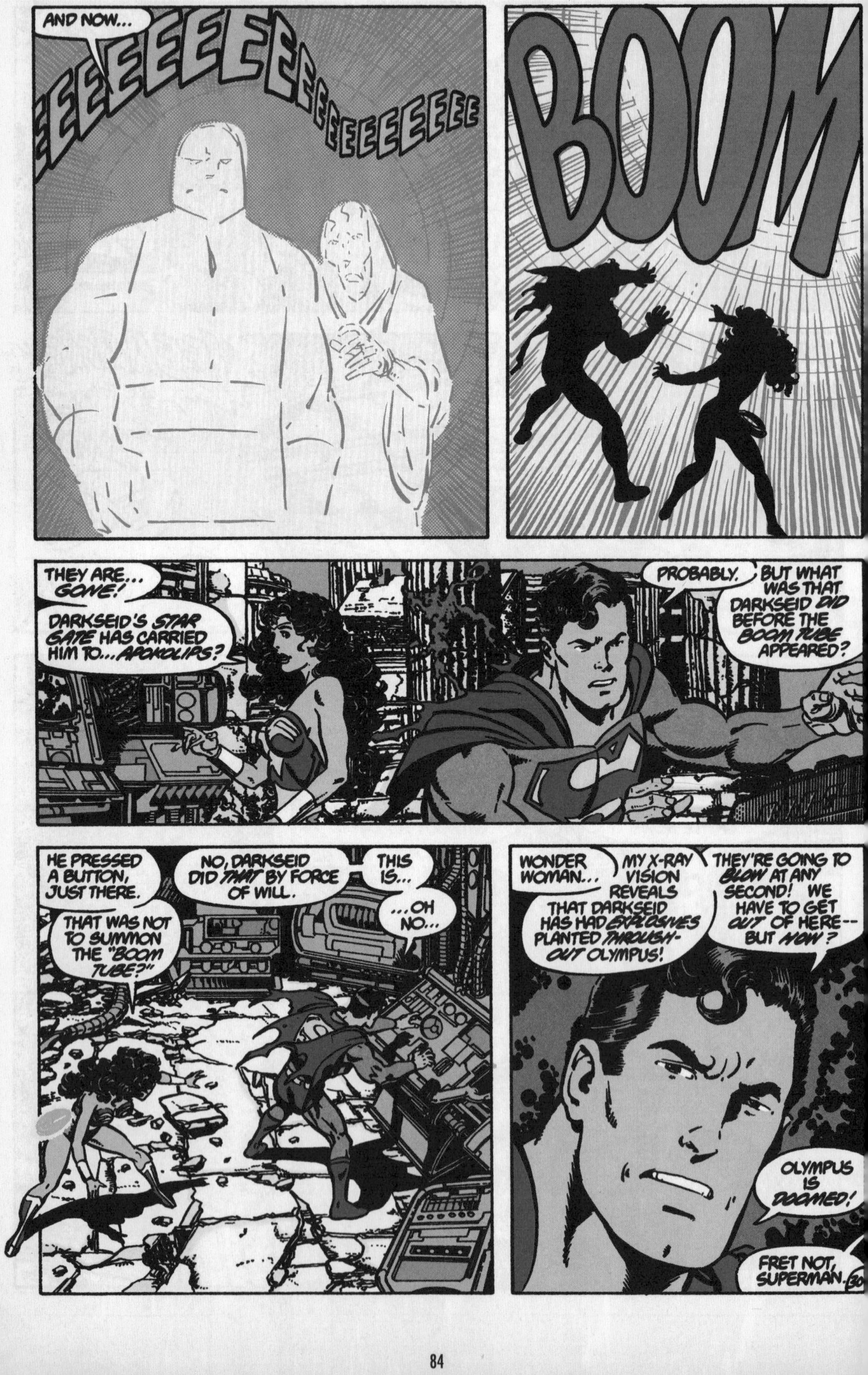

AND NOW...
EEEEEEEEEEEEEEEEEEEE
BOOM
THEY ARE... GONE!
DARKSEID'S STAR GATE HAS CARRIED HIM TO... APOKOLIPS?
PROBABLY.
BUT WHAT WAS THAT DARKSEID DID BEFORE THE BOOM TUBE APPEARED?
HE PRESSED A BUTTON, JUST THERE.
THAT WAS NOT TO SUMMON THE "BOOM TUBE?"
NO, DARKSEID DID THAT BY FORCE OF WILL.
THIS IS...
...OH NO...
WONDER WOMAN...
MY X-RAY VISION REVEALS THAT DARKSEID HAS HAD EXPLOSIVES PLANTED THROUGH-OUT OLYMPUS!
THEY'RE GOING TO BLOW AT ANY SECOND! WE HAVE TO GET OUT OF HERE-- BUT HOW?
OLYMPUS IS DOOMED!
FRET NOT, SUPERMAN.
30

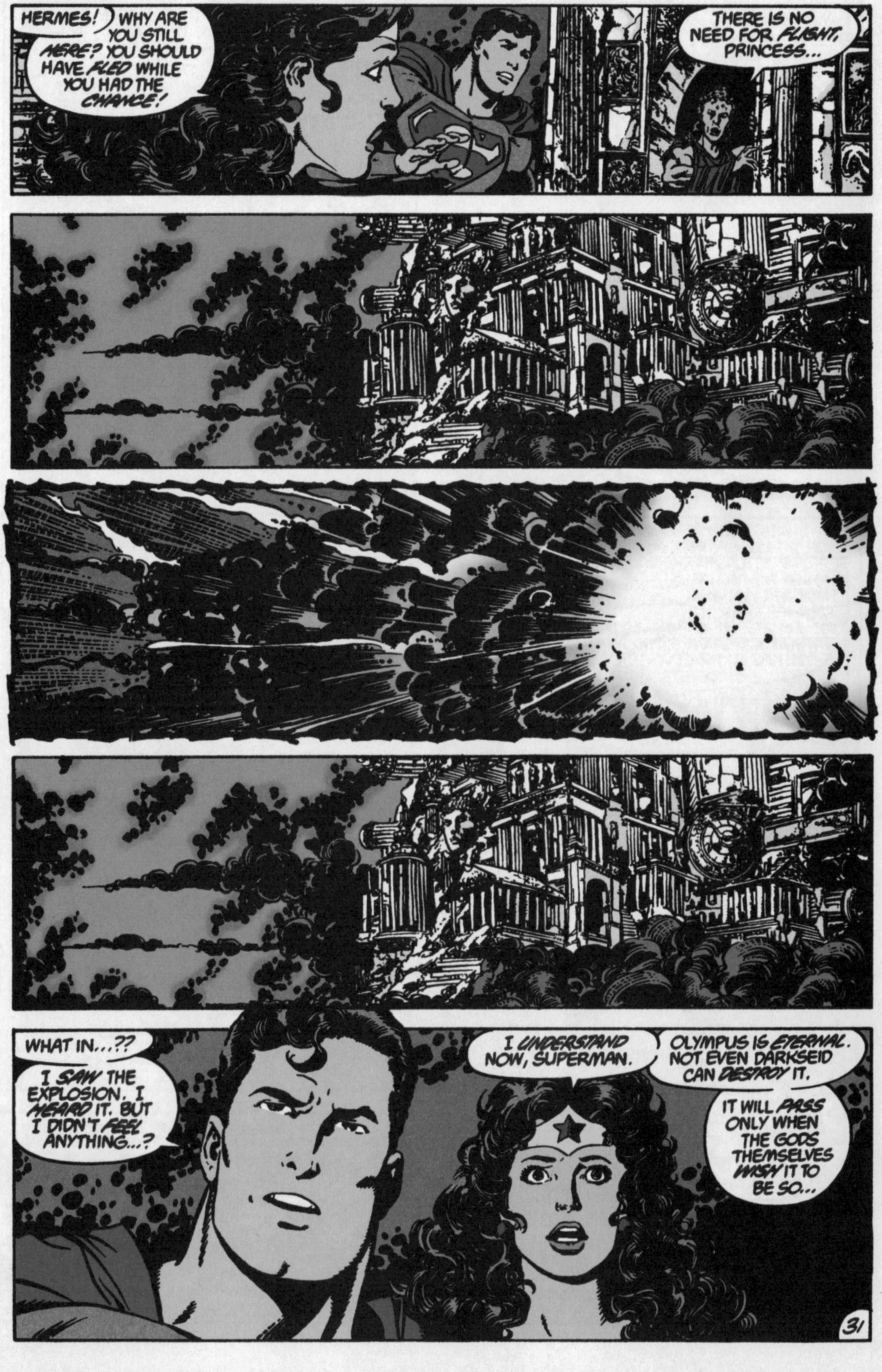
HERMES!
WHY ARE YOU STILL HERE? YOU SHOULD HAVE FLED WHILE YOU HAD THE CHANCE!
THERE IS NO NEED FOR FLIGHT, PRINCESS...
WHAT IN...??
I SAW THE EXPLOSION. I HEARD IT. BUT I DIDN'T FEEL ANYTHING...?
I UNDERSTAND NOW, SUPERMAN.
OLYMPUS IS ETERNAL. NOT EVEN DARKSEID CAN DESTROY IT.
IT WILL PASS ONLY WHEN THE GODS THEMSELVES WISH IT TO BE SO...
31

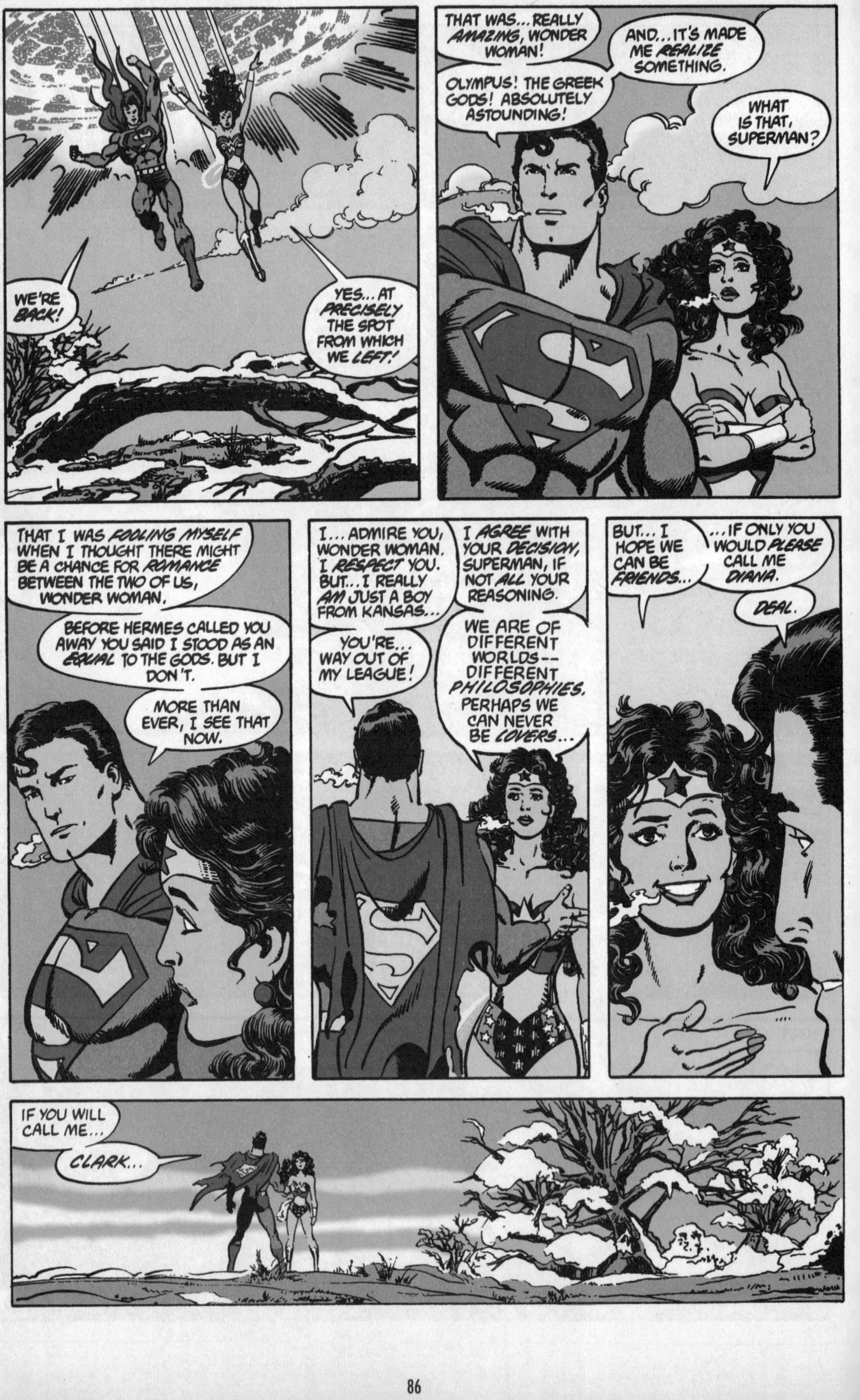
WE'RE BACK!
YES... AT PRECISELY THE SPOT FROM WHICH WE LEFT!
THAT WAS... REALLY AMAZING, WONDER WOMAN!
OLYMPUS! THE GREEK GODS! ABSOLUTELY ASTOUNDING!
AND... IT'S MADE ME REALIZE SOMETHING.
WHAT IS THAT, SUPERMAN?
THAT I WAS FOOLING MYSELF WHEN I THOUGHT THERE MIGHT BE A CHANCE FOR ROMANCE BETWEEN THE TWO OF US, WONDER WOMAN.
BEFORE HERMES CALLED YOU AWAY YOU SAID I STOOD AS AN EQUAL TO THE GODS. BUT I DON'T.
MORE THAN EVER, I SEE THAT NOW.
I... ADMIRE YOU, WONDER WOMAN. I RESPECT YOU. BUT... I REALLY AM JUST A BOY FROM KANSAS...
YOU'RE... WAY OUT OF MY LEAGUE!
I AGREE WITH YOUR DECISION, SUPERMAN, IF NOT ALL YOUR REASONING.
WE ARE OF DIFFERENT WORLDS-- DIFFERENT PHILOSOPHIES. PERHAPS WE CAN NEVER BE LOVERS...
BUT... I HOPE WE CAN BE FRIENDS...
...IF ONLY YOU WOULD PLEASE CALL ME DIANA.
DEAL.
IF YOU WILL CALL ME...
CLARK...

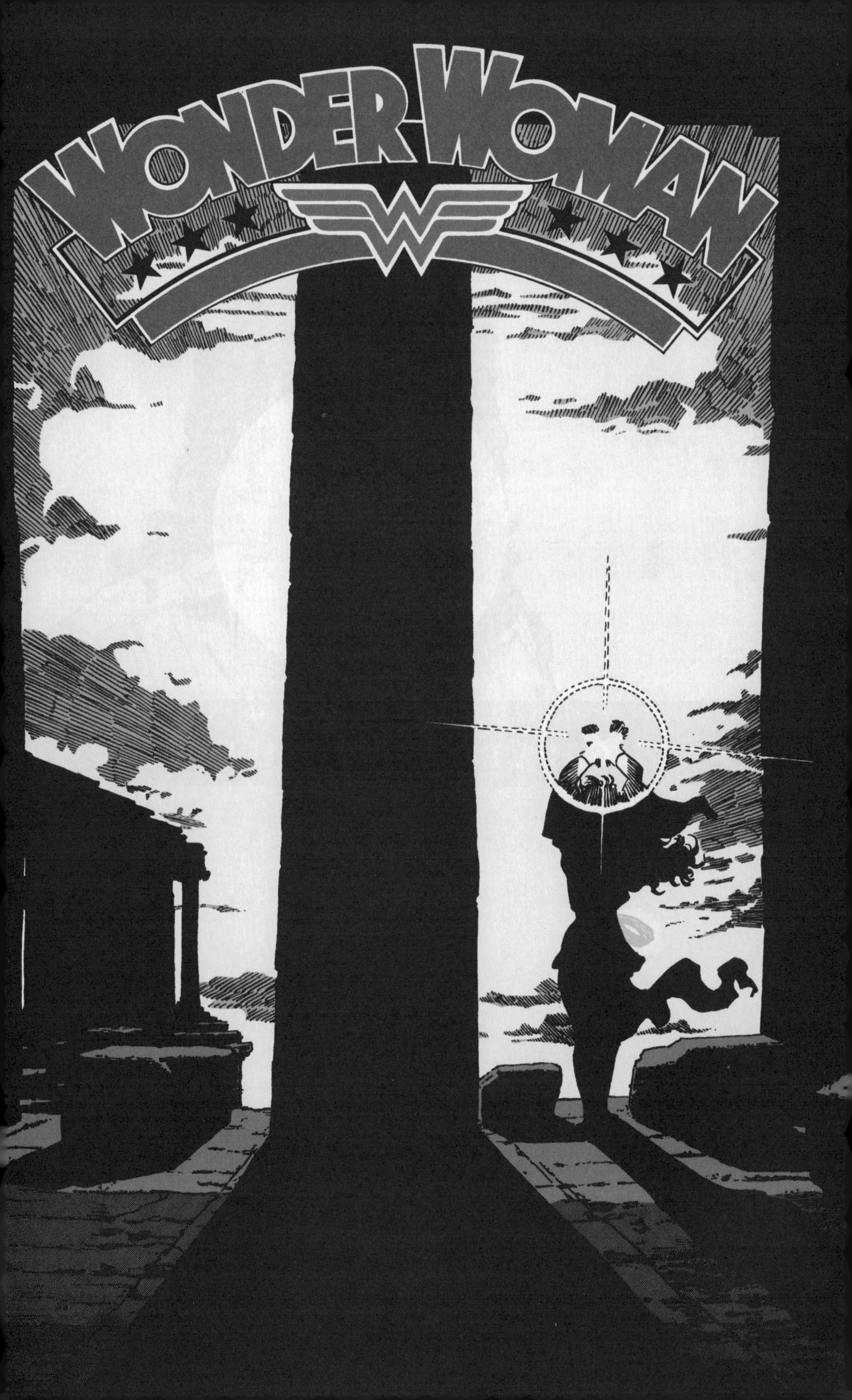
WONDER WOMAN

WONDER WOMAN

CHAPTER FOUR

CHAOS:

BLACK MASSES COLLIDE, THRUST BY VIOLENT WINDS.

THE DARKNESS RENT SPORADICALLY BY SHARDS OF BLISTERING LIGHT.

FEW HAVE EVER ENTERED THIS SAVAGE REALM, AND FEWER HAVE SURVIVED.

YET, INTO THIS RAGING FURY FLIES A TINY, DELICATE BIRD, UNDAUNTED BY THE EBON TERROR AROUND IT.

FOR THIS MESSENGER'S SPECIAL JOURNEY HAS BEEN SANCTIONED BY THE GRACE OF THE GODS...

...AND THE LOVE OF A QUEEN.

WITH NO STARS TO GUIDE IT, NO LANDMARKS TO DIRECT IT, THE PINIONED TRAVELER GLIDES DEEPER INTO THE ABYSS...

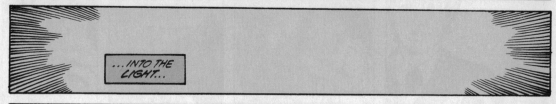

...UNTIL IT REACHES ITS GOAL...

...AND INSTINCTIVELY CROSSES FROM THE DARK AND DIN...

...INTO THE LIGHT...

...AND PEACE.

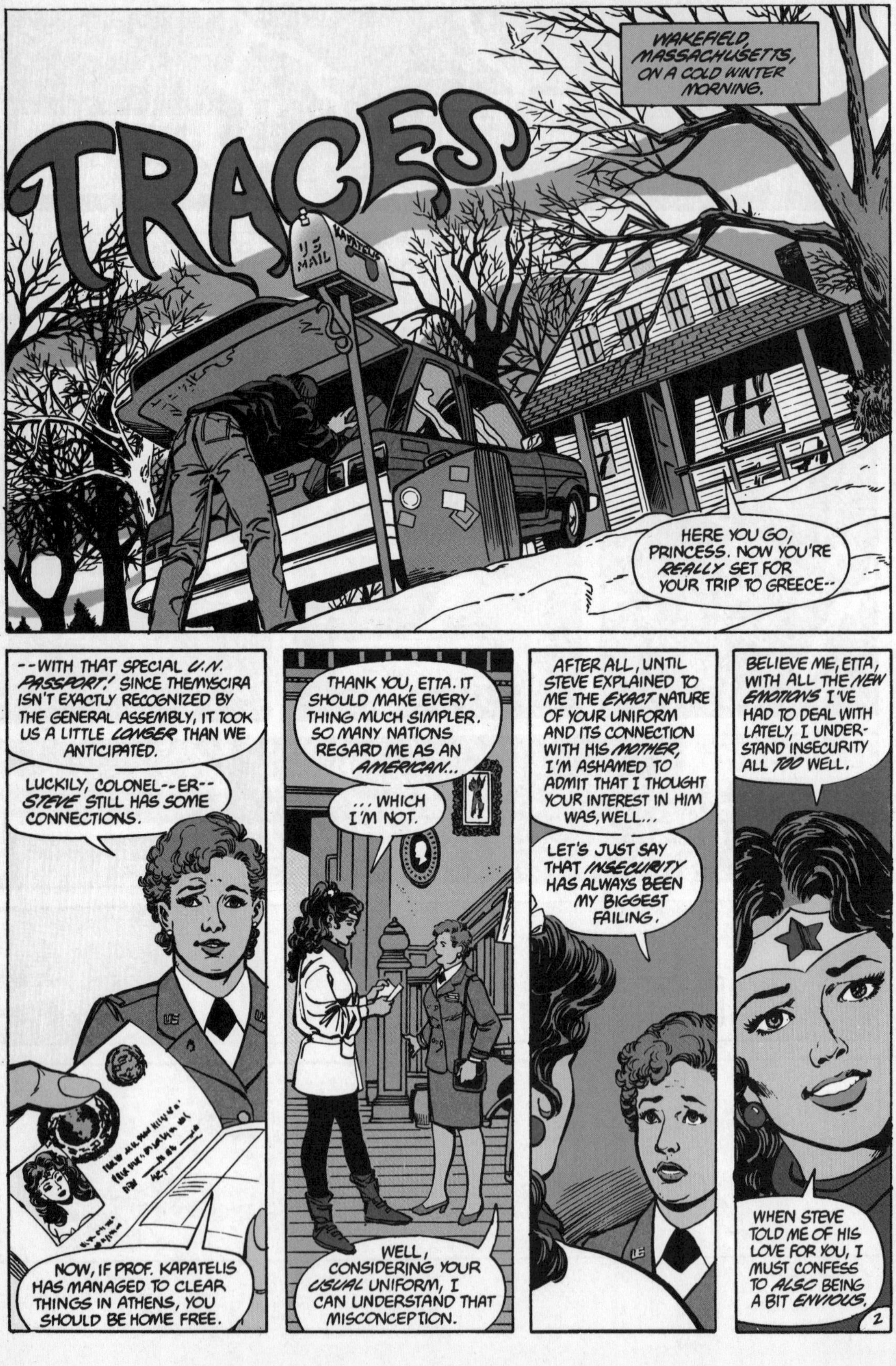
WAKEFIELD, MASSACHUSETTS, ON A COLD WINTER MORNING.
TRACES
U S MAIL
KAPATELIS
HERE YOU GO, PRINCESS. NOW YOU'RE REALLY SET FOR YOUR TRIP TO GREECE--
--WITH THAT SPECIAL U.N. PASSPORT! SINCE THEMYSCIRA ISN'T EXACTLY RECOGNIZED BY THE GENERAL ASSEMBLY, IT TOOK US A LITTLE LONGER THAN WE ANTICIPATED.
LUCKILY, COLONEL--ER--STEVE STILL HAS SOME CONNECTIONS.
NOW, IF PROF. KAPATELIS HAS MANAGED TO CLEAR THINGS IN ATHENS, YOU SHOULD BE HOME FREE.
THANK YOU, ETTA. IT SHOULD MAKE EVERYTHING MUCH SIMPLER. SO MANY NATIONS REGARD ME AS AN AMERICAN...
...WHICH I'M NOT.
WELL, CONSIDERING YOUR USUAL UNIFORM, I CAN UNDERSTAND THAT MISCONCEPTION.
AFTER ALL, UNTIL STEVE EXPLAINED TO ME THE EXACT NATURE OF YOUR UNIFORM AND ITS CONNECTION WITH HIS MOTHER, I'M ASHAMED TO ADMIT THAT I THOUGHT YOUR INTEREST IN HIM WAS, WELL...
LET'S JUST SAY THAT INSECURITY HAS ALWAYS BEEN MY BIGGEST FAILING.
BELIEVE ME, ETTA, WITH ALL THE NEW EMOTIONS I'VE HAD TO DEAL WITH LATELY, I UNDERSTAND INSECURITY ALL TOO WELL.
WHEN STEVE TOLD ME OF HIS LOVE FOR YOU, I MUST CONFESS TO ALSO BEING A BIT ENVIOUS.
2

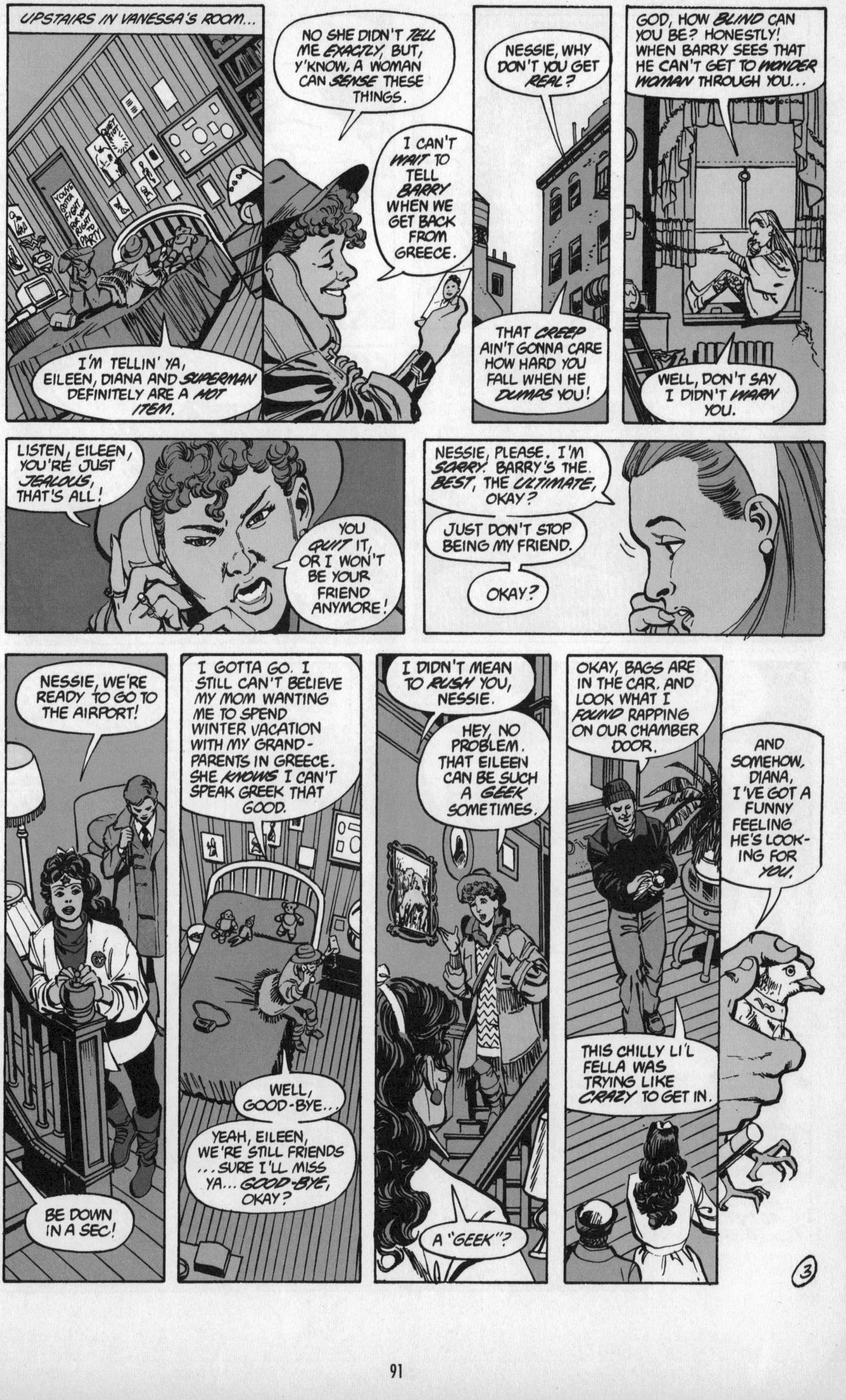

UPSTAIRS IN VANESSA'S ROOM...
I'M TELLIN' YA, EILEEN, DIANA AND SUPERMAN DEFINITELY ARE A HOT ITEM.
NO SHE DIDN'T TELL ME EXACTLY, BUT, Y'KNOW, A WOMAN CAN SENSE THESE THINGS.
I CAN'T WAIT TO TELL BARRY WHEN WE GET BACK FROM GREECE.
NESSIE, WHY DON'T YOU GET REAL?
THAT CREEP AIN'T GONNA CARE HOW HARD YOU FALL WHEN HE DUMPS YOU!
GOD, HOW BLIND CAN YOU BE? HONESTLY! WHEN BARRY SEES THAT HE CAN'T GET TO WONDER WOMAN THROUGH YOU...
WELL, DON'T SAY I DIDN'T WARN YOU.
LISTEN, EILEEN, YOU'RE JUST JEALOUS, THAT'S ALL!
YOU QUIT IT, OR I WON'T BE YOUR FRIEND ANYMORE!
NESSIE, PLEASE. I'M SORRY. BARRY'S THE. BEST, THE ULTIMATE, OKAY?
JUST DON'T STOP BEING MY FRIEND.
OKAY?
NESSIE, WE'RE READY TO GO TO THE AIRPORT!
BE DOWN IN A SEC!
I GOTTA GO. I STILL CAN'T BELIEVE MY MOM WANTING ME TO SPEND WINTER VACATION WITH MY GRAND-PARENTS IN GREECE. SHE KNOWS I CAN'T SPEAK GREEK THAT GOOD.
WELL, GOOD-BYE...
YEAH, EILEEN, WE'RE STILL FRIENDS ...SURE I'LL MISS YA... GOOD-BYE, OKAY?
I DIDN'T MEAN TO RUSH YOU, NESSIE.
HEY, NO PROBLEM. THAT EILEEN CAN BE SUCH A GEEK SOMETIMES.
A "GEEK"?
OKAY, BAGS ARE IN THE CAR. AND LOOK WHAT I FOUND RAPPING ON OUR CHAMBER DOOR.
THIS CHILLY LI'L FELLA WAS TRYING LIKE CRAZY TO GET IN.
AND SOMEHOW, DIANA, I'VE GOT A FUNNY FEELING HE'S LOOK-ING FOR YOU.
3

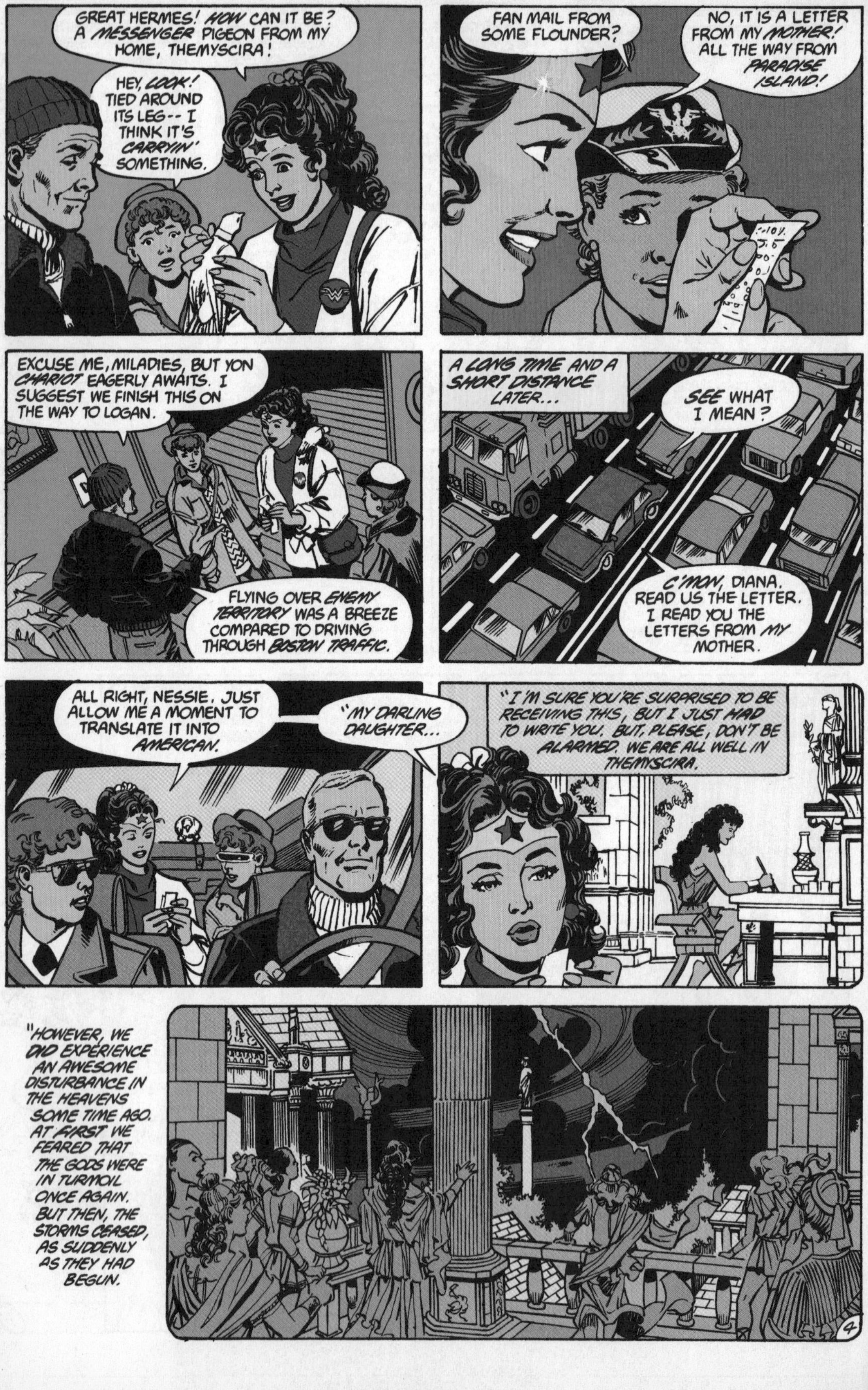
GREAT HERMES! HOW CAN IT BE? A MESSENGER PIGEON FROM MY HOME, THEMYSCIRA!
HEY, LOOK! TIED AROUND ITS LEG-- I THINK IT'S CARRYIN' SOMETHING.
FAN MAIL FROM SOME FLOUNDER?
NO, IT IS A LETTER FROM MY MOTHER! ALL THE WAY FROM PARADISE ISLAND!
EXCUSE ME, MILADIES, BUT YON CHARIOT EAGERLY AWAITS. I SUGGEST WE FINISH THIS ON THE WAY TO LOGAN.
FLYING OVER ENEMY TERRITORY WAS A BREEZE COMPARED TO DRIVING THROUGH BOSTON TRAFFIC.
A LONG TIME AND A SHORT DISTANCE LATER...
SEE WHAT I MEAN?
C'MON, DIANA. READ US THE LETTER. I READ YOU THE LETTERS FROM MY MOTHER.
ALL RIGHT, NESSIE. JUST ALLOW ME A MOMENT TO TRANSLATE IT INTO AMERICAN.
"MY DARLING DAUGHTER...
"I'M SURE YOU'RE SURPRISED TO BE RECEIVING THIS, BUT I JUST HAD TO WRITE YOU. BUT, PLEASE, DON'T BE ALARMED. WE ARE ALL WELL IN THEMYSCIRA.
"HOWEVER, WE DID EXPERIENCE AN AWESOME DISTURBANCE IN THE HEAVENS SOME TIME AGO. AT FIRST WE FEARED THAT THE GODS WERE IN TURMOIL ONCE AGAIN. BUT THEN, THE STORMS CEASED, AS SUDDENLY AS THEY HAD BEGUN.
4

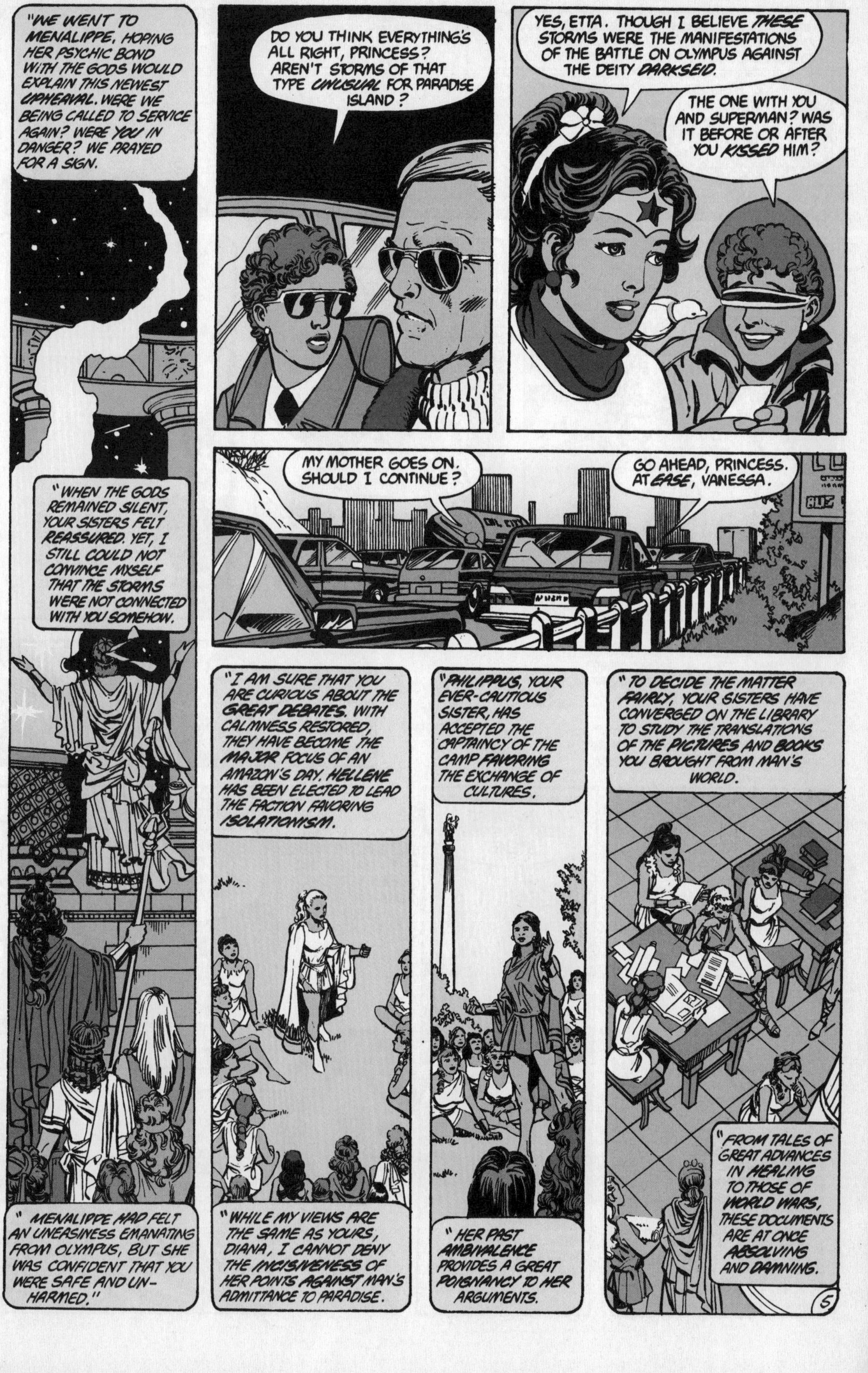
"WE WENT TO MENALIPPE, HOPING HER PSYCHIC BOND WITH THE GODS WOULD EXPLAIN THIS NEWEST UPHEAVAL. WERE WE BEING CALLED TO SERVICE AGAIN? WERE YOU IN DANGER? WE PRAYED FOR A SIGN.
DO YOU THINK EVERYTHING'S ALL RIGHT, PRINCESS? AREN'T STORMS OF THAT TYPE UNUSUAL FOR PARADISE ISLAND?
YES, ETTA. THOUGH I BELIEVE THESE STORMS WERE THE MANIFESTATIONS OF THE BATTLE ON OLYMPUS AGAINST THE DEITY DARKSEID.
THE ONE WITH YOU AND SUPERMAN? WAS IT BEFORE OR AFTER YOU KISSED HIM?
"WHEN THE GODS REMAINED SILENT, YOUR SISTERS FELT REASSURED. YET, I STILL COULD NOT CONVINCE MYSELF THAT THE STORMS WERE NOT CONNECTED WITH YOU SOMEHOW.
MY MOTHER GOES ON. SHOULD I CONTINUE?
GO AHEAD, PRINCESS. AT EASE, VANESSA.
"MENALIPPE HAD FELT AN UNEASINESS EMANATING FROM OLYMPUS, BUT SHE WAS CONFIDENT THAT YOU WERE SAFE AND UNHARMED."
"I AM SURE THAT YOU ARE CURIOUS ABOUT THE GREAT DEBATES. WITH CALMNESS RESTORED, THEY HAVE BECOME THE MAJOR FOCUS OF AN AMAZON'S DAY. HELLENE HAS BEEN ELECTED TO LEAD THE FACTION FAVORING ISOLATIONISM.
"WHILE MY VIEWS ARE THE SAME AS YOURS, DIANA, I CANNOT DENY THE INCISIVENESS OF HER POINTS AGAINST MAN'S ADMITTANCE TO PARADISE.
"PHILIPPUS, YOUR EVER-CAUTIOUS SISTER, HAS ACCEPTED THE CAPTAINCY OF THE CAMP FAVORING THE EXCHANGE OF CULTURES.
"HER PAST AMBIVALENCE PROVIDES A GREAT POIGNANCY TO HER ARGUMENTS.
"TO DECIDE THE MATTER FAIRLY, YOUR SISTERS HAVE CONVERGED ON THE LIBRARY TO STUDY THE TRANSLATIONS OF THE PICTURES AND BOOKS YOU BROUGHT FROM MAN'S WORLD.
"FROM TALES OF GREAT ADVANCES IN HEALING TO THOSE OF WORLD WARS, THESE DOCUMENTS ARE AT ONCE ABSOLVING AND DAMNING.
5

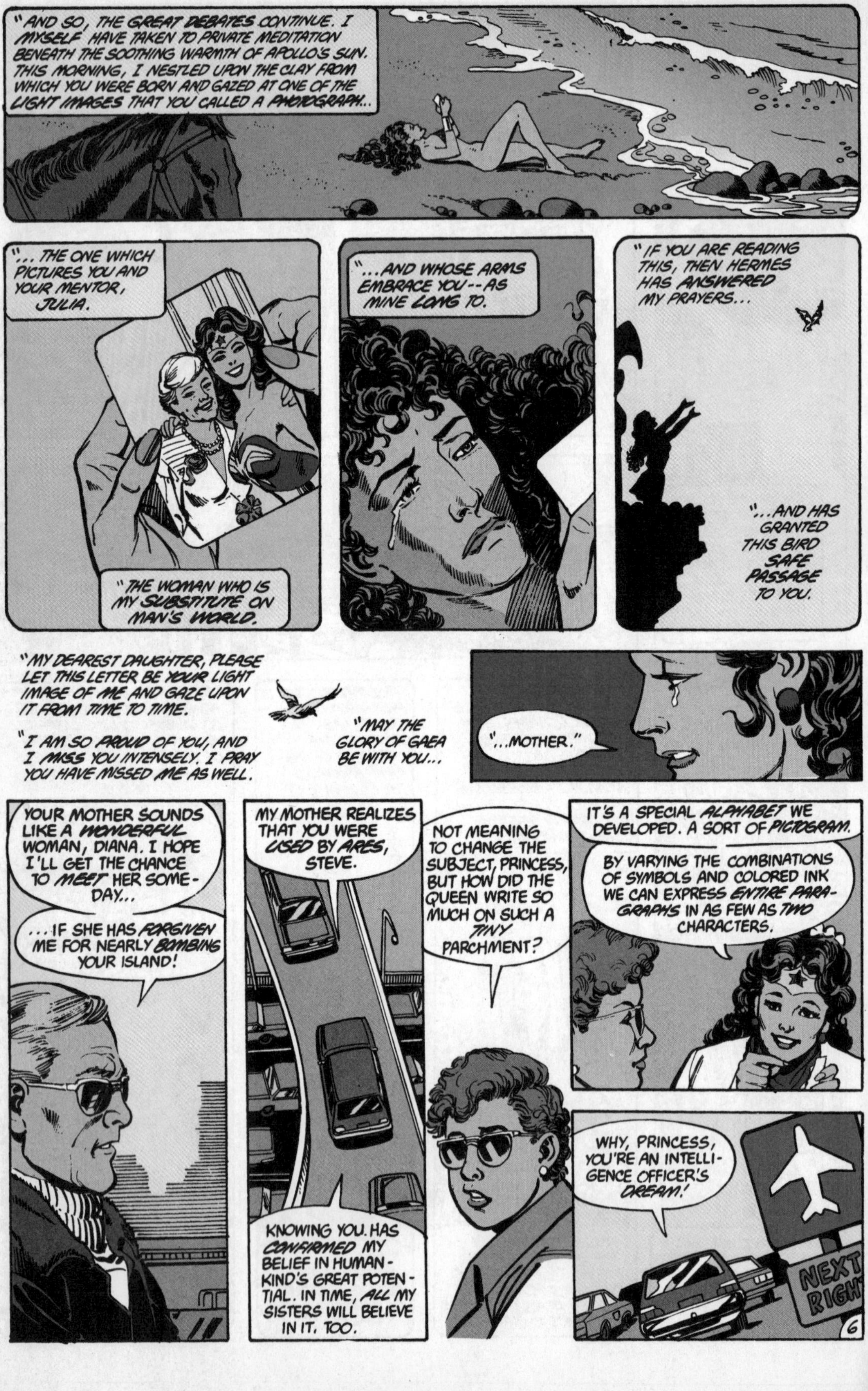

"AND SO, THE GREAT DEBATES CONTINUE. I MYSELF HAVE TAKEN TO PRIVATE MEDITATION BENEATH THE SOOTHING WARMTH OF APOLLO'S SUN. THIS MORNING, I NESTLED UPON THE CLAY FROM WHICH YOU WERE BORN AND GAZED AT ONE OF THE LIGHT IMAGES THAT YOU CALLED A PHOTOGRAPH...
"... THE ONE WHICH PICTURES YOU AND YOUR MENTOR, JULIA.
"THE WOMAN WHO IS MY SUBSTITUTE ON MAN'S WORLD.
"...AND WHOSE ARMS EMBRACE YOU--AS MINE LONG TO.
"IF YOU ARE READING THIS, THEN HERMES HAS ANSWERED MY PRAYERS...
"...AND HAS GRANTED THIS BIRD SAFE PASSAGE TO YOU.
"MY DEAREST DAUGHTER, PLEASE LET THIS LETTER BE YOUR LIGHT IMAGE OF ME AND GAZE UPON IT FROM TIME TO TIME.
"I AM SO PROUD OF YOU, AND I MISS YOU INTENSELY. I PRAY YOU HAVE MISSED ME AS WELL.
"MAY THE GLORY OF GAEA BE WITH YOU...
"...MOTHER."
YOUR MOTHER SOUNDS LIKE A WONDERFUL WOMAN, DIANA. I HOPE I'LL GET THE CHANCE TO MEET HER SOME-DAY...
...IF SHE HAS FORGIVEN ME FOR NEARLY BOMBING YOUR ISLAND!
MY MOTHER REALIZES THAT YOU WERE USED BY ARES, STEVE.
KNOWING YOU. HAS CONFIRMED MY BELIEF IN HUMAN-KIND'S GREAT POTEN-TIAL. IN TIME, ALL MY SISTERS WILL BELIEVE IN IT, TOO.
NOT MEANING TO CHANGE THE SUBJECT, PRINCESS, BUT HOW DID THE QUEEN WRITE SO MUCH ON SUCH A TINY PARCHMENT?
IT'S A SPECIAL ALPHABET WE DEVELOPED. A SORT OF PICTOGRAM.
BY VARYING THE COMBINATIONS OF SYMBOLS AND COLORED INK WE CAN EXPRESS ENTIRE PARA-GRAPHS IN AS FEW AS TWO CHARACTERS.
WHY, PRINCESS, YOU'RE AN INTELLI-GENCE OFFICER'S DREAM!
NEXT RIGHT
6

MOMMY, LOOK! WONDER WOMAN!

WHAT HAVE I TOLD YOU ABOUT MAKING UP STORIES!?

BUT, MOMMY...

DID YOU *HEAR* ME? NOW, BE QUIET!

"BESIDES, WHAT WOULD *WONDER WOMAN* BE DOING IN AN *AIRPORT* ANYWAY?"

C'MON, DIANA. IT'S *FREEZING* OUT HERE. YOUR MOM'LL BE HAPPY WITH A *SHORT* NOTE.

RELAX, KID, WE HAVE ENOUGH TIME.

LT. CANDY IS STILL MAKING SPECIAL ARRANGEMENTS AT *CUSTOMS.*

PLEASE, NESSIE, I HAVE TO SEND THIS NOTE BACK QUICKLY.

MY MOTHER MUST *NEVER* DOUBT THAT I LOVE HER AND MISS HER WITH ALL MY HEART.

NOW, TINY ONE, TAKE WING, AND MAY HERMES GUIDE YOUR *RETURN* HOME.

I OFFER YOU THIS *KISS* AS A TOKEN OF A *GRATEFUL* PRINCESS.

THE GLORY OF GAEA BE WITH YOU.

"*NOW, FLY!*"

"WELL, THERE THEY GO, STEVE. I HOPE GREECE IS ALL THAT DIANA EXPECTS IT TO BE."

"SO FAR, EVERYTHING'S GONE RATHER SMOOTHLY. DIANA'S *PRIORITY CLEARANCE* ALLOWED HER TO CARRY HER LARIAT ON BOARD WITH NO PROBLEM."

GOOD. THOUGH I'D HATE TO BE THE ONE WHO TRIES TO *TAKE* IT AWAY FROM HER!

SO, ETTA, WHAT ARE *YOUR* PLANS FOR THE REST OF THE DAY?

OH, I FIGURED I'D HIT THE *GYM.* THOSE *LAST 15 LBS.* ARE THE *TOUGHEST.* YOU?

SINCE I HAVEN'T HEARD FROM ANY OF THE *AIRCRAFT COMPANIES* YET, I *HAD* HOPED THAT I COULD *COERCE* YOU INTO AN *ALTERNATIVE* METHOD OF *CALORIC CONSUMPTION.*

SIR, I *DO* LIKE THE WAY YOU *THINK!*

7

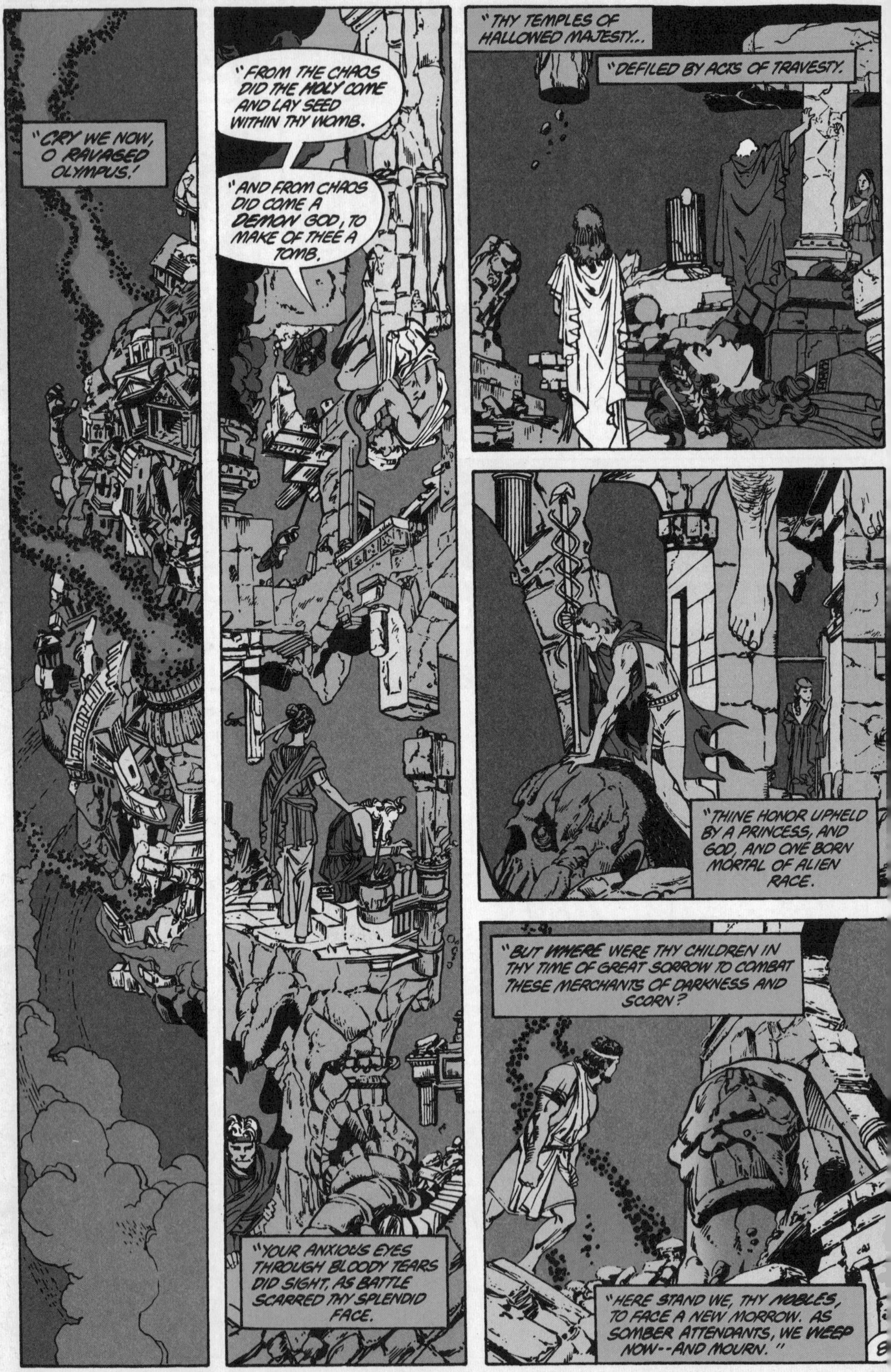
"CRY WE NOW, O RAVAGED OLYMPUS!
"FROM THE CHAOS DID THE MOLY COME AND LAY SEED WITHIN THY WOMB.
"AND FROM CHAOS DID COME A DEMON GOD, TO MAKE OF THEE A TOMB.
"YOUR ANXIOUS EYES THROUGH BLOODY TEARS DID SIGHT, AS BATTLE SCARRED THY SPLENDID FACE.
"THY TEMPLES OF HALLOWED MAJESTY...
"DEFILED BY ACTS OF TRAVESTY.
"THINE HONOR UPHELD BY A PRINCESS, AND GOD, AND ONE BORN MORTAL OF ALIEN RACE.
"BUT WHERE WERE THY CHILDREN IN THY TIME OF GREAT SORROW TO COMBAT THESE MERCHANTS OF DARKNESS AND SCORN?
"HERE STAND WE, THY NOBLES, TO FACE A NEW MORROW. AS SOMBER ATTENDANTS, WE WEEP NOW--AND MOURN."

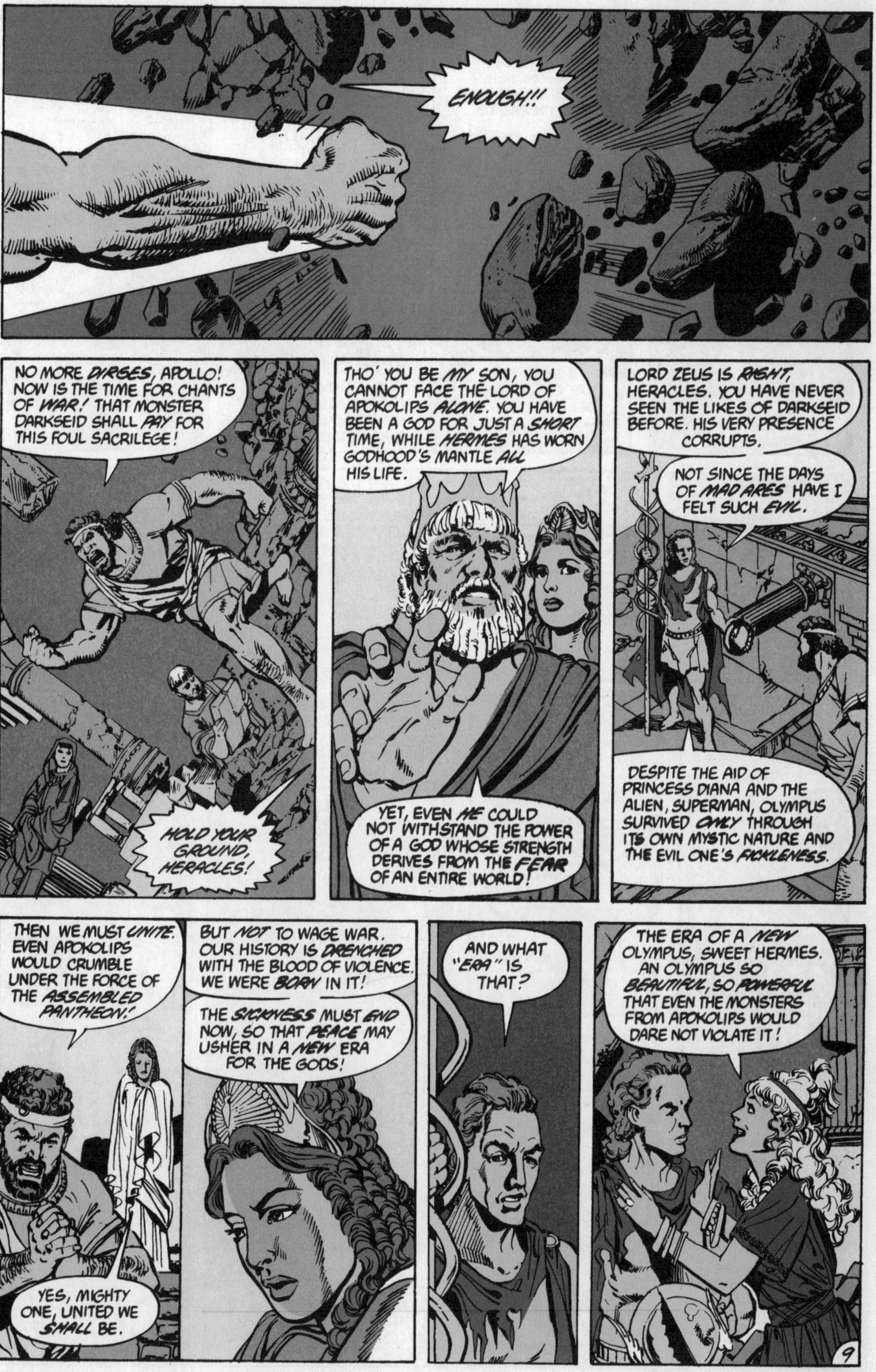
ENOUGH!!
NO MORE DIRGES, APOLLO! NOW IS THE TIME FOR CHANTS OF WAR! THAT MONSTER DARKSEID SHALL PAY FOR THIS FOUL SACRILEGE!
HOLD YOUR GROUND, HERACLES!
THO' YOU BE MY SON, YOU CANNOT FACE THE LORD OF APOKOLIPS ALONE. YOU HAVE BEEN A GOD FOR JUST A SHORT TIME, WHILE HERMES HAS WORN GODHOOD'S MANTLE ALL HIS LIFE.
YET, EVEN HE COULD NOT WITHSTAND THE POWER OF A GOD WHOSE STRENGTH DERIVES FROM THE FEAR OF AN ENTIRE WORLD!
LORD ZEUS IS RIGHT, HERACLES. YOU HAVE NEVER SEEN THE LIKES OF DARKSEID BEFORE. HIS VERY PRESENCE CORRUPTS.
NOT SINCE THE DAYS OF MAD ARES HAVE I FELT SUCH EVIL.
DESPITE THE AID OF PRINCESS DIANA AND THE ALIEN, SUPERMAN, OLYMPUS SURVIVED ONLY THROUGH ITS OWN MYSTIC NATURE AND THE EVIL ONE'S FICKLENESS.
THEN WE MUST UNITE. EVEN APOKOLIPS WOULD CRUMBLE UNDER THE FORCE OF THE ASSEMBLED PANTHEON!
YES, MIGHTY ONE, UNITED WE SHALL BE.
BUT NOT TO WAGE WAR. OUR HISTORY IS DRENCHED WITH THE BLOOD OF VIOLENCE. WE WERE BORN IN IT!
THE SICKNESS MUST END NOW, SO THAT PEACE MAY USHER IN A NEW ERA FOR THE GODS!
AND WHAT "ERA" IS THAT?
THE ERA OF A NEW OLYMPUS, SWEET HERMES. AN OLYMPUS SO BEAUTIFUL, SO POWERFUL THAT EVEN THE MONSTERS FROM APOKOLIPS WOULD DARE NOT VIOLATE IT!
9

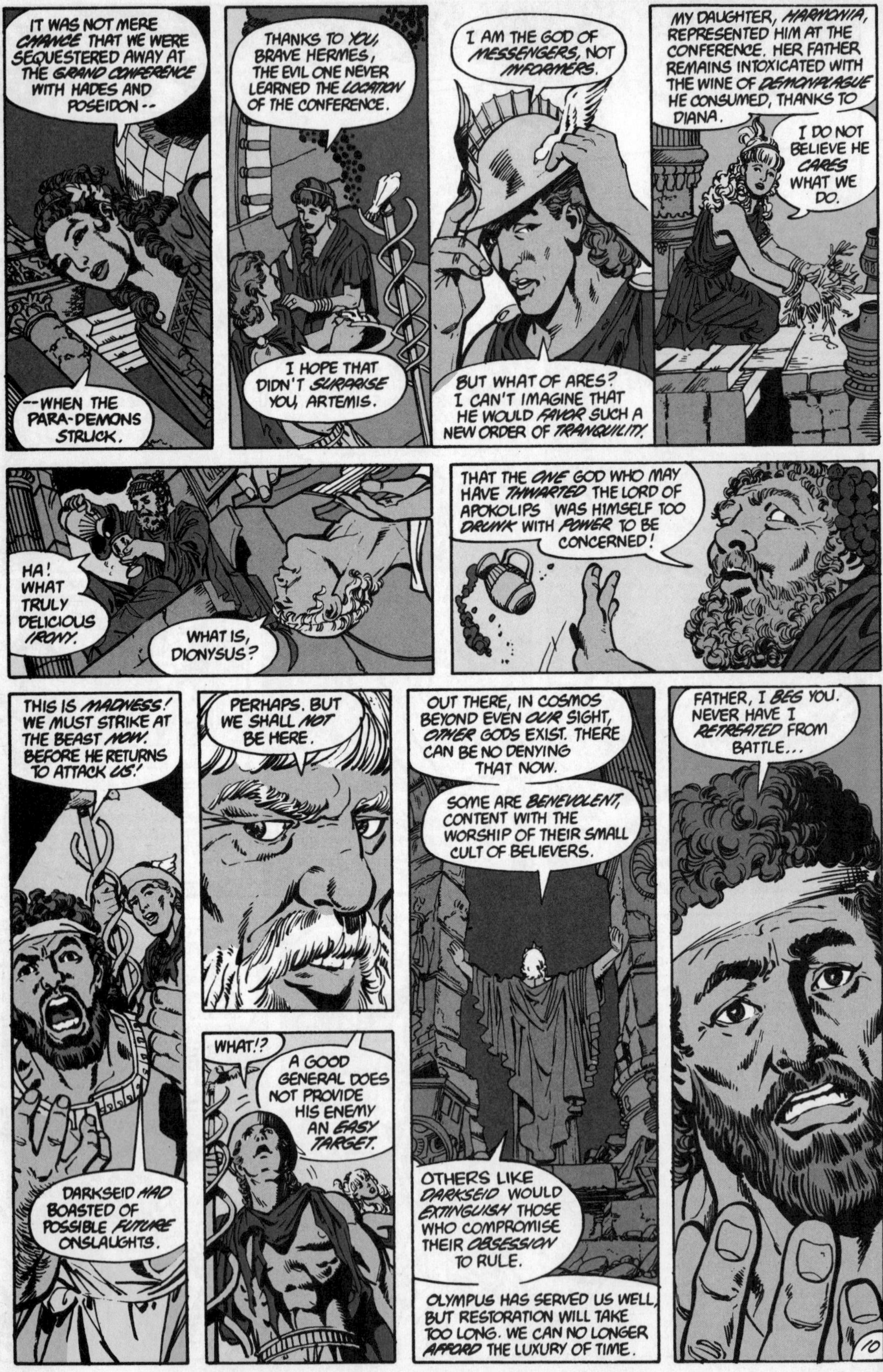
IT WAS NOT MERE CHANCE THAT WE WERE SEQUESTERED AWAY AT THE GRAND CONFERENCE WITH HADES AND POSEIDON --
--WHEN THE PARA-DEMONS STRUCK.
THANKS TO YOU, BRAVE HERMES, THE EVIL ONE NEVER LEARNED THE LOCATION OF THE CONFERENCE.
I HOPE THAT DIDN'T SURPRISE YOU, ARTEMIS.
I AM THE GOD OF MESSENGERS, NOT INFORMERS.
BUT WHAT OF ARES? I CAN'T IMAGINE THAT HE WOULD FAVOR SUCH A NEW ORDER OF TRANQUILITY.
MY DAUGHTER, HARMONIA, REPRESENTED HIM AT THE CONFERENCE. HER FATHER REMAINS INTOXICATED WITH THE WINE OF DEMONPLAGUE HE CONSUMED, THANKS TO DIANA.
I DO NOT BELIEVE HE CARES WHAT WE DO.
HA! WHAT TRULY DELICIOUS IRONY.
WHAT IS, DIONYSUS?
THAT THE ONE GOD WHO MAY HAVE THWARTED THE LORD OF APOKOLIPS WAS HIMSELF TOO DRUNK WITH POWER TO BE CONCERNED!
THIS IS MADNESS! WE MUST STRIKE AT THE BEAST NOW. BEFORE HE RETURNS TO ATTACK US!
DARKSEID HAD BOASTED OF POSSIBLE FUTURE ONSLAUGHTS.
PERHAPS. BUT WE SHALL NOT BE HERE.
WHAT!?
A GOOD GENERAL DOES NOT PROVIDE HIS ENEMY AN EASY TARGET.
OUT THERE, IN COSMOS BEYOND EVEN OUR SIGHT, OTHER GODS EXIST. THERE CAN BE NO DENYING THAT NOW.
SOME ARE BENEVOLENT, CONTENT WITH THE WORSHIP OF THEIR SMALL CULT OF BELIEVERS.
OTHERS LIKE DARKSEID WOULD EXTINGUISH THOSE WHO COMPROMISE THEIR OBSESSION TO RULE.
OLYMPUS HAS SERVED US WELL, BUT RESTORATION WILL TAKE TOO LONG. WE CAN NO LONGER AFFORD THE LUXURY OF TIME.
FATHER, I BEG YOU. NEVER HAVE I RETREATED FROM BATTLE...
10

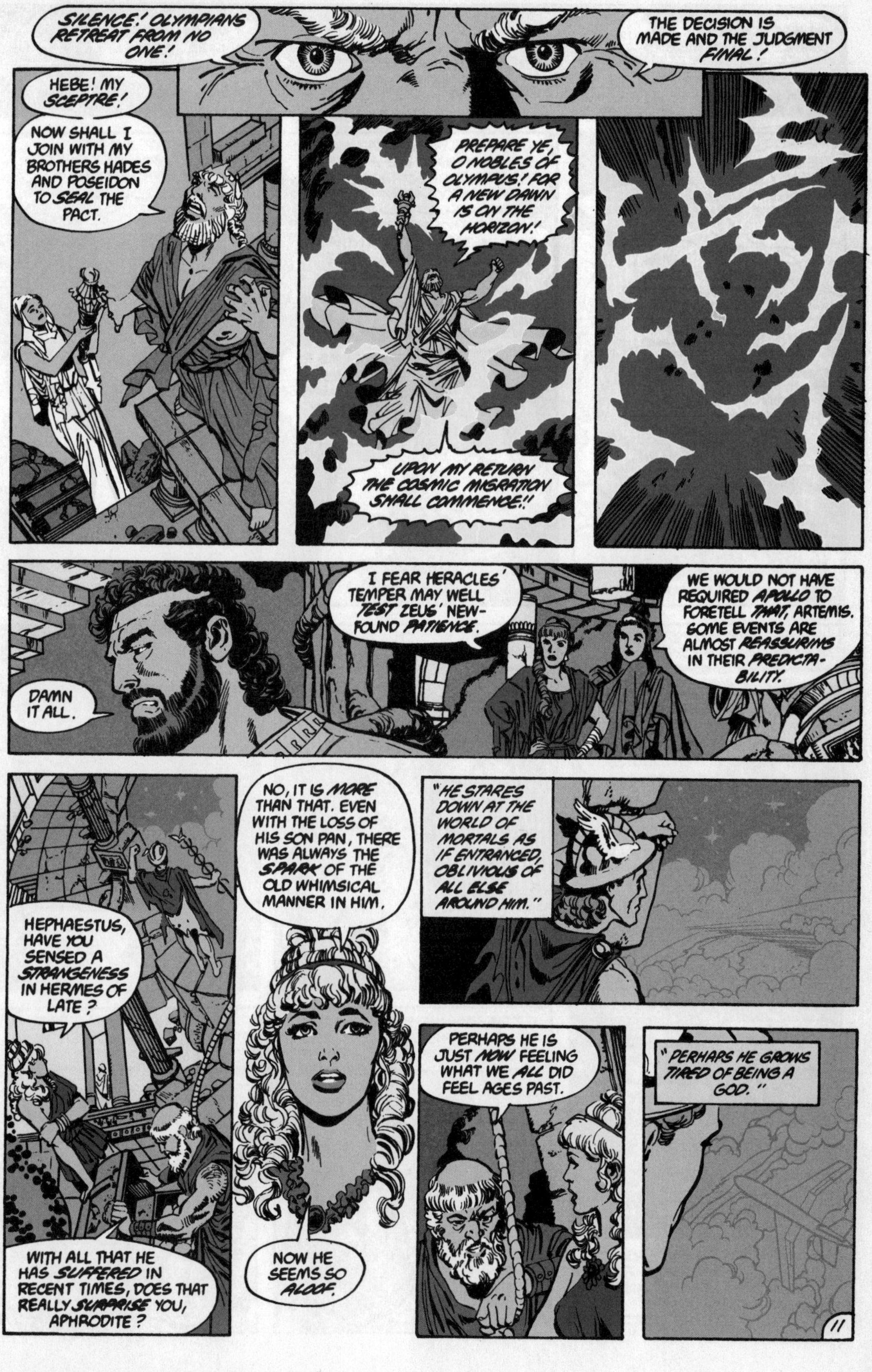
SILENCE! OLYMPIANS RETREAT FROM NO ONE!
THE DECISION IS MADE AND THE JUDGMENT FINAL!
HEBE! MY SCEPTRE!
NOW SHALL I JOIN WITH MY BROTHERS HADES AND POSEIDON TO SEAL THE PACT.
PREPARE YE, O NOBLES OF OLYMPUS! FOR A NEW DAWN IS ON THE HORIZON!
UPON MY RETURN THE COSMIC MIGRATION SHALL COMMENCE!!
DAMN IT ALL.
I FEAR HERACLES' TEMPER MAY WELL TEST ZEUS' NEW-FOUND PATIENCE.
WE WOULD NOT HAVE REQUIRED APOLLO TO FORETELL THAT, ARTEMIS. SOME EVENTS ARE ALMOST REASSURING IN THEIR PREDICTA-BILITY.
HEPHAESTUS, HAVE YOU SENSED A STRANGENESS IN HERMES OF LATE?
WITH ALL THAT HE HAS SUFFERED IN RECENT TIMES, DOES THAT REALLY SURPRISE YOU, APHRODITE?
NO, IT IS MORE THAN THAT. EVEN WITH THE LOSS OF HIS SON PAN, THERE WAS ALWAYS THE SPARK OF THE OLD WHIMSICAL MANNER IN HIM.
NOW HE SEEMS SO ALOOF.
"HE STARES DOWN AT THE WORLD OF MORTALS AS IF ENTRANCED, OBLIVIOUS OF ALL ELSE AROUND HIM."
PERHAPS HE IS JUST NOW FEELING WHAT WE ALL DID FEEL AGES PAST.
"PERHAPS HE GROWS TIRED OF BEING A GOD."
11

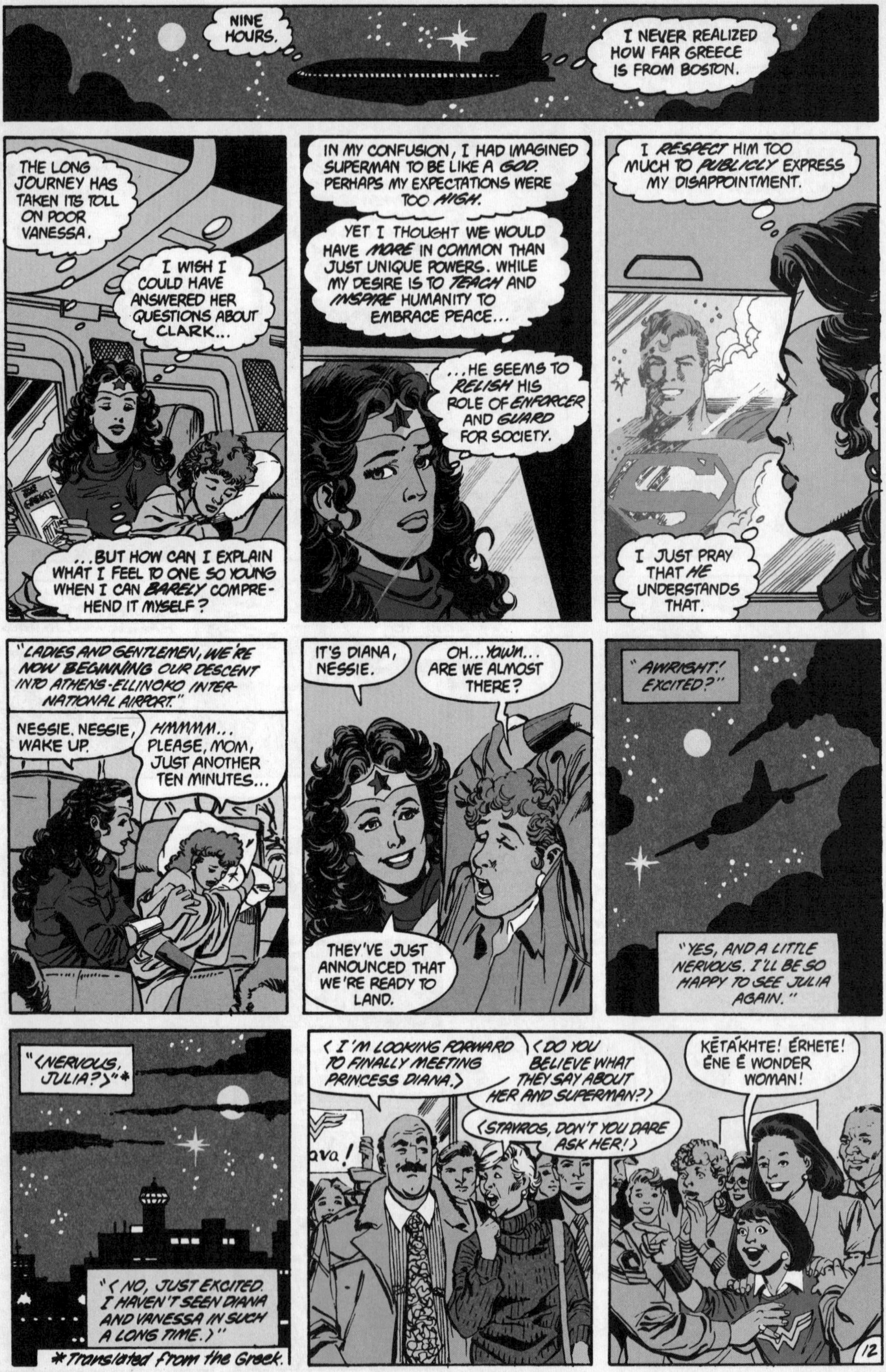
NINE HOURS.
I NEVER REALIZED HOW FAR GREECE IS FROM BOSTON.
THE LONG JOURNEY HAS TAKEN ITS TOLL ON POOR VANESSA.
I WISH I COULD HAVE ANSWERED HER QUESTIONS ABOUT CLARK...
...BUT HOW CAN I EXPLAIN WHAT I FEEL TO ONE SO YOUNG WHEN I CAN BARELY COMPREHEND IT MYSELF?
IN MY CONFUSION, I HAD IMAGINED SUPERMAN TO BE LIKE A GOD. PERHAPS MY EXPECTATIONS WERE TOO HIGH.
YET I THOUGHT WE WOULD HAVE MORE IN COMMON THAN JUST UNIQUE POWERS. WHILE MY DESIRE IS TO TEACH AND INSPIRE HUMANITY TO EMBRACE PEACE...
...HE SEEMS TO RELISH HIS ROLE OF ENFORCER AND GUARD FOR SOCIETY.
I RESPECT HIM TOO MUCH TO PUBLICLY EXPRESS MY DISAPPOINTMENT.
I JUST PRAY THAT HE UNDERSTANDS THAT.
"LADIES AND GENTLEMEN, WE'RE NOW BEGINNING OUR DESCENT INTO ATHENS-ELLINOKO INTERNATIONAL AIRPORT."
NESSIE. NESSIE, WAKE UP.
HMMMM... PLEASE, MOM, JUST ANOTHER TEN MINUTES...
IT'S DIANA, NESSIE.
OH...YAWN... ARE WE ALMOST THERE?
THEY'VE JUST ANNOUNCED THAT WE'RE READY TO LAND.
"AWRIGHT! EXCITED?"
"YES, AND A LITTLE NERVOUS. I'LL BE SO HAPPY TO SEE JULIA AGAIN."
"⟨NERVOUS, JULIA?⟩"*
"⟨NO, JUST EXCITED. I HAVEN'T SEEN DIANA AND VANESSA IN SUCH A LONG TIME.⟩"
*Translated from the Greek.
⟨I'M LOOKING FORWARD TO FINALLY MEETING PRINCESS DIANA.⟩
⟨DO YOU BELIEVE WHAT THEY SAY ABOUT HER AND SUPERMAN?⟩
⟨STAVROS, DON'T YOU DARE ASK HER!⟩
KĒTÁKHTE! ÉRHETE! ĒNE Ē WONDER WOMAN!
12

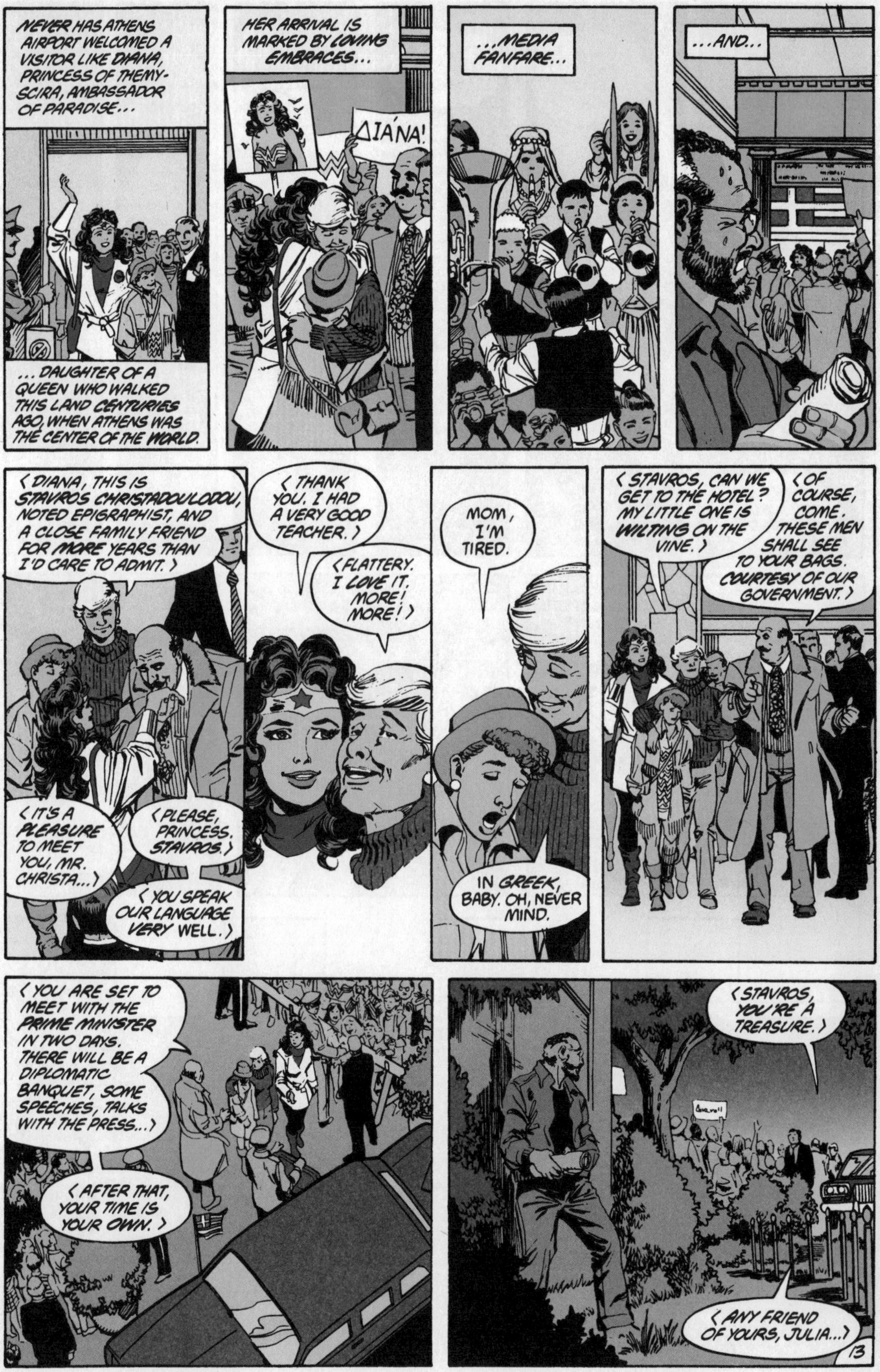
NEVER HAS ATHENS AIRPORT WELCOMED A VISITOR LIKE DIANA, PRINCESS OF THEMYSCIRA, AMBASSADOR OF PARADISE...
...DAUGHTER OF A QUEEN WHO WALKED THIS LAND CENTURIES AGO, WHEN ATHENS WAS THE CENTER OF THE WORLD.
HER ARRIVAL IS MARKED BY LOVING EMBRACES...
ΔIÁNA!
...MEDIA FANFARE...
...AND...
‹DIANA, THIS IS STAVROS CHRISTADOULODOU, NOTED EPIGRAPHIST, AND A CLOSE FAMILY FRIEND FOR MORE YEARS THAN I'D CARE TO ADMIT.›
‹IT'S A PLEASURE TO MEET YOU, MR. CHRISTA...›
‹PLEASE, PRINCESS. STAVROS.›
‹YOU SPEAK OUR LANGUAGE VERY WELL.›
‹THANK YOU. I HAD A VERY GOOD TEACHER.›
‹FLATTERY. I LOVE IT. MORE! MORE!›
MOM, I'M TIRED.
IN GREEK, BABY. OH, NEVER MIND.
‹STAVROS, CAN WE GET TO THE HOTEL? MY LITTLE ONE IS WILTING ON THE VINE.›
‹OF COURSE, COME. THESE MEN SHALL SEE TO YOUR BAGS. COURTESY OF OUR GOVERNMENT.›
‹YOU ARE SET TO MEET WITH THE PRIME MINISTER IN TWO DAYS. THERE WILL BE A DIPLOMATIC BANQUET, SOME SPEECHES, TALKS WITH THE PRESS...›
‹AFTER THAT, YOUR TIME IS YOUR OWN.›
‹STAVROS, YOU'RE A TREASURE.›
‹ANY FRIEND OF YOURS, JULIA...›
13

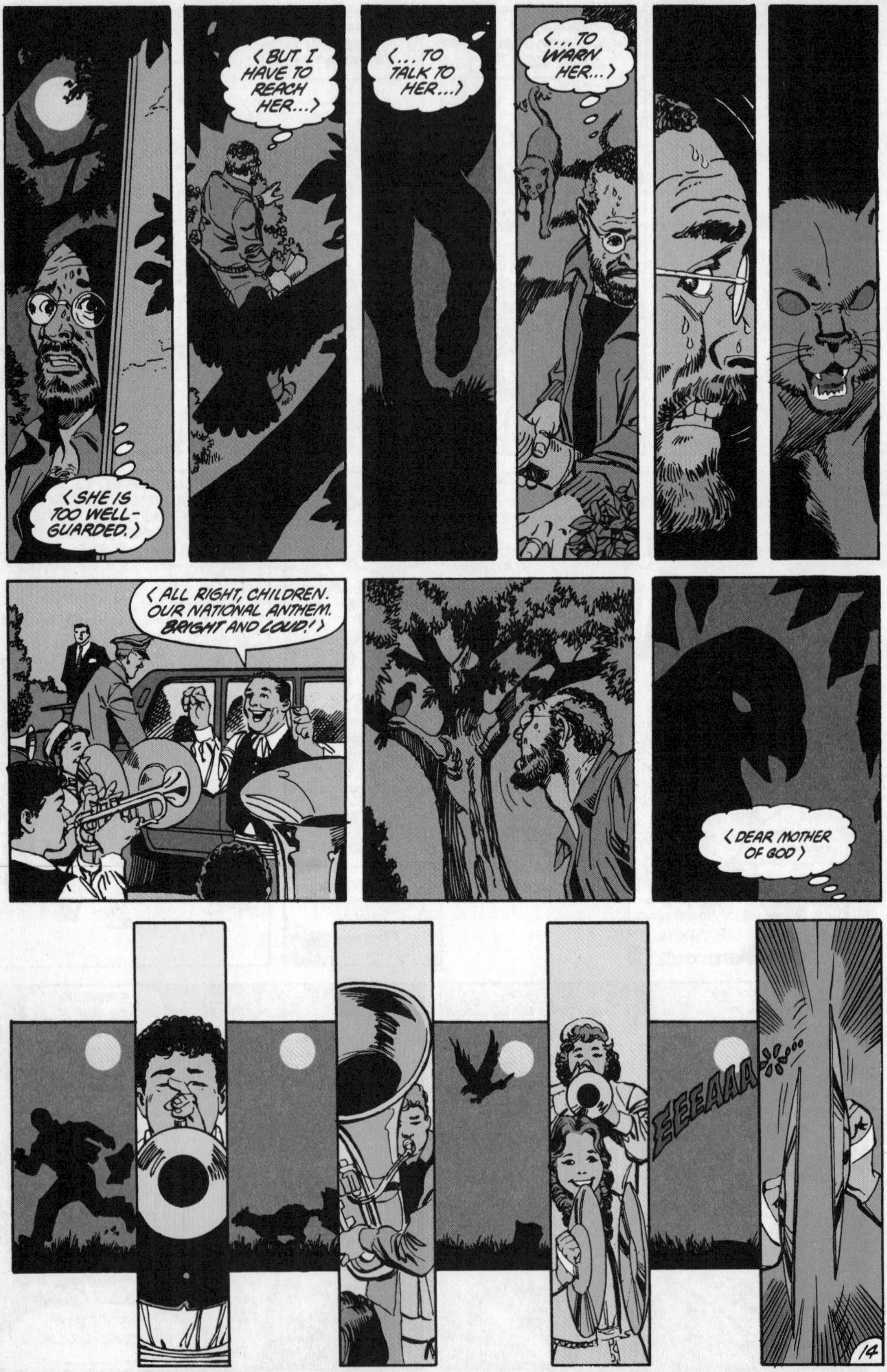

⟨ SHE IS TOO WELL-GUARDED. ⟩
⟨ BUT I HAVE TO REACH HER... ⟩
⟨ ... TO TALK TO HER... ⟩
⟨ ..., TO WARN HER... ⟩
⟨ ALL RIGHT, CHILDREN. OUR NATIONAL ANTHEM. BRIGHT AND LOUD! ⟩
⟨ DEAR MOTHER OF GOD ⟩
EEEAAA
14

BOSTON GLOBE

WONDER WOMAN WOWS'EM IN GREECE

Diana made honorary Greek Citizen

Princess Diana

I am a Citizen of the World

CHRISSIE!!

YOU RANG, MS. MAYER?

GET THIS MEMO OUT. TOMORROW, I WANT TO MEET WITH ALL DEPARTMENT HEADS AT 11 AM. *NO* EXCUSES.

DO I GIVE A *REASON*?

THEY'LL KNOW WHAT IT'S ABOUT.

AND *CALL UP* FEIST'S LIQUOR. THE WELL'S RUNNING *DRY* AGAIN.

MYNDI, DON'T YOU THINK YOU'VE BEEN *OVERDOING* IT A BIT?

DON'T START WITH ME. I'VE HAD ONE *LOUSY* DAY.

BEING MY COLLEGE ROOMMATE DOES NOT ENTITLE YOU TO *LECTURE* ME.

THEY'VE *ALL* BEEN PICKING AT ME. PROF. KAPATELIS, ALL THE WAY FROM GREECE, THAT CLOONEY WOMAN FROM THE NEEDY CHILDREN FOUNDATION, THE CITY COUNCIL, THE LAWYERS...

EVERYONE WANTS A PIECE OF MYNDI MAYER.

THE *ONLY* ONE WHO *HASN'T* TAKEN ME TO THE CARPET OVER THIS *FAIR FIASCO* IS *DIANA.* NO, SHE'S GOTTA BE SO DAMN *UNDERSTANDING!*

BOSTON'S PERFECT LITTLE *CHEERLEADER.* MAKES ME WANNA PUKE.

HELL, WILL YOU *PLEASE* CALL UP FEIST'S!?

MYNDI, YOU'RE NOT YOURSELF. YOU *KNOW* WHO'S RESPONSIBLE FOR ALL THIS. WHY DON'T YOU JUST *FIRE* THE CREEP?

DON'T START GETTING ON SKEETER'S CASE. STEVE LONDON AND... OTHER PEOPLE... WERE SUPPOSED TO *HELP* HIM AND...

WHY AM I EXPLAINING MYSELF TO *YOU*? YOU'RE *ONLY* A SECRETARY!

GET THAT MEMO OUT AND CALL THE LIQUOR STORE.

UNLESS YOU DON'T *LIKE* YOUR JOB, MS. FENTON.

OKAY, MS. MAYER. I'LL TAKE CARE OF IT.

BOSS LADY GIVING YOU A HARD TIME, SWEETHEART?

STUFF IT, SLEAZEBAG!

15

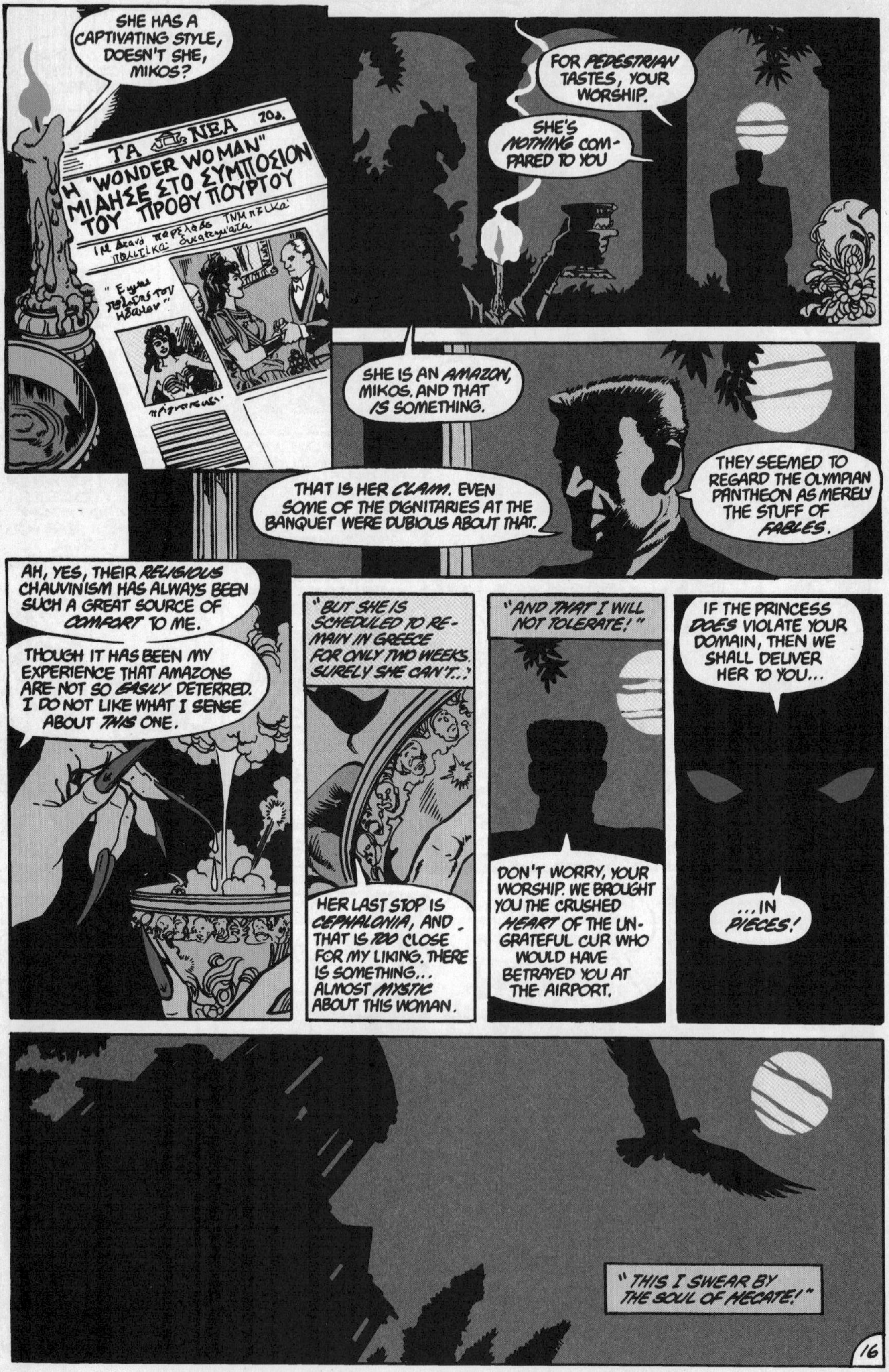
SHE HAS A CAPTIVATING STYLE, DOESN'T SHE, MIKOS?
ΤΑ ΝΕΑ 20δ.
Η "WONDER WOMAN" ΜΙΑΗΣΕ ΣΤΟ ΣΥΜΠΟΣΙΟΝ ΤΟΥ ΠΡΟΘΥ ΠΟΥΡΤΟΥ
FOR PEDESTRIAN TASTES, YOUR WORSHIP.
SHE'S NOTHING COMPARED TO YOU
SHE IS AN AMAZON, MIKOS. AND THAT IS SOMETHING.
THAT IS HER CLAIM. EVEN SOME OF THE DIGNITARIES AT THE BANQUET WERE DUBIOUS ABOUT THAT.
THEY SEEMED TO REGARD THE OLYMPIAN PANTHEON AS MERELY THE STUFF OF FABLES.
AH, YES, THEIR RELIGIOUS CHAUVINISM HAS ALWAYS BEEN SUCH A GREAT SOURCE OF COMFORT TO ME.
THOUGH IT HAS BEEN MY EXPERIENCE THAT AMAZONS ARE NOT SO EASILY DETERRED. I DO NOT LIKE WHAT I SENSE ABOUT THIS ONE.
"BUT SHE IS SCHEDULED TO REMAIN IN GREECE FOR ONLY TWO WEEKS. SURELY SHE CAN'T..."
HER LAST STOP IS CEPHALONIA, AND THAT IS TOO CLOSE FOR MY LIKING. THERE IS SOMETHING... ALMOST MYSTIC ABOUT THIS WOMAN.
"AND THAT I WILL NOT TOLERATE!"
DON'T WORRY, YOUR WORSHIP. WE BROUGHT YOU THE CRUSHED HEART OF THE UNGRATEFUL CUR WHO WOULD HAVE BETRAYED YOU AT THE AIRPORT.
IF THE PRINCESS DOES VIOLATE YOUR DOMAIN, THEN WE SHALL DELIVER HER TO YOU...
...IN PIECES!
"THIS I SWEAR BY THE SOUL OF HECATE!"
16

THE ACROPOLIS, THE NEXT MORNING:

I CAN *FEEL* IT.

LIKE A FADING ECHO OR A DIMMING LIGHT...

...THE *TRACES* REMAIN.

THE GODS *WERE* HERE!

EVEN SEEING *PHOTOS* AND *FILMS* OF THIS ACROPOLIS COULD NOT HAVE PREPARED ME FOR SUCH *SENSATIONS.*

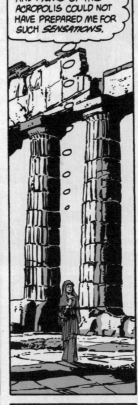

I CAN SEE THE GLINTS OF SUNLIGHT DANCING ON THE DRAWN SWORDS AS MY MOTHER'S ARMY MARCHED OVER THIS LAND, CENTURIES BEFORE THESE TEMPLES WERE EVEN ERECTED.

I CAN HEAR THE SONGS OF THE POETS...

...AND I CAN SMELL THE BLOOD.

THE GODS WERE IN THEIR *GREATEST* GLORY THEN. ONLY GREAT *FAITH* COULD HAVE INSPIRED SUCH MONUMENTS.

AS IT IS ON THEMYSCIRA, SO WAS IT *ONCE* HERE.

NOW I BEGIN TO FULLY UNDERSTAND THE GREAT SENSE OF *LOSS* THE GODS MUST HAVE FELT WHEN MAN NO LONGER WANTED THEM...

...AND THE GREAT TRUST THEY HAVE PLACED IN ME.

DESPITE THE CRUEL WINDS OF TIME AND THE VIOLENT ONSLAUGHTS OF WAR, THIS ACROPOLIS AND OTHER SUCH STRUCTURES STILL STAND. CITIES BEAR THE GODS' NAMES.

THEY MAY NOT BE *WORSHIPPED,* BUT THEY HAVE NOT BEEN *FORGOTTEN.*

AND *THAT* ITSELF IS A *START.*

O ATHENA! FROM YOUR TEMPLE I PRAY THAT I BE GRANTED THE WISDOM TO FIND THE VOICE THAT WILL INSPIRE.

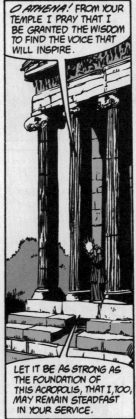

LET IT BE AS STRONG AS THE FOUNDATION OF THIS ACROPOLIS, THAT I, TOO, MAY REMAIN STEADFAST IN YOUR SERVICE.

I HAVE MUCH TO *TEACH* AND MUCH TO *LEARN.* GRANT ME THE *PATIENCE* TO DO BOTH.

FOR THE GLORY OF GAEA!

17

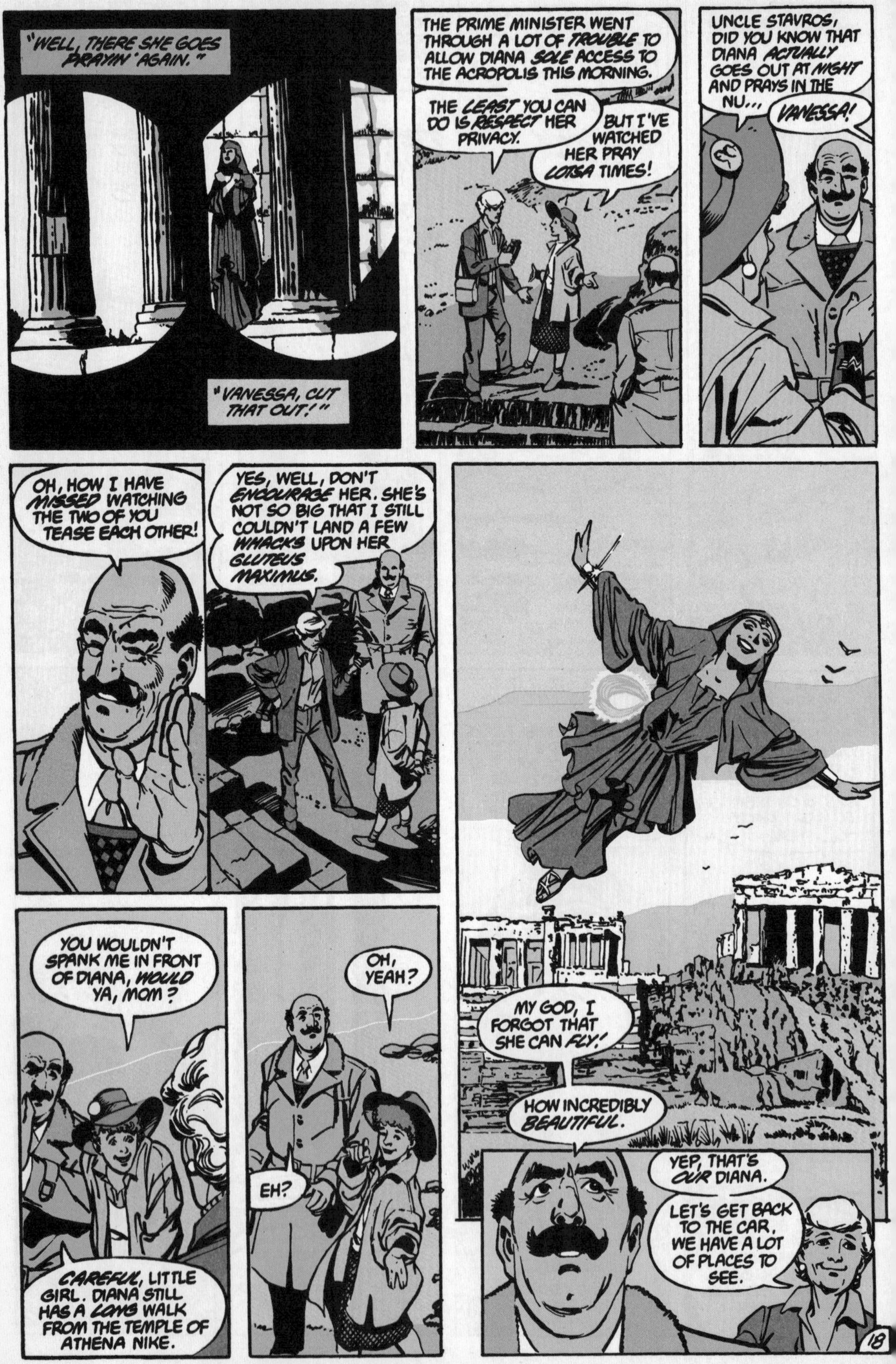
"WELL, THERE SHE GOES PRAYIN' AGAIN."
"VANESSA, CUT THAT OUT!"
THE PRIME MINISTER WENT THROUGH A LOT OF TROUBLE TO ALLOW DIANA SOLE ACCESS TO THE ACROPOLIS THIS MORNING.
THE LEAST YOU CAN DO IS RESPECT HER PRIVACY.
BUT I'VE WATCHED HER PRAY LOTSA TIMES!
UNCLE STAVROS, DID YOU KNOW THAT DIANA ACTUALLY GOES OUT AT NIGHT AND PRAYS IN THE NU...
VANESSA!
OH, HOW I HAVE MISSED WATCHING THE TWO OF YOU TEASE EACH OTHER!
YES, WELL, DON'T ENCOURAGE HER. SHE'S NOT SO BIG THAT I STILL COULDN'T LAND A FEW WHACKS UPON HER GLUTEUS MAXIMUS.
YOU WOULDN'T SPANK ME IN FRONT OF DIANA, WOULD YA, MOM?
CAREFUL, LITTLE GIRL. DIANA STILL HAS A LONG WALK FROM THE TEMPLE OF ATHENA NIKE.
OH, YEAH?
EH?
MY GOD, I FORGOT THAT SHE CAN FLY!
HOW INCREDIBLY BEAUTIFUL.
YEP, THAT'S OUR DIANA.
LET'S GET BACK TO THE CAR. WE HAVE A LOT OF PLACES TO SEE.
18

AS DIANA TOURS THROUGH GREECE, SHE REALIZES JUST HOW *MAGNIFICENTLY* MAN ONCE WORSHIPPED THE GODS.

GREAT MARBLE TRIBUTES RECALLING OLYMPUS' GOLDEN AGE...

THE HILL OF THE MUSES IN ATHENS...

...NAMED FOR THOSE WHO INSPIRE THE SOULS OF *ARTISTS.*

HEPHAESTEUM...

...COMMEMORATING THE GOD WHO FORGED HER MAGIC LASSO FROM THE GOLDEN GIRDLE OF GAEA.

THE *HERAION* IN OLYMPIA...

...WHERE GREAT ATHLETIC GAMES WERE HELD IN THE NAME OF ZEUS.

THE TEMPLE OF APOLLO IN DELPHI...

...HOME OF THE ORACLE WHOM THE SUN-GOD BLESSED WITH THE GIFT OF PRECOGNITION.

AND *LESBOS*...

...BIRTHPLACE OF THE GREEK POETESS *SAPPHO* AND ONCE THE SITE OF AN *AMAZON* CITY...

...A CITY DESTROYED BY MAN'S IGNORANCE AND FEAR CENTURIES AGO...

...LEAVING NO TRACE...

...EXCEPT IN THE EYES OF AN AMAZON PRINCESS.

SLEEP WELL, MY SISTERS. ENJOY THE SPLENDORS OF YOUR *AFTERLIFE* IN THE ELYSIAN FIELDS AND TAKE COMFORT IN THE KNOWLEDGE THAT THE *AMAZON IDEALS* HAVE NOT PERISHED.

AS LONG AS ONE OF US STILL LIVES, THE LESSONS OF PEACE AND EQUALITY SHALL BE TAUGHT. I BELIEVE MAN IS *NOW* READY TO LEARN.

19

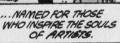

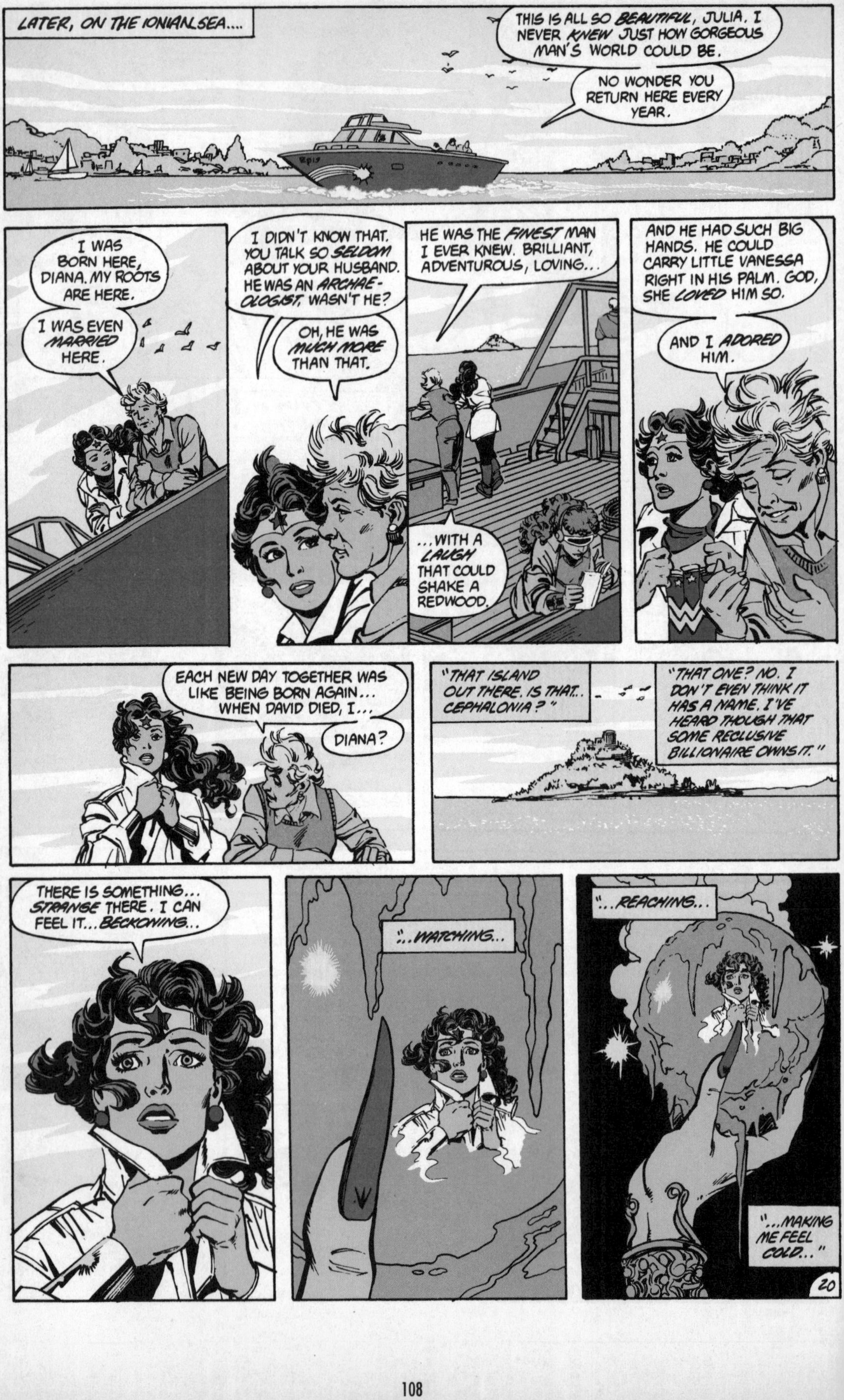
LATER, ON THE IONIAN SEA....
THIS IS ALL SO BEAUTIFUL, JULIA. I NEVER KNEW JUST HOW GORGEOUS MAN'S WORLD COULD BE.
NO WONDER YOU RETURN HERE EVERY YEAR.
I WAS BORN HERE, DIANA. MY ROOTS ARE HERE.
I WAS EVEN MARRIED HERE.
I DIDN'T KNOW THAT. YOU TALK SO SELDOM ABOUT YOUR HUSBAND. HE WAS AN ARCHAE-OLOGIST, WASN'T HE?
OH, HE WAS MUCH MORE THAN THAT.
HE WAS THE FINEST MAN I EVER KNEW. BRILLIANT, ADVENTUROUS, LOVING...
...WITH A LAUGH THAT COULD SHAKE A REDWOOD.
AND HE HAD SUCH BIG HANDS. HE COULD CARRY LITTLE VANESSA RIGHT IN HIS PALM. GOD, SHE LOVED HIM SO.
AND I ADORED HIM.
EACH NEW DAY TOGETHER WAS LIKE BEING BORN AGAIN... WHEN DAVID DIED, I...
DIANA?
"THAT ISLAND OUT THERE. IS THAT... CEPHALONIA?"
"THAT ONE? NO. I DON'T EVEN THINK IT HAS A NAME. I'VE HEARD THOUGH THAT SOME RECLUSIVE BILLIONAIRE OWNS IT."
THERE IS SOMETHING... STRANGE THERE. I CAN FEEL IT... BECKONING...
"...WATCHING...
"...REACHING...
"...MAKING ME FEEL COLD..."
20

...SO...COLD...

DIANA!

PRINCESS!

MOM, WHAT HAPPENED?

I DON'T KNOW. SHE JUST KEELED OVER.

SHE WAS LOOKING OUT AT THAT *ISLAND*...

MOM! HER SKIN IS LIKE *ICE*!

STAVROS!

MAGIA...

STAVROS!!

EH?

HELP ME GET HER BELOW. VANESSA, CALL THE HOSPITAL IN CEPHALONIA.

SHE'S GONNA BE ALL RIGHT, ISN'T SHE?

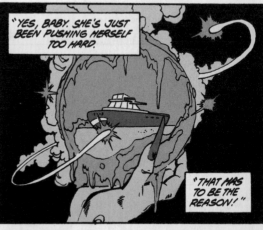

"YES, BABY. SHE'S JUST BEEN PUSHING HERSELF TOO HARD.

"THAT HAS TO BE THE REASON!"

LET THAT BE YOUR *FIRST* WARNING, AMAZON.

21

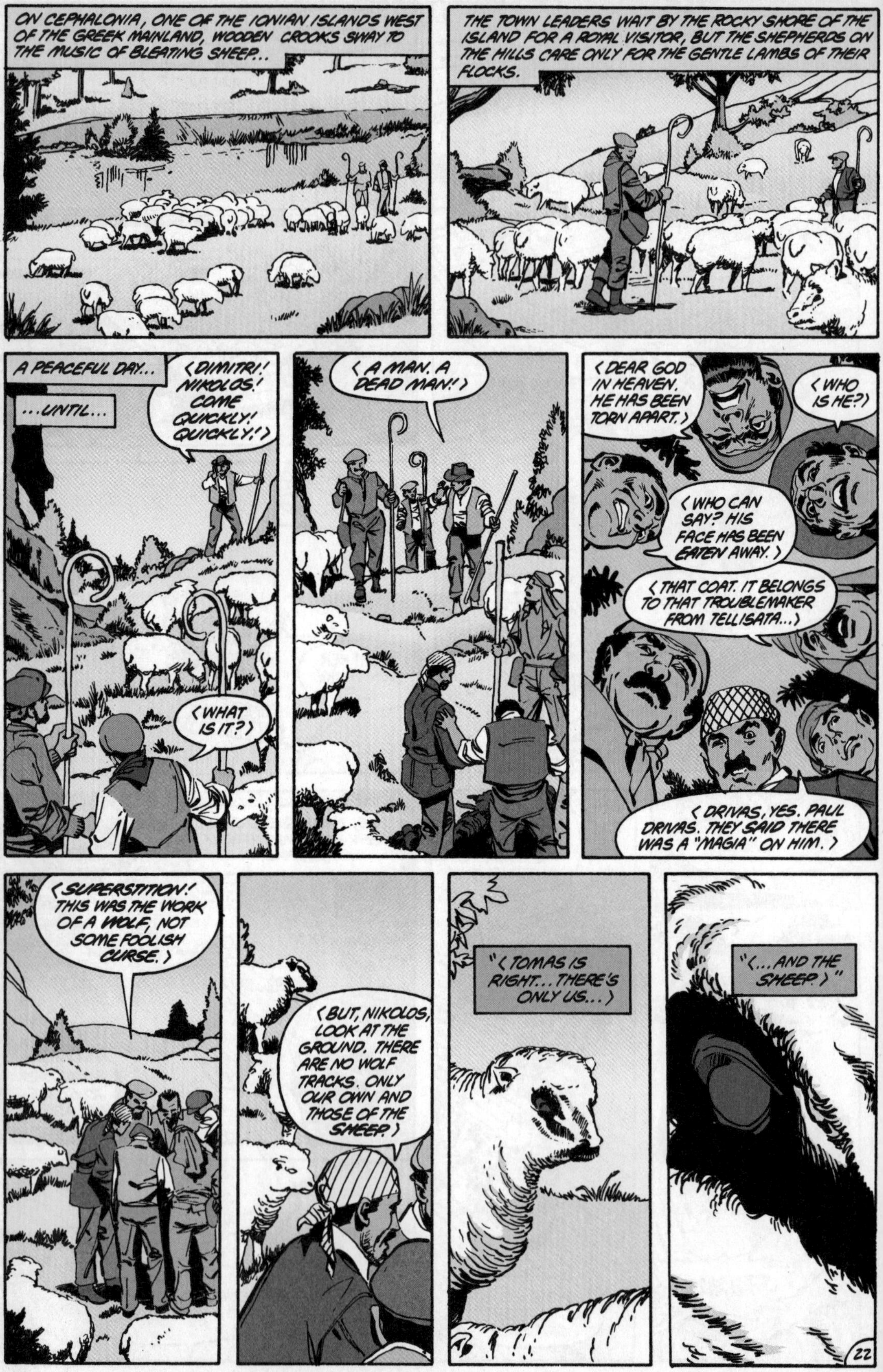
ON CEPHALONIA, ONE OF THE IONIAN ISLANDS WEST OF THE GREEK MAINLAND, WOODEN CROOKS SWAY TO THE MUSIC OF BLEATING SHEEP...
THE TOWN LEADERS WAIT BY THE ROCKY SHORE OF THE ISLAND FOR A ROYAL VISITOR, BUT THE SHEPHERDS ON THE HILLS CARE ONLY FOR THE GENTLE LAMBS OF THEIR FLOCKS.
A PEACEFUL DAY...
...UNTIL...
⟨DIMITRI! NIKOLOS! COME QUICKLY! QUICKLY!⟩
⟨WHAT IS IT?⟩
⟨A MAN. A DEAD MAN!⟩
⟨DEAR GOD IN HEAVEN. HE HAS BEEN TORN APART.⟩
⟨WHO IS HE?⟩
⟨WHO CAN SAY? HIS FACE HAS BEEN EATEN AWAY.⟩
⟨THAT COAT. IT BELONGS TO THAT TROUBLEMAKER FROM TELLISATA...⟩
⟨DRIVAS, YES. PAUL DRIVAS. THEY SAID THERE WAS A "MAGIA" ON HIM.⟩
⟨SUPERSTITION! THIS WAS THE WORK OF A WOLF, NOT SOME FOOLISH CURSE.⟩
⟨BUT, NIKOLOS, LOOK AT THE GROUND. THERE ARE NO WOLF TRACKS. ONLY OUR OWN AND THOSE OF THE SHEEP.⟩
"⟨TOMAS IS RIGHT... THERE'S ONLY US...⟩
"⟨...AND THE SHEEP.⟩"
22

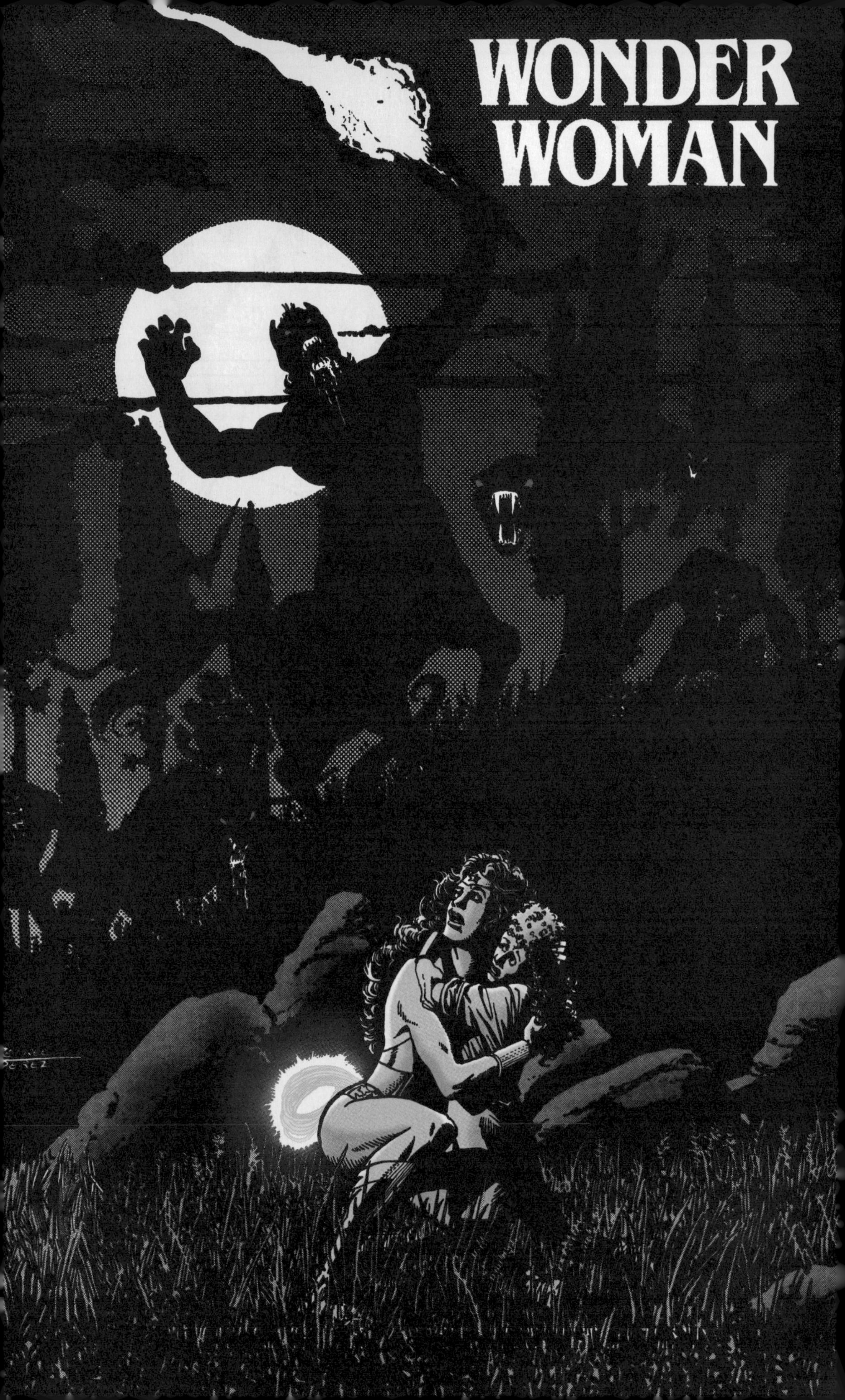
WONDER
WOMAN

WONDER WOMAN

WONDER WOMAN

CHAPTER FIVE

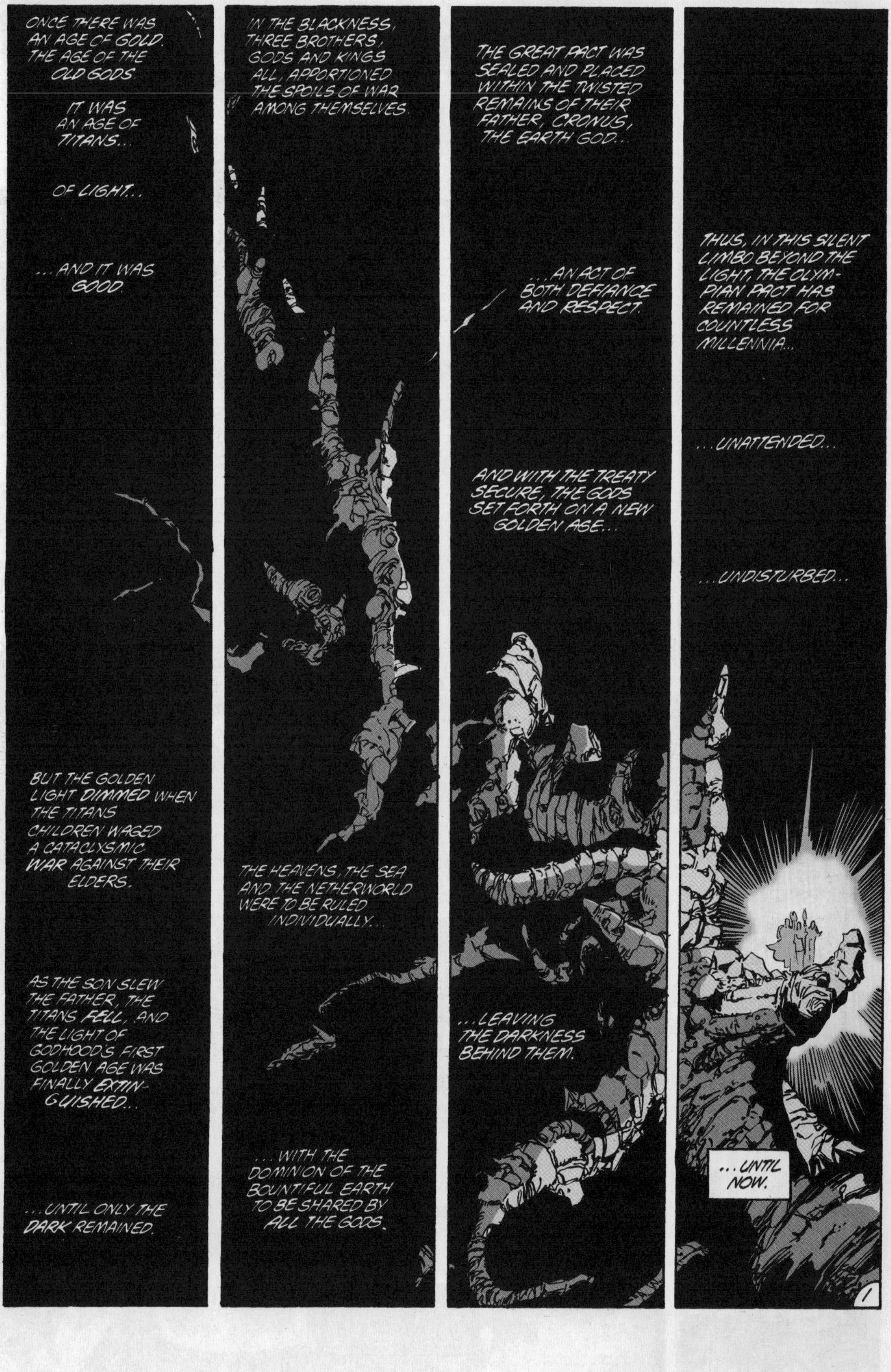
ONCE THERE WAS AN AGE OF GOLD. THE AGE OF THE OLD GODS.
IT WAS AN AGE OF TITANS...
OF LIGHT...
...AND IT WAS GOOD.
BUT THE GOLDEN LIGHT DIMMED WHEN THE TITANS CHILDREN WAGED A CATACLYSMIC WAR AGAINST THEIR ELDERS.
AS THE SON SLEW THE FATHER, THE TITANS FELL, AND THE LIGHT OF GODHOOD'S FIRST GOLDEN AGE WAS FINALLY EXTINGUISHED...
...UNTIL ONLY THE DARK REMAINED.
IN THE BLACKNESS, THREE BROTHERS, GODS AND KINGS ALL, APPORTIONED THE SPOILS OF WAR AMONG THEMSELVES.
THE HEAVENS, THE SEA AND THE NETHERWORLD WERE TO BE RULED INDIVIDUALLY...
...WITH THE DOMINION OF THE BOUNTIFUL EARTH TO BE SHARED BY ALL THE GODS.
THE GREAT PACT WAS SEALED AND PLACED WITHIN THE TWISTED REMAINS OF THEIR FATHER, CRONUS, THE EARTH GOD...
...AN ACT OF BOTH DEFIANCE AND RESPECT.
AND WITH THE TREATY SECURE, THE GODS SET FORTH ON A NEW GOLDEN AGE...
...LEAVING THE DARKNESS BEHIND THEM.
THUS, IN THIS SILENT LIMBO BEYOND THE LIGHT, THE OLYMPIAN PACT HAS REMAINED FOR COUNTLESS MILLENNIA...
...UNATTENDED...
...UNDISTURBED...
...UNTIL NOW.
1

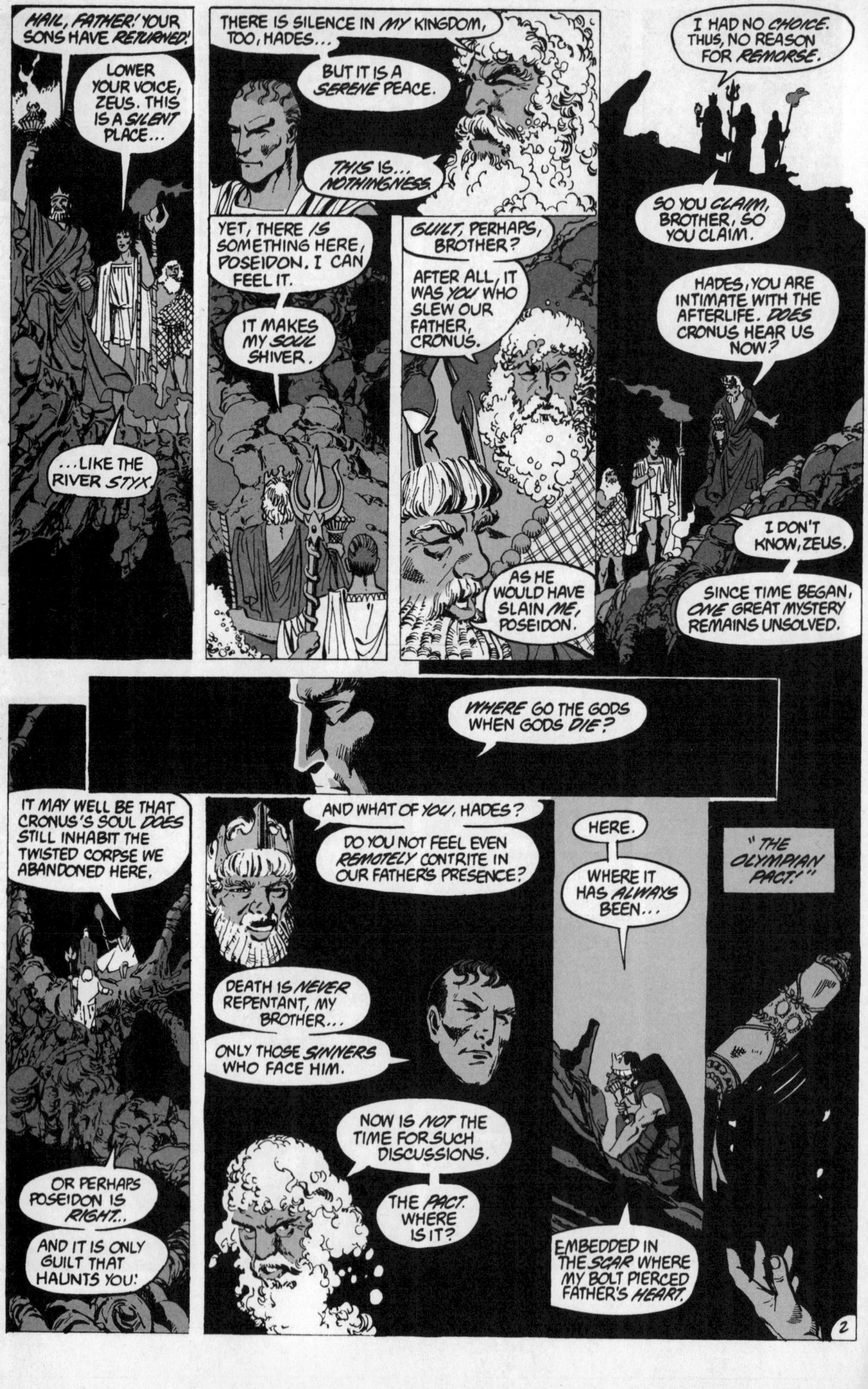
HAIL, FATHER! YOUR SONS HAVE RETURNED!
LOWER YOUR VOICE, ZEUS. THIS IS A SILENT PLACE...
...LIKE THE RIVER STYX.
THERE IS SILENCE IN MY KINGDOM, TOO, HADES...
BUT IT IS A SERENE PEACE.
THIS IS... NOTHINGNESS.
I HAD NO CHOICE. THUS, NO REASON FOR REMORSE.
YET, THERE IS SOMETHING HERE, POSEIDON. I CAN FEEL IT.
IT MAKES MY SOUL SHIVER.
GUILT, PERHAPS, BROTHER?
AFTER ALL, IT WAS YOU WHO SLEW OUR FATHER, CRONUS.
AS HE WOULD HAVE SLAIN ME, POSEIDON.
SO YOU CLAIM, BROTHER, SO YOU CLAIM.
HADES, YOU ARE INTIMATE WITH THE AFTERLIFE. DOES CRONUS HEAR US NOW?
I DON'T KNOW, ZEUS.
SINCE TIME BEGAN, ONE GREAT MYSTERY REMAINS UNSOLVED.
WHERE GO THE GODS WHEN GODS DIE?
IT MAY WELL BE THAT CRONUS'S SOUL DOES STILL INHABIT THE TWISTED CORPSE WE ABANDONED HERE.
OR PERHAPS POSEIDON IS RIGHT...
AND IT IS ONLY GUILT THAT HAUNTS YOU!
AND WHAT OF YOU, HADES?
DO YOU NOT FEEL EVEN REMOTELY CONTRITE IN OUR FATHER'S PRESENCE?
DEATH IS NEVER REPENTANT, MY BROTHER...
ONLY THOSE SINNERS WHO FACE HIM.
NOW IS NOT THE TIME FOR SUCH DISCUSSIONS.
THE PACT. WHERE IS IT?
HERE.
WHERE IT HAS ALWAYS BEEN...
EMBEDDED IN THE SCAR WHERE MY BOLT PIERCED FATHER'S HEART.
"THE OLYMPIAN PACT!"
2

IT SEEMS TO HAVE LOST SOME OF ITS LUSTER.

AS HAS OLYMPUS.

WE KNOW NOW THAT THE GODS ARE NOT MEANT TO BE DIVIDED...

BUT TO RULE JOINTLY, EQUALLY, OVER A UNITED PANTHEON.

IT TOOK A MORTAL GIRL TO MAKE ME SEE THAT.

PRINCESS DIANA HAS PROVED HERSELF NO MERE MORTAL, BROTHER ZEUS.

SHE HAS EARNED THE APPELLATION THE HUMANS HAVE BESTOWED ON HER.

SHE IS A WONDER WOMAN.

AYE. I KNEW IT FROM THE START.

WHEN I CLEARED THEIR PATH TO THEMYSCIRA, I COULD SEE THAT THE AMAZONS WERE DESTINED FOR GREATNESS.

SO YOU CLAIM, BROTHER, SO YOU CLAIM.

BUT NOW, LET US PROCEED...

...SO THAT WE MAY FORM A NEW OLYMPUS.

AND SO, AS IT WAS COUNTLESS MILLENNIA AGO, THREE BROTHERS, GODS AND KINGS ALL, GATHER IN THE BLACKNESS TO SEAL A HOLY PACT.

POSEIDON, LORD OF THE SEAS, RAISES HIS ROYAL TRIDENT, PRESENTED TO HIM BY HIS WIFE AMPHITRITE...

AS HADES, RULER OF THE UNDERWORLD, ELEVATES HIS STAFF OF REWARD AND PUNISHMENT, CARVED FROM THE TOOTH OF THE GUARDHOUND CERBERUS...

AND ZEUS, MIGHTY MONARCH OF THE HEAVENS, UPLIFTS HIS SCEPTER OF LIGHTNING, FORGED BY HIS BLACKSMITH SON, HEPHAESTUS.

THE GREAT SYMBOLS OF POWER CROSS, JOINING FOR THE FIRST TIME.

A FIRE BURSTS FORTH FROM THE AXIS...

...BURNING AWAY THE OLD...

...AND SEALING THE NEW.

THE DARK GIVES WAY TO A GOLDEN LIGHT...

..AND IT IS GOOD.

3

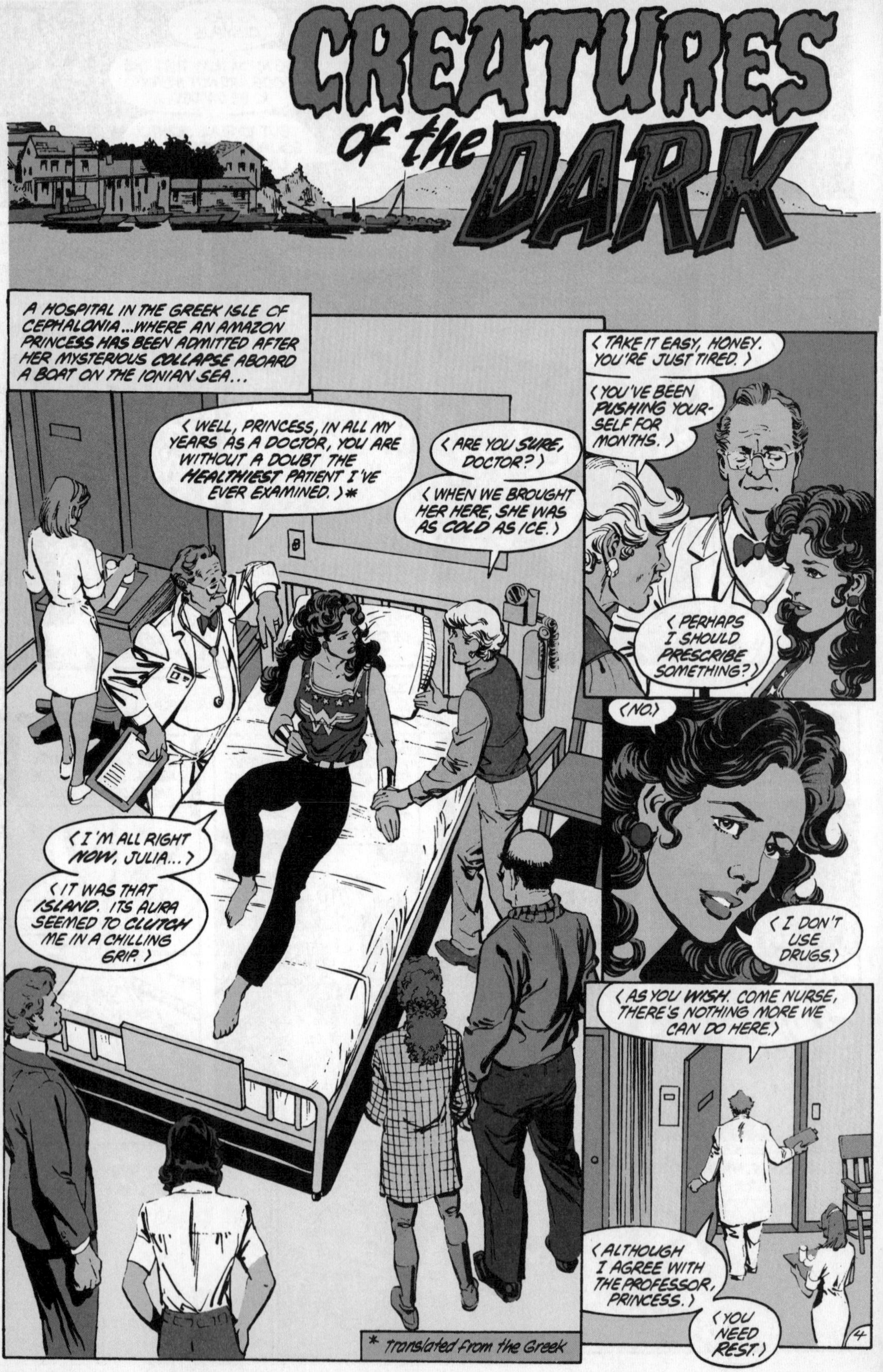
CREATURES of the DARK
A HOSPITAL IN THE GREEK ISLE OF CEPHALONIA...WHERE AN AMAZON PRINCESS HAS BEEN ADMITTED AFTER HER MYSTERIOUS COLLAPSE ABOARD A BOAT ON THE IONIAN SEA...
‹ WELL, PRINCESS, IN ALL MY YEARS AS A DOCTOR, YOU ARE WITHOUT A DOUBT THE HEALTHIEST PATIENT I'VE EVER EXAMINED. ›*
‹ ARE YOU SURE, DOCTOR? ›
‹ WHEN WE BROUGHT HER HERE, SHE WAS AS COLD AS ICE. ›
‹ I'M ALL RIGHT NOW, JULIA... ›
‹ IT WAS THAT ISLAND. ITS AURA SEEMED TO CLUTCH ME IN A CHILLING GRIP. ›
* Translated from the Greek
‹ TAKE IT EASY, HONEY. YOU'RE JUST TIRED. ›
‹ YOU'VE BEEN PUSHING YOURSELF FOR MONTHS. ›
‹ PERHAPS I SHOULD PRESCRIBE SOMETHING? ›
‹NO.›
‹ I DON'T USE DRUGS. ›
‹ AS YOU WISH. COME NURSE, THERE'S NOTHING MORE WE CAN DO HERE. ›
‹ ALTHOUGH I AGREE WITH THE PROFESSOR, PRINCESS. ›
‹ YOU NEED REST. ›
4

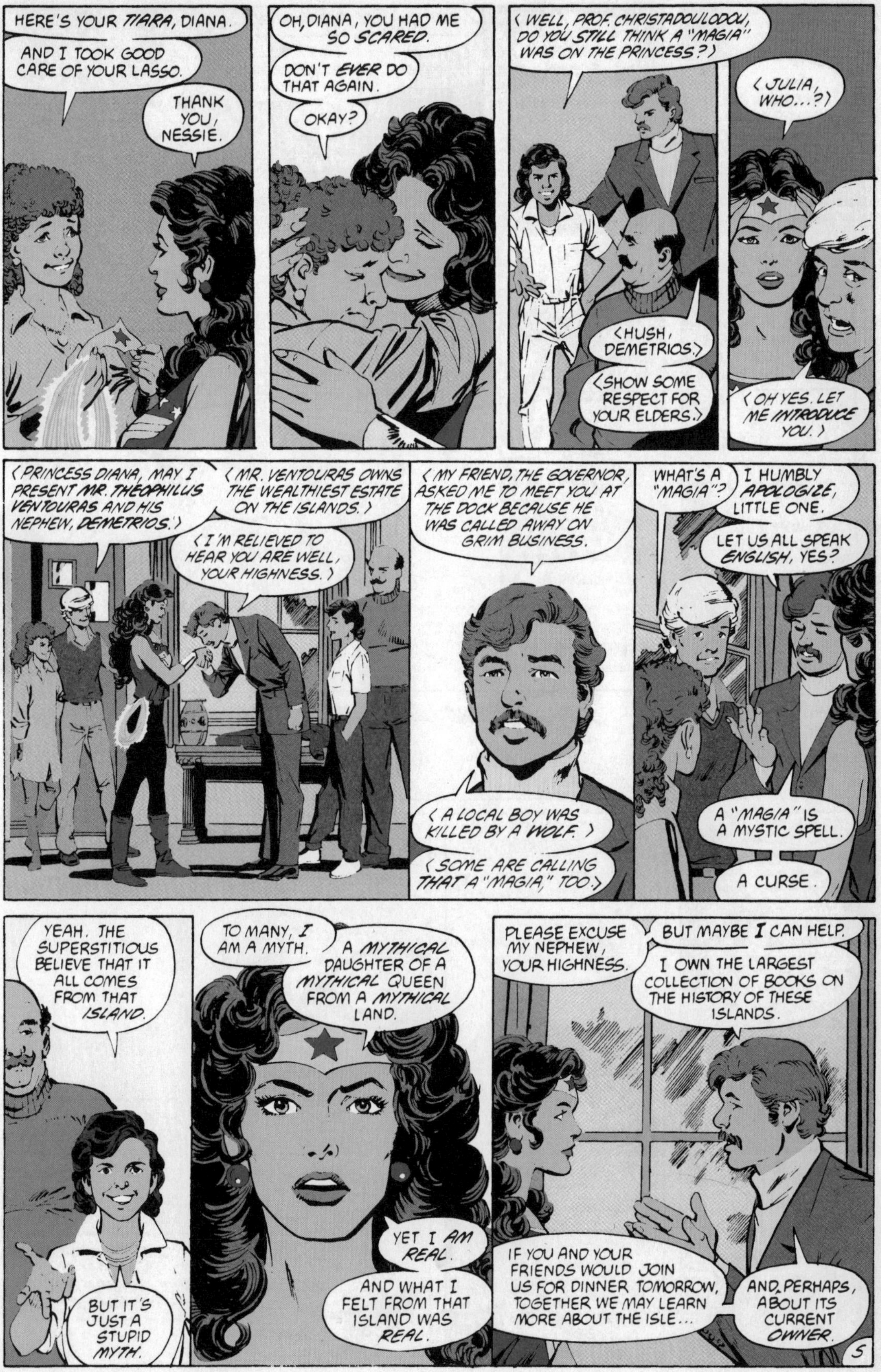
HERE'S YOUR TIARA, DIANA.
AND I TOOK GOOD CARE OF YOUR LASSO.
THANK YOU, NESSIE.
OH, DIANA, YOU HAD ME SO SCARED.
DON'T EVER DO THAT AGAIN.
OKAY?
<WELL, PROF. CHRISTADOULODOU, DO YOU STILL THINK A "MAGIA" WAS ON THE PRINCESS?>
<HUSH, DEMETRIOS.>
<SHOW SOME RESPECT FOR YOUR ELDERS.>
<JULIA, WHO...?>
<OH YES. LET ME INTRODUCE YOU.>
<PRINCESS DIANA, MAY I PRESENT MR. THEOPHILUS VENTOURAS AND HIS NEPHEW, DEMETRIOS.>
<MR. VENTOURAS OWNS THE WEALTHIEST ESTATE ON THE ISLANDS.>
<I'M RELIEVED TO HEAR YOU ARE WELL, YOUR HIGHNESS.>
<MY FRIEND, THE GOVERNOR, ASKED ME TO MEET YOU AT THE DOCK BECAUSE HE WAS CALLED AWAY ON GRIM BUSINESS.
<A LOCAL BOY WAS KILLED BY A WOLF.>
<SOME ARE CALLING THAT A "MAGIA," TOO.>
WHAT'S A "MAGIA"?
I HUMBLY APOLOGIZE, LITTLE ONE.
LET US ALL SPEAK ENGLISH, YES?
A "MAGIA" IS A MYSTIC SPELL.
A CURSE.
YEAH. THE SUPERSTITIOUS BELIEVE THAT IT ALL COMES FROM THAT ISLAND.
BUT IT'S JUST A STUPID MYTH.
TO MANY, I AM A MYTH.
A MYTHICAL DAUGHTER OF A MYTHICAL QUEEN FROM A MYTHICAL LAND.
YET I AM REAL.
AND WHAT I FELT FROM THAT ISLAND WAS REAL.
PLEASE EXCUSE MY NEPHEW, YOUR HIGHNESS.
BUT MAYBE I CAN HELP.
I OWN THE LARGEST COLLECTION OF BOOKS ON THE HISTORY OF THESE ISLANDS.
IF YOU AND YOUR FRIENDS WOULD JOIN US FOR DINNER TOMORROW, TOGETHER WE MAY LEARN MORE ABOUT THE ISLE...
AND, PERHAPS, ABOUT ITS CURRENT OWNER.
5

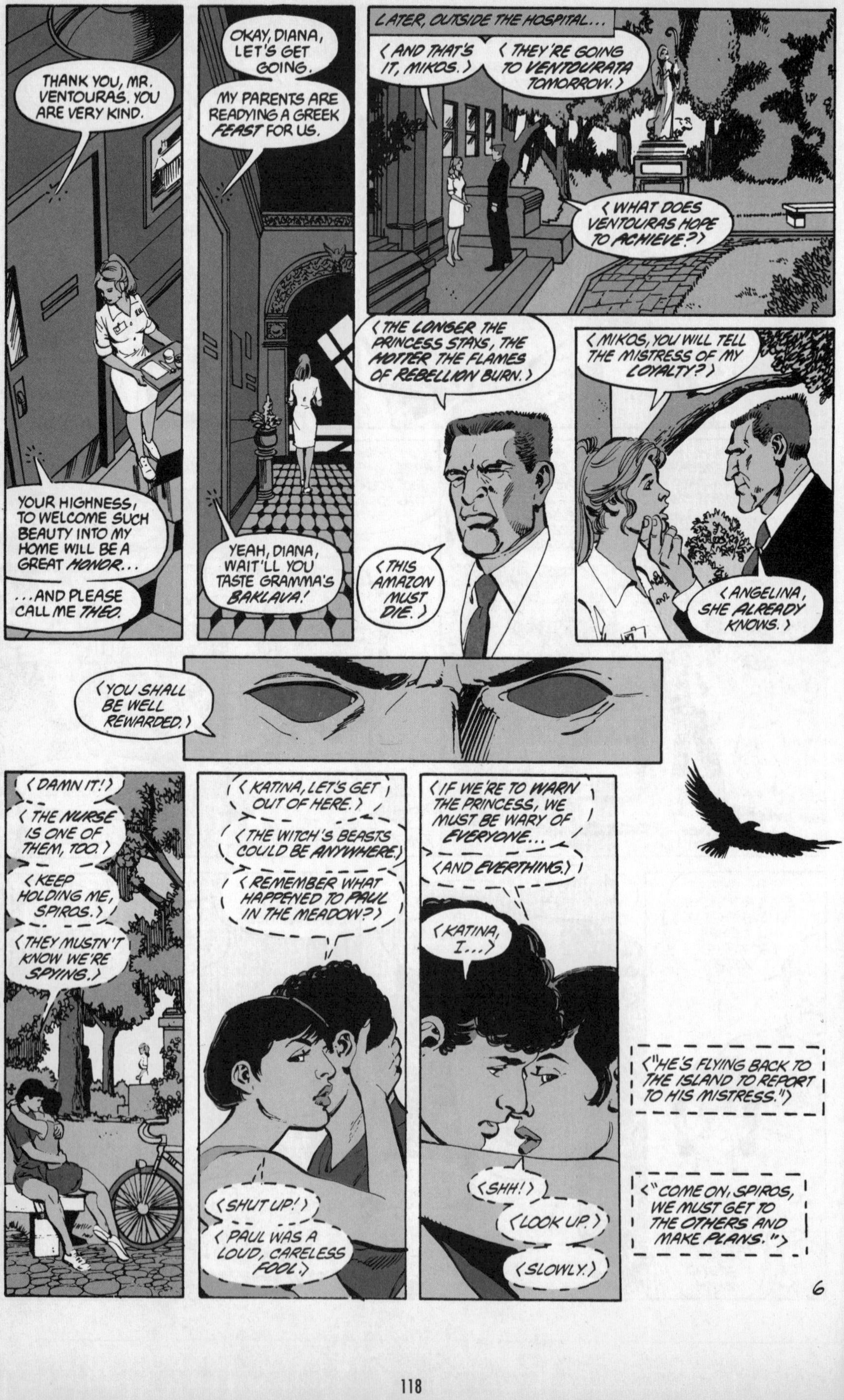

THANK YOU, MR. VENTOURAS. YOU ARE VERY KIND.
YOUR HIGHNESS, TO WELCOME SUCH BEAUTY INTO MY HOME WILL BE A GREAT HONOR...
...AND PLEASE CALL ME THEO.
OKAY, DIANA, LET'S GET GOING.
MY PARENTS ARE READYING A GREEK FEAST FOR US.
YEAH, DIANA, WAIT'LL YOU TASTE GRAMMA'S BAKLAVA!
LATER, OUTSIDE THE HOSPITAL...
⟨AND THAT'S IT, MIKOS.⟩
⟨THEY'RE GOING TO VENTOURATA TOMORROW.⟩
⟨WHAT DOES VENTOURAS HOPE TO ACHIEVE?⟩
⟨THE LONGER THE PRINCESS STAYS, THE HOTTER THE FLAMES OF REBELLION BURN.⟩
⟨THIS AMAZON MUST DIE.⟩
⟨MIKOS, YOU WILL TELL THE MISTRESS OF MY LOYALTY?⟩
⟨ANGELINA, SHE ALREADY KNOWS.⟩
⟨YOU SHALL BE WELL REWARDED.⟩
⟨DAMN IT!⟩
⟨THE NURSE IS ONE OF THEM, TOO.⟩
⟨KEEP HOLDING ME, SPIROS.⟩
⟨THEY MUSTN'T KNOW WE'RE SPYING.⟩
⟨KATINA, LET'S GET OUT OF HERE.⟩
⟨THE WITCH'S BEASTS COULD BE ANYWHERE.⟩
⟨REMEMBER WHAT HAPPENED TO PAUL IN THE MEADOW?⟩
⟨SHUT UP!⟩
⟨PAUL WAS A LOUD, CARELESS FOOL.⟩
⟨IF WE'RE TO WARN THE PRINCESS, WE MUST BE WARY OF EVERYONE...
⟨AND EVERTHING.⟩
⟨KATINA, I...⟩
⟨SHH!⟩
⟨LOOK UP.⟩
⟨SLOWLY.⟩
⟨"HE'S FLYING BACK TO THE ISLAND TO REPORT TO HIS MISTRESS."⟩
⟨"COME ON, SPIROS, WE MUST GET TO THE OTHERS AND MAKE PLANS."⟩
6

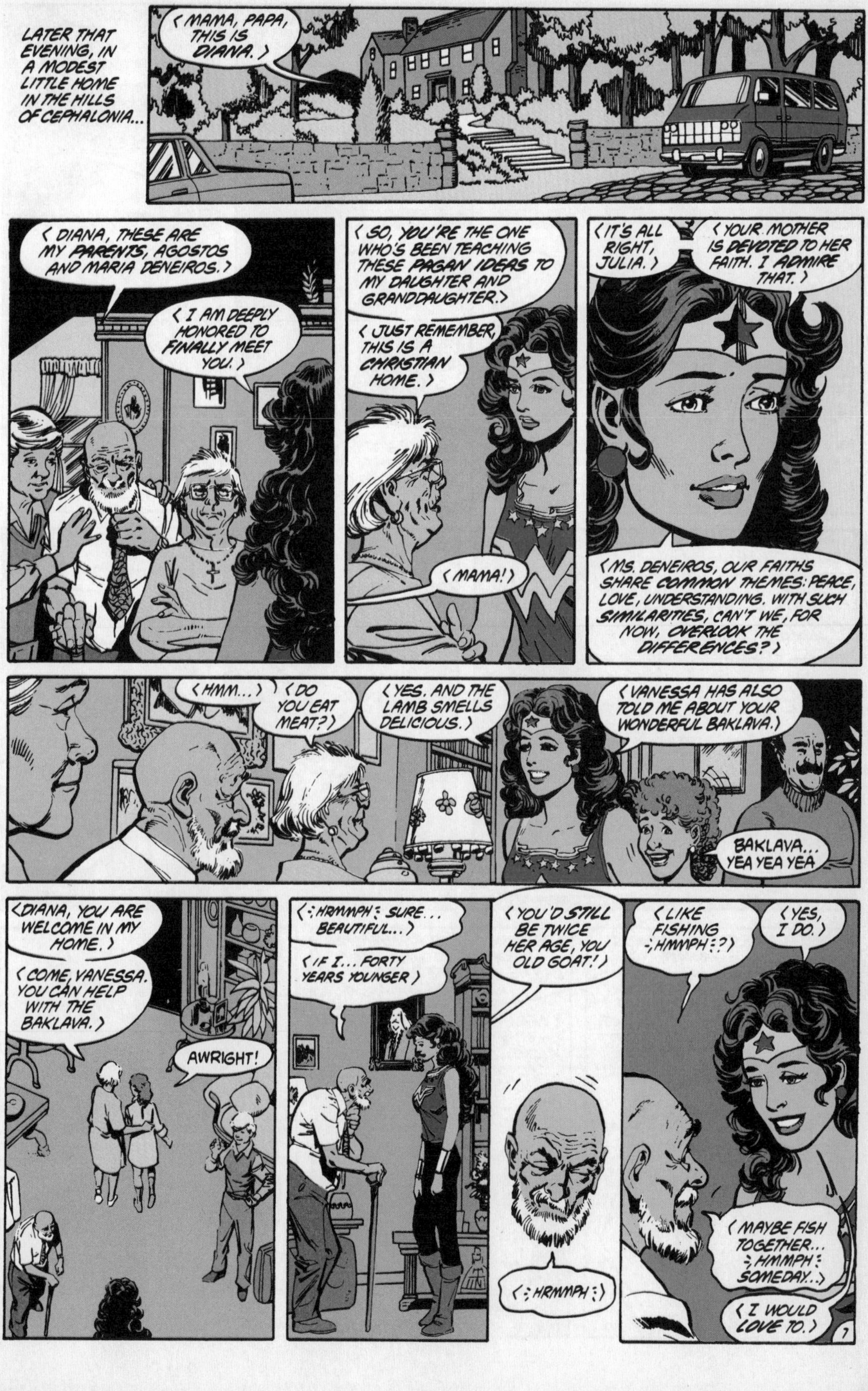
LATER THAT EVENING, IN A MODEST LITTLE HOME IN THE HILLS OF CEPHALONIA...
‹ MAMA, PAPA, THIS IS DIANA. ›
‹ DIANA, THESE ARE MY PARENTS, AGOSTOS AND MARIA DENEIROS. ›
‹ I AM DEEPLY HONORED TO FINALLY MEET YOU. ›
‹ SO, YOU'RE THE ONE WHO'S BEEN TEACHING THESE PAGAN IDEAS TO MY DAUGHTER AND GRANDDAUGHTER. ›
‹ JUST REMEMBER, THIS IS A CHRISTIAN HOME. ›
‹ MAMA! ›
‹ IT'S ALL RIGHT, JULIA. ›
‹ YOUR MOTHER IS DEVOTED TO HER FAITH. I ADMIRE THAT. ›
‹ MS. DENEIROS, OUR FAITHS SHARE COMMON THEMES: PEACE, LOVE, UNDERSTANDING. WITH SUCH SIMILARITIES, CAN'T WE, FOR NOW, OVERLOOK THE DIFFERENCES? ›
‹ HMM... ›
‹ DO YOU EAT MEAT? ›
‹ YES. AND THE LAMB SMELLS DELICIOUS. ›
‹ VANESSA HAS ALSO TOLD ME ABOUT YOUR WONDERFUL BAKLAVA. ›
BAKLAVA... YEA YEA YEA
‹ DIANA, YOU ARE WELCOME IN MY HOME. ›
‹ COME, VANESSA. YOU CAN HELP WITH THE BAKLAVA. ›
AWRIGHT!
‹ :HRMMPH: SURE... BEAUTIFUL... ›
‹ IF I... FORTY YEARS YOUNGER ›
‹ YOU'D STILL BE TWICE HER AGE, YOU OLD GOAT! ›
‹ :HRMMPH: ›
‹ LIKE FISHING :HMMPH:? ›
‹ YES, I DO. ›
‹ MAYBE FISH TOGETHER... :HMMPH: SOMEDAY... ›
‹ I WOULD LOVE TO. ›
7

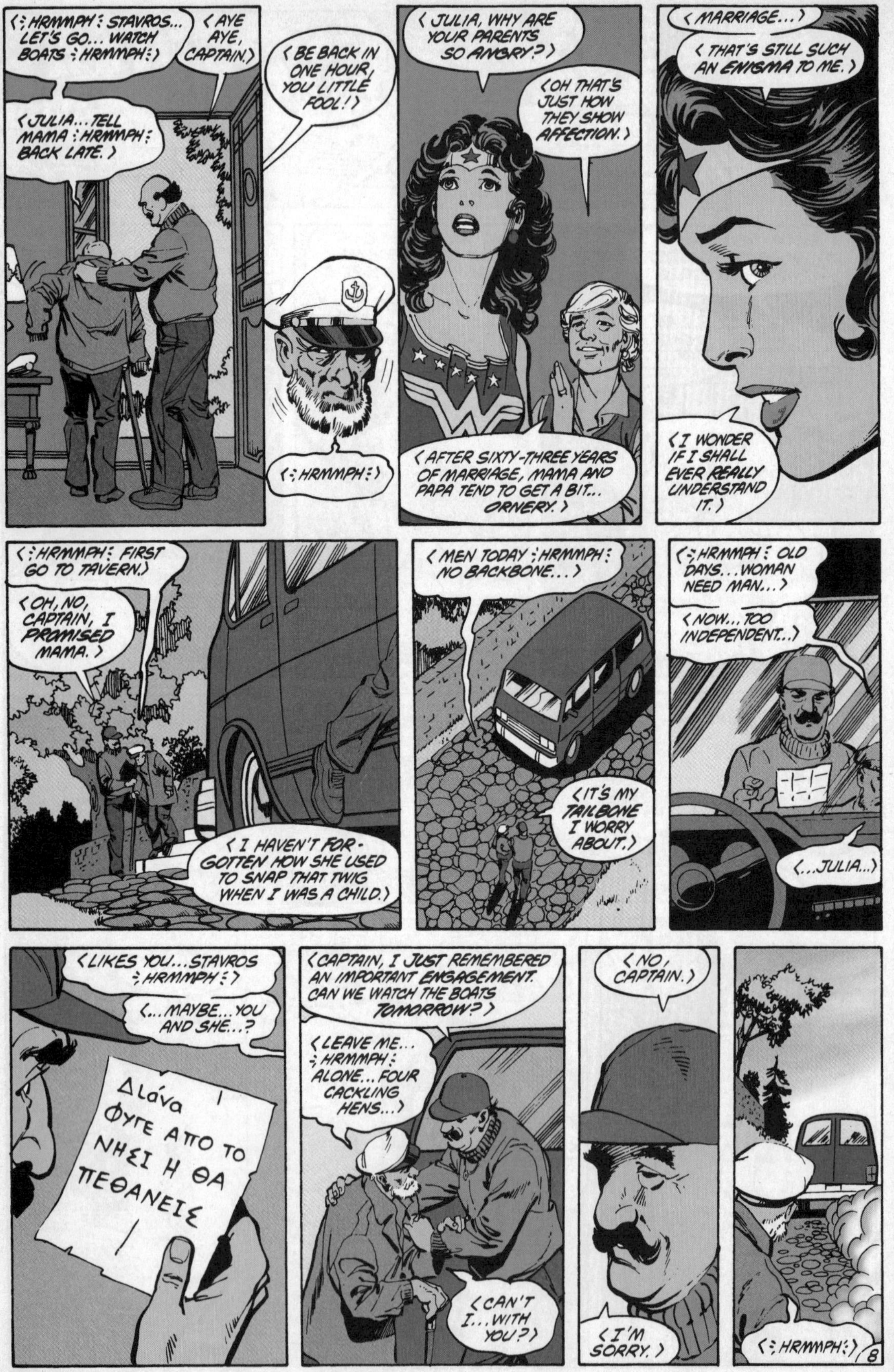
<:HRMMPH: STAVROS... LET'S GO... WATCH BOATS :HRMMPH:>
<AYE AYE, CAPTAIN.>
<JULIA... TELL MAMA :HRMMPH: BACK LATE.>
<BE BACK IN ONE HOUR, YOU LITTLE FOOL!>
<:HRMMPH:>
<JULIA, WHY ARE YOUR PARENTS SO ANGRY?>
<OH THAT'S JUST HOW THEY SHOW AFFECTION.>
<AFTER SIXTY-THREE YEARS OF MARRIAGE, MAMA AND PAPA TEND TO GET A BIT... ORNERY.>
<MARRIAGE...>
<THAT'S STILL SUCH AN ENIGMA TO ME.>
<I WONDER IF I SHALL EVER REALLY UNDERSTAND IT.>
<:HRMMPH: FIRST GO TO TAVERN.>
<OH, NO, CAPTAIN, I PROMISED MAMA.>
<I HAVEN'T FORGOTTEN HOW SHE USED TO SNAP THAT TWIG WHEN I WAS A CHILD.>
<MEN TODAY :HRMMPH: NO BACKBONE...>
<IT'S MY TAILBONE I WORRY ABOUT.>
<:HRMMPH: OLD DAYS... WOMAN NEED MAN...>
<NOW... TOO INDEPENDENT...>
<...JULIA...>
<LIKES YOU... STAVROS :HRMMPH:>
<...MAYBE... YOU AND SHE...?>
Διάνα ΦΥΓΕ ΑΠΟ ΤΟ ΝΗΣΙ Η ΘΑ ΠΕΘΑΝΕΙΣ
<CAPTAIN, I JUST REMEMBERED AN IMPORTANT ENGAGEMENT. CAN WE WATCH THE BOATS TOMORROW?>
<LEAVE ME... :HRMMPH: ALONE... FOUR CACKLING HENS...>
<CAN'T I... WITH YOU?>
<NO, CAPTAIN.>
<I'M SORRY.>
<:HRMMPH:>
8

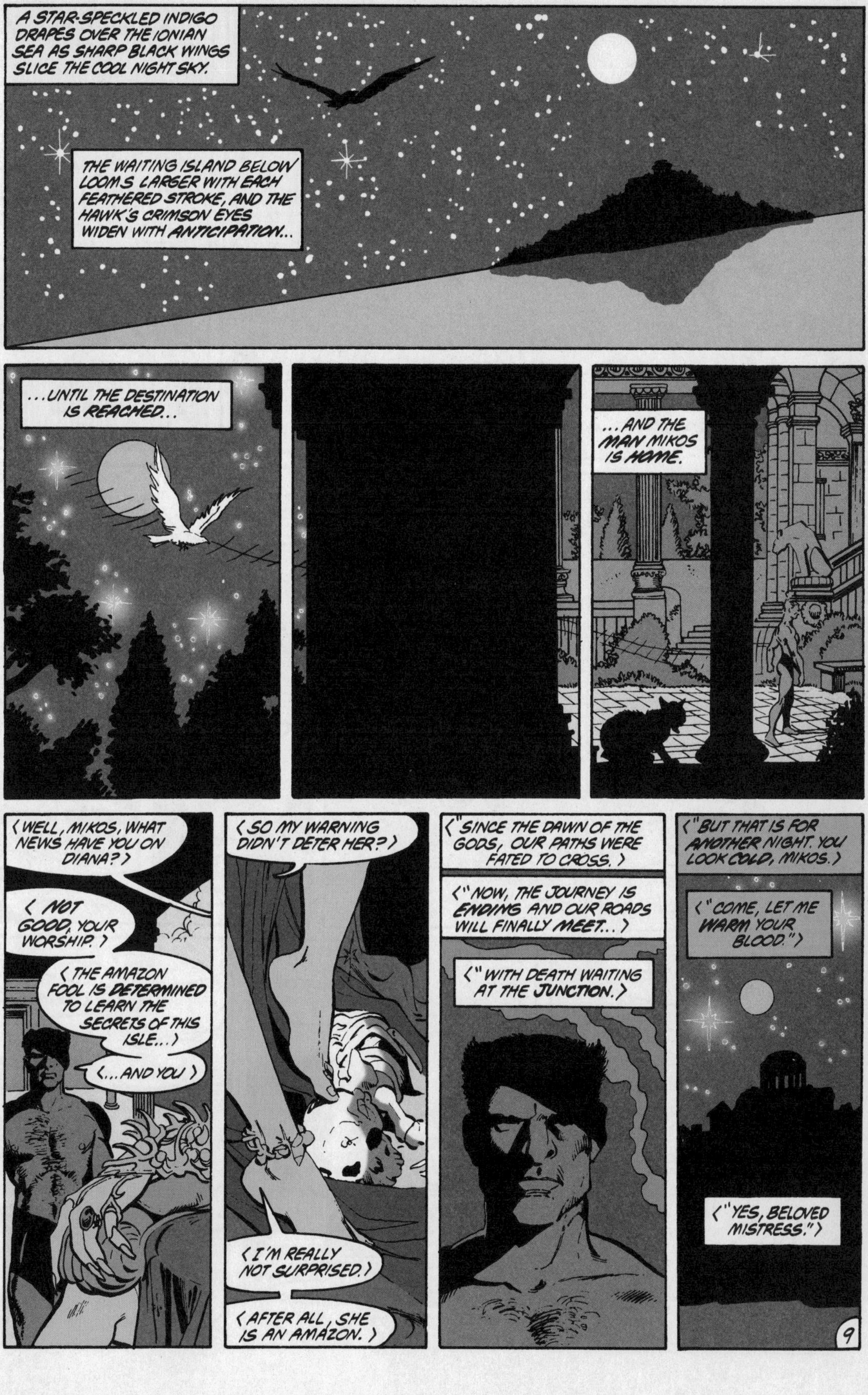
A STAR-SPECKLED INDIGO DRAPES OVER THE IONIAN SEA AS SHARP BLACK WINGS SLICE THE COOL NIGHT SKY.
THE WAITING ISLAND BELOW LOOMS LARGER WITH EACH FEATHERED STROKE, AND THE HAWK'S CRIMSON EYES WIDEN WITH ANTICIPATION...
...UNTIL THE DESTINATION IS REACHED...
...AND THE MAN MIKOS IS HOME.
⟨WELL, MIKOS, WHAT NEWS HAVE YOU ON DIANA?⟩
⟨NOT GOOD, YOUR WORSHIP.⟩
⟨THE AMAZON FOOL IS DETERMINED TO LEARN THE SECRETS OF THIS ISLE...⟩
⟨...AND YOU⟩
⟨SO MY WARNING DIDN'T DETER HER?⟩
⟨I'M REALLY NOT SURPRISED.⟩
⟨AFTER ALL, SHE IS AN AMAZON.⟩
⟨"SINCE THE DAWN OF THE GODS, OUR PATHS WERE FATED TO CROSS.⟩
⟨"NOW, THE JOURNEY IS ENDING AND OUR ROADS WILL FINALLY MEET...⟩
⟨"WITH DEATH WAITING AT THE JUNCTION.⟩
⟨"BUT THAT IS FOR ANOTHER NIGHT. YOU LOOK COLD, MIKOS.⟩
⟨"COME, LET ME WARM YOUR BLOOD."⟩
⟨"YES, BELOVED MISTRESS."⟩
9

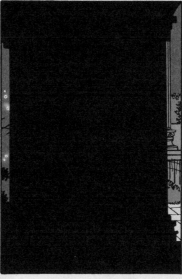

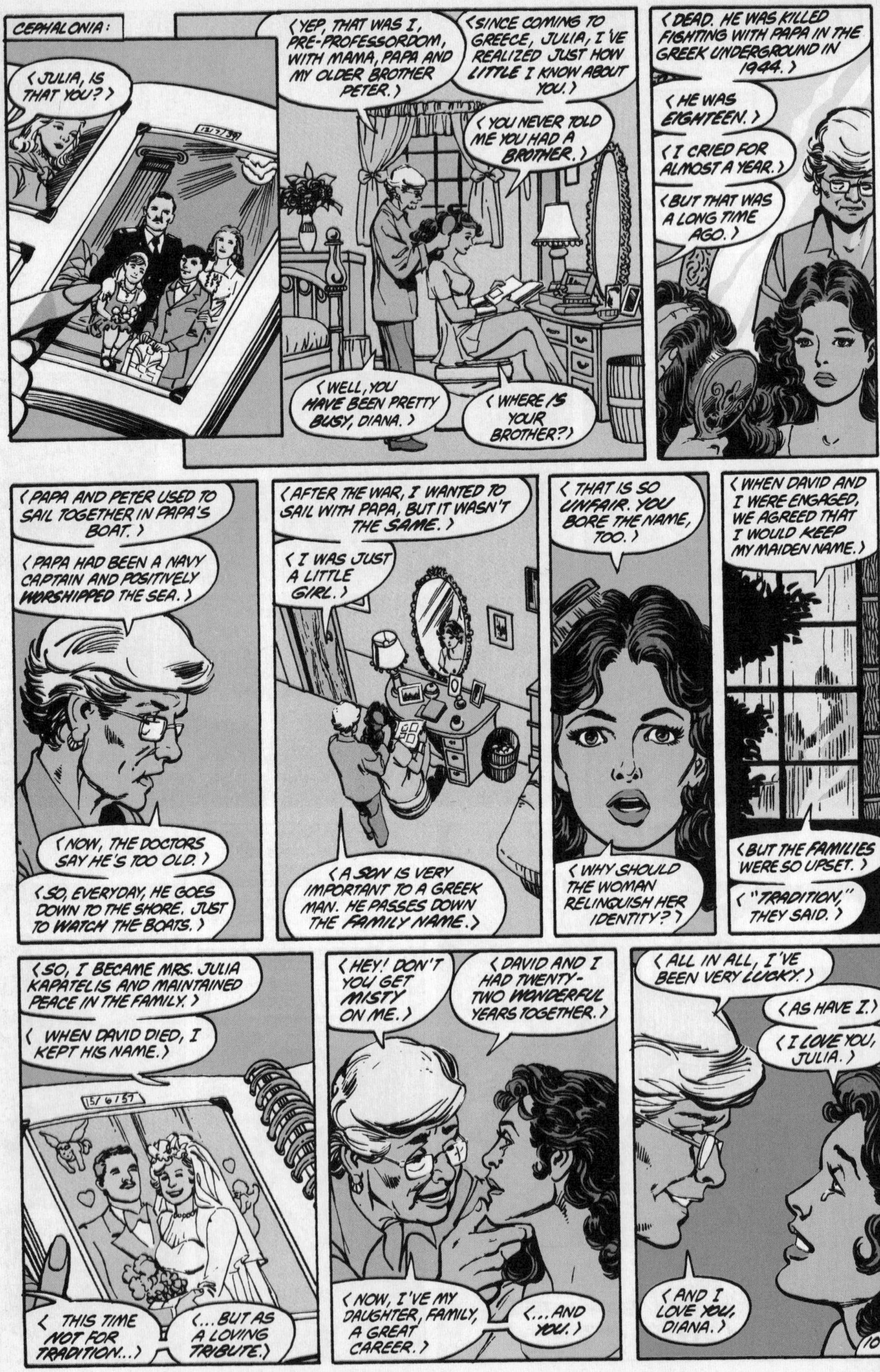
CEPHALONIA:
⟨JULIA, IS THAT YOU?⟩
12/7/38
⟨YEP, THAT WAS I, PRE-PROFESSORDOM, WITH MAMA, PAPA AND MY OLDER BROTHER PETER.⟩
⟨SINCE COMING TO GREECE, JULIA, I'VE REALIZED JUST HOW LITTLE I KNOW ABOUT YOU.⟩
⟨YOU NEVER TOLD ME YOU HAD A BROTHER.⟩
⟨WELL, YOU HAVE BEEN PRETTY BUSY, DIANA.⟩
⟨WHERE IS YOUR BROTHER?⟩
⟨DEAD. HE WAS KILLED FIGHTING WITH PAPA IN THE GREEK UNDERGROUND IN 1944.⟩
⟨HE WAS EIGHTEEN.⟩
⟨I CRIED FOR ALMOST A YEAR.⟩
⟨BUT THAT WAS A LONG TIME AGO.⟩
⟨PAPA AND PETER USED TO SAIL TOGETHER IN PAPA'S BOAT.⟩
⟨PAPA HAD BEEN A NAVY CAPTAIN AND POSITIVELY WORSHIPPED THE SEA.⟩
⟨NOW, THE DOCTORS SAY HE'S TOO OLD.⟩
⟨SO, EVERYDAY, HE GOES DOWN TO THE SHORE. JUST TO WATCH THE BOATS.⟩
⟨AFTER THE WAR, I WANTED TO SAIL WITH PAPA, BUT IT WASN'T THE SAME.⟩
⟨I WAS JUST A LITTLE GIRL.⟩
⟨A SON IS VERY IMPORTANT TO A GREEK MAN. HE PASSES DOWN THE FAMILY NAME.⟩
⟨THAT IS SO UNFAIR. YOU BORE THE NAME, TOO.⟩
⟨WHY SHOULD THE WOMAN RELINQUISH HER IDENTITY?⟩
⟨WHEN DAVID AND I WERE ENGAGED, WE AGREED THAT I WOULD KEEP MY MAIDEN NAME.⟩
⟨BUT THE FAMILIES WERE SO UPSET.⟩
⟨"TRADITION," THEY SAID.⟩
⟨SO, I BECAME MRS. JULIA KAPATELIS AND MAINTAINED PEACE IN THE FAMILY.⟩
⟨WHEN DAVID DIED, I KEPT HIS NAME.⟩
15/6/57
⟨THIS TIME NOT FOR TRADITION...⟩
⟨...BUT AS A LOVING TRIBUTE.⟩
⟨HEY! DON'T YOU GET MISTY ON ME.⟩
⟨DAVID AND I HAD TWENTY-TWO WONDERFUL YEARS TOGETHER.⟩
⟨NOW, I'VE MY DAUGHTER, FAMILY, A GREAT CAREER.⟩
⟨...AND YOU.⟩
⟨ALL IN ALL, I'VE BEEN VERY LUCKY.⟩
⟨AS HAVE I.⟩
⟨I LOVE YOU, JULIA.⟩
⟨AND I LOVE YOU, DIANA.⟩
10

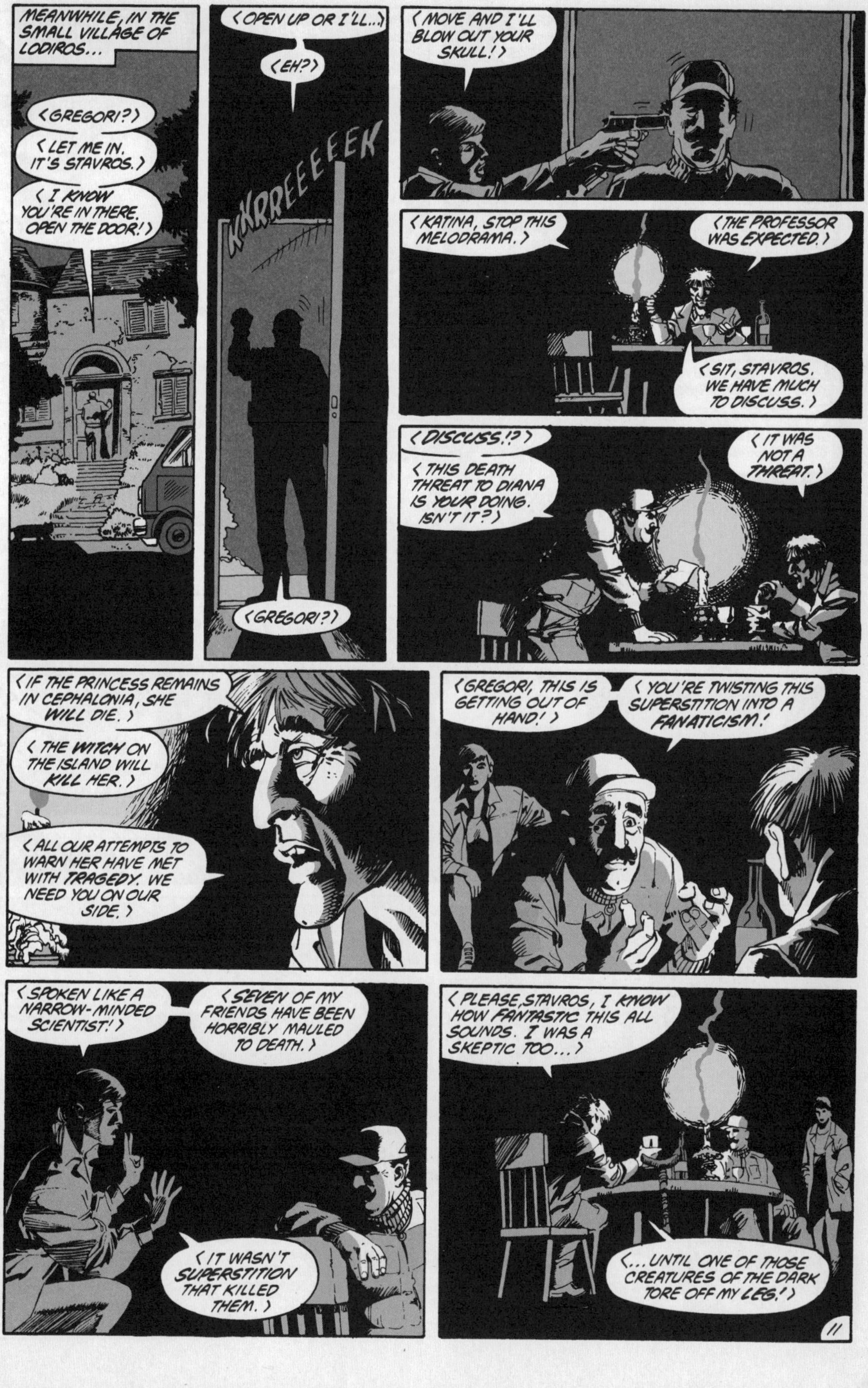
MEANWHILE, IN THE SMALL VILLAGE OF LODIROS...
<GREGORI?>
<LET ME IN. IT'S STAVROS.>
<I KNOW YOU'RE IN THERE. OPEN THE DOOR!>
<OPEN UP OR I'LL...>
<EH?>
KKRREEEEEEK
<GREGORI?>
<MOVE AND I'LL BLOW OUT YOUR SKULL!>
<KATINA, STOP THIS MELODRAMA.>
<THE PROFESSOR WAS EXPECTED.>
<SIT, STAVROS. WE HAVE MUCH TO DISCUSS.>
<DISCUSS!?>
<THIS DEATH THREAT TO DIANA IS YOUR DOING. ISN'T IT?>
<IT WAS NOT A THREAT.>
<IF THE PRINCESS REMAINS IN CEPHALONIA, SHE WILL DIE.>
<THE WITCH ON THE ISLAND WILL KILL HER.>
<ALL OUR ATTEMPTS TO WARN HER HAVE MET WITH TRAGEDY. WE NEED YOU ON OUR SIDE.>
<GREGORI, THIS IS GETTING OUT OF HAND!>
<YOU'RE TWISTING THIS SUPERSTITION INTO A FANATICISM!>
<SPOKEN LIKE A NARROW-MINDED SCIENTIST!>
<SEVEN OF MY FRIENDS HAVE BEEN HORRIBLY MAULED TO DEATH.>
<IT WASN'T SUPERSTITION THAT KILLED THEM.>
<PLEASE, STAVROS, I KNOW HOW FANTASTIC THIS ALL SOUNDS. I WAS A SKEPTIC TOO...>
<...UNTIL ONE OF THOSE CREATURES OF THE DARK TORE OFF MY LEGS!>
11

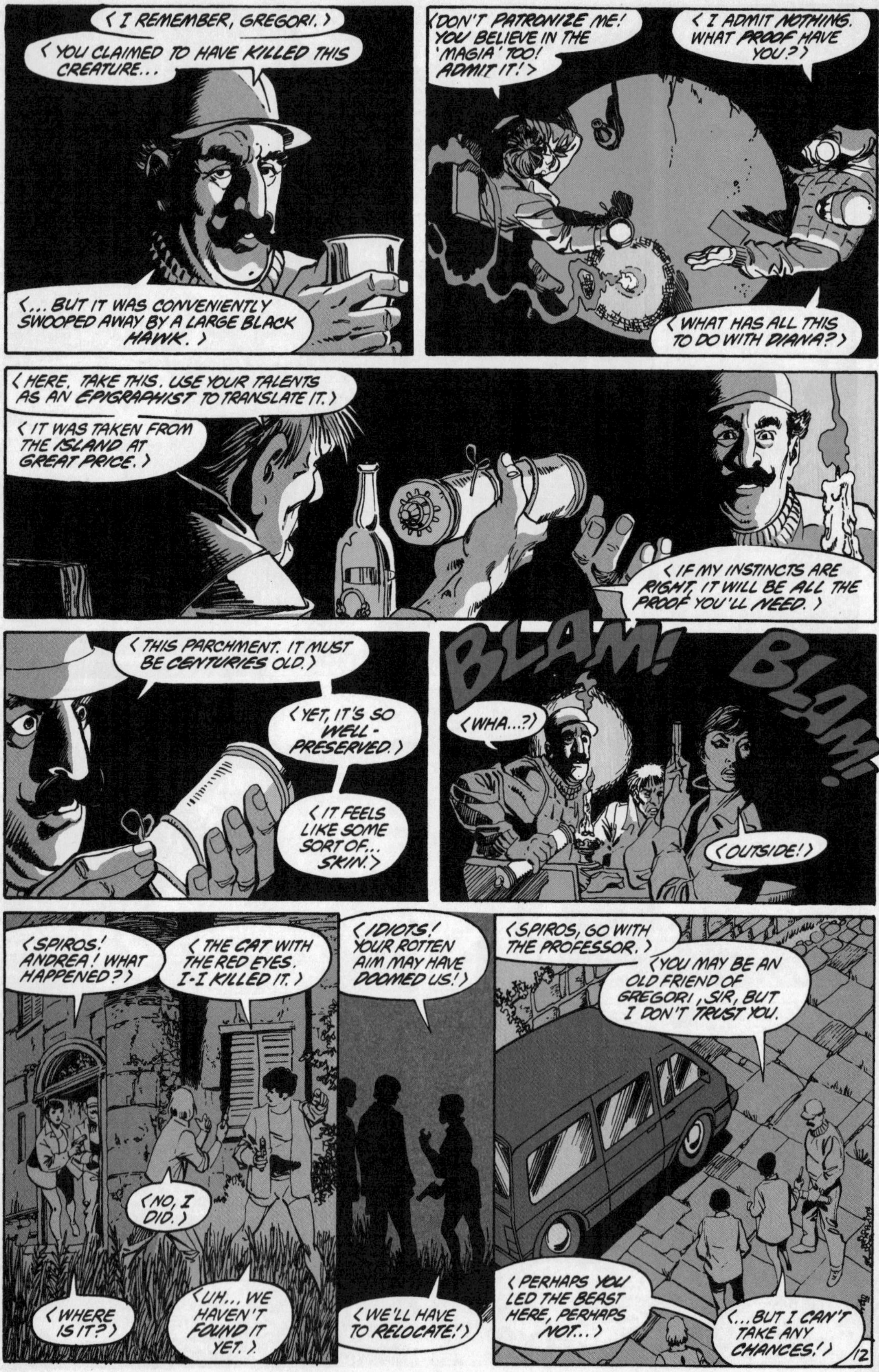
⟨I REMEMBER, GREGORI.⟩
⟨YOU CLAIMED TO HAVE KILLED THIS CREATURE...
⟨...BUT IT WAS CONVENIENTLY SWOOPED AWAY BY A LARGE BLACK HAWK.⟩
⟨DON'T PATRONIZE ME! YOU BELIEVE IN THE 'MAGIA' TOO! ADMIT IT!⟩
⟨I ADMIT NOTHING. WHAT PROOF HAVE YOU?⟩
⟨WHAT HAS ALL THIS TO DO WITH DIANA?⟩
⟨HERE, TAKE THIS. USE YOUR TALENTS AS AN EPIGRAPHIST TO TRANSLATE IT.⟩
⟨IT WAS TAKEN FROM THE ISLAND AT GREAT PRICE.⟩
⟨IF MY INSTINCTS ARE RIGHT, IT WILL BE ALL THE PROOF YOU'LL NEED.⟩
⟨THIS PARCHMENT. IT MUST BE CENTURIES OLD.⟩
⟨YET, IT'S SO WELL-PRESERVED.⟩
⟨IT FEELS LIKE SOME SORT OF... SKIN.⟩
BLAM!
BLAM!
⟨WHA...?⟩
⟨OUTSIDE!⟩
⟨SPIROS! ANDREA! WHAT HAPPENED?⟩
⟨THE CAT WITH THE RED EYES. I-I KILLED IT.⟩
⟨NO, I DID.⟩
⟨WHERE IS IT?⟩
⟨UH... WE HAVEN'T FOUND IT YET.⟩
⟨IDIOTS! YOUR ROTTEN AIM MAY HAVE DOOMED US!⟩
⟨WE'LL HAVE TO RELOCATE!⟩
⟨SPIROS, GO WITH THE PROFESSOR.⟩
⟨YOU MAY BE AN OLD FRIEND OF GREGORI, SIR, BUT I DON'T TRUST YOU.
⟨PERHAPS YOU LED THE BEAST HERE, PERHAPS NOT...⟩
⟨...BUT I CAN'T TAKE ANY CHANCES!⟩
12

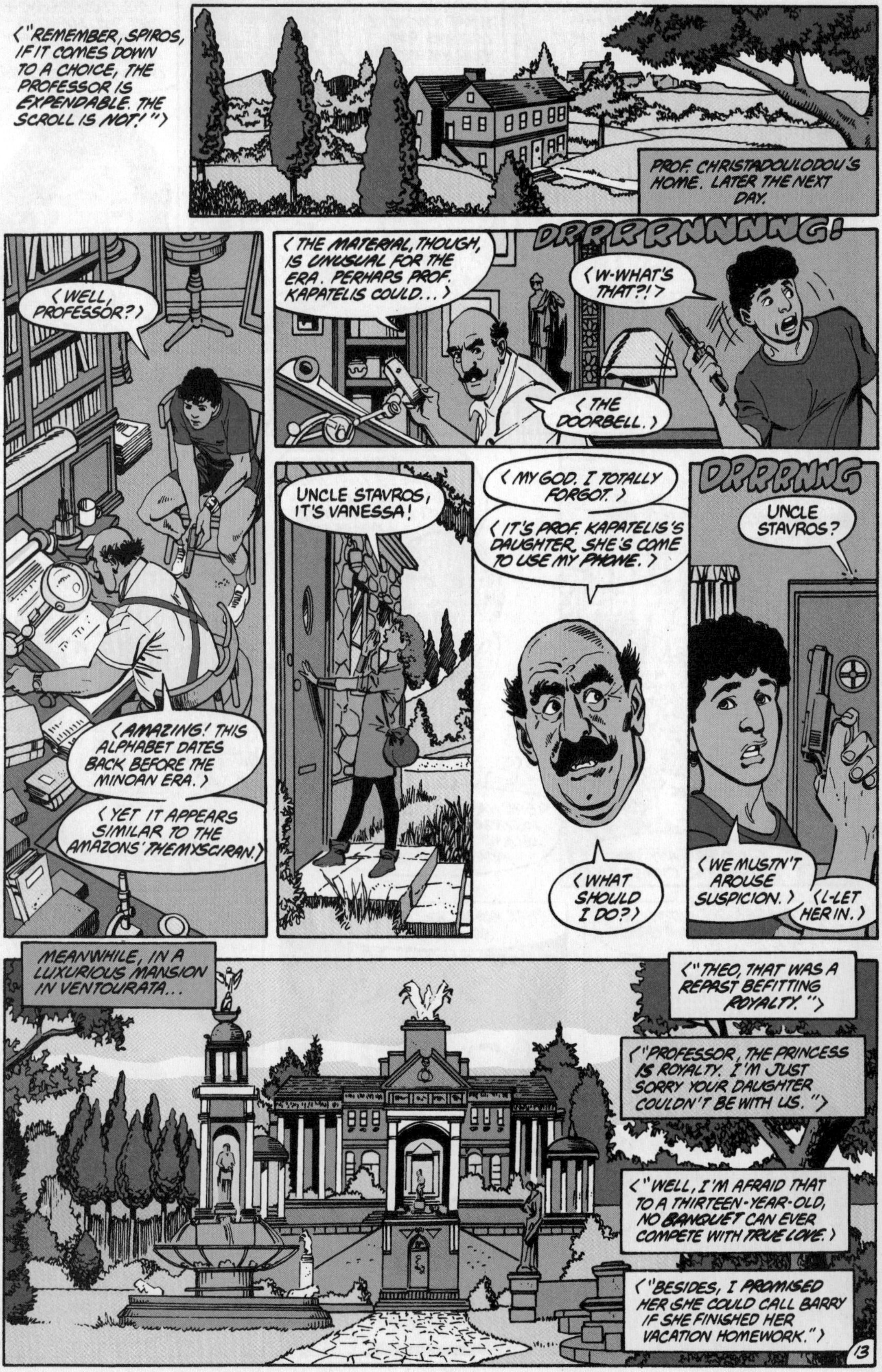
〈"REMEMBER, SPIROS, IF IT COMES DOWN TO A CHOICE, THE PROFESSOR IS EXPENDABLE. THE SCROLL IS NOT!"〉
PROF. CHRISTADOULODOU'S HOME. LATER THE NEXT DAY.
〈WELL, PROFESSOR?〉
〈AMAZING! THIS ALPHABET DATES BACK BEFORE THE MINOAN ERA.〉
〈YET IT APPEARS SIMILAR TO THE AMAZONS' THEMYSCIRAN.〉
〈THE MATERIAL, THOUGH, IS UNUSUAL FOR THE ERA. PERHAPS PROF. KAPATELIS COULD...〉
DRRRRNNNNG!
〈W-WHAT'S THAT?!〉
〈THE DOORBELL.〉
UNCLE STAVROS, IT'S VANESSA!
〈MY GOD. I TOTALLY FORGOT.〉
〈IT'S PROF. KAPATELIS'S DAUGHTER. SHE'S COME TO USE MY PHONE.〉
〈WHAT SHOULD I DO?〉
DRRRNNG
UNCLE STAVROS?
〈WE MUSTN'T AROUSE SUSPICION.〉
〈L-LET HER IN.〉
MEANWHILE, IN A LUXURIOUS MANSION IN VENTOURATA...
〈"THEO, THAT WAS A REPAST BEFITTING ROYALTY."〉
〈"PROFESSOR, THE PRINCESS IS ROYALTY. I'M JUST SORRY YOUR DAUGHTER COULDN'T BE WITH US."〉
〈"WELL, I'M AFRAID THAT TO A THIRTEEN-YEAR-OLD, NO BANQUET CAN EVER COMPETE WITH TRUE LOVE.〉
〈"BESIDES, I PROMISED HER SHE COULD CALL BARRY IF SHE FINISHED HER VACATION HOMEWORK."〉
13

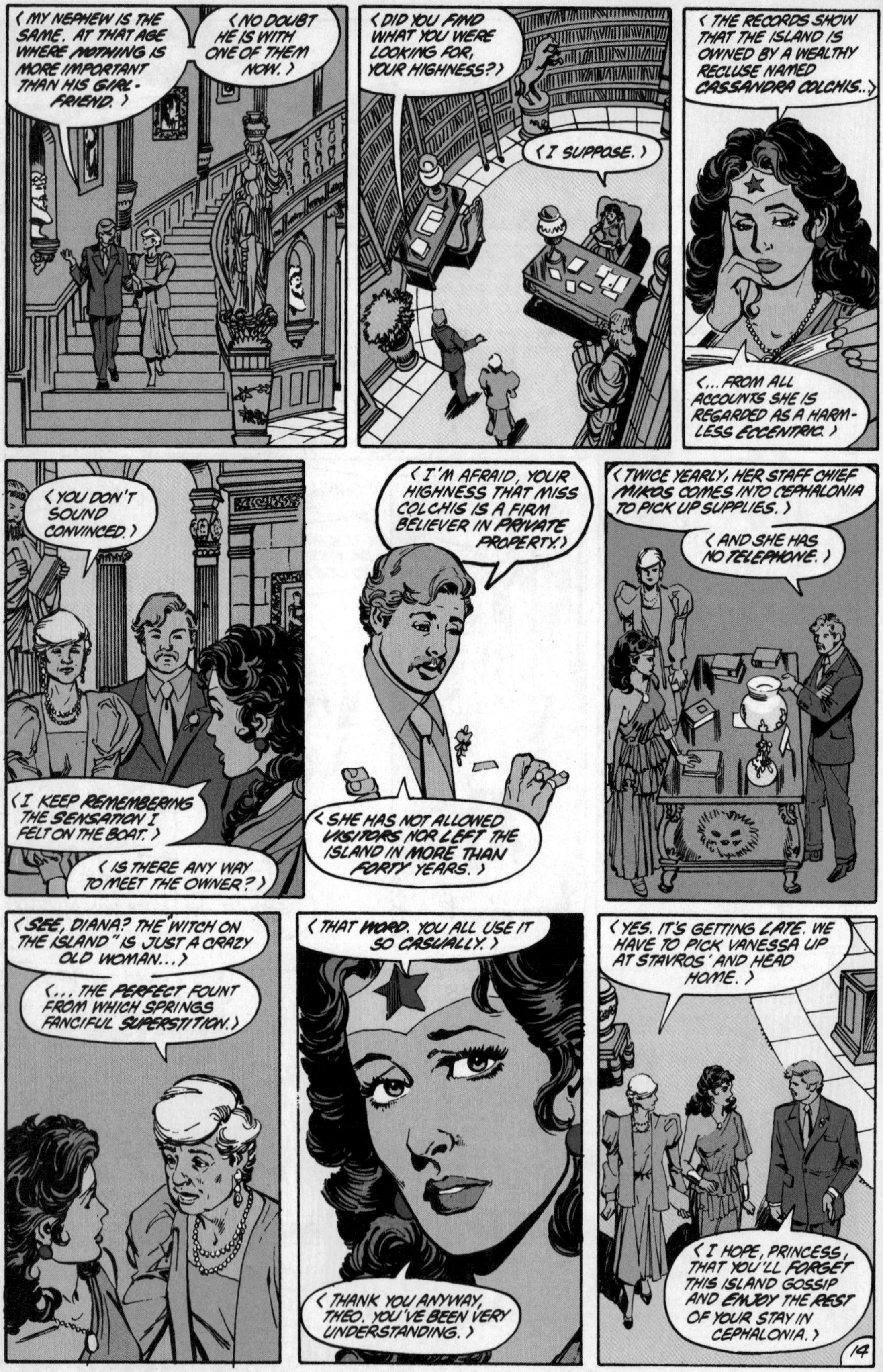

⟨ MY NEPHEW IS THE SAME. AT THAT AGE WHERE NOTHING IS MORE IMPORTANT THAN HIS GIRL-FRIEND. ⟩
⟨ NO DOUBT HE IS WITH ONE OF THEM NOW. ⟩
⟨ DID YOU FIND WHAT YOU WERE LOOKING FOR, YOUR HIGHNESS? ⟩
⟨ I SUPPOSE. ⟩
⟨ THE RECORDS SHOW THAT THE ISLAND IS OWNED BY A WEALTHY RECLUSE NAMED CASSANDRA COLCHIS.. ⟩
⟨...FROM ALL ACCOUNTS SHE IS REGARDED AS A HARM-LESS ECCENTRIC. ⟩
⟨ YOU DON'T SOUND CONVINCED. ⟩
⟨ I KEEP REMEMBERING THE SENSATION I FELT ON THE BOAT. ⟩
⟨ IS THERE ANY WAY TO MEET THE OWNER? ⟩
⟨ I'M AFRAID, YOUR HIGHNESS THAT MISS COLCHIS IS A FIRM BELIEVER IN PRIVATE PROPERTY. ⟩
⟨ SHE HAS NOT ALLOWED VISITORS NOR LEFT THE ISLAND IN MORE THAN FORTY YEARS. ⟩
⟨ TWICE YEARLY, HER STAFF CHIEF MIKOS COMES INTO CEPHALONIA TO PICK UP SUPPLIES. ⟩
⟨ AND SHE HAS NO TELEPHONE. ⟩
⟨ SEE, DIANA? THE "WITCH ON THE ISLAND" IS JUST A CRAZY OLD WOMAN... ⟩
⟨... THE PERFECT FOUNT FROM WHICH SPRINGS FANCIFUL SUPERSTITION. ⟩
⟨ THAT WORD. YOU ALL USE IT SO CASUALLY. ⟩
⟨ THANK YOU ANYWAY, THEO. YOU'VE BEEN VERY UNDERSTANDING. ⟩
⟨ YES. IT'S GETTING LATE. WE HAVE TO PICK VANESSA UP AT STAVROS' AND HEAD HOME. ⟩
⟨ I HOPE, PRINCESS, THAT YOU'LL FORGET THIS ISLAND GOSSIP AND ENJOY THE REST OF YOUR STAY IN CEPHALONIA. ⟩
14

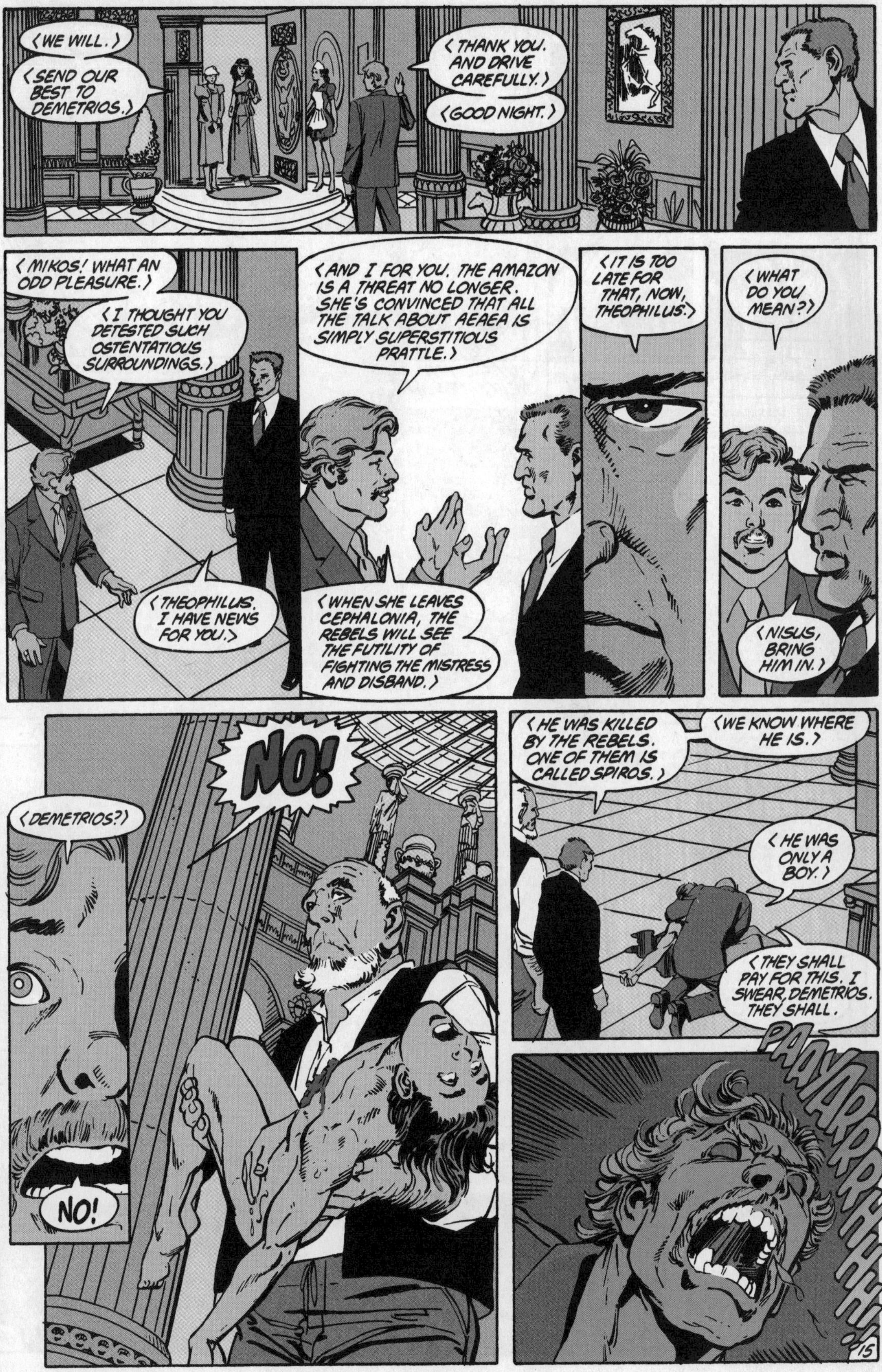

⟨WE WILL.⟩
⟨SEND OUR BEST TO DEMETRIOS.⟩
⟨THANK YOU. AND DRIVE CAREFULLY.⟩
⟨GOOD NIGHT.⟩
⟨MIKOS! WHAT AN ODD PLEASURE.⟩
⟨I THOUGHT YOU DETESTED SUCH OSTENTATIOUS SURROUNDINGS.⟩
⟨THEOPHILUS. I HAVE NEWS FOR YOU.⟩
⟨AND I FOR YOU. THE AMAZON IS A THREAT NO LONGER. SHE'S CONVINCED THAT ALL THE TALK ABOUT AEAEA IS SIMPLY SUPERSTITIOUS PRATTLE.⟩
⟨WHEN SHE LEAVES CEPHALONIA, THE REBELS WILL SEE THE FUTILITY OF FIGHTING THE MISTRESS AND DISBAND.⟩
⟨IT IS TOO LATE FOR THAT, NOW, THEOPHILUS.⟩
⟨WHAT DO YOU MEAN?⟩
⟨NISUS, BRING HIM IN.⟩
⟨DEMETRIOS?⟩
NO!
NO!
⟨HE WAS KILLED BY THE REBELS. ONE OF THEM IS CALLED SPIROS.⟩
⟨WE KNOW WHERE HE IS.⟩
⟨HE WAS ONLY A BOY.⟩
⟨THEY SHALL PAY FOR THIS. I SWEAR, DEMETRIOS. THEY SHALL.
PAAYARRHHHH!!
15

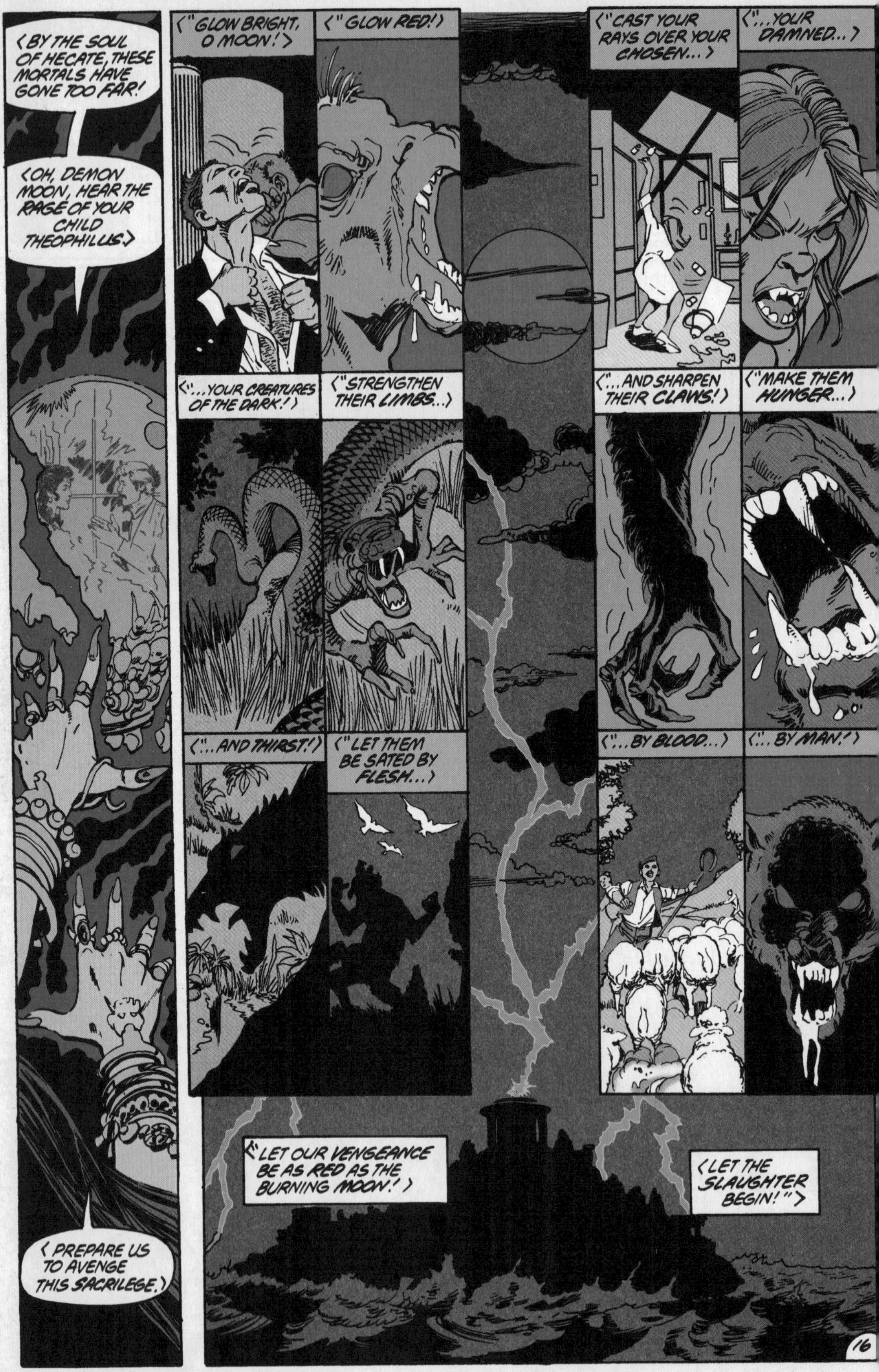

<BY THE SOUL OF HECATE, THESE MORTALS HAVE GONE TOO FAR!
<OH, DEMON MOON, HEAR THE RAGE OF YOUR CHILD THEOPHILUS.>
<PREPARE US TO AVENGE THIS SACRILEGE.>
<"GLOW BRIGHT, O MOON!>
<"GLOW RED!>
<"CAST YOUR RAYS OVER YOUR CHOSEN...>
<"...YOUR DAMNED...>
<"...YOUR CREATURES OF THE DARK!>
<"STRENGTHEN THEIR LIMBS...>
<"...AND SHARPEN THEIR CLAWS!>
<"MAKE THEM HUNGER...>
<"...AND THIRST!>
<"LET THEM BE SATED BY FLESH...>
<"...BY BLOOD...>
<"...BY MAN!>
<"LET OUR VENGEANCE BE AS RED AS THE BURNING MOON!>
<LET THE SLAUGHTER BEGIN!">
16

< DIANA. DO YOU HEAR SOMETHING? >

< YES. THE SOUNDS OF ANIMALS IN A FRENZY. >

< IT'S ALL AROUND US! >

< JULIA, LOOK! >

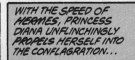
< "DEAR GOD IN HEAVEN! THAT'S STAVROS' HOUSE!" >

< "VANESSA IS IN THERE!" >

WITH THE SPEED OF HERMES, PRINCESS DIANA UNFLINCHINGLY PROPELS HERSELF INTO THE CONFLAGRATION...

...PRAYING WITH ALL HER HEART THAT SHE IS NOT TOO LATE!

STAVROS! NESSIE!

< ...DIANA... >

GREAT GAEA!

17

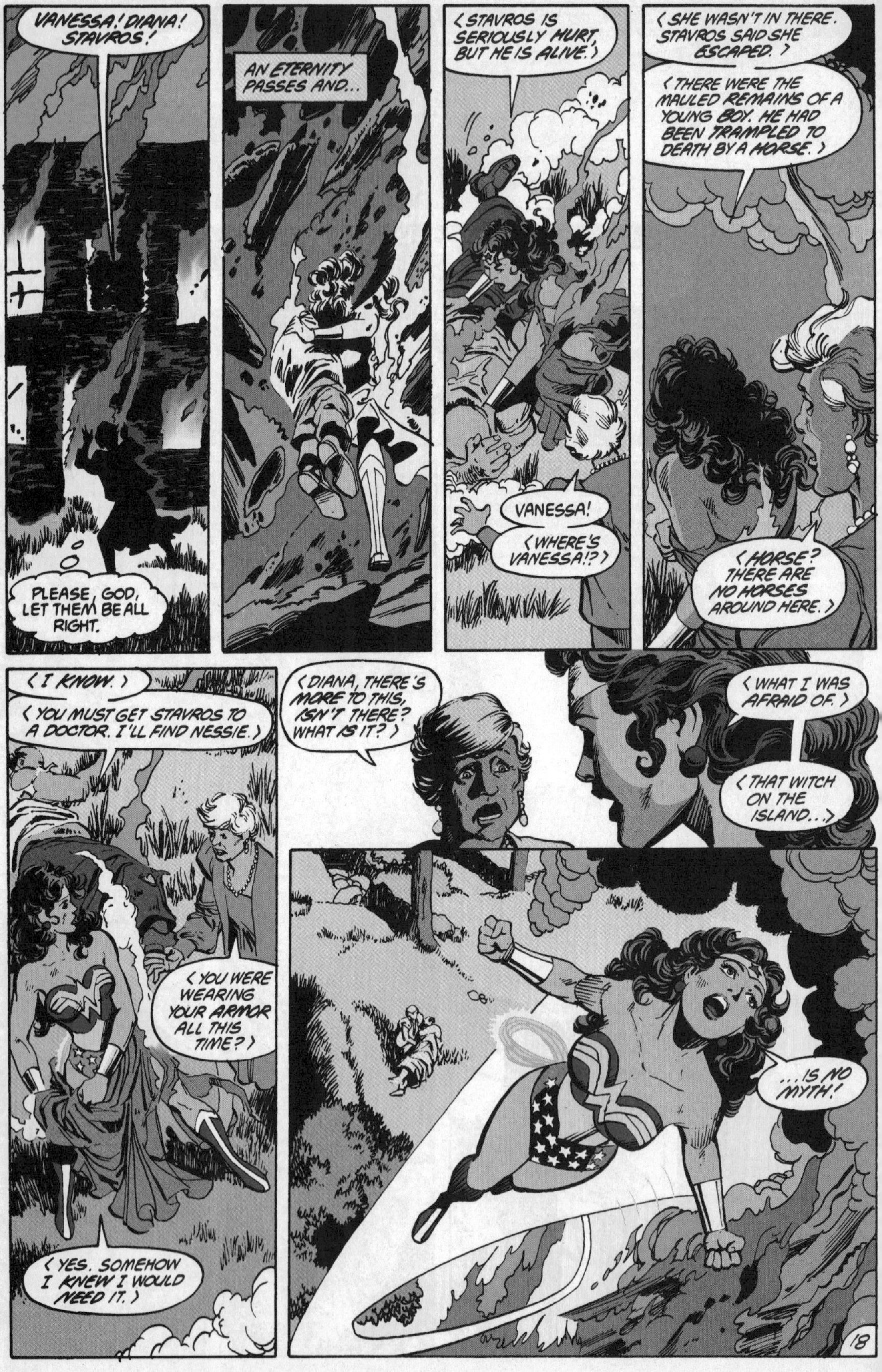
VANESSA! DIANA! STAVROS!
PLEASE, GOD, LET THEM BE ALL RIGHT.
AN ETERNITY PASSES AND...
‹ STAVROS IS SERIOUSLY HURT, BUT HE IS ALIVE. ›
VANESSA!
‹ WHERE'S VANESSA!? ›
‹ SHE WASN'T IN THERE. STAVROS SAID SHE ESCAPED. ›
‹ THERE WERE THE MAULED REMAINS OF A YOUNG BOY. HE HAD BEEN TRAMPLED TO DEATH BY A HORSE. ›
‹ HORSE? THERE ARE NO HORSES AROUND HERE. ›
‹ I KNOW. ›
‹ YOU MUST GET STAVROS TO A DOCTOR. I'LL FIND NESSIE. ›
‹ YOU WERE WEARING YOUR ARMOR ALL THIS TIME? ›
‹ YES. SOMEHOW I KNEW I WOULD NEED IT. ›
‹ DIANA, THERE'S MORE TO THIS, ISN'T THERE? WHAT IS IT? ›
‹ WHAT I WAS AFRAID OF. ›
‹ THAT WITCH ON THE ISLAND... ›
...IS NO MYTH!
18

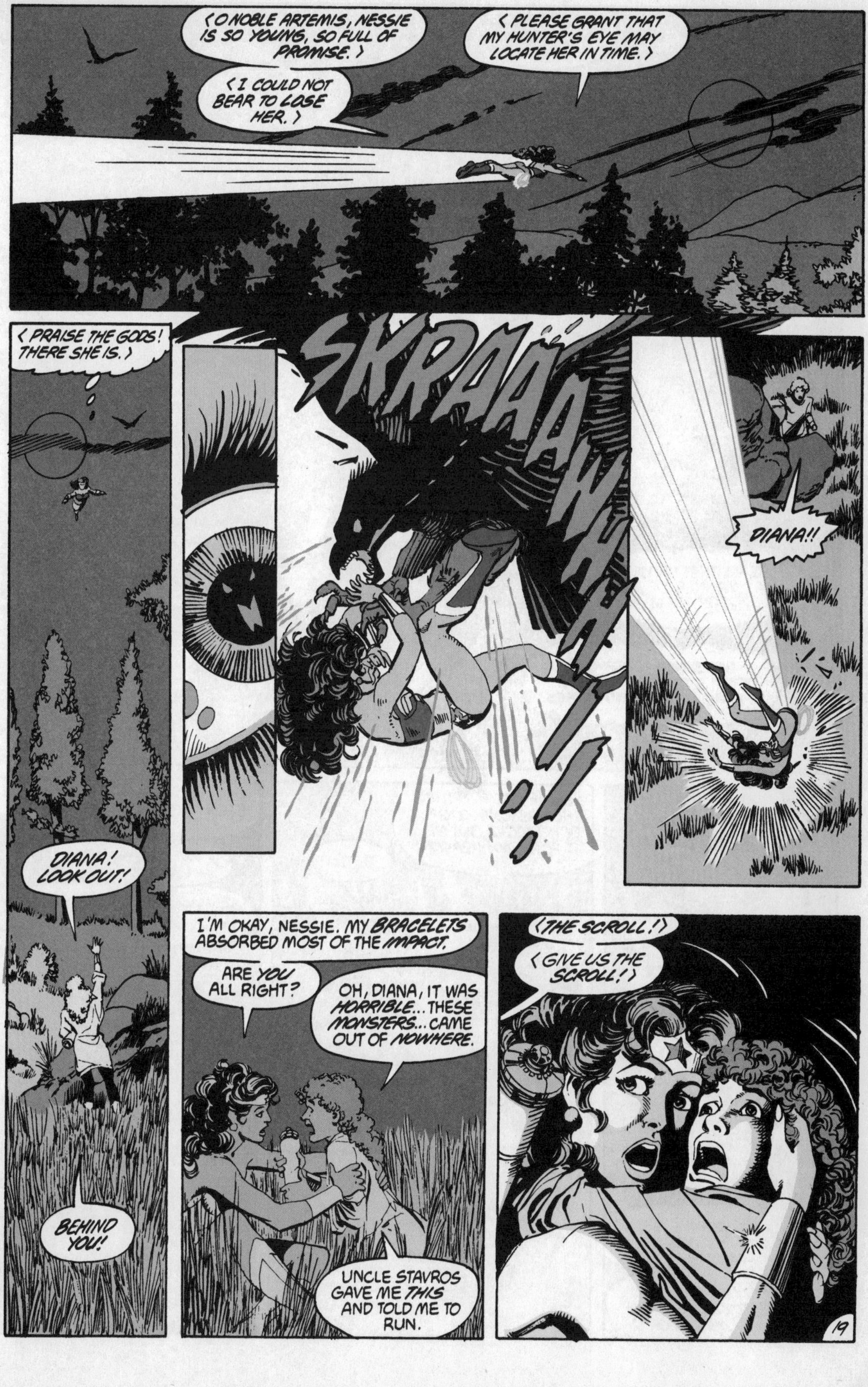

‹ O NOBLE ARTEMIS, NESSIE IS SO YOUNG, SO FULL OF PROMISE. ›
‹ I COULD NOT BEAR TO LOSE HER. ›
‹ PLEASE GRANT THAT MY HUNTER'S EYE MAY LOCATE HER IN TIME. ›
‹ PRAISE THE GODS! THERE SHE IS. ›
SKRAAAWWK!!
DIANA!!
DIANA! LOOK OUT!
BEHIND YOU!
I'M OKAY, NESSIE. MY BRACELETS ABSORBED MOST OF THE IMPACT.
ARE YOU ALL RIGHT?
OH, DIANA, IT WAS HORRIBLE... THESE MONSTERS... CAME OUT OF NOWHERE.
UNCLE STAVROS GAVE ME THIS AND TOLD ME TO RUN.
‹ THE SCROLL! ›
‹ GIVE US THE SCROLL! ›
19

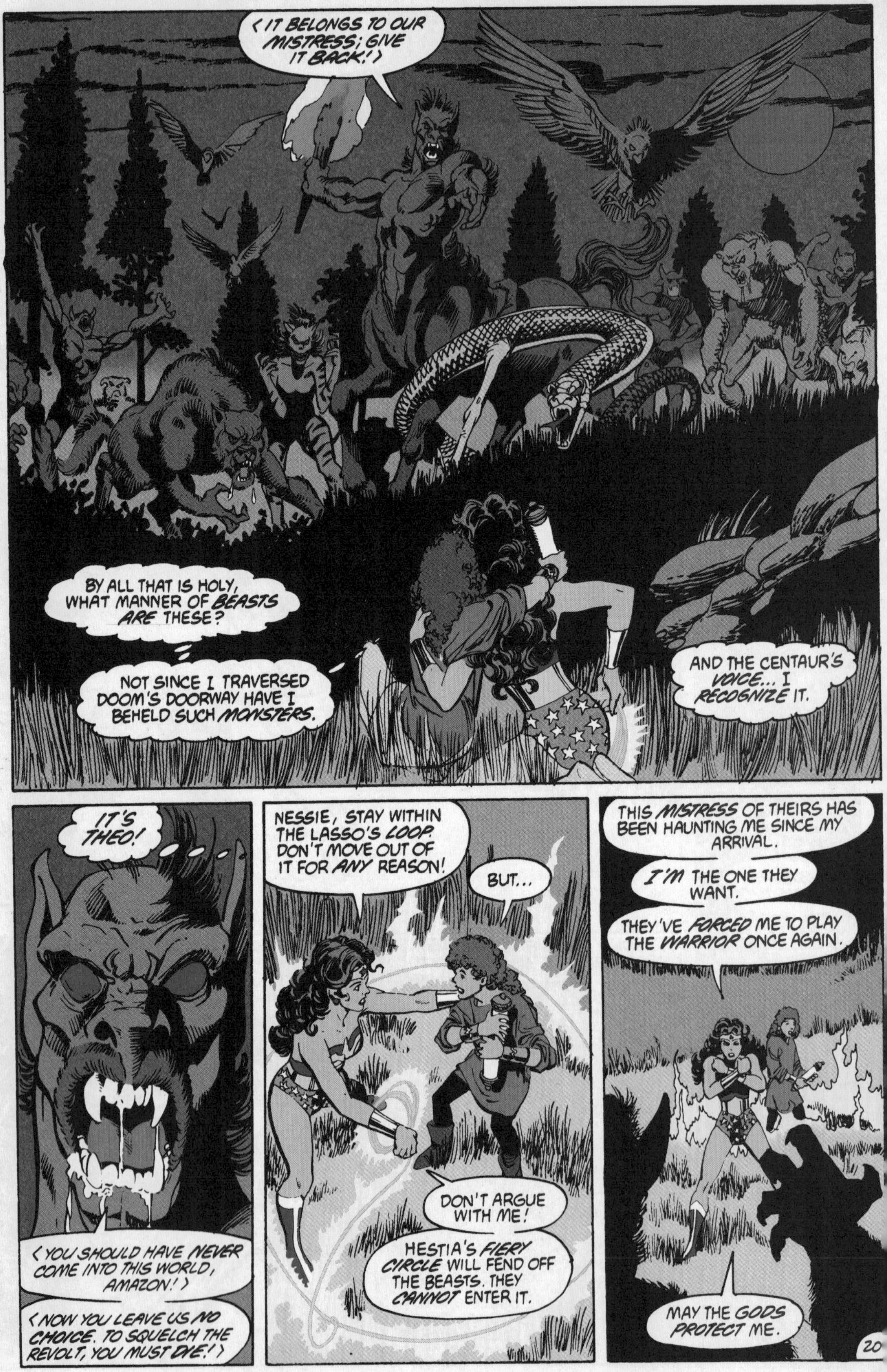

‹IT BELONGS TO OUR MISTRESS; GIVE IT BACK!›
BY ALL THAT IS HOLY, WHAT MANNER OF BEASTS ARE THESE?
NOT SINCE I TRAVERSED DOOM'S DOORWAY HAVE I BEHELD SUCH MONSTERS.
AND THE CENTAUR'S VOICE... I RECOGNIZE IT.
IT'S THEO!
‹YOU SHOULD HAVE NEVER COME INTO THIS WORLD, AMAZON!›
‹NOW YOU LEAVE US NO CHOICE. TO SQUELCH THE REVOLT, YOU MUST DIE!›
NESSIE, STAY WITHIN THE LASSO'S LOOP. DON'T MOVE OUT OF IT FOR ANY REASON!
BUT...
DON'T ARGUE WITH ME!
HESTIA'S FIERY CIRCLE WILL FEND OFF THE BEASTS. THEY CANNOT ENTER IT.
THIS MISTRESS OF THEIRS HAS BEEN HAUNTING ME SINCE MY ARRIVAL.
I'M THE ONE THEY WANT.
THEY'VE FORCED ME TO PLAY THE WARRIOR ONCE AGAIN.
MAY THE GODS PROTECT ME.
20

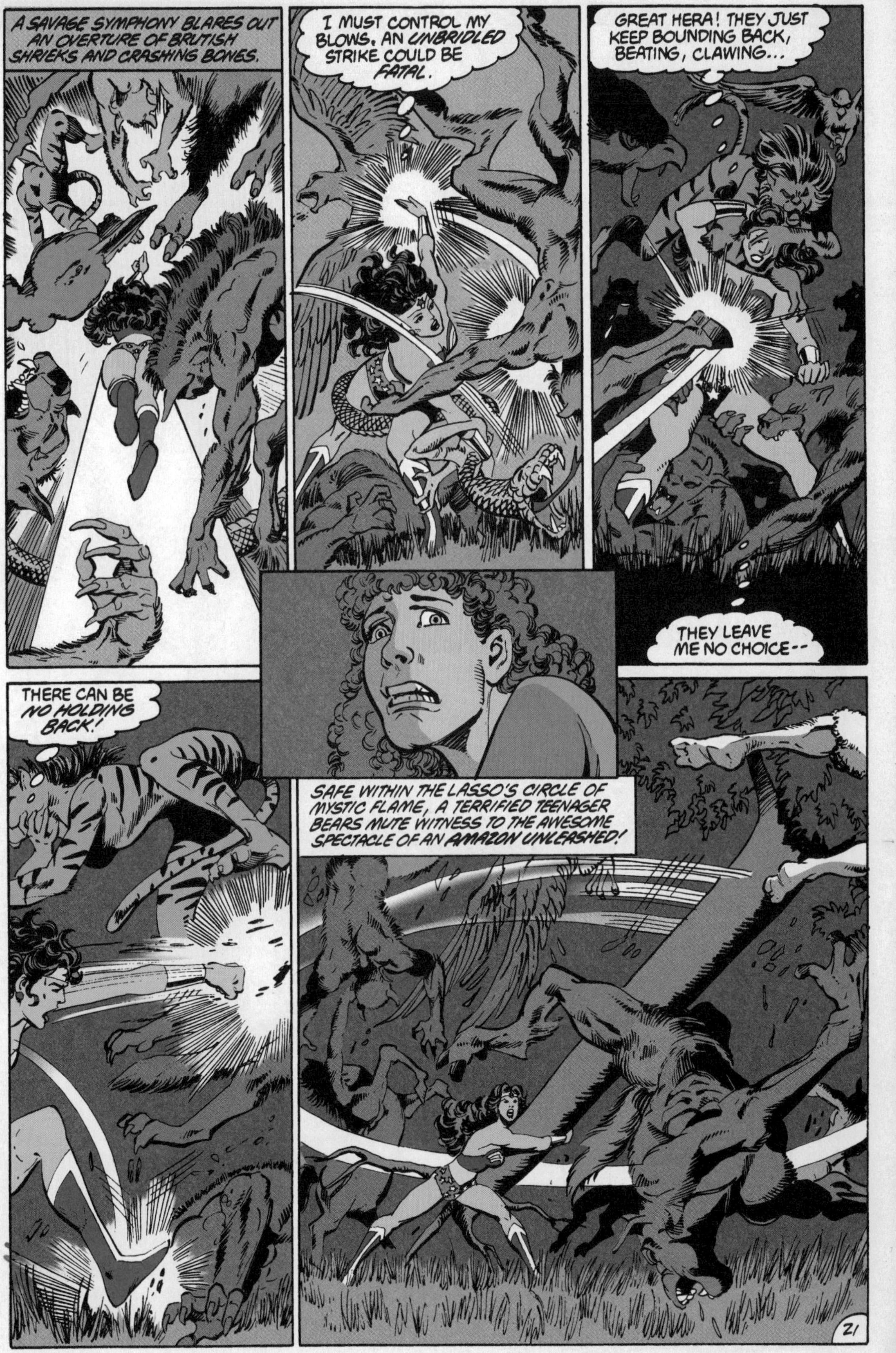
A SAVAGE SYMPHONY BLARES OUT AN OVERTURE OF BRUTISH SHRIEKS AND CRASHING BONES.
I MUST CONTROL MY BLOWS. AN UNBRIDLED STRIKE COULD BE FATAL.
GREAT HERA! THEY JUST KEEP BOUNDING BACK, BEATING, CLAWING...
THEY LEAVE ME NO CHOICE--
THERE CAN BE NO HOLDING BACK!
SAFE WITHIN THE LASSO'S CIRCLE OF MYSTIC FLAME, A TERRIFIED TEENAGER BEARS MUTE WITNESS TO THE AWESOME SPECTACLE OF AN AMAZON UNLEASHED!
21

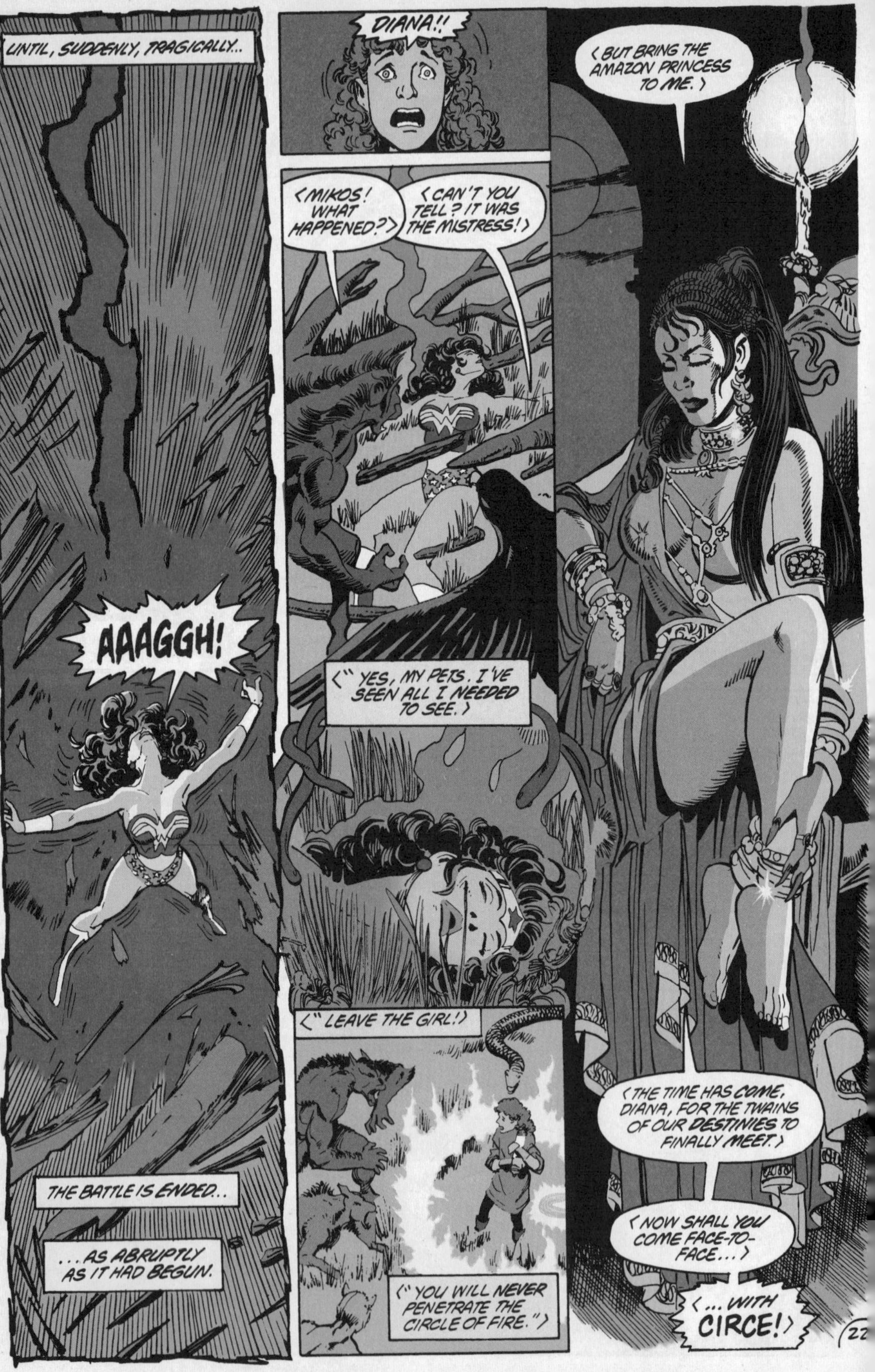
UNTIL, SUDDENLY, TRAGICALLY...
AAAGGH!
THE BATTLE IS ENDED...
...AS ABRUPTLY AS IT HAD BEGUN.
DIANA!!
<MIKOS! WHAT HAPPENED?>
<CAN'T YOU TELL? IT WAS THE MISTRESS!>
<"YES, MY PETS. I'VE SEEN ALL I NEEDED TO SEE.>
<"LEAVE THE GIRL!>
<"YOU WILL NEVER PENETRATE THE CIRCLE OF FIRE.">
<BUT BRING THE AMAZON PRINCESS TO ME.>
<THE TIME HAS COME, DIANA, FOR THE TWAINS OF OUR DESTINIES TO FINALLY MEET.>
<NOW SHALL YOU COME FACE-TO-FACE...>
<...WITH CIRCE!>
22

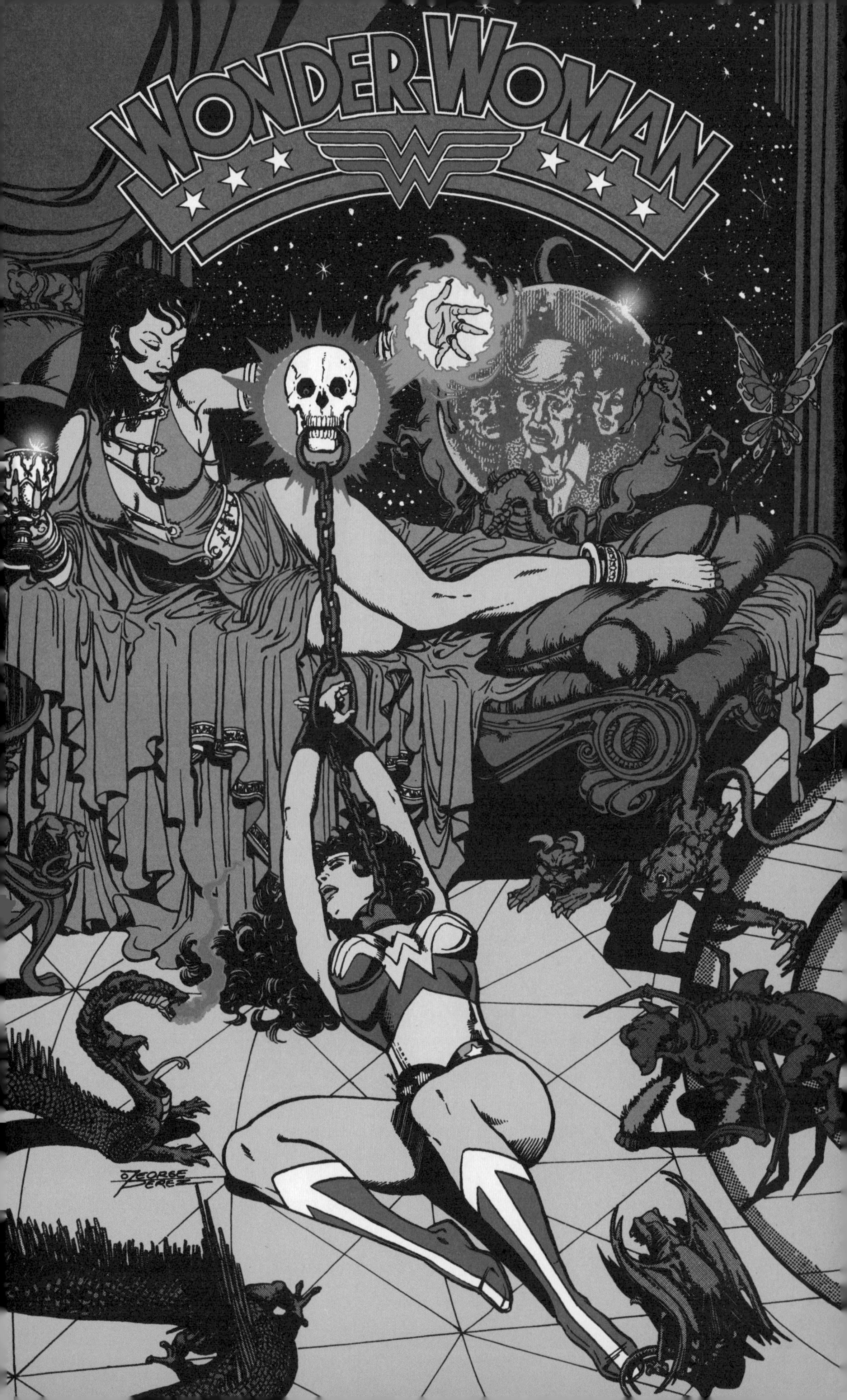
WONDER WOMAN
GEORGE PEREZ

WONDER WOMAN

CHAPTER SIX

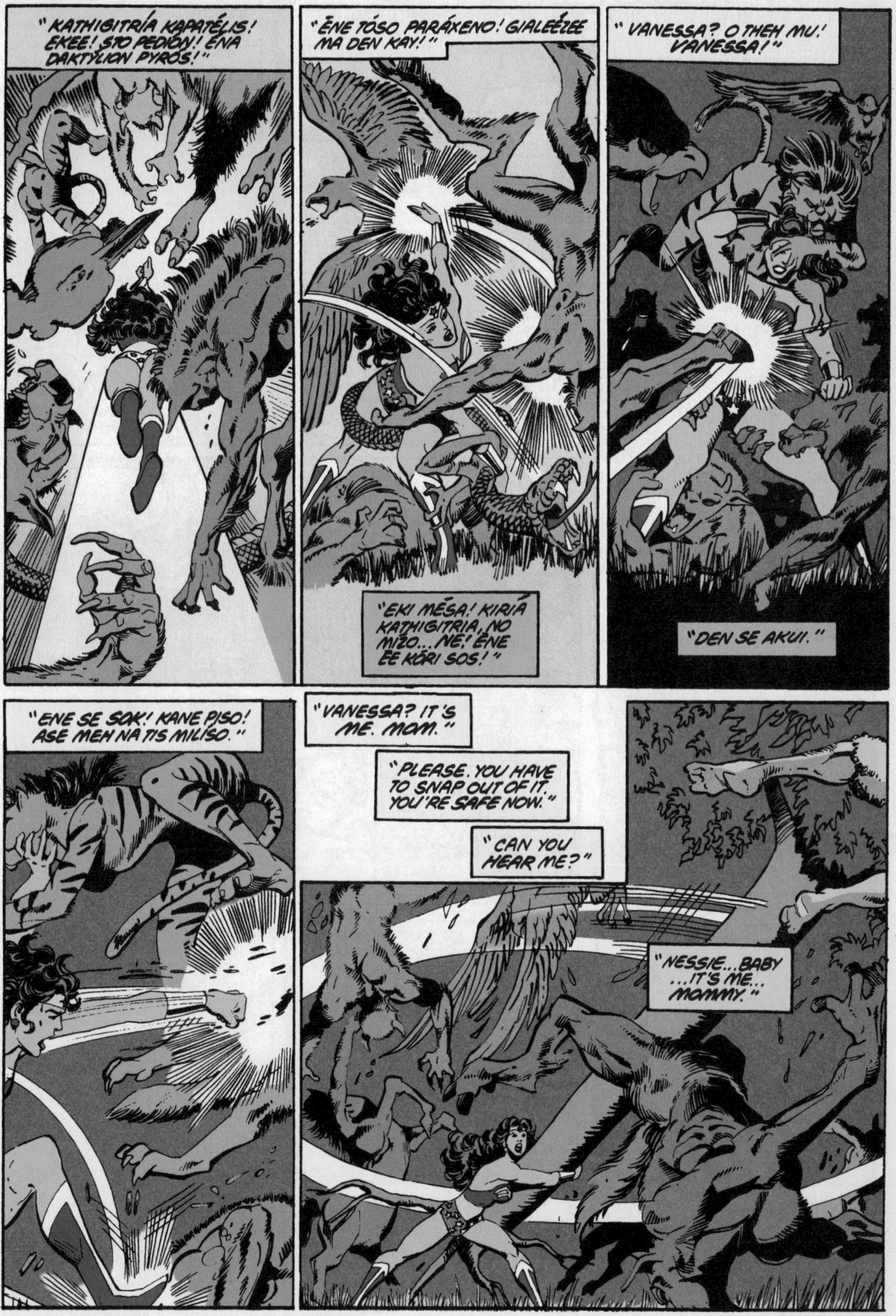
"KATHIGITRÍA KAPATÉLIS! EKEE! STO PEDIÓN! ÉNA DAKTÝLION PYRÓS!"
"ĒNE TÓSO PARÁXENO! GIALEÉZEE MA DEN KAY!"
"EKI MĒSA! KIRIÁ KATHIGITRIA, NO MIZO... NE! ĒNE ĒE KÖRI SOS!"
"VANESSA? O THEH MU! VANESSA!"
"DEN SE AKUI."
"ENE SE SOK! KANE PISO! ASE MEH NA TIS MILISO."
"VANESSA? IT'S ME. MOM."
"PLEASE. YOU HAVE TO SNAP OUT OF IT. YOU'RE SAFE NOW."
"CAN YOU HEAR ME?"
"NESSIE...BABY ...IT'S ME... MOMMY."

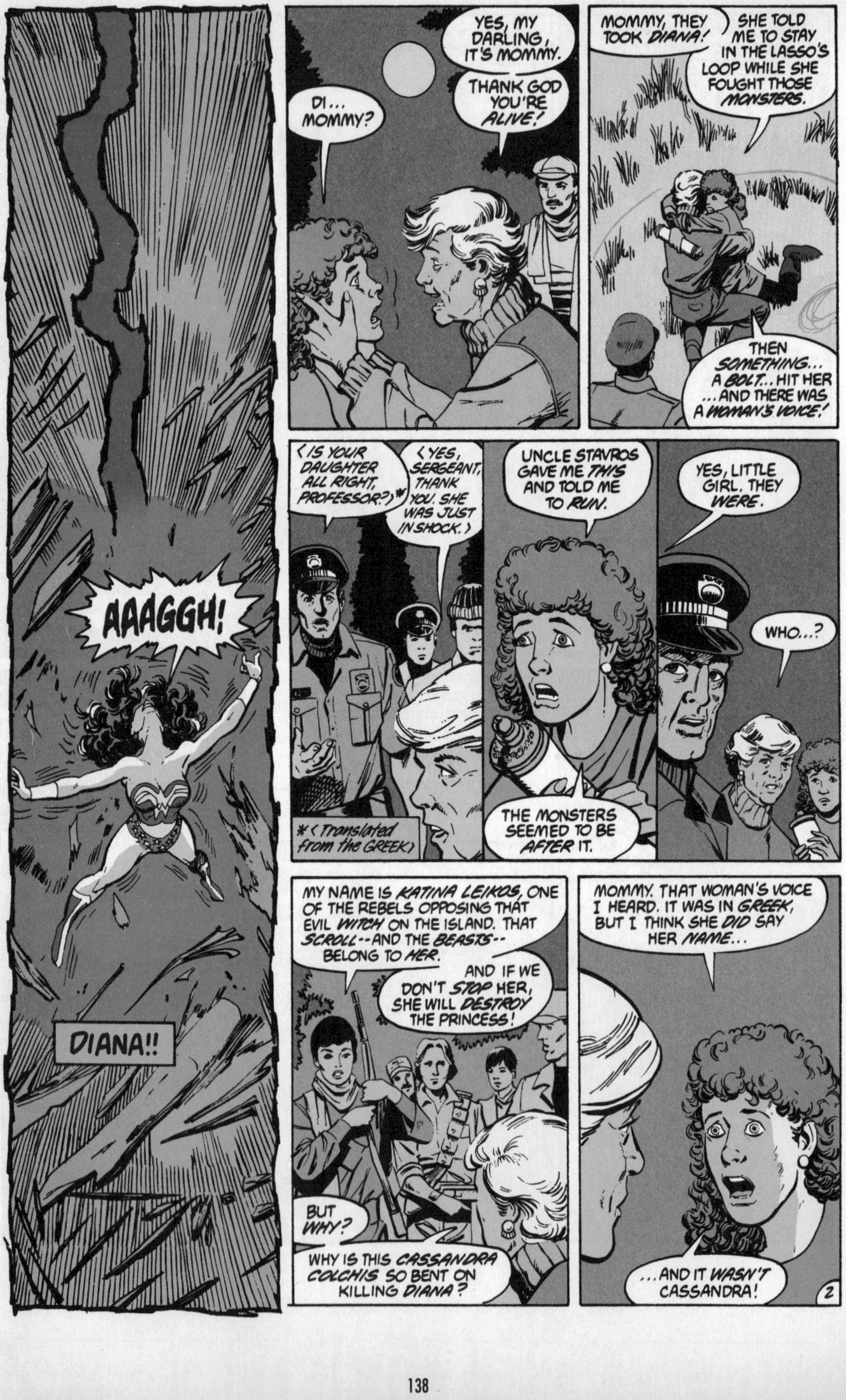
AAAGGH!
DIANA!!
DI... MOMMY?
YES, MY DARLING, IT'S MOMMY.
THANK GOD YOU'RE ALIVE!
MOMMY, THEY TOOK DIANA!
SHE TOLD ME TO STAY IN THE LASSO'S LOOP WHILE SHE FOUGHT THOSE MONSTERS.
THEN SOMETHING... A BOLT... HIT HER ...AND THERE WAS A WOMAN'S VOICE!
<IS YOUR DAUGHTER ALL RIGHT, PROFESSOR?>*
<YES, SERGEANT, THANK YOU. SHE WAS JUST IN SHOCK.>
*<Translated from the GREEK>
UNCLE STAVROS GAVE ME THIS AND TOLD ME TO RUN.
THE MONSTERS SEEMED TO BE AFTER IT.
YES, LITTLE GIRL, THEY WERE.
WHO...?
MY NAME IS KATINA LEIKOS, ONE OF THE REBELS OPPOSING THAT EVIL WITCH ON THE ISLAND. THAT SCROLL--AND THE BEASTS--BELONG TO HER.
AND IF WE DON'T STOP HER, SHE WILL DESTROY THE PRINCESS!
BUT WHY?
WHY IS THIS CASSANDRA COLCHIS SO BENT ON KILLING DIANA?
MOMMY. THAT WOMAN'S VOICE I HEARD. IT WAS IN GREEK, BUT I THINK SHE DID SAY HER NAME...
...AND IT WASN'T CASSANDRA!
2

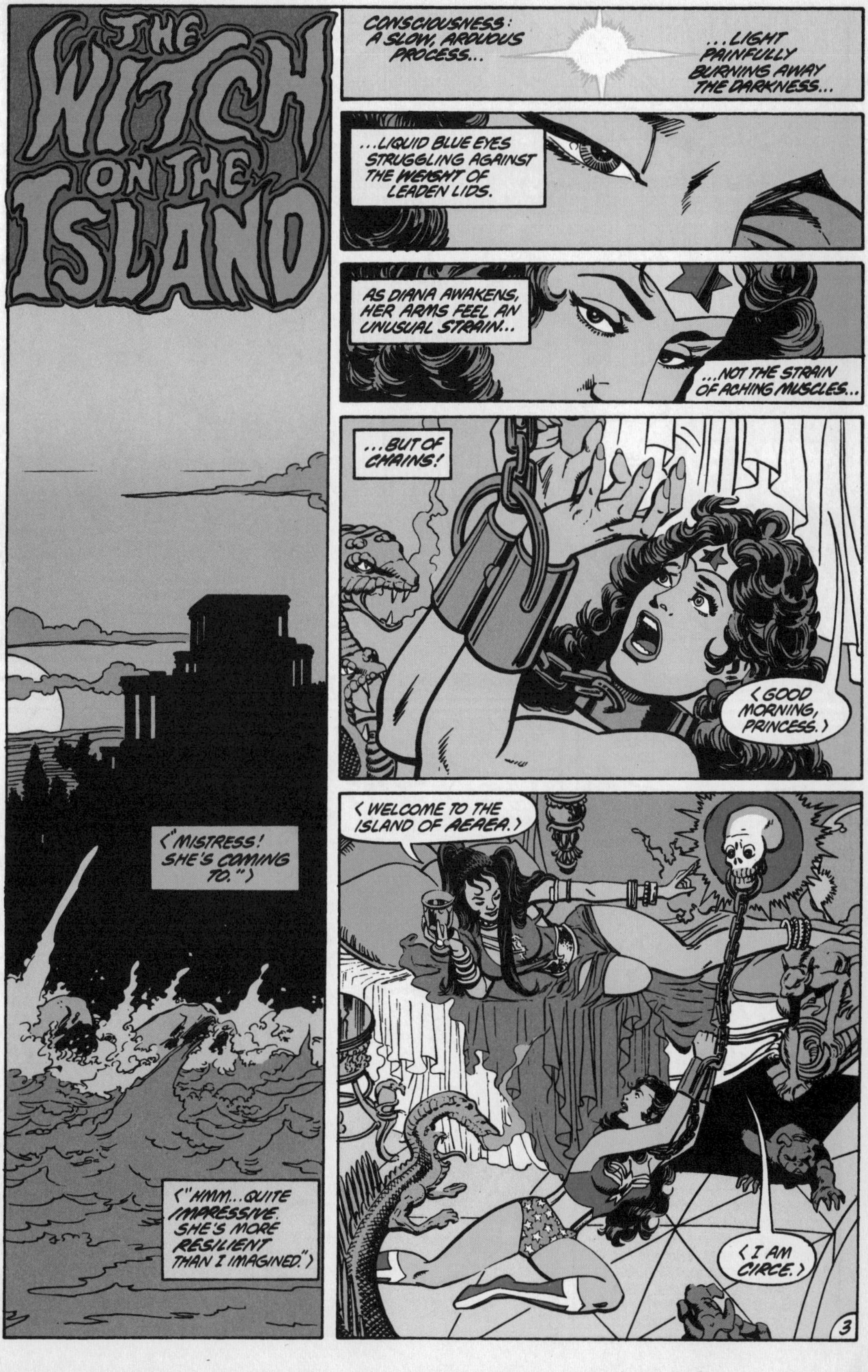
THE WITCH ON THE ISLAND
CONSCIOUSNESS: A SLOW, ARDUOUS PROCESS...
...LIGHT PAINFULLY BURNING AWAY THE DARKNESS...
...LIQUID BLUE EYES STRUGGLING AGAINST THE WEIGHT OF LEADEN LIDS.
AS DIANA AWAKENS, HER ARMS FEEL AN UNUSUAL STRAIN...
...NOT THE STRAIN OF ACHING MUSCLES...
...BUT OF CHAINS!
〈GOOD MORNING, PRINCESS.〉
〈"MISTRESS! SHE'S COMING TO."〉
〈"HMM... QUITE IMPRESSIVE. SHE'S MORE RESILIENT THAN I IMAGINED."〉
〈WELCOME TO THE ISLAND OF AEAEA.〉
〈I AM CIRCE.〉
3

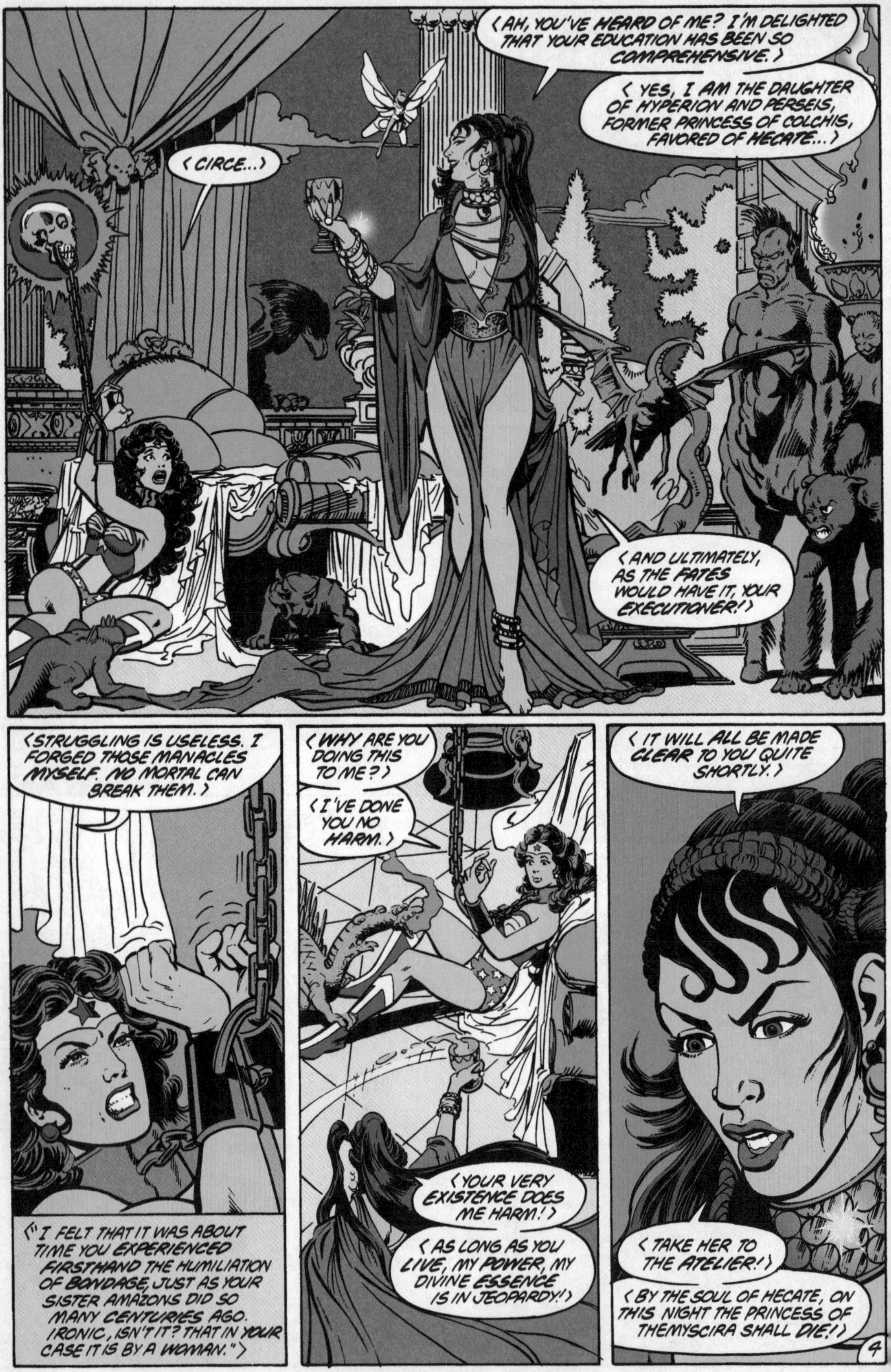

⟨CIRCE...⟩
⟨AH, YOU'VE HEARD OF ME? I'M DELIGHTED THAT YOUR EDUCATION HAS BEEN SO COMPREHENSIVE.⟩
⟨YES, I AM THE DAUGHTER OF HYPERION AND PERSEIS, FORMER PRINCESS OF COLCHIS, FAVORED OF HECATE...⟩
⟨AND ULTIMATELY, AS THE FATES WOULD HAVE IT, YOUR EXECUTIONER!⟩
⟨STRUGGLING IS USELESS. I FORGED THOSE MANACLES MYSELF. NO MORTAL CAN BREAK THEM.⟩
⟨"I FELT THAT IT WAS ABOUT TIME YOU EXPERIENCED FIRSTHAND THE HUMILIATION OF BONDAGE, JUST AS YOUR SISTER AMAZONS DID SO MANY CENTURIES AGO. IRONIC, ISN'T IT? THAT IN YOUR CASE IT IS BY A WOMAN."⟩
⟨WHY ARE YOU DOING THIS TO ME?⟩
⟨I'VE DONE YOU NO HARM.⟩
⟨YOUR VERY EXISTENCE DOES ME HARM!⟩
⟨AS LONG AS YOU LIVE, MY POWER, MY DIVINE ESSENCE IS IN JEOPARDY!⟩
⟨IT WILL ALL BE MADE CLEAR TO YOU QUITE SHORTLY.⟩
⟨TAKE HER TO THE ATELIER!⟩
⟨BY THE SOUL OF HECATE, ON THIS NIGHT THE PRINCESS OF THEMYSCIRA SHALL DIE!⟩
4

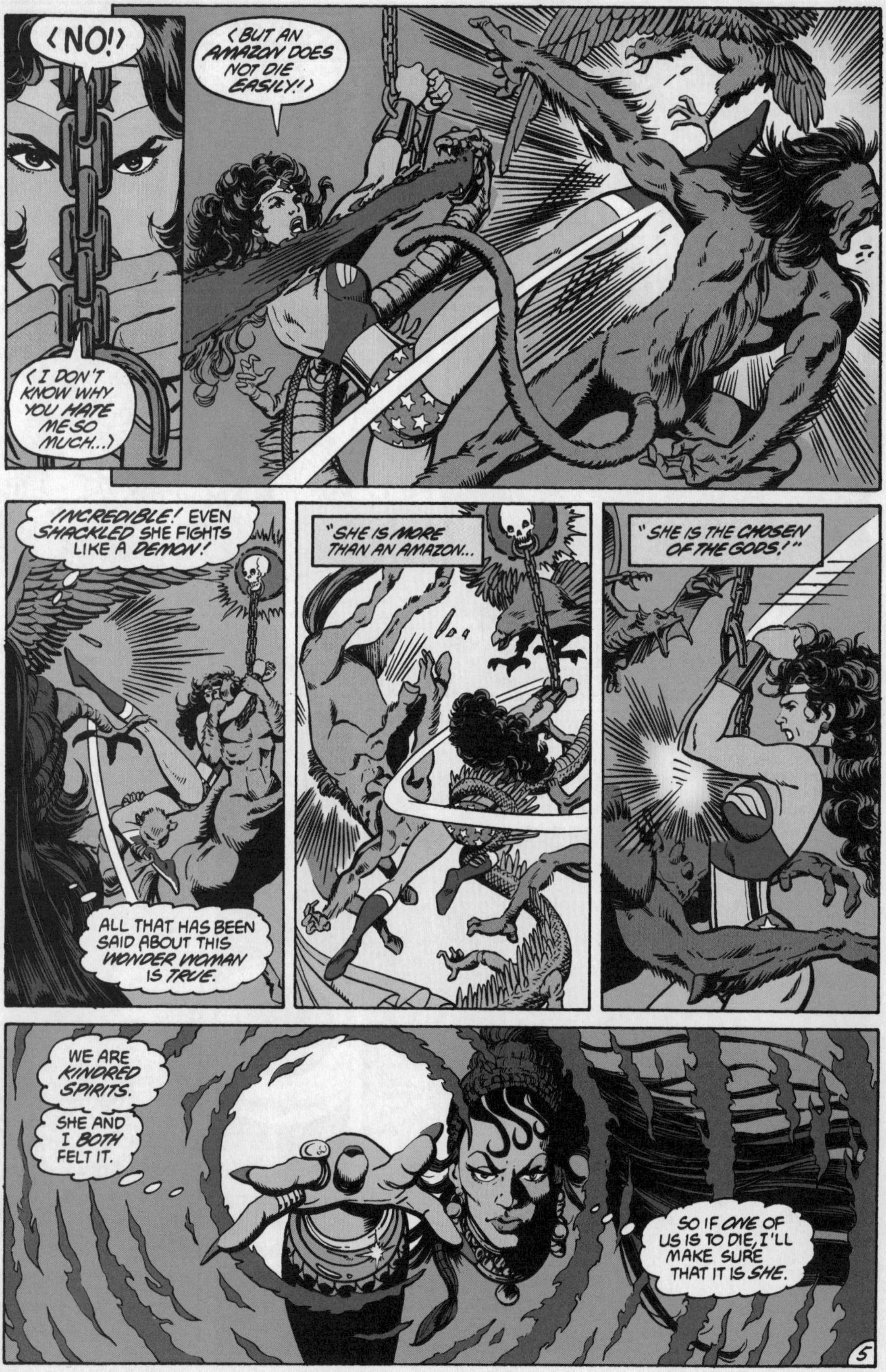
‹NO!›
‹BUT AN AMAZON DOES NOT DIE EASILY!›
‹I DON'T KNOW WHY YOU HATE ME SO MUCH...›
INCREDIBLE! EVEN SHACKLED SHE FIGHTS LIKE A DEMON!
ALL THAT HAS BEEN SAID ABOUT THIS WONDER WOMAN IS TRUE.
"SHE IS MORE THAN AN AMAZON...
"SHE IS THE CHOSEN OF THE GODS!"
WE ARE KINDRED SPIRITS.
SHE AND I BOTH FELT IT.
SO IF ONE OF US IS TO DIE, I'LL MAKE SURE THAT IT IS SHE.
5

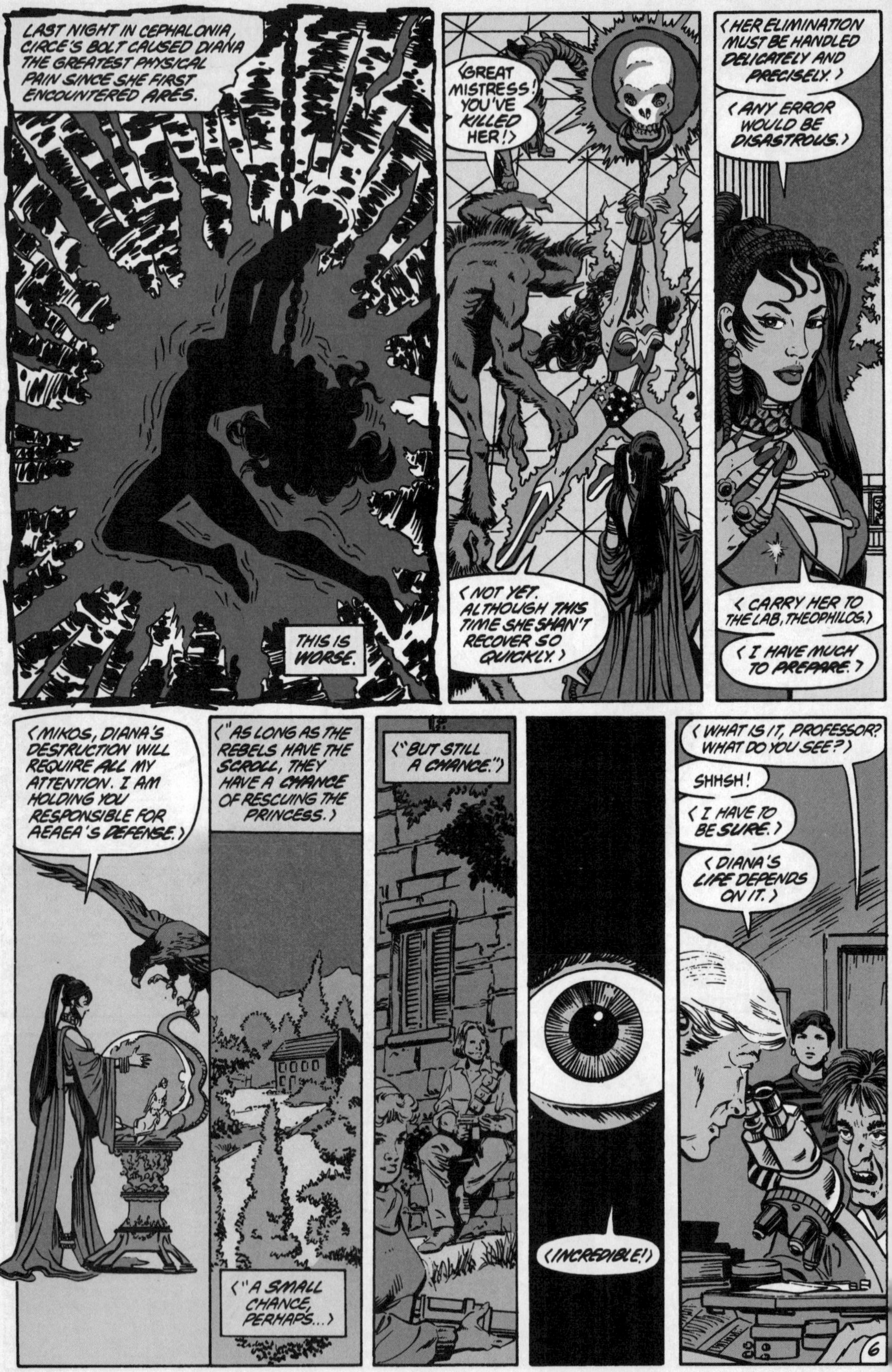
LAST NIGHT IN CEPHALONIA, CIRCE'S BOLT CAUSED DIANA THE GREATEST PHYSICAL PAIN SINCE SHE FIRST ENCOUNTERED ARES.
THIS IS WORSE.
‹GREAT MISTRESS! YOU'VE KILLED HER!›
‹NOT YET. ALTHOUGH THIS TIME SHE SHAN'T RECOVER SO QUICKLY.›
‹HER ELIMINATION MUST BE HANDLED DELICATELY AND PRECISELY.›
‹ANY ERROR WOULD BE DISASTROUS.›
‹CARRY HER TO THE LAB, THEOPHILOS.›
‹I HAVE MUCH TO PREPARE.›
‹MIKOS, DIANA'S DESTRUCTION WILL REQUIRE ALL MY ATTENTION. I AM HOLDING YOU RESPONSIBLE FOR AEAEA'S DEFENSE.›
‹"AS LONG AS THE REBELS HAVE THE SCROLL, THEY HAVE A CHANCE OF RESCUING THE PRINCESS.›
‹"A SMALL CHANCE, PERHAPS...›
‹"BUT STILL A CHANCE."›
‹INCREDIBLE!›
‹WHAT IS IT, PROFESSOR? WHAT DO YOU SEE?›
SHHSH!
‹I HAVE TO BE SURE.›
‹DIANA'S LIFE DEPENDS ON IT.›
6

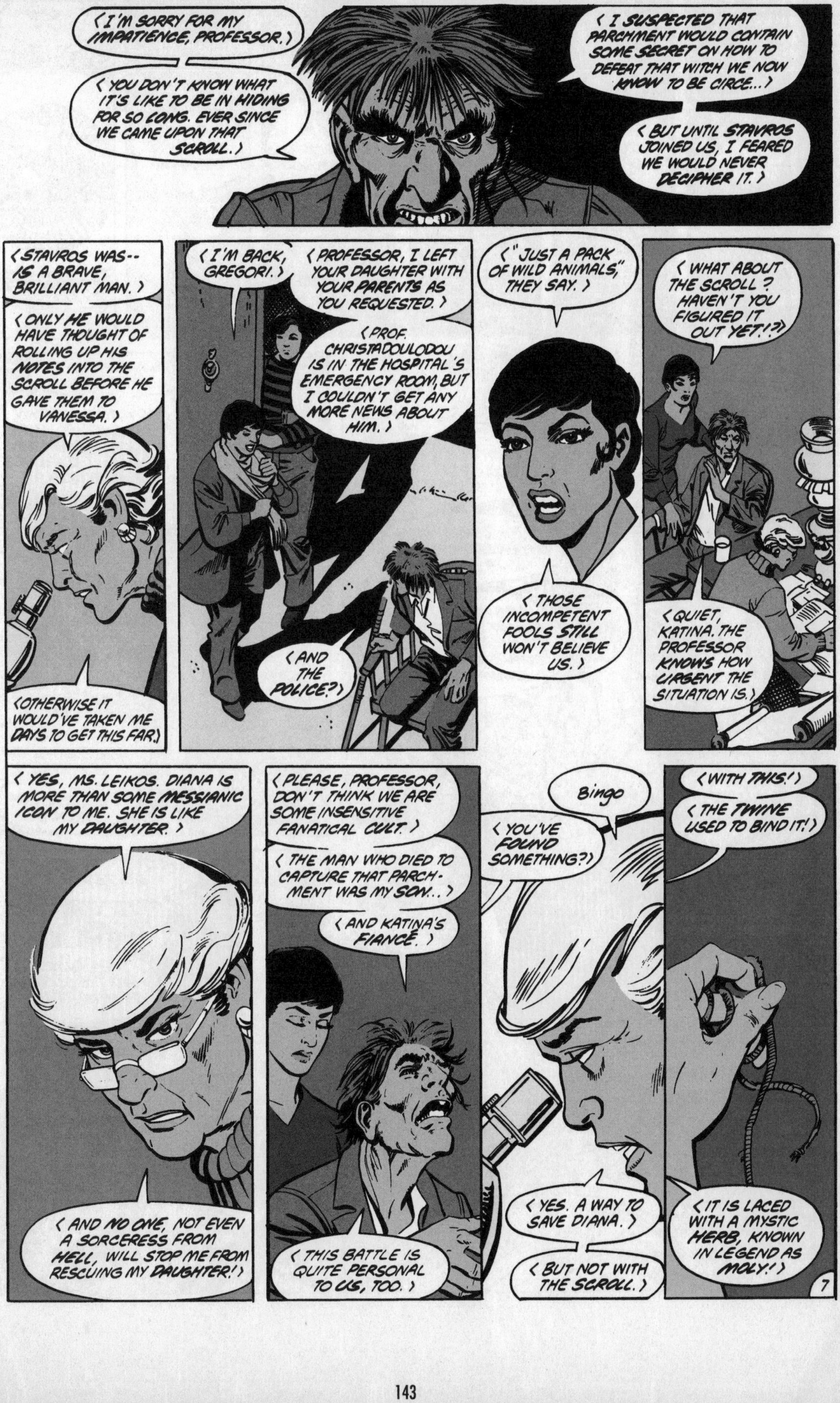

‹ I'M SORRY FOR MY IMPATIENCE, PROFESSOR. ›
‹ YOU DON'T KNOW WHAT IT'S LIKE TO BE IN HIDING FOR SO LONG. EVER SINCE WE CAME UPON THAT SCROLL. ›
‹ I SUSPECTED THAT PARCHMENT WOULD CONTAIN SOME SECRET ON HOW TO DEFEAT THAT WITCH WE NOW KNOW TO BE CIRCE... ›
‹ BUT UNTIL STAVROS JOINED US, I FEARED WE WOULD NEVER DECIPHER IT. ›
‹ STAVROS WAS-- IS A BRAVE, BRILLIANT MAN. ›
‹ ONLY HE WOULD HAVE THOUGHT OF ROLLING UP HIS NOTES INTO THE SCROLL BEFORE HE GAVE THEM TO VANESSA. ›
‹ OTHERWISE IT WOULD'VE TAKEN ME DAYS TO GET THIS FAR. ›
‹ I'M BACK, GREGORI. ›
‹ PROFESSOR, I LEFT YOUR DAUGHTER WITH YOUR PARENTS AS YOU REQUESTED. ›
‹ PROF. CHRISTADOULODOU IS IN THE HOSPITAL'S EMERGENCY ROOM, BUT I COULDN'T GET ANY MORE NEWS ABOUT HIM. ›
‹ AND THE POLICE? ›
‹ "JUST A PACK OF WILD ANIMALS," THEY SAY. ›
‹ THOSE INCOMPETENT FOOLS STILL WON'T BELIEVE US. ›
‹ WHAT ABOUT THE SCROLL ? HAVEN'T YOU FIGURED IT OUT YET!?›
‹ QUIET, KATINA. THE PROFESSOR KNOWS HOW URGENT THE SITUATION IS. ›
‹ YES, MS. LEIKOS. DIANA IS MORE THAN SOME MESSIANIC ICON TO ME. SHE IS LIKE MY DAUGHTER. ›
‹ AND NO ONE, NOT EVEN A SORCERESS FROM HELL, WILL STOP ME FROM RESCUING MY DAUGHTER! ›
‹ PLEASE, PROFESSOR, DON'T THINK WE ARE SOME INSENSITIVE FANATICAL CULT. ›
‹ THE MAN WHO DIED TO CAPTURE THAT PARCHMENT WAS MY SON... ›
‹ AND KATINA'S FIANCÉ. ›
‹ THIS BATTLE IS QUITE PERSONAL TO US, TOO. ›
Bingo
‹ YOU'VE FOUND SOMETHING? ›
‹ YES. A WAY TO SAVE DIANA. ›
‹ BUT NOT WITH THE SCROLL. ›
‹ WITH THIS! ›
‹ THE TWINE USED TO BIND IT! ›
‹ IT IS LACED WITH A MYSTIC HERB, KNOWN IN LEGEND AS MOLY! ›
7

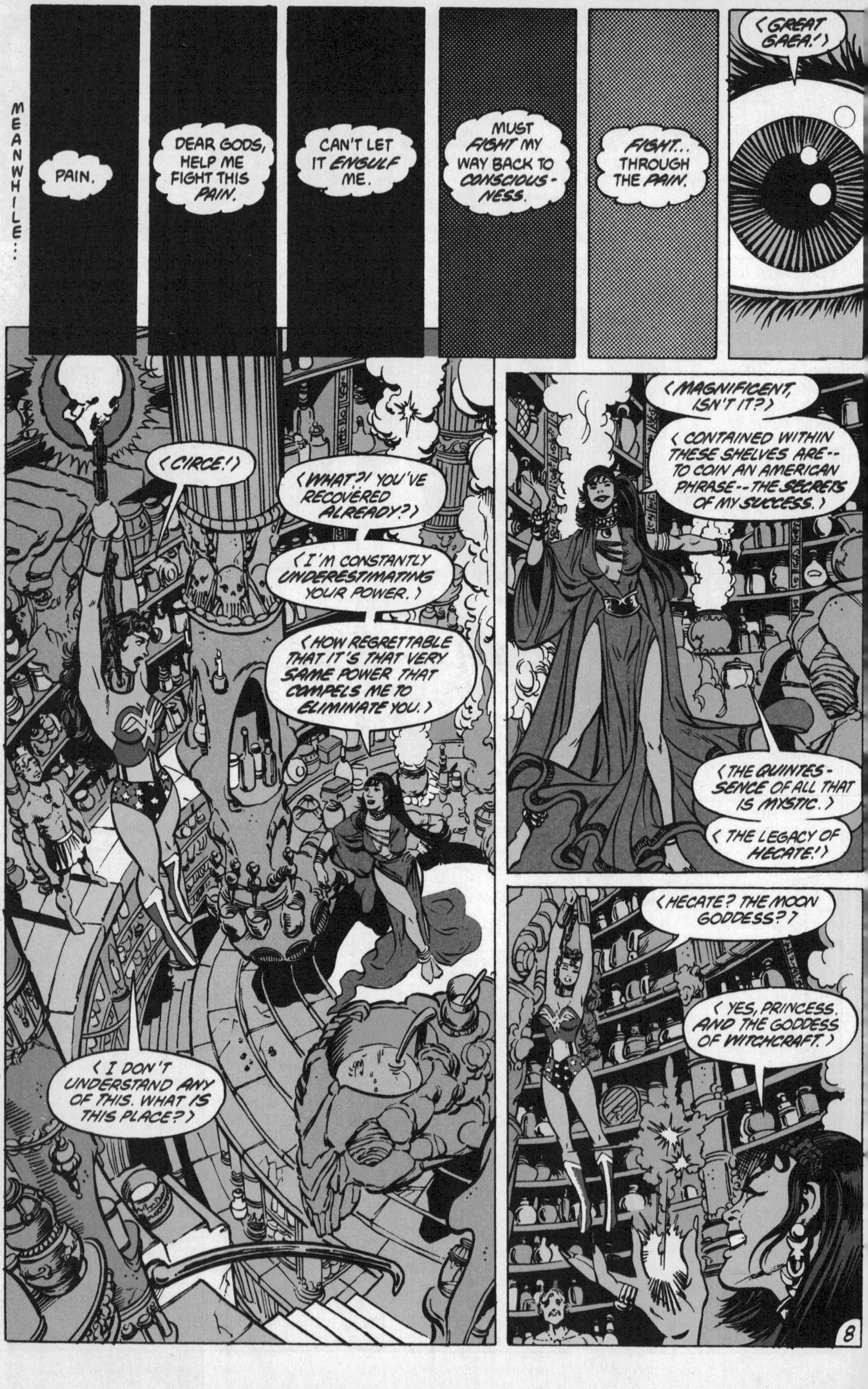
MEANWHILE...
PAIN.
DEAR GODS, HELP ME FIGHT THIS PAIN.
CAN'T LET IT ENGULF ME.
MUST FIGHT MY WAY BACK TO CONSCIOUS-NESS.
FIGHT... THROUGH THE PAIN.
<GREAT GAEA!>
<CIRCE!>
<WHAT?! YOU'VE RECOVERED ALREADY?>
<I'M CONSTANTLY UNDERESTIMATING YOUR POWER.>
<HOW REGRETTABLE THAT IT'S THAT VERY SAME POWER THAT COMPELS ME TO ELIMINATE YOU.>
<I DON'T UNDERSTAND ANY OF THIS. WHAT IS THIS PLACE?>
<MAGNIFICENT, ISN'T IT?>
<CONTAINED WITHIN THESE SHELVES ARE--TO COIN AN AMERICAN PHRASE--THE SECRETS OF MY SUCCESS.>
<THE QUINTES-SENCE OF ALL THAT IS MYSTIC.>
<THE LEGACY OF HECATE!>
<HECATE? THE MOON GODDESS?>
<YES, PRINCESS. AND THE GODDESS OF WITCHCRAFT.>
8

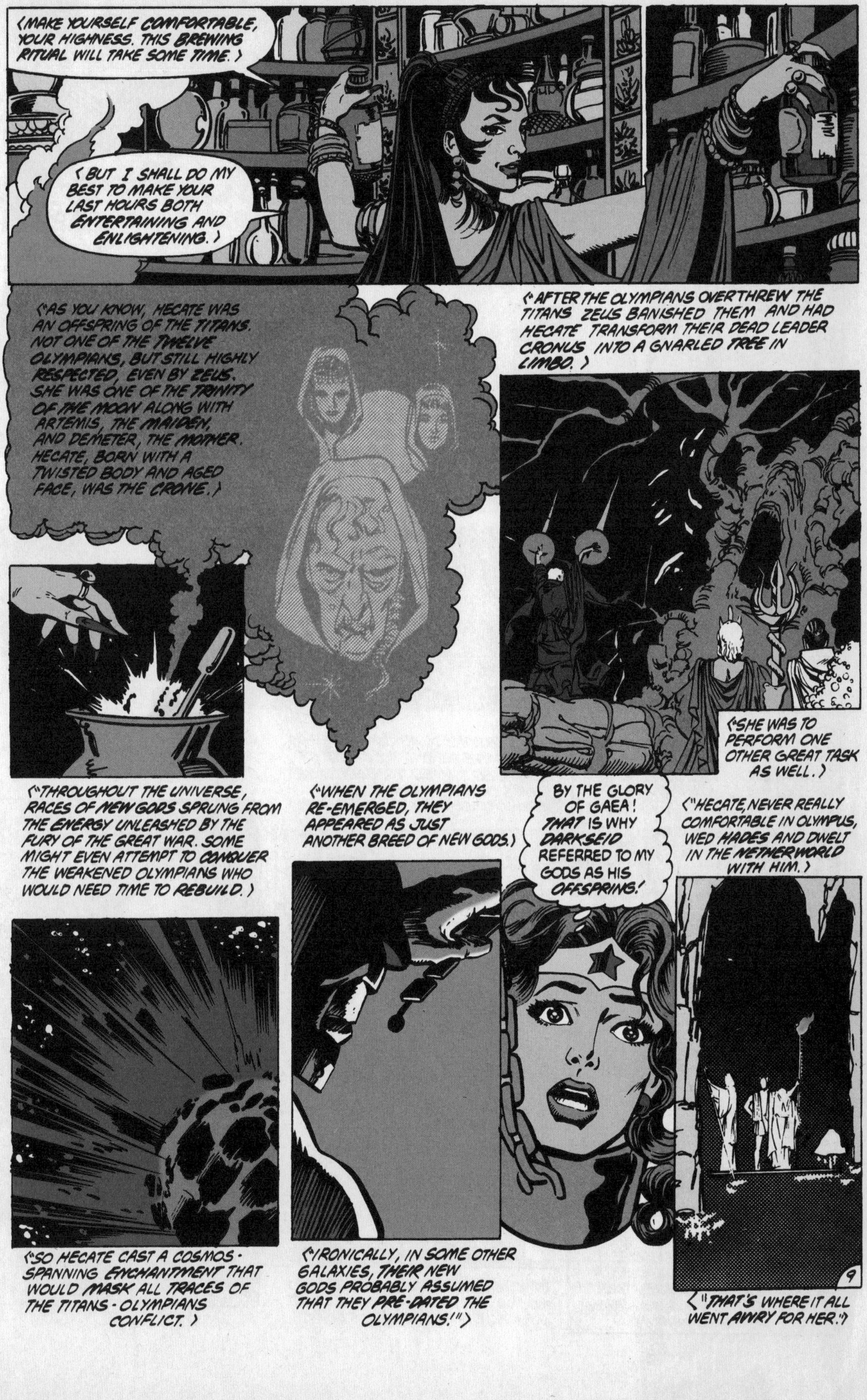
<MAKE YOURSELF COMFORTABLE, YOUR HIGHNESS. THIS BREWING RITUAL WILL TAKE SOME TIME.>
<BUT I SHALL DO MY BEST TO MAKE YOUR LAST HOURS BOTH ENTERTAINING AND ENLIGHTENING.>
<"AS YOU KNOW, HECATE WAS AN OFFSPRING OF THE TITANS. NOT ONE OF THE TWELVE OLYMPIANS, BUT STILL HIGHLY RESPECTED, EVEN BY ZEUS. SHE WAS ONE OF THE TRINITY OF THE MOON ALONG WITH ARTEMIS, THE MAIDEN, AND DEMETER, THE MOTHER. HECATE, BORN WITH A TWISTED BODY AND AGED FACE, WAS THE CRONE.>
<"AFTER THE OLYMPIANS OVERTHREW THE TITANS ZEUS BANISHED THEM AND HAD HECATE TRANSFORM THEIR DEAD LEADER CRONUS INTO A GNARLED TREE IN LIMBO.>
<"SHE WAS TO PERFORM ONE OTHER GREAT TASK AS WELL.>
<"THROUGHOUT THE UNIVERSE, RACES OF NEW GODS SPRUNG FROM THE ENERGY UNLEASHED BY THE FURY OF THE GREAT WAR. SOME MIGHT EVEN ATTEMPT TO CONQUER THE WEAKENED OLYMPIANS WHO WOULD NEED TIME TO REBUILD.>
<"SO HECATE CAST A COSMOS-SPANNING ENCHANTMENT THAT WOULD MASK ALL TRACES OF THE TITANS-OLYMPIANS CONFLICT.>
<"WHEN THE OLYMPIANS RE-EMERGED, THEY APPEARED AS JUST ANOTHER BREED OF NEW GODS.>
<"IRONICALLY, IN SOME OTHER GALAXIES, THEIR NEW GODS PROBABLY ASSUMED THAT THEY PRE-DATED THE OLYMPIANS!">
BY THE GLORY OF GAEA! THAT IS WHY DARKSEID REFERRED TO MY GODS AS HIS OFFSPRING!
<"HECATE, NEVER REALLY COMFORTABLE IN OLYMPUS, WED HADES AND DWELT IN THE NETHERWORLD WITH HIM.>
<"THAT'S WHERE IT ALL WENT AWRY FOR HER.">

< HMM. HAVE TO BE EXTRA CAREFUL HERE. >

< THEOPHILOS, BRING ME THE HEART. THE FRESH ONE. >

< YES, MISTRESS. >

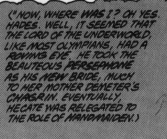

("NOW, WHERE WAS I? OH YES. HADES. WELL, IT SEEMED THAT THE LORD OF THE UNDERWORLD, LIKE MOST OLYMPIANS, HAD A ROVING EYE. HE TOOK THE BEAUTEOUS PERSEPHONE AS HIS NEW BRIDE, MUCH TO HER MOTHER DEMETER'S CHAGRIN. EVENTUALLY, HECATE WAS RELEGATED TO THE ROLE OF HANDMAIDEN.)

<"HERA, RESENTFUL OF ZEUS' RESPECT FOR HECATE, FORBADE ANY OLYMPIAN TO AID THE HUMBLED MOON GODDESS. >

<"IT WAS AN INSULT THAT HECATE WOULD NEVER FORGET. >

<"AS TIME PASSED THE BITTERNESS GREW AND SHE LONGED FOR THE SWEETNESS OF REVENGE. FOR THE FINAL TIME, HECATE RETURNED TO THE EARTH THAT WAS MOTHER TO US ALL. >

<"AND THAT'S WHERE MY STORY BEGINS. ")

< I TOO WAS ONCE A PRINCESS OF COLCHIS. >

<..BUT MY TRAITOROUS SUBJECTS OBJECTED TO MY KILLING MY WEAKLING HUSBAND. >

< SO I FOUND REFUGE ON THIS ISLAND AND SWORE I WOULD USE MY MAGIC AND POTIONS TO AVENGE MYSELF ON THE INFERIORS WHO DARED STAND AGAINST ME! >

<" UNFORTUNATELY, MY SORCERY WAS INEFFECTIVE BEYOND THE LIMITS OF AEAEA. SO I USED THE SEDUCTIVE SONGS OF THE SIREN TO LURE WAYWARD SEAFARERS TO MY LAIR. >

<"THOSE WHO SURVIVED THE JAGGED ROCKS FACED ME. I MADE THEM BEG FOR THE COMFORT OF DEATH. >

<"BUT IT WASN'T ENOUGH. I WANTED MORE POWER. I NEEDED IT. I WOULD HAVE SOLD MY SOUL FOR IT. >

<"AND I DID. ")

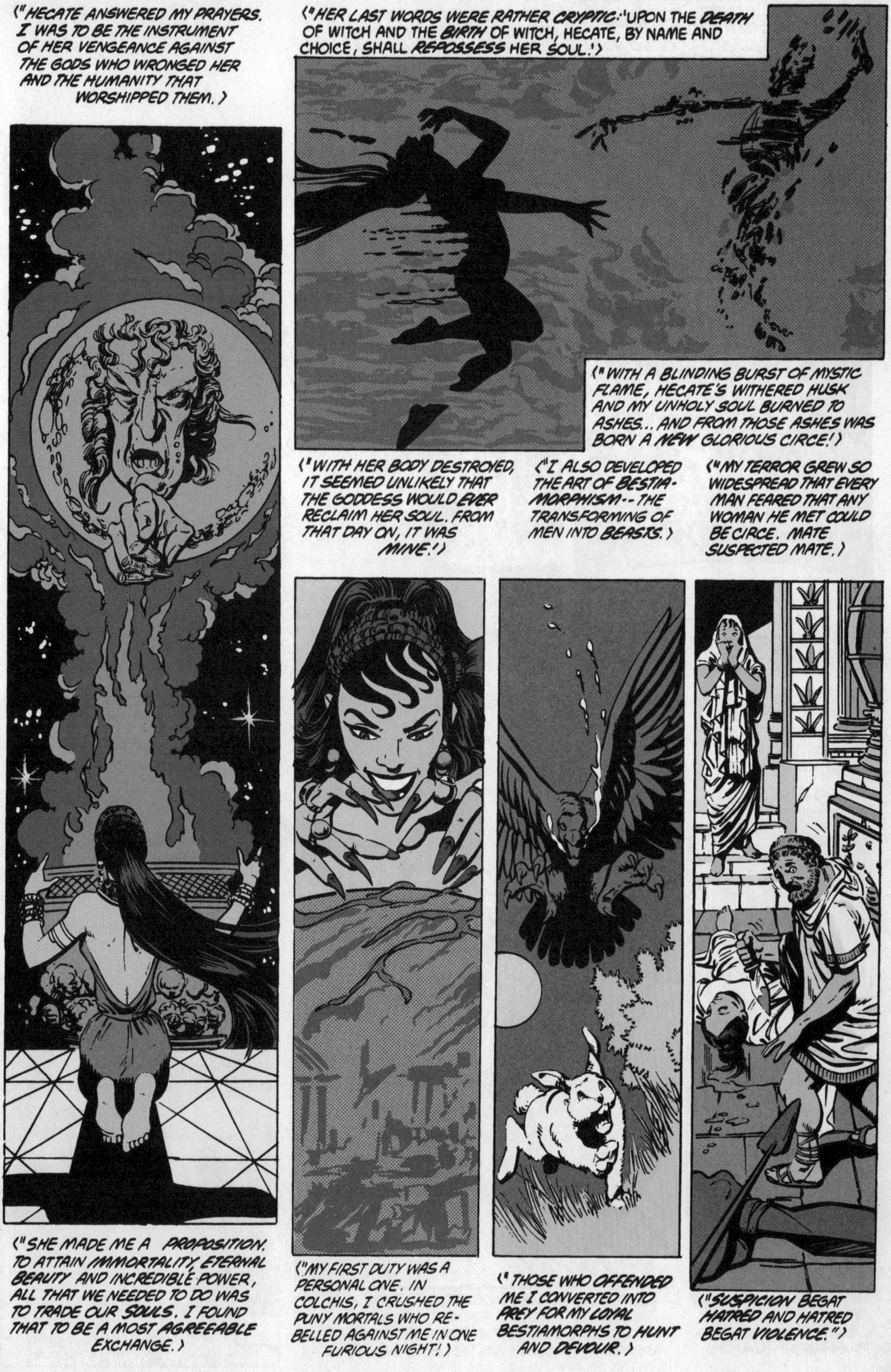
("HECATE ANSWERED MY PRAYERS. I WAS TO BE THE INSTRUMENT OF HER VENGEANCE AGAINST THE GODS WHO WRONGED HER AND THE HUMANITY THAT WORSHIPPED THEM.)
("SHE MADE ME A PROPOSITION. TO ATTAIN IMMORTALITY, ETERNAL BEAUTY AND INCREDIBLE POWER, ALL THAT WE NEEDED TO DO WAS TO TRADE OUR SOULS. I FOUND THAT TO BE A MOST AGREEABLE EXCHANGE.)
("HER LAST WORDS WERE RATHER CRYPTIC: 'UPON THE DEATH OF WITCH AND THE BIRTH OF WITCH, HECATE, BY NAME AND CHOICE, SHALL REPOSSESS HER SOUL.')
("WITH A BLINDING BURST OF MYSTIC FLAME, HECATE'S WITHERED HUSK AND MY UNHOLY SOUL BURNED TO ASHES... AND FROM THOSE ASHES WAS BORN A NEW GLORIOUS CIRCE!)
("WITH HER BODY DESTROYED, IT SEEMED UNLIKELY THAT THE GODDESS WOULD EVER RECLAIM HER SOUL. FROM THAT DAY ON, IT WAS MINE!)
("MY FIRST DUTY WAS A PERSONAL ONE. IN COLCHIS, I CRUSHED THE PUNY MORTALS WHO RE-BELLED AGAINST ME IN ONE FURIOUS NIGHT!)
("I ALSO DEVELOPED THE ART OF BESTIA-MORPHISM -- THE TRANSFORMING OF MEN INTO BEASTS.)
("THOSE WHO OFFENDED ME I CONVERTED INTO PREY FOR MY LOYAL BESTIAMORPHS TO HUNT AND DEVOUR.)
("MY TERROR GREW SO WIDESPREAD THAT EVERY MAN FEARED THAT ANY WOMAN HE MET COULD BE CIRCE. MATE SUSPECTED MATE.)
("SUSPICION BEGAT HATRED AND HATRED BEGAT VIOLENCE.")

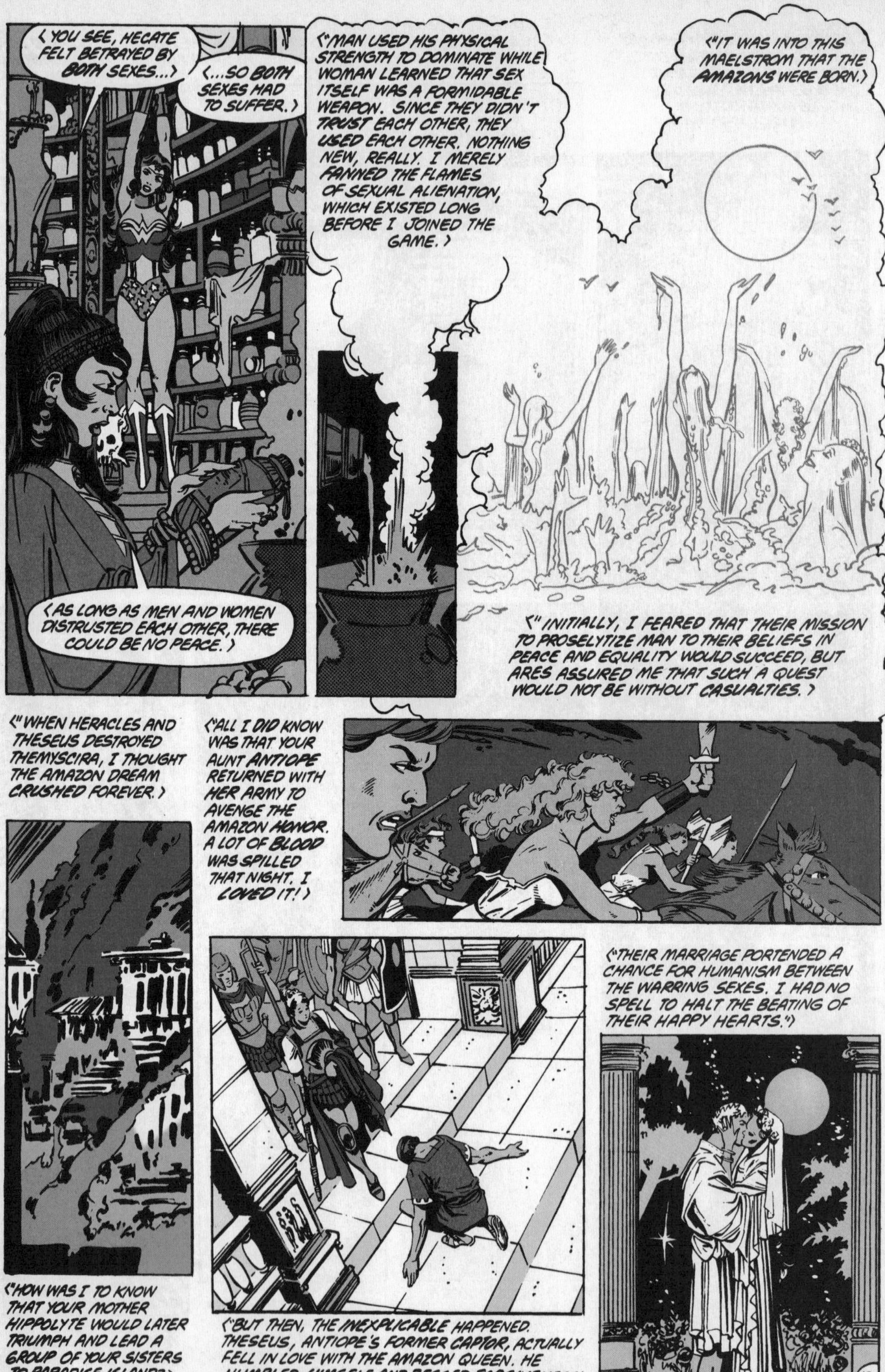
‹YOU SEE, HECATE FELT BETRAYED BY BOTH SEXES...›
‹...SO BOTH SEXES HAD TO SUFFER.›
‹AS LONG AS MEN AND WOMEN DISTRUSTED EACH OTHER, THERE COULD BE NO PEACE.›
‹"MAN USED HIS PHYSICAL STRENGTH TO DOMINATE WHILE WOMAN LEARNED THAT SEX ITSELF WAS A FORMIDABLE WEAPON. SINCE THEY DIDN'T TRUST EACH OTHER, THEY USED EACH OTHER. NOTHING NEW, REALLY. I MERELY FANNED THE FLAMES OF SEXUAL ALIENATION, WHICH EXISTED LONG BEFORE I JOINED THE GAME.›
‹"IT WAS INTO THIS MAELSTROM THAT THE AMAZONS WERE BORN.›
‹"INITIALLY, I FEARED THAT THEIR MISSION TO PROSELYTIZE MAN TO THEIR BELIEFS IN PEACE AND EQUALITY WOULD SUCCEED, BUT ARES ASSURED ME THAT SUCH A QUEST WOULD NOT BE WITHOUT CASUALTIES.›
‹"WHEN HERACLES AND THESEUS DESTROYED THEMYSCIRA, I THOUGHT THE AMAZON DREAM CRUSHED FOREVER.›
‹"ALL I DID KNOW WAS THAT YOUR AUNT ANTIOPE RETURNED WITH HER ARMY TO AVENGE THE AMAZON HONOR. A LOT OF BLOOD WAS SPILLED THAT NIGHT. I LOVED IT!›
‹"HOW WAS I TO KNOW THAT YOUR MOTHER HIPPOLYTE WOULD LATER TRIUMPH AND LEAD A GROUP OF YOUR SISTERS TO PARADISE ISLAND?›
‹"BUT THEN, THE INEXPLICABLE HAPPENED. THESEUS, ANTIOPE'S FORMER CAPTOR, ACTUALLY FELL IN LOVE WITH THE AMAZON QUEEN. HE HUMBLED HIMSELF AND BEGGED FORGIVENESS.›
‹"THEIR MARRIAGE PORTENDED A CHANCE FOR HUMANISM BETWEEN THE WARRING SEXES. I HAD NO SPELL TO HALT THE BEATING OF THEIR HAPPY HEARTS."›
12

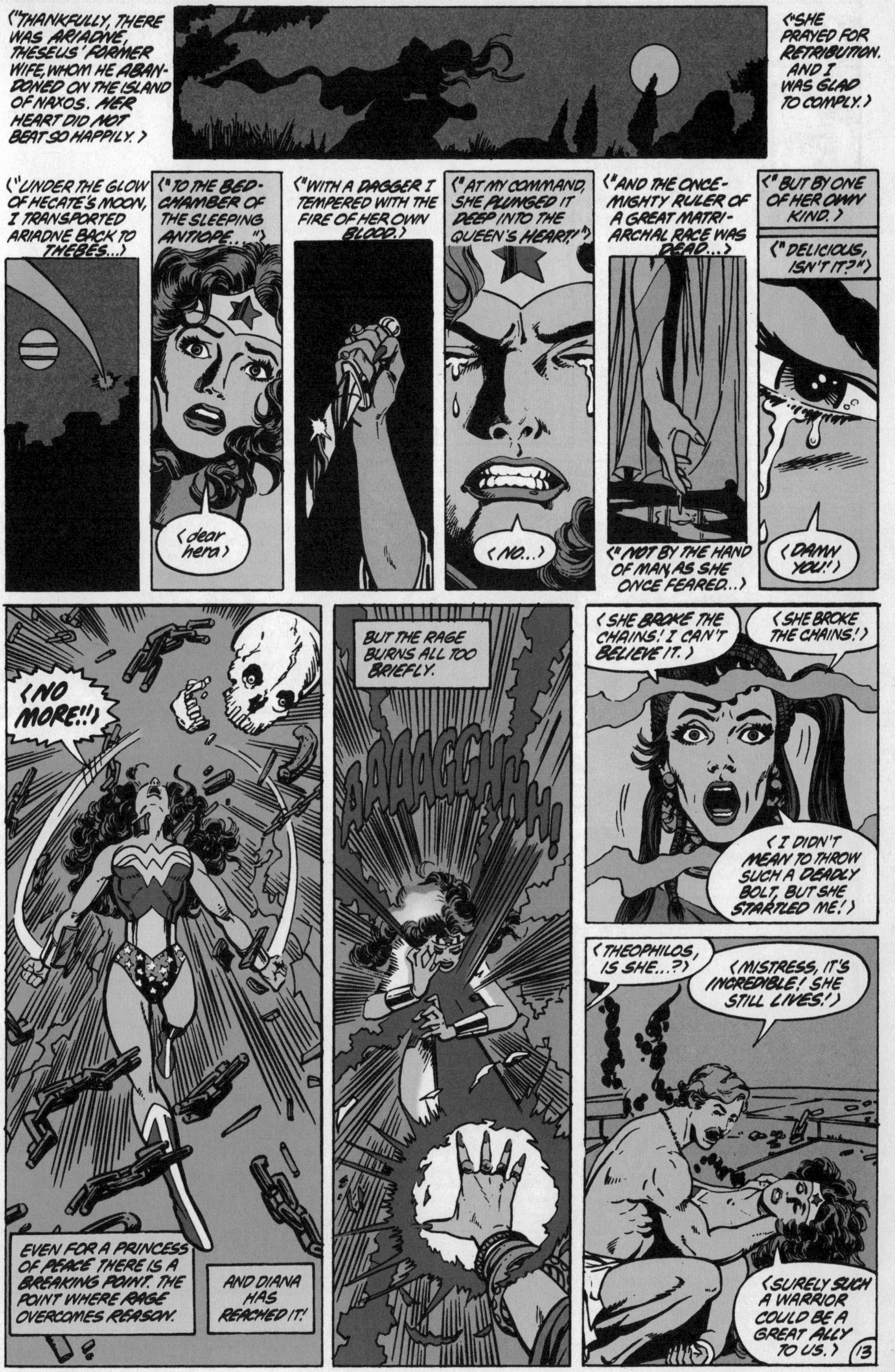

("THANKFULLY, THERE WAS ARIADNE, THESEUS' FORMER WIFE, WHOM HE ABANDONED ON THE ISLAND OF NAXOS. HER HEART DID NOT BEAT SO HAPPILY.)
("SHE PRAYED FOR RETRIBUTION. AND I WAS GLAD TO COMPLY.)
("UNDER THE GLOW OF HECATE'S MOON, I TRANSPORTED ARIADNE BACK TO THEBES...)
("TO THE BED-CHAMBER OF THE SLEEPING ANTIOPE...")
(dear hera)
("WITH A DAGGER I TEMPERED WITH THE FIRE OF HER OWN BLOOD.)
("AT MY COMMAND, SHE PLUNGED IT DEEP INTO THE QUEEN'S HEART!")
(NO...)
("AND THE ONCE-MIGHTY RULER OF A GREAT MATRI-ARCHAL RACE WAS DEAD...)
("NOT BY THE HAND OF MAN, AS SHE ONCE FEARED...)
(" BUT BY ONE OF HER OWN KIND.)
("DELICIOUS, ISN'T IT?")
(DAMN YOU!)
(NO MORE!!)
EVEN FOR A PRINCESS OF PEACE THERE IS A BREAKING POINT. THE POINT WHERE RAGE OVERCOMES REASON.
AND DIANA HAS REACHED IT!
BUT THE RAGE BURNS ALL TOO BRIEFLY.
AAAAGGHHH!
(SHE BROKE THE CHAINS! I CAN'T BELIEVE IT.)
(SHE BROKE THE CHAINS!)
(I DIDN'T MEAN TO THROW SUCH A DEADLY BOLT, BUT SHE STARTLED ME!)
(THEOPHILOS, IS SHE...?)
(MISTRESS, IT'S INCREDIBLE! SHE STILL LIVES!)
(SURELY SUCH A WARRIOR COULD BE A GREAT ALLY TO US.)
13

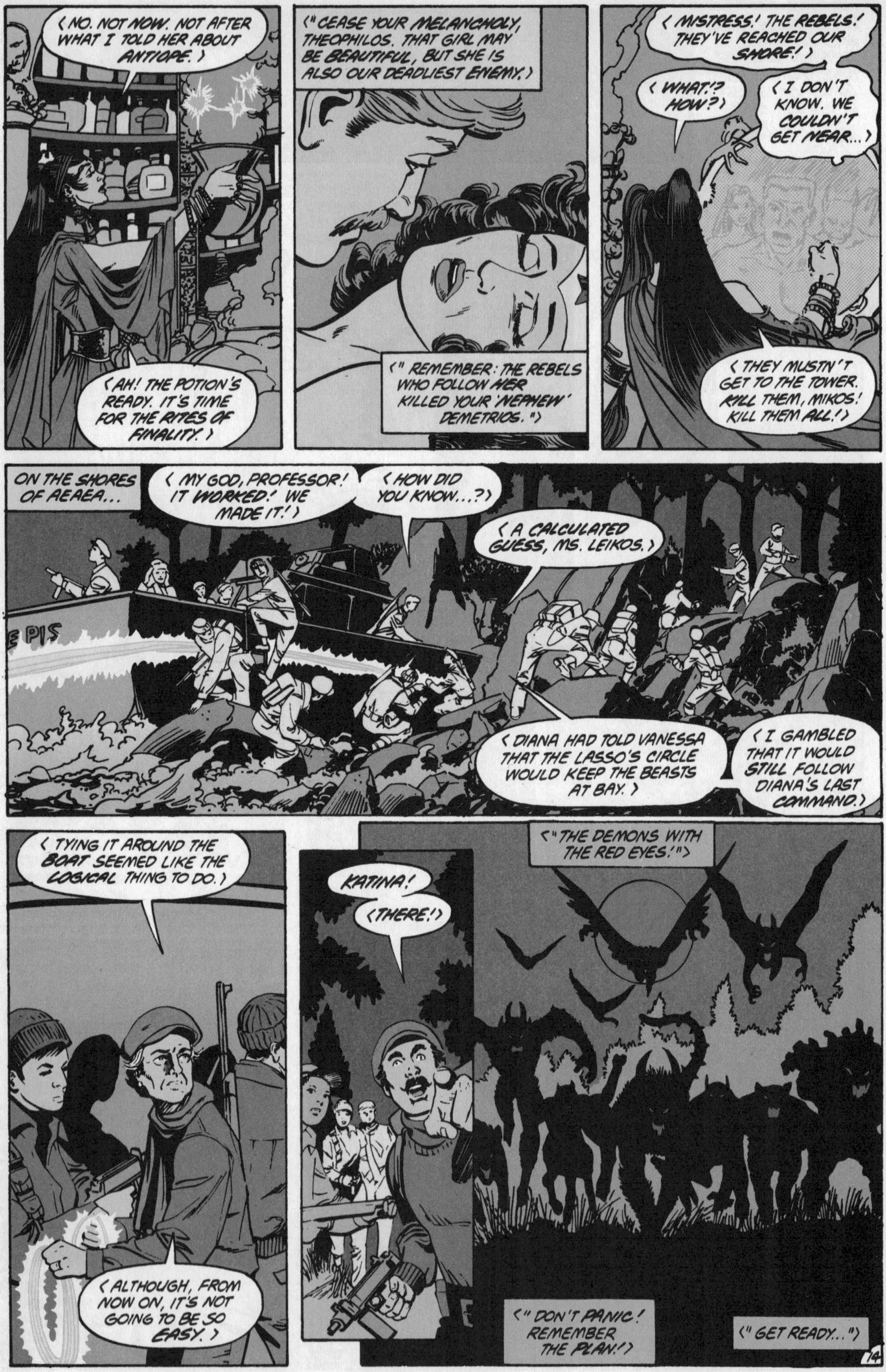
‹NO. NOT NOW. NOT AFTER WHAT I TOLD HER ABOUT ANTIOPE.›
‹AH! THE POTION'S READY. IT'S TIME FOR THE RITES OF FINALITY.›
‹"CEASE YOUR MELANCHOLY, THEOPHILOS. THAT GIRL MAY BE BEAUTIFUL, BUT SHE IS ALSO OUR DEADLIEST ENEMY.›
‹"REMEMBER: THE REBELS WHO FOLLOW HER KILLED YOUR 'NEPHEW' DEMETRIOS."›
‹MISTRESS! THE REBELS! THEY'VE REACHED OUR SHORE!›
‹WHAT!? HOW?›
‹I DON'T KNOW. WE COULDN'T GET NEAR...›
‹THEY MUSTN'T GET TO THE TOWER. KILL THEM, MIKOS! KILL THEM ALL!›
ON THE SHORES OF AEAEA...
‹MY GOD, PROFESSOR! IT WORKED! WE MADE IT!›
‹HOW DID YOU KNOW...?›
‹A CALCULATED GUESS, MS. LEIKOS.›
E PIS
‹DIANA HAD TOLD VANESSA THAT THE LASSO'S CIRCLE WOULD KEEP THE BEASTS AT BAY.›
‹I GAMBLED THAT IT WOULD STILL FOLLOW DIANA'S LAST COMMAND.›
‹TYING IT AROUND THE BOAT SEEMED LIKE THE LOGICAL THING TO DO.›
‹ALTHOUGH, FROM NOW ON, IT'S NOT GOING TO BE SO EASY.›
KATINA!
‹THERE!›
‹"THE DEMONS WITH THE RED EYES!"›
‹"DON'T PANIC! REMEMBER THE PLAN!"›
‹"GET READY..."›
14

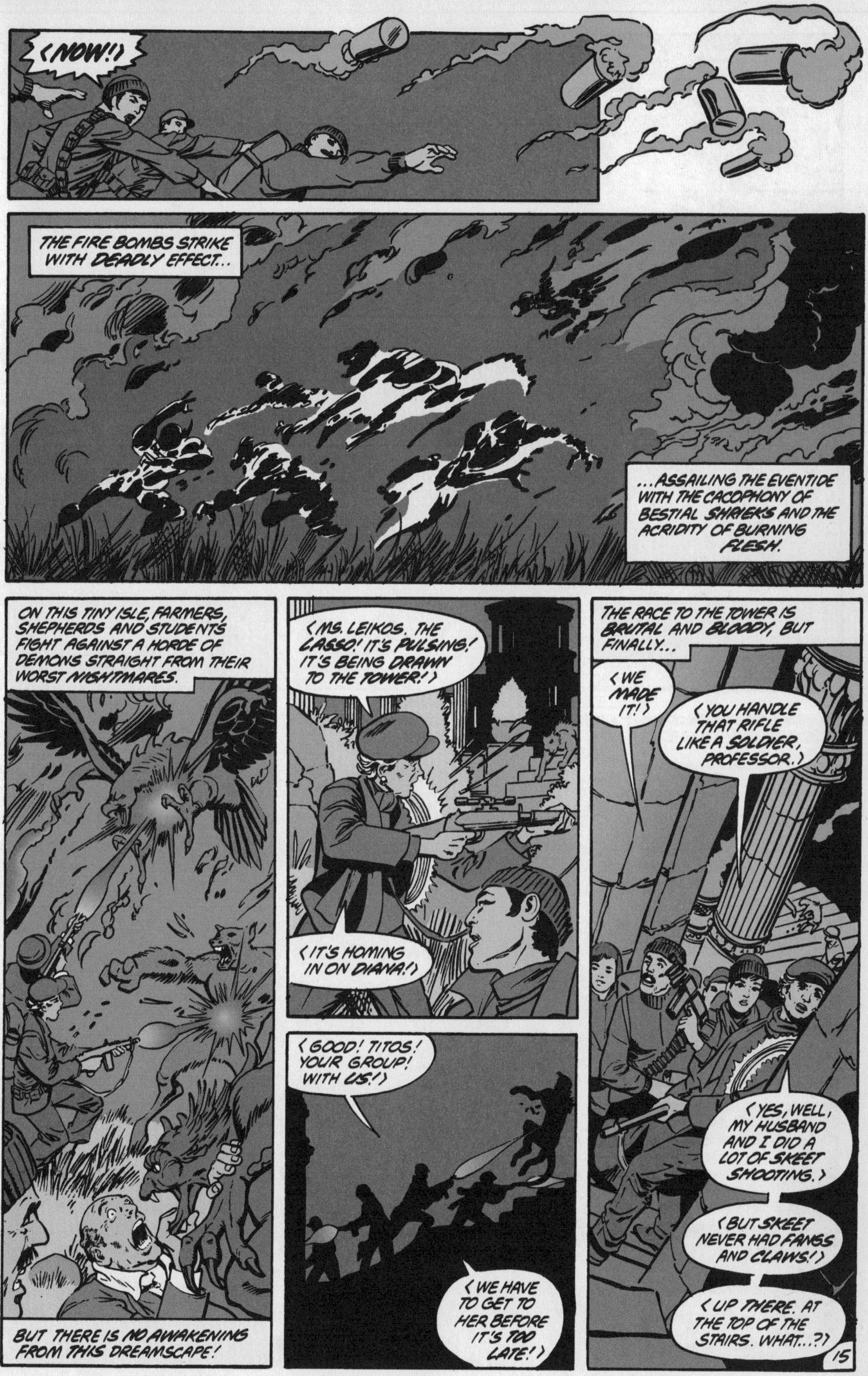

‹NOW!›
THE FIRE BOMBS STRIKE WITH DEADLY EFFECT...
...ASSAILING THE EVENTIDE WITH THE CACOPHONY OF BESTIAL SHRIEKS AND THE ACRIDITY OF BURNING FLESH.
ON THIS TINY ISLE, FARMERS, SHEPHERDS AND STUDENTS FIGHT AGAINST A HORDE OF DEMONS STRAIGHT FROM THEIR WORST NIGHTMARES.
BUT THERE IS NO AWAKENING FROM THIS DREAMSCAPE!
‹MS. LEIKOS. THE LASSO! IT'S PULSING! IT'S BEING DRAWN TO THE TOWER!›
‹IT'S HOMING IN ON DIANA!›
‹GOOD! TITOS! YOUR GROUP! WITH US!›
‹WE HAVE TO GET TO HER BEFORE IT'S TOO LATE!›
THE RACE TO THE TOWER IS BRUTAL AND BLOODY, BUT FINALLY...
‹WE MADE IT!›
‹YOU HANDLE THAT RIFLE LIKE A SOLDIER, PROFESSOR.›
‹YES, WELL, MY HUSBAND AND I DID A LOT OF SKEET SHOOTING.›
‹BUT SKEET NEVER HAD FANGS AND CLAWS!›
‹UP THERE. AT THE TOP OF THE STAIRS. WHAT...?›
15

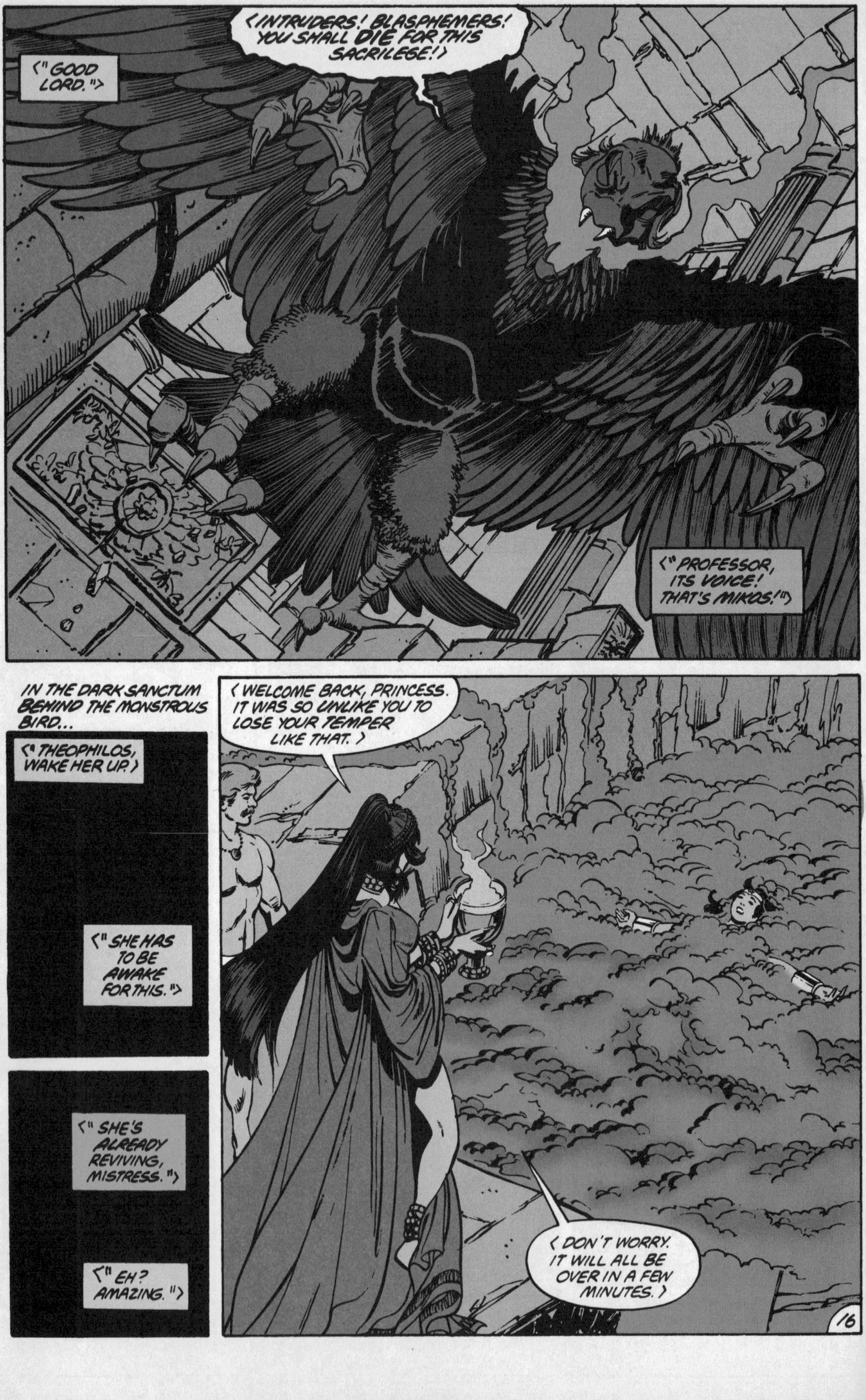

<("GOOD LORD.">
<INTRUDERS! BLASPHEMERS! YOU SHALL DIE FOR THIS SACRILEGE!>
<"PROFESSOR, ITS VOICE! THAT'S MIKOS!">
IN THE DARK SANCTUM BEHIND THE MONSTROUS BIRD...
<"THEOPHILOS, WAKE HER UP.>
<WELCOME BACK, PRINCESS. IT WAS SO UNLIKE YOU TO LOSE YOUR TEMPER LIKE THAT.>
<"SHE HAS TO BE AWAKE FOR THIS.">
<"SHE'S ALREADY REVIVING, MISTRESS.">
<"EH? AMAZING.">
<DON'T WORRY. IT WILL ALL BE OVER IN A FEW MINUTES.>
16

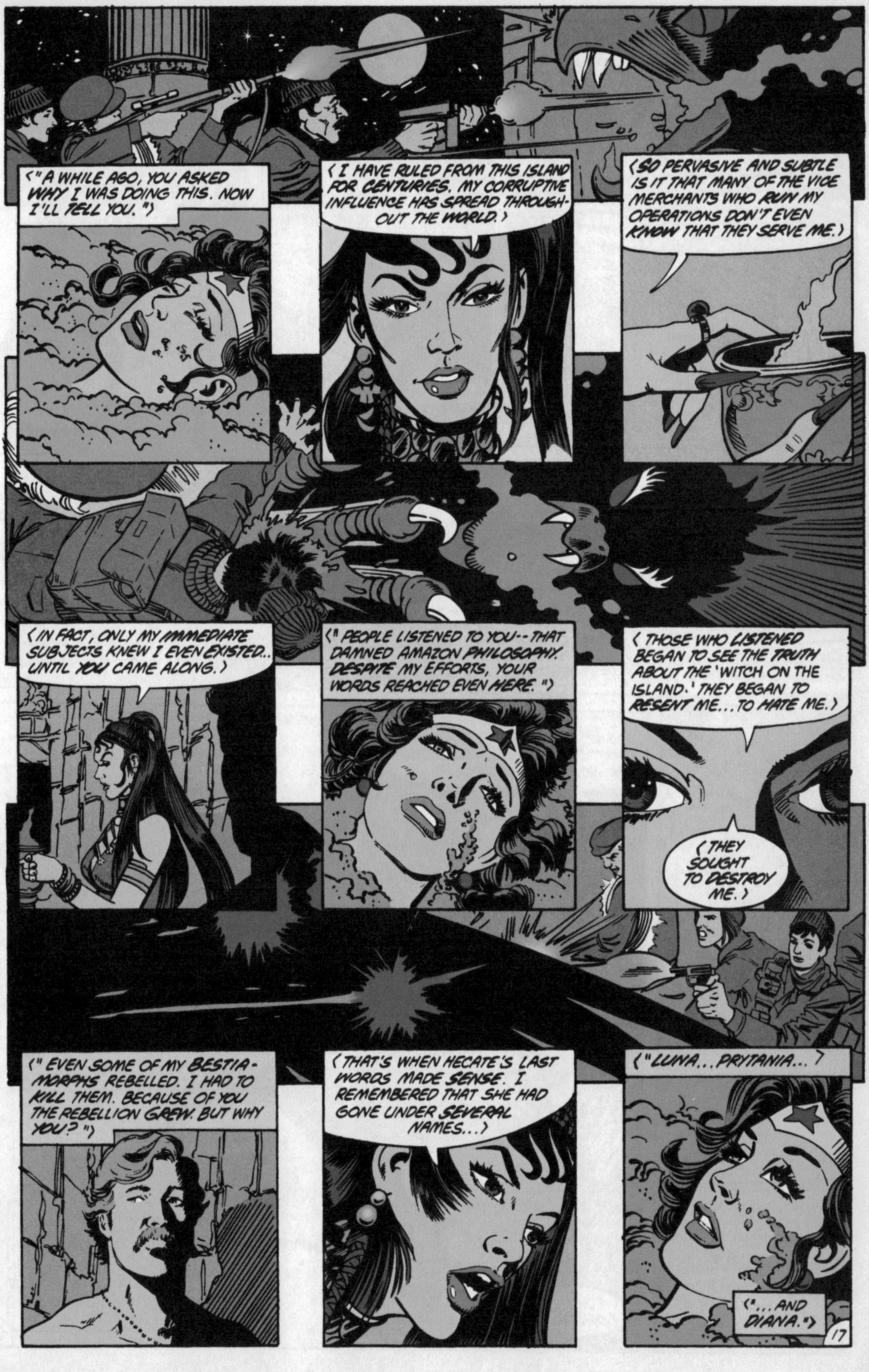
("A WHILE AGO, YOU ASKED WHY I WAS DOING THIS. NOW I'LL TELL YOU.")
(I HAVE RULED FROM THIS ISLAND FOR CENTURIES. MY CORRUPTIVE INFLUENCE HAS SPREAD THROUGHOUT THE WORLD.)
(SO PERVASIVE AND SUBTLE IS IT THAT MANY OF THE VICE MERCHANTS WHO RUN MY OPERATIONS DON'T EVEN KNOW THAT THEY SERVE ME.)
(IN FACT, ONLY MY IMMEDIATE SUBJECTS KNEW I EVEN EXISTED... UNTIL YOU CAME ALONG.)
("PEOPLE LISTENED TO YOU--THAT DAMNED AMAZON PHILOSOPHY. DESPITE MY EFFORTS, YOUR WORDS REACHED EVEN HERE.")
(THOSE WHO LISTENED BEGAN TO SEE THE TRUTH ABOUT THE 'WITCH ON THE ISLAND.' THEY BEGAN TO RESENT ME... TO HATE ME.)
(THEY SOUGHT TO DESTROY ME.)
("EVEN SOME OF MY BESTIAMORPHS REBELLED. I HAD TO KILL THEM. BECAUSE OF YOU THE REBELLION GREW. BUT WHY YOU?")
(THAT'S WHEN HECATE'S LAST WORDS MADE SENSE. I REMEMBERED THAT SHE HAD GONE UNDER SEVERAL NAMES...)
("LUNA... PRYTANIA...)
("...AND DIANA.")
17

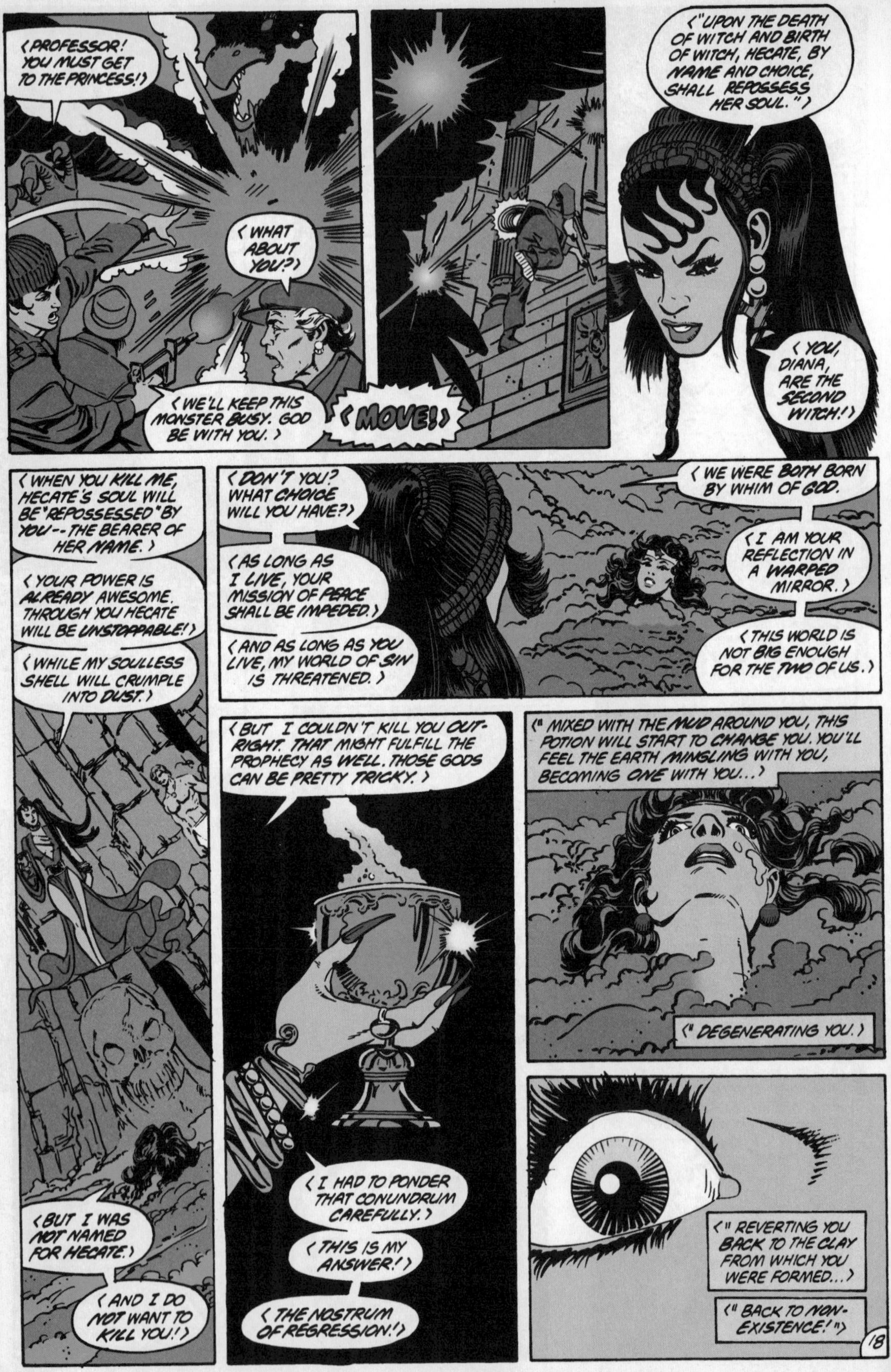
<PROFESSOR! YOU MUST GET TO THE PRINCESS!>
<WHAT ABOUT YOU?>
<WE'LL KEEP THIS MONSTER BUSY. GOD BE WITH YOU.>
<MOVE!>
<"UPON THE DEATH OF WITCH AND BIRTH OF WITCH, HECATE, BY NAME AND CHOICE, SHALL REPOSSESS HER SOUL.">
<YOU, DIANA, ARE THE SECOND WITCH!>
<WHEN YOU KILL ME, HECATE'S SOUL WILL BE "REPOSSESSED" BY YOU--THE BEARER OF HER NAME.>
<YOUR POWER IS ALREADY AWESOME. THROUGH YOU HECATE WILL BE UNSTOPPABLE!>
<WHILE MY SOULLESS SHELL WILL CRUMPLE INTO DUST.>
<BUT I WAS NOT NAMED FOR HECATE.>
<AND I DO NOT WANT TO KILL YOU!>
<DON'T YOU? WHAT CHOICE WILL YOU HAVE?>
<AS LONG AS I LIVE, YOUR MISSION OF PEACE SHALL BE IMPEDED.>
<AND AS LONG AS YOU LIVE, MY WORLD OF SIN IS THREATENED.>
<WE WERE BOTH BORN BY WHIM OF GOD.
<I AM YOUR REFLECTION IN A WARPED MIRROR.>
<THIS WORLD IS NOT BIG ENOUGH FOR THE TWO OF US.>
<BUT I COULDN'T KILL YOU OUTRIGHT. THAT MIGHT FULFILL THE PROPHECY AS WELL. THOSE GODS CAN BE PRETTY TRICKY.>
<I HAD TO PONDER THAT CONUNDRUM CAREFULLY.>
<THIS IS MY ANSWER!>
<THE NOSTRUM OF REGRESSION!>
<" MIXED WITH THE MUD AROUND YOU, THIS POTION WILL START TO CHANGE YOU. YOU'LL FEEL THE EARTH MINGLING WITH YOU, BECOMING ONE WITH YOU...>
<" DEGENERATING YOU.>
<" REVERTING YOU BACK TO THE CLAY FROM WHICH YOU WERE FORMED...>
<" BACK TO NON-EXISTENCE!">
18

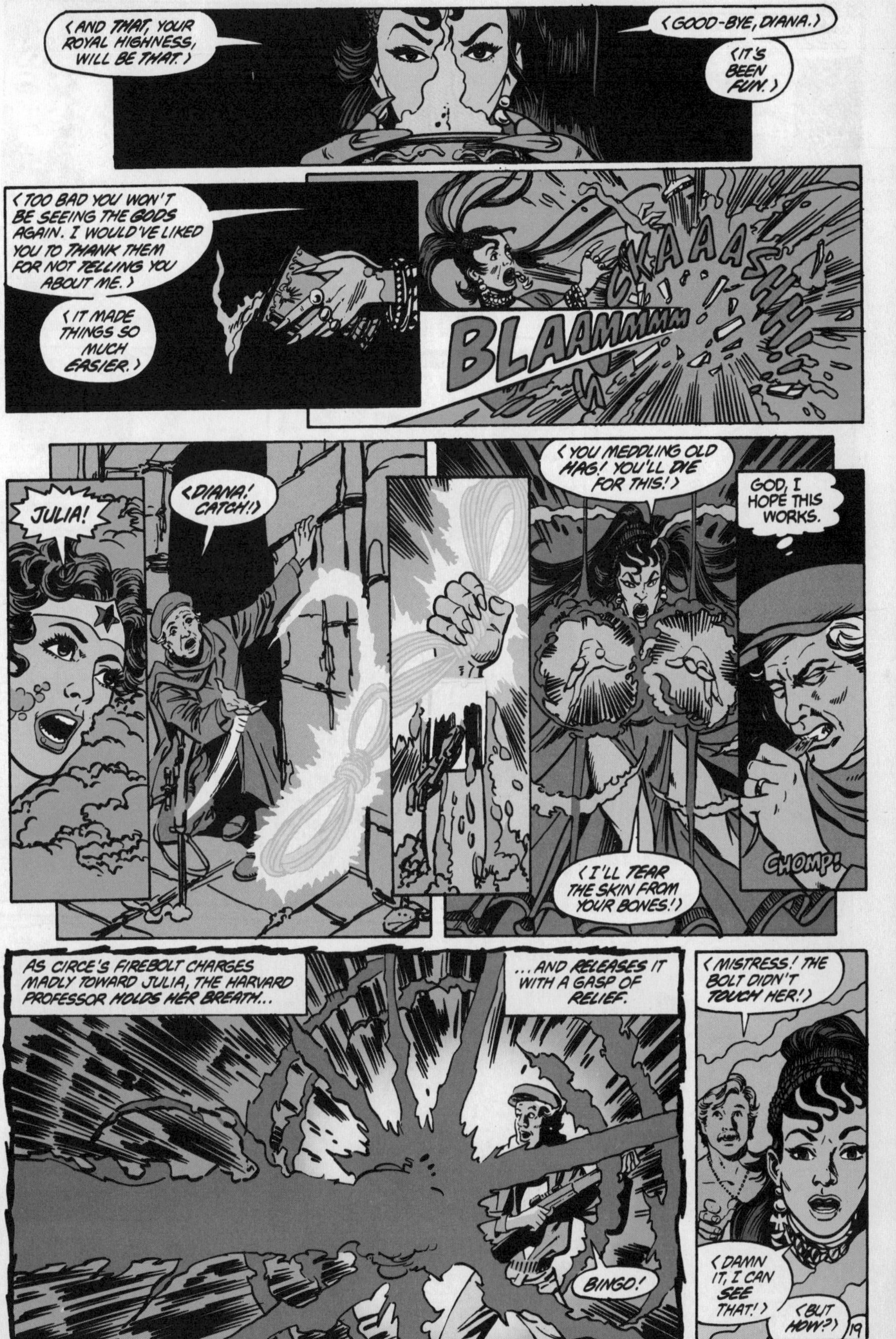

(AND THAT, YOUR ROYAL HIGHNESS, WILL BE THAT.)
(GOOD-BYE, DIANA.)
(IT'S BEEN FUN.)
(TOO BAD YOU WON'T BE SEEING THE GODS AGAIN. I WOULD'VE LIKED YOU TO THANK THEM FOR NOT TELLING YOU ABOUT ME.)
(IT MADE THINGS SO MUCH EASIER.)
CKAAAASHH!
BLAAMMMM
JULIA!
(DIANA! CATCH!)
(YOU MEDDLING OLD HAG! YOU'LL DIE FOR THIS!)
(I'LL TEAR THE SKIN FROM YOUR BONES!)
GOD, I HOPE THIS WORKS.
CHOMP!
AS CIRCE'S FIREBOLT CHARGES MADLY TOWARD JULIA, THE HARVARD PROFESSOR HOLDS HER BREATH...
...AND RELEASES IT WITH A GASP OF RELIEF.
BINGO!
(MISTRESS! THE BOLT DIDN'T TOUCH HER!)
(DAMN IT, I CAN SEE THAT!)
(BUT HOW?)
19

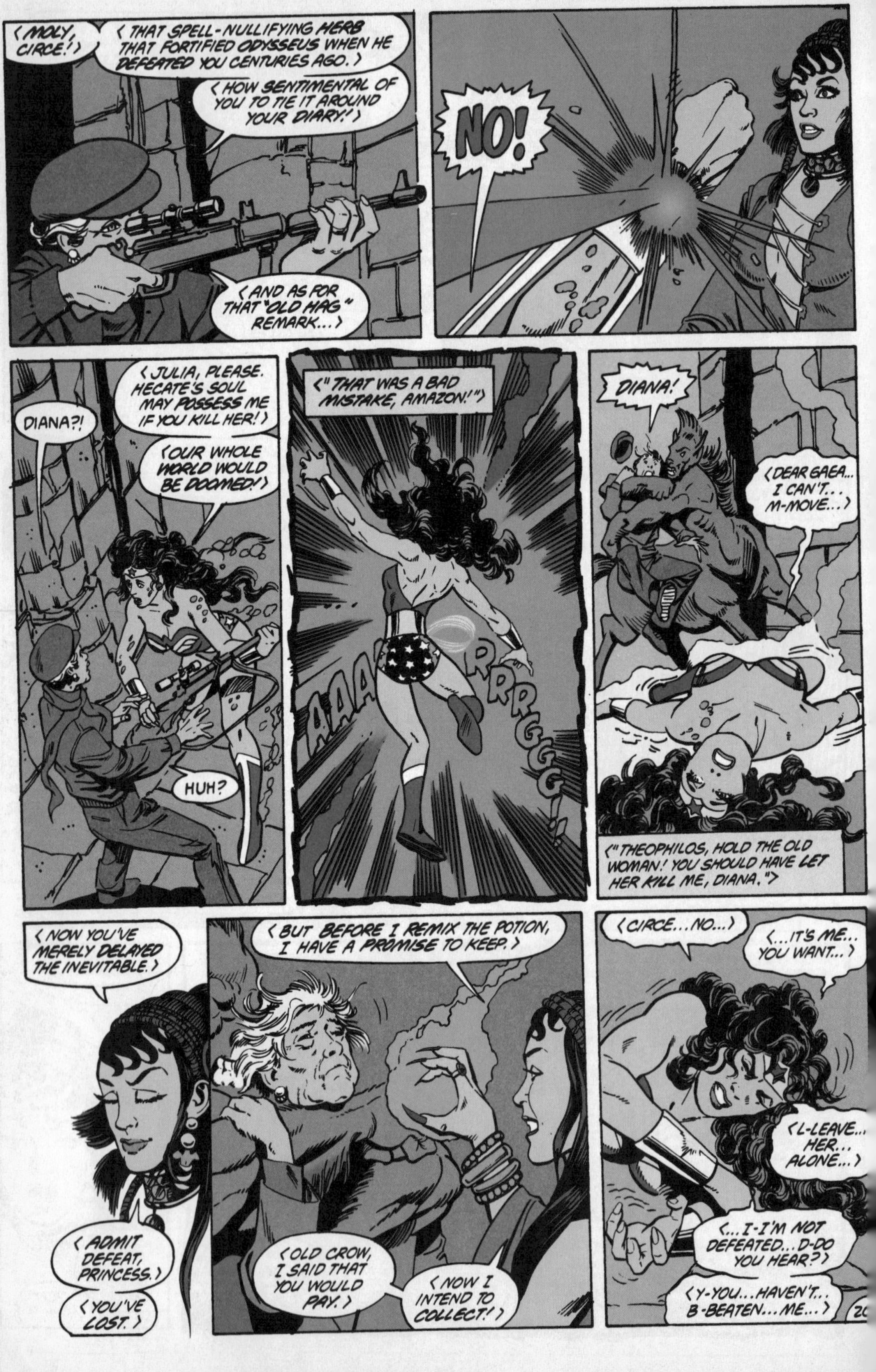

‹MOLY, CIRCE!›
‹THAT SPELL-NULLIFYING HERB THAT FORTIFIED ODYSSEUS WHEN HE DEFEATED YOU CENTURIES AGO.›
‹HOW SENTIMENTAL OF YOU TO TIE IT AROUND YOUR DIARY!›
‹AND AS FOR THAT "OLD HAG" REMARK...›
NO!
DIANA?!
‹JULIA, PLEASE. HECATE'S SOUL MAY POSSESS ME IF YOU KILL HER!›
‹OUR WHOLE WORLD WOULD BE DOOMED!›
HUH?
‹"THAT WAS A BAD MISTAKE, AMAZON!"›
AAAARRRGGG
DIANA!
‹DEAR GAEA... I CAN'T... M-MOVE...›
‹"THEOPHILOS, HOLD THE OLD WOMAN! YOU SHOULD HAVE LET HER KILL ME, DIANA."›
‹NOW YOU'VE MERELY DELAYED THE INEVITABLE.›
‹ADMIT DEFEAT, PRINCESS.›
‹YOU'VE LOST.›
‹BUT BEFORE I REMIX THE POTION, I HAVE A PROMISE TO KEEP.›
‹OLD CROW, I SAID THAT YOU WOULD PAY.›
‹NOW I INTEND TO COLLECT!›
‹CIRCE... NO...›
‹...IT'S ME... YOU WANT...›
‹L-LEAVE... HER... ALONE...›
‹...I-I'M NOT DEFEATED... D-DO YOU HEAR?›
‹Y-YOU... HAVEN'T... B-BEATEN... ME...›

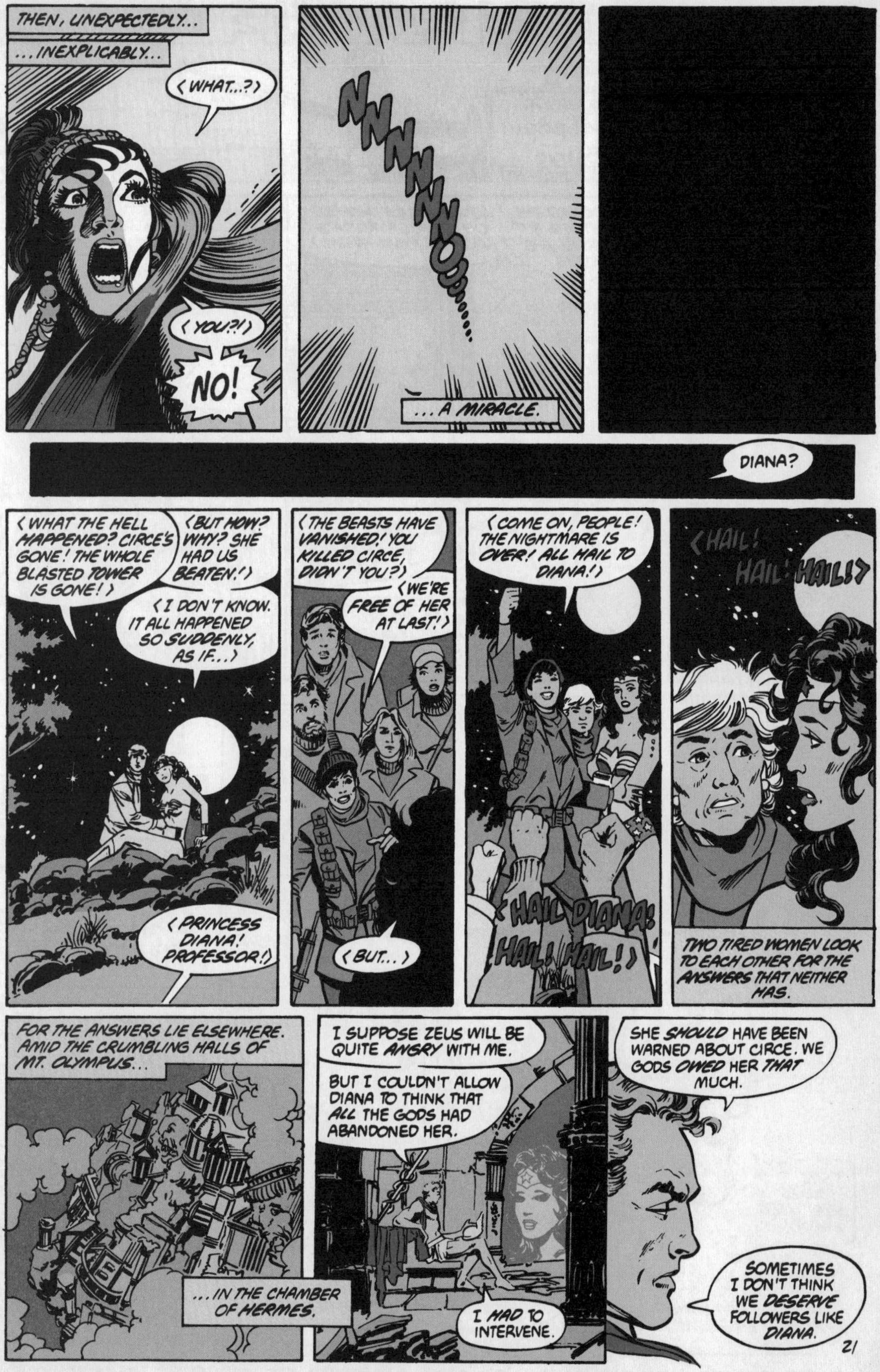

THEN, UNEXPECTEDLY...
...INEXPLICABLY...
‹WHAT...?›
‹YOU?!›
NO!
NNNNNNNOOOOOO......
...A MIRACLE.
DIANA?
‹WHAT THE HELL HAPPENED? CIRCE'S GONE! THE WHOLE BLASTED TOWER IS GONE!›
‹BUT HOW? WHY? SHE HAD US BEATEN!›
‹I DON'T KNOW. IT ALL HAPPENED SO SUDDENLY, AS IF...›
‹PRINCESS DIANA! PROFESSOR!›
‹THE BEASTS HAVE VANISHED! YOU KILLED CIRCE, DIDN'T YOU?›
‹WE'RE FREE OF HER AT LAST!›
‹BUT...›
‹COME ON, PEOPLE! THE NIGHTMARE IS OVER! ALL HAIL TO DIANA!›
‹HAIL DIANA! HAIL! HAIL!›
‹HAIL! HAIL! HAIL!›
TWO TIRED WOMEN LOOK TO EACH OTHER FOR THE ANSWERS THAT NEITHER HAS.
FOR THE ANSWERS LIE ELSEWHERE. AMID THE CRUMBLING HALLS OF MT. OLYMPUS...
...IN THE CHAMBER OF HERMES.
I SUPPOSE ZEUS WILL BE QUITE ANGRY WITH ME.
BUT I COULDN'T ALLOW DIANA TO THINK THAT ALL THE GODS HAD ABANDONED HER.
I HAD TO INTERVENE.
SHE SHOULD HAVE BEEN WARNED ABOUT CIRCE. WE GODS OWED HER THAT MUCH.
SOMETIMES I DON'T THINK WE DESERVE FOLLOWERS LIKE DIANA.
21

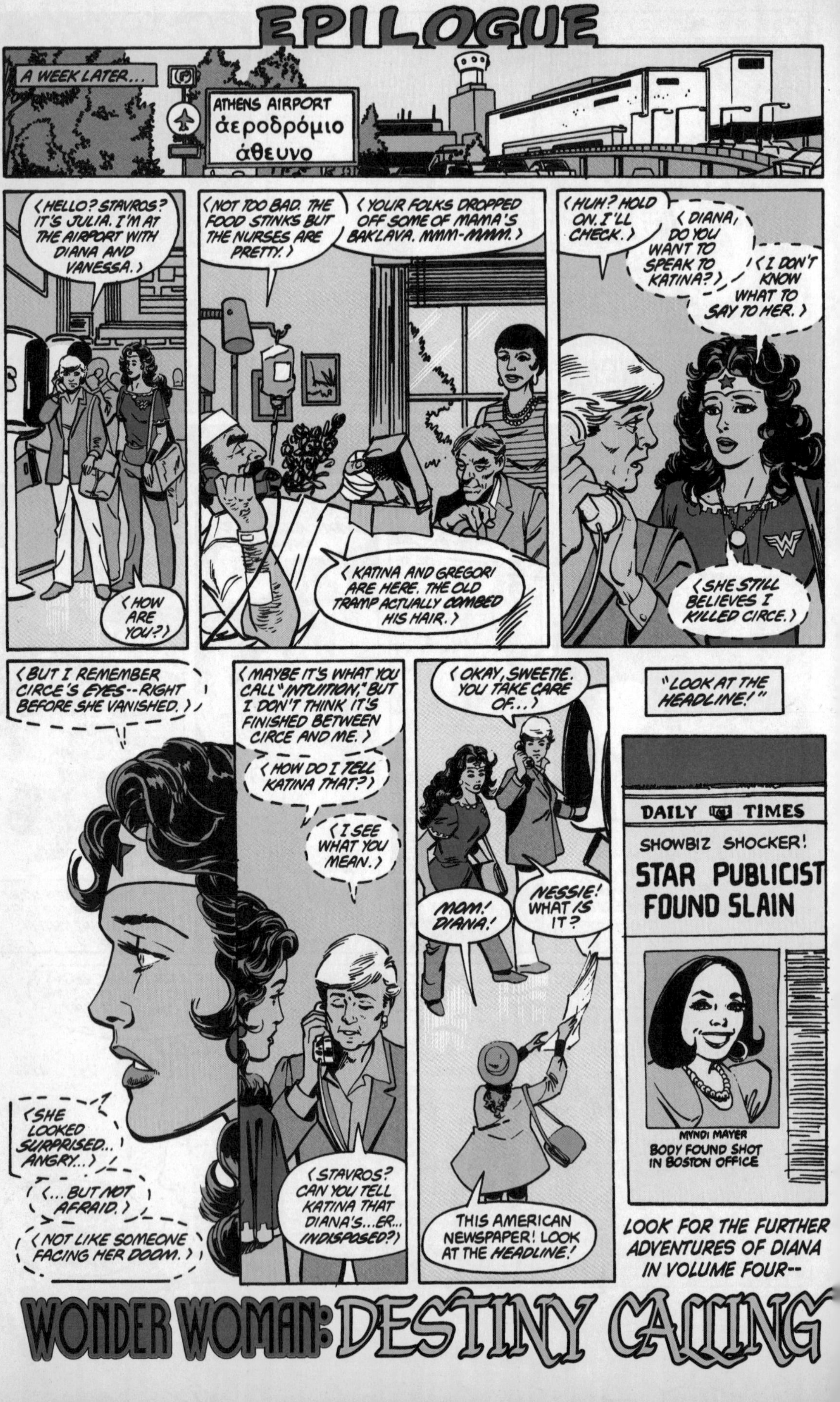
EPILOGUE
A WEEK LATER...
ATHENS AIRPORT
άεροδρόμιο
άθευνο
⟨HELLO? STAVROS? IT'S JULIA. I'M AT THE AIRPORT WITH DIANA AND VANESSA.⟩
⟨HOW ARE YOU?⟩
⟨NOT TOO BAD. THE FOOD STINKS BUT THE NURSES ARE PRETTY.⟩
⟨YOUR FOLKS DROPPED OFF SOME OF MAMA'S BAKLAVA. MMM-MMM.⟩
⟨KATINA AND GREGORI ARE HERE. THE OLD TRAMP ACTUALLY COMBED HIS HAIR.⟩
⟨HUH? HOLD ON. I'LL CHECK.⟩
⟨DIANA, DO YOU WANT TO SPEAK TO KATINA?⟩
⟨I DON'T KNOW WHAT TO SAY TO HER.⟩
⟨SHE STILL BELIEVES I KILLED CIRCE.⟩
⟨BUT I REMEMBER CIRCE'S EYES--RIGHT BEFORE SHE VANISHED.⟩
⟨SHE LOOKED SURPRISED... ANGRY...⟩
⟨...BUT NOT AFRAID.⟩
⟨NOT LIKE SOMEONE FACING HER DOOM.⟩
⟨MAYBE IT'S WHAT YOU CALL "INTUITION," BUT I DON'T THINK IT'S FINISHED BETWEEN CIRCE AND ME.⟩
⟨HOW DO I TELL KATINA THAT?⟩
⟨I SEE WHAT YOU MEAN.⟩
⟨STAVROS? CAN YOU TELL KATINA THAT DIANA'S...ER... INDISPOSED?⟩
⟨OKAY, SWEETIE. YOU TAKE CARE OF...⟩
MOM! DIANA!
NESSIE! WHAT IS IT?
THIS AMERICAN NEWSPAPER! LOOK AT THE HEADLINE!
"LOOK AT THE HEADLINE!"
DAILY TIMES
SHOWBIZ SHOCKER!
STAR PUBLICIST FOUND SLAIN
MYNDI MAYER
BODY FOUND SHOT IN BOSTON OFFICE
LOOK FOR THE FURTHER ADVENTURES OF DIANA IN VOLUME FOUR--
WONDER WOMAN: DESTINY CALLING

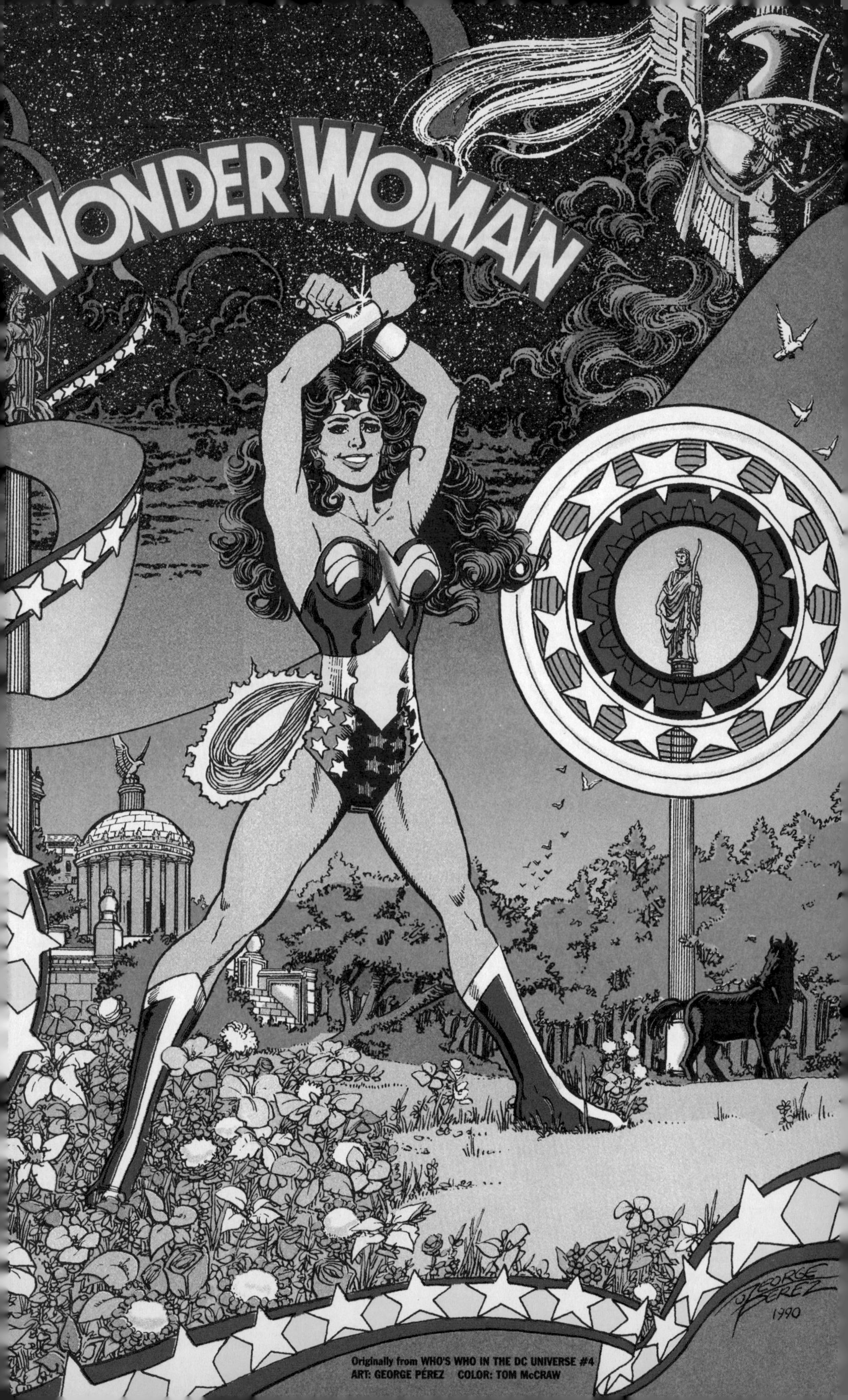
WONDER WOMAN
GEORGE PEREZ
1990

Originally from WHO'S WHO IN THE DC UNIVERSE #4
ART: GEORGE PÉREZ   COLOR: TOM McCRAW